System Modelling and Control

Second Edition

J. Schwarzenbach
K. F. Gill

Mechanical Engineering Department
University of Leeds

Edward Arnold

© J. Schwarzenbach and K. F. Gill 1984

First published in Great Britain 1978 by
Edward Arnold (Publishers) Ltd, 41 Bedford Square, London WC1B 3DQ

Edward Arnold, 300 North Charles Street, Baltimore, Maryland 21201, U.S.A.

Edward Arnold (Australia) Pty Ltd, 80 Waverley Road, Caulfield East, Victoria 3145, Australia

Reprinted with corrections 1979
Second edition 1984

ISBN 0 7131 3518 2

Typeset and printed in Great Britain at
The Pitman Press, Bath

Preface to First Edition

Since the early 1940s, the number of practical applications of the principle of feedback has grown rapidly and the range of application has become very wide, with the consequence that an increasing proportion of engineers, scientists, and technologists require a basic appreciation of the fundamentals of automatic control theory. As the requirements for system dynamic performance have become more exacting so also have the demands on the engineer. Many who are new to the subject find feedback control theory difficult to understand, largely because of the rather abstract nature of some of the concepts involved. Of the textbooks available many are so comprehensive in their coverage that they are more suited to the reader who already has some understanding of the subject rather than to the beginner. The sheer volume of theoretical material tends to discourage the latter type of reader, and the detail often obscures the significance of the main principles.

The primary objective in writing this book has therefore been to sift from the large volume of literature on control theory the material believed to be most pertinent to industrial practice, and to present it in such a way that the student or practising engineer can attain a sound physical understanding of the basic principles of control. Familiarity with the material presented in the book will enable the reader to converse with specialists in the field, to design simple control loops adequate for many industrial applications, and with the aid of more advanced texts to design more complex control schemes. The aim throughout has been to present the fundamental theory in such a way that the reader can see the practical relevance of the material and that he can build up a clear mental picture to aid understanding. The mathematical manipulations can readily be mastered with practice; understanding the significance of the procedures and of their results is the real problem.

The principles of feedback control theory are very general; thus the topic is broadly based and is of relevance for a wide range of dynamic systems. The main variation in the potential areas of application lies in the differing characteristics and complexity of the systems to be controlled. Electrical engineers probably have the least difficulty in understanding control theory since many of the concepts are relevant to their other areas of study. They probably also face the fewest problems of application since the systems with which they deal, although often complex, are well defined because of the discrete lumped nature of most components and of the ease of measurement of system variables.

Many existing textbooks are intended primarily for the electrical engineer. The method of approach used in this book should make it particularly useful for mechanical engineers, chemical engineers, and other technologists and scientists (and in part also for life scientists, economists and others with an interest in the dynamic behaviour of systems and in the concept of feedback). The main problem in designing a control loop for non-electrical systems normally arises when attempting to obtain an adequate mathematical model for the system since, in general, components cannot readily be represented by simple discrete ideal elements; often non-linearities are dominant, measurement is difficult, and noise is significant.

In our teaching of control to undergraduates, postgraduates, industrial engineers and non-engineers we have experimented with the method of approach, the topics included, and the order of presentation. The approach that has evolved, and appears to be the most effective, forms the basis for this book. We have found that the 'classical' approach based on the transfer function and associated techniques of analysis is more easily comprehended and related to practice by the beginner than is 'modern control theory' which is based on a state space approach. The emphasis in this book is accordingly on classical linear control theory. Some understanding of the ideas of the state space approach and its relationship to the classical approach is nevertheless highly desirable; hence a chapter is included to introduce the reader to the more advanced theoretical procedures which have been developed over the last decade or so and which are particularly useful for the mathematical analysis of multivariable systems. The material is presented in such a way as to make the transition from the classical to the modern approach as smooth as possible. With regard to the order of presentation of material we have found definite advantage in analysing in some detail the dynamic behaviour of components of systems in both the time and the frequency domain prior to any detailed consideration of a closed loop system. This gives the student a clear awareness of the nature of the dynamic response of a system component and how the response varies with the form of the transfer function and the input excitation. It shows him how the response to any given input can be calculated from a knowledge of the transfer function and conversely how a transfer function can be determined by practical testing of a system component. The latter, the process of system identification, is used for verifying mathematical models derived theoretically and may be the only means, or the easiest means, of obtaining a transfer function representation where theoretical derivation is difficult. When this foundation has been laid the principle of feedback can be introduced and rapid progress made in analysing the dynamic behaviour of closed loop systems and, in particular, how accuracy and stability are affected by components within the loop. This then leads logically and easily to the most important stage, consideration of the design of feedback control systems to meet specific dynamic performance specifications.

The material presented in this book should cover the control engineering content of most undergraduate degree schemes which include the subject of automatic control. The book should be of equal value to the engineer in industry who did not include control in his studies but who is now faced with having to deal with some aspect of control or to communicate with others working in the field. It is suggested that at a first reading (or where a minimum of time is available) Chapters 5 and 7 can be omitted without detriment to the understanding of later material. Where time is not available for these chapters it is nevertheless recommended that the reader tries to gain a general idea of the contents.

We wish to express our thanks to those who have contributed most to the development of this book—the many students of differing backgrounds who by their attempts at learning control theory have highlighted points of particular difficulty in understanding. We are especially indebted to our colleague Mr. J. L. Douglas who has endeavoured to learn the fundamentals of the subject by using this book for self-teaching. In doing so he has made valuable suggestions which have enabled us to remove some of our errors and ambiguities, and to make minor additions where our steps have been rather large. We thank also Mrs M. Fernando for her valuable contribution of a neatly typed text.

Leeds   J. Schwarzenbach
1978   K. F. Gill

Preface to Second Edition

It is encouraging to find that this book appears to a large extent to have attained its primary objectives and that it is therefore helping to meet the need for textbooks which explain simply and clearly the basic fundamentals of control engineering. In the period since it was first published digital computers and microprocessors have come to play a very prominent role both as control system components and as tools for analysis, and the main purpose of this second edition is to introduce supplementary material to reflect this change. Sections have been incorporated describing digital simulation and simulation languages, Section 7.5 has been rewritten to include digital computation of correlation functions and power spectra, and a new chapter has been included to deal with the analysis of discrete data systems. The important topic of design has also been given greater emphasis by expanding the final chapter. Solutions to the problems have been included, and the bibliography has been updated.

Leeds
1984

J. Schwarzenbach
K. F. Gill

Contents

List of Principal Symbols

Symbols which appear in one part of the book only, and whose meaning is clear from the accompanying text or figures, have been omitted from this list.

Variables which are functions of time are normally represented by lower case letters, and the Laplace transforms of the variables are normally represented by the corresponding capital letters e.g. $F(s)$ is the Laplace transform of $f(t)$, i.e. $F(s) = \mathcal{L}[f(t)]$.

Subscripts are used where more than one of a given variable is used, e.g. $f_1(t), f_2(t), \ldots, F_1(s), F_2(s), \ldots$

Variables are assumed to be relative to appropriate datum or design values (system components are normally assumed to be linear).

Starred symbols are used to indicate time functions that are in sampled form e.g. $f^*(t)$, the sampled version of $f(t)$, is the series of values $f(0), f(T), f(2T), f(3T) \ldots$; it has Laplace transform $F^*(s)$ and z transform $F(z) = \mathcal{Z}[f(t)]$.

$u(t)$	$U(s)$	Input signal to system or system component
$r(t)$	$R(s)$	Reference input to (or set point of) feedback system
$c(t)$	$C(s)$	
$y(t)$	$Y(s)$	Output signal from system or system component
$e(t)$	$E(s)$	Error signal
$n(t)$	$N(s)$	Noise signal
$m(t)$	$M(s)$	Manipulated variable, output from controller
$s = \sigma + j\omega$		Laplace operator, (real part σ, imaginary part ω)
$G(s)$		Transfer function of component of a system
$H(s)$		Transfer function of component in a feedback path
$\delta(t)$		Unit impulse function
$g(t)$, or $w(t)$		Unit impulse response, or weighting function, $\mathcal{L}^{-1}[G(s)]$
$G(j\omega)$		Transfer function with $s = j\omega$; gives harmonic characteristics of system, i.e. $|G(j\omega)|$ = magnitude, $\angle G(j\omega)$ = phase angle φ of output relative to input for input frequency ω
$p_1, p_2, p_3, \ldots$		Poles of a transfer function (factors of denominator) i.e. roots of the characteristic equation
$z_1, z_2, z_3, \ldots$		Zeros of a transfer function (factors of numerator)
K		Gain constant
τ		Time constant of a first order component (in Chapter 7, τ represents time shift of a signal)
ζ and ω_n		Damping factor and undamped natural frequency, respec-

	tively, for a second order system component (or associated with a pair of complex conjugate roots)
ω_s	Sampling frequency
T	Sampling interval, $T = 2\pi/\omega_s$
z	Alternative to Laplace operator used with sampled signals, $z = e^{sT}$
$G(z)$	Pulse transfer function
K_p, K_v, K_a	Positional, velocity, and acceleration error coefficients respectively
M_p and ω_p	Peak magnification of a closed loop system, and the frequency at which it occurs
M	Closed loop magnification
$\left.\begin{array}{l} k_1, k_2, k_3 \\ k_c, T_i, T_d \end{array}\right\}$	Coefficients of P + I + D controller
$\{x(t)\}$	State vector, comprising the n state variables $x_1(t)$, $x_2(t)$, $x_3(t) \ldots x_n(t)$
$\{y(t)\}$	Response or output vector
$\{u(t)\}$	Control or input vector
A	Coefficient matrix
B	Driving matrix
C	Output matrix
D	Transmission matrix
I	Unit matrix
$\varphi(t)$	Solution matrix or transition matrix
$\varphi_{xx}(\tau)$	Autocorrelation function of a variable $x(t)$
$\varphi_{xy}(\tau), \varphi_{yx}(\tau)$	Cross correlation function of a pair of variables $x(t)$, $y(t)$
$\Phi_{xx}(\omega)$	Power spectral density of a variable $x(t)$, i.e. the Fourier transform of $\varphi_{xx}(\tau)$
$\Phi_{xy}(\omega)$	Cross spectral density, Fourier transform of $\varphi_{xy}(\tau)$

1
Introduction

As technological processes increase in complexity, and the required performance specifications become more severe, analytical design procedures assume great importance. It has become essential for engineers to have an understanding of the nature of the dynamic behaviour of systems, and of the methods available for analysing and improving dynamic performance.

These requirements are making the use of mathematical modelling techniques an essential part of design. The nature of the model and the methods employed in obtaining it are dependent on the depth of understanding needed at a particular stage of the design study, and on the use to which the model will be put.

It is hoped that this book will give to both the student and the practising engineer a clear insight into the main facets of system modelling, linear control theory, and control system design, and that it will form a sound foundation for practical application or more advanced study. The level of mathematical knowledge assumed is a familiarity with simple differential equations and with complex numbers.

1.1 What is a system?

It is desirable first to define what is meant by a *system*, a word which is frequently used in conversation. Broadly, a system can be thought of as a collection of interacting components, although sometimes interest might lie just in one single component. These components will often be discrete physical elements of hardware, but can equally well be functional parts of such physical components. The system of interest might be a power station, a steam turbine in the power station, or a control valve on the turbine; it might be an aeroplane, its air conditioning, an engine, or part of an engine; a process plant for the production of a chemical, or a large or small part of the plant; a human being, or some part of the body such as the muscle control mechanism for a limb; or it might be the economic system of a country, or any other from a wide range of fields.

The system would normally be considered conceptually as being that part of the universe in which interest lay. There would be interaction between the system and certain parts of the surroundings known as the environment. The two would be separated by an imaginary boundary. In defining the system and its environment it is necessary to decide where this boundary should be placed; this decision depends both on the physical entities involved and on the purpose of the investigation.

In studying a power station, interest might lie primarily in the relationship between the power station and the community, in which case the system and its environment might be envisaged as in Fig. 1.1. There might, however, be a more specific interest in the speed control system of the turbogenerator, in which case the system could be as in Fig. 1.2.

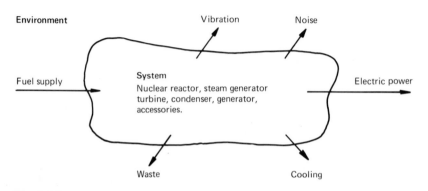

Fig. 1.1 Power station system and its relationship to the environment

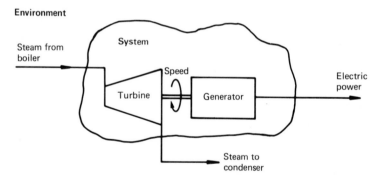

Fig. 1.2 Turbogenerator speed control system

In abstracting from the whole the system of interest, it is necessary to consider carefully where the boundary shall be placed, and closely allied is the need to decide what relevant signals cross the system boundary. In addition, there will be signals of interest within the system boundary, variables which help to describe and define the detailed system behaviour. Some of these signals will be measurable, some not or only indirectly; some will be useful from the viewpoint of analysis, and some not.

The signals which pass to the system from the environment will be termed the *system inputs*, while those passing out across the boundary will be the *system outputs*. Often there will be only one system input that is varying and one system output which is affected. The systems to be considered in this book will be predominantly single-input–single-output systems, the type which occurs most frequently in practice.

1.2 System control

The aim of studying dynamic system behaviour is generally one of gaining an understanding of the system, with a view to controlling it to give specific values of certain important variables, to satisfy a required specification.

For the purpose of controlling the system it is necessary to adjust the values of one or more of the inputs to the system. Only certain of the inputs will be available for adjustment and these are referred to as the controlled inputs, whereas others will be disturbance inputs over which no control exists. In the heating of a room, for example, the heat input from the heating device can be altered as required, but the heat flow to or from the environment cannot be controlled in the same way. The variable chosen to be a measure of the desired system output may or may not give a true indication that the control is satisfactory. In the room heating control, the temperature of interest is probably the average temperature or the temperature in the part of the room where people sit, whereas the temperature measured is that at one specific point, the location of the thermostat. This may not even be positioned in the same room, so that appropriate allowances must be made in the design and utilization of the heating system.

Sometimes the incentive for studying a system will be purely one of seeking an understanding of the way in which it functions. In this category come some physiological systems, for which possibilities for designing control loops or improving system behaviour are rather limited.

Two broad classes of control system are available, *open loop control* and *closed loop control* and these are depicted schematically in Fig. 1.3.

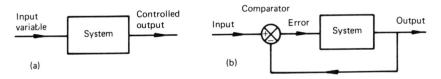

Fig. 1.3 Open loop and closed loop control (a) open loop (b) closed loop.

(a) *Open loop or scheduling control.* On the basis of knowledge about the system and of past experience, a prediction is made of what the input should be to give the desired output; the input is adjusted accordingly. Familiar examples are automatic toasters, programmable washing machines, and interest rate variations as they are used to affect economic systems. Such control is frequently unsatisfactory because any unexpected disturbances to the system can cause a deviation in the output from the desired value. The quality of the toast will vary with the type of bread and the initial temperature of the toaster, the cleanliness of the clothes will depend on correct assessment of amount of soap powder and length of washing cycle required, the effectiveness of an interest rate change will depend on a host of other factors affecting the economy.

(b) *Closed loop or feedback control.* The system output is measured and compared with the desired value; the system continually attempts to reduce the error between the two. Familiar examples are thermostatic controls on domestic and industrial ovens and other heating systems, level controls on water cisterns, and speed regulation by means of engine governors. Frequently the loop is closed through a human being; this is the case with road vehicles, as when a car is driven along an undulating road at a steady speed, or when the car is positioned in its garage at the end of the run.

1.3 The need for analysis

There are many examples of early control systems such as a device of Hero of Alexandria which opened a set of temple doors when a ceremonial fire was lit, and closed them again when the fire died down, or the much later centrifugal governor developed by James Watt for the speed control of steam engines. These systems were produced almost entirely by a trial and observation design process and without the assistance of any theoretical analysis. Simple control loops can still often be made to operate satisfactorily in this way because the specifications have a wide tolerance. As performance requirements become more demanding it becomes necessary to resort to a more analytical approach, since without this the cost in terms of time, manpower, and unnecessary complexity of equipment is not justifiable.

Closing the loop can make the system more accurate by giving a much smaller or a zero steady state error, but it can make the system very oscillatory or even unstable. Basically, problems arise when delays occur within the system; this causes corrective action to be applied too late, leading to alternating overcorrection and undercorrection. It is necessary to achieve a satisfactory compromise between the conflicting requirements of accuracy and stability.

1.4 Methods of system representation

It has been shown that the first step in the study of a system is the important one of defining clearly what constitutes the system of interest, and in what ways the system interacts with the surrounding environment. Having drawn a conceptual boundary round the system it is necessary to represent the system in a convenient pictorial and mathematical way.

A useful and very frequently used pictorial representation of a system is the *block diagram* where individual blocks are used to represent separate functional parts of the system. Fig. 1.3a is a simple block diagram representing a system with a single input and a single output, the lines indicating the signal flow paths, with direction of signal transmission given by the arrows. Where signals are added to or subtracted from one another, summing points are indicated, as shown in Fig. 1.3b. Although any single-input–single-output system could be represented by a single block as in Fig. 1.3a, if the system comprises a number of interacting components it is more useful if it is represented by several blocks interconnected by the appropriate signal flow paths.

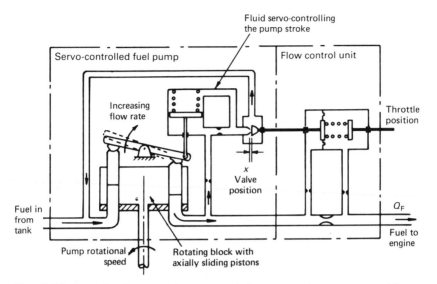

Fig. 1.4 Schematic diagram of pump and flow control on a gas turbine speed control system (with symbols for pressures, flows, springrates, diaphragm areas, flow restrictions, etc. omitted)

In arriving at a block diagram representation, an intermediate schematic diagram in which the functional parts are clearly shown would often be utilized. Consider as an illustration that the system of interest is an aircraft gas turbine speed control system. The engineering drawings, although showing the physical arrangement, are too congested with detail and would not show the type of information required for a dynamic study. A schematic diagram of the form shown in Fig. 1.4 would however show how the system components function and form the basis for an analytical study, and enable the production of a block diagram of the form shown in Fig. 1.5.

Block diagrams show only the interrelationships between the different parts of the system, and for analysis must be supplemented by a quantitative

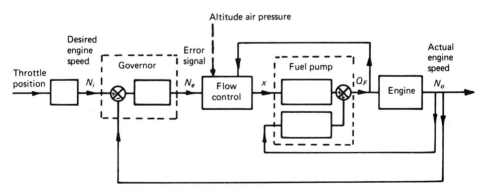

Fig. 1.5 Block diagram of engine and speed control system

description in the form of appropriate mathematical expressions for each of the blocks on the diagram. Such a mathematical description of the system is termed a *model*. Evaluation of an accurate model is often difficult. Since dynamic conditions are being considered the equations relating the outputs to the inputs of the blocks will in general be differential equations. It will be seen in the next chapter that for control engineering purposes these are often written as *transfer functions*, defined as the ratio of the Laplace transforms of the output and input when initial conditions are zero. When these equations are combined to give an overall output–input relationship a single differential equation of high order results.

An alternative method of mathematical representation which is particularly amenable to solution by means of the digital computer is the *state space* technique. Instead of a single nth order equation the problem is transformed to one of solving n first order equations. Unlike the classical approach, the complexity of the method of solution does not increase rapidly with the complexity of the problem, and hence this approach is particularly suitable for complex systems.

An alternative pictorial representation is the *signal flow graph*. This type of representation does not have to cater for the transfer function normally associated with the block diagram and so is capable of giving a more detailed schematic representation of a complex system if needed. It illustrates the passage of signals through a system, as does the block diagram, but also includes a more basic description of the feedback paths associated with a system, and enables the effects of variation in all system parameters to be seen directly.

The analytical equations would generally be obtained by a combination of theoretical analysis and experimental testing. If the component of the system is sufficiently simple, then it is possible to write down equations which govern the variables concerned, and hence obtain both the form of the equations and the values of the parameters of the equations. This is described for a number of physical components in Chapter 2. Subsequently the component would often be tested to verify the parameter values obtained. If the system is more complex, then simplifying assumptions must be made to arrive at the likely form of the equations; these assumptions must be confirmed and parameters obtained by testing. If the contents of the block are unknown (a so-called *black box* problem) then it will be necessary to arrive at the characteristics entirely experimentally.

The resulting equations will be a parametric model of the component, and ideally the parameters will be associated with specific physical characteristics of the system. In the black box type of situation the latter would not be the case, and sometimes no attempt is made to fit equations to the experimental response. In this situation the component is described by the actual response curve, and the model would be non-parametric.

1.5 Methods of analysis and design

When the input to a system changes as a function of time, the form of the resulting response is clearly dependent both on the nature of the input function and on the equations describing the dynamic characteristics of the system and, provided that these equations are available, the output response can be calculated for any input function of known mathematical form. In practice external disturbances, often of unpredictable form, may act as additional inputs and modify the response in a random manner. Such disturbance inputs, generally referred to as *noise* when they consist of random fluctuations about a mean value, have negligible effect in many situations and hence are usually ignored in the earlier stages of the analysis of a system. The disturbance can also be a change in mean value of a variable which causes an alteration in the system datum operating point, and hence in the parameters of the system equations. It is unrealistic for the purposes of analysis to consider attempting to investigate the response of the system for all conceivable types of input function; thus usually only certain specific types of function are studied. These are chosen primarily for reasons of analytical simplicity and because design criteria have been developed for them. They include an instantaneous change, which is the most severe input change that a system can undergo, and certain other typically encountered input functions such as an input changing in a sinusoidal manner, or one changing at a constant rate.

The input forcing functions most commonly considered are of three types:

    (i) transient disturbances such as step changes of magnitude, ramp changes, or impulsive changes,

    (ii) sinusoidal signals,

    (iii) statistical signals, which have random characteristics.

The output response as a function of time can be obtained for any specific forcing function by analytical or computer solution of the differential equations. Study of the effects on the response which result from alterations in the mathematical model yields an understanding of the dynamic significance of the various terms in the governing equations, and hence the significance of the corresponding parameters in a physical system. For experimental verification of theoretically obtained dynamic equations, or for a black box approach to the identification of a mathematical model, a practical system component can be tested by recording the output for one or more of these input functions. Subsequently the measured response is compared with the response from a range of mathematical models; the model with the closest fit can then be chosen to represent the tested system component.

Solution of a system differential equation can, in principle, be carried out using either a digital or an analogue computer. Chapter 3 describes the basic elements of an electronic analogue computer, and the method for deriving a circuit diagram which defines the appropriate interconnection of these elements, to produce a circuit whose governing differential equation is the same as that to be solved. The circuit is thus an analogue or simulation of the system and, if forced with a voltage input of the desired waveform, then the variation of the output voltage represents the time response of the system. The variation of any system variables other than the output can be noted by recording the voltages at appropriate points in the circuit. This is followed by a description of how the mode control buttons on the computer switch the circuit to enable the computation to be started, stopped, and otherwise controlled in a useful manner, a list of some non-linear elements which are available for solving non-linear differential equations, and a discussion about time scaling and amplitude scaling. The chapter concludes with two sections on digital computer solution of differential equations. These explain first the discrete approach which is needed and the way in which integration routines are used to obtain an approximation to the solution, and then the use of a high level simulation language to simplify program writing and often to enable the digital computer to be used in an on-line interactive manner.

Solution of the system differential equation can alternatively be carried out by hand for simple transient changes of input and for sinusoidal input changes, the first two types of forcing function listed above. Chapters 4 and 6, which deal respectively with time domain analysis and frequency domain analysis, describe how the Laplace transform technique can be utilized to determine the response of a linear system of known transfer function or differential equation to such input functions. Systems of gradually increasing complexity are analysed; in this way a clear mental picture can be built up of the nature of dynamic response and of the way in which changes in the form of the governing equation influence the response. The latter part of each chapter describes the converse process—testing an actual system component with one of these forms of input function, noting the resulting response, and determining a transfer function which would give a very similar response and which could be used as a mathematical model of the system component. Statistical signals, which have random characteristics and must be described by appropriate statistical functions rather than by analytical functions of time, form the third class of important forcing functions. They are particularly useful for this process of system identification for experimental testing in situations where the level of inherent system noise is significant; by appropriate mathematical manipulation the effect of the noise can largely be eliminated and time or frequency response information obtained. Chapter 7 defines and illustrates the significance of autocorrelation functions and power spectral densities which are respectively time and frequency domain descriptions of such signals; it also describes this method of system identification with particular reference to the most frequently used signal, the pseudo random binary sequence.

The chapters whose contents are outlined above all utilize a dynamic system description which is in the form of a transfer function or the equivalent nth order differential equation relating output to input. The methods of analysis and design associated with this form of description are referred to as the *classical methods*. Chapter 5 describes the alternative state space approach to system representation and analysis, an approach which is fundamental to a range of techniques of analysis and design referred to as *modern control theory*. Methods are presented for deriving the state vector differential equation, the n first order differential equations which constitute the state space description of a system component, a form of description which can be used equally well where there is more than one input and output. A method of solving the state vector differential equation is presented, and for a simple input function it is demonstrated that the analytical solution is the same as that obtained by the Laplace transform approach of Chapter 4. Normally however solution must be carried out by digital computer methods, and it is here, in the unified approach that is possible, that the power of the state space description lies. The chapter concludes by giving an insight into the way in which such solution is carried out. The methods of analysis and design described in the later chapters are the classical methods, chosen because of the unrivalled understanding of system behaviour which is offered by time and frequency response techniques. Once a fundamental understanding has been gained in this way a deeper study of the modern approach is recommended particularly where design work must be carried out for systems with more than one input or output.

The final four chapters are concerned broadly with designing or modifying a system to ensure that its dynamic behaviour is acceptable. Chapter 8 returns to the topic of system control already introduced in Section 1.2, and describes the main characteristics of feedback control systems. The steady state accuracy is evaluated in terms of the transfer function and of the input function; it is also shown that an increase of accuracy is accompanied by a tendency towards more oscillatory behaviour and might give rise to instability. The two main methods of stability analysis are described and illustrated, and the chapter concludes by showing how the overall response of the closed loop system can be evaluated from a knowledge of the dynamic response of the system components within the loop. Chapter 9 describes the root locus method of analysis, a technique which assists the engineer to gain an understanding of system behaviour by showing what effect variation of system gain or some other variable has on the transient response. Chapter 10 explains the effect on system performance of introducing a sampler within the loop, thus converting a continuous signal to a discrete data form, and describes how the analytical techniques must be modified to extend to sampled-data systems. The final chapter explains the functioning of integral action and derivative action within a controller, and describes the general approach to system improvement by the use of additional compensation networks within the control loop. To conclude, the many facets of system modelling and control described throughout the book are brought together by presenting in outline form a case study for a practical system, an electrohydraulic position control for the slideway of a milling machine, designed to be numerically controlled.

2
Mathematical Description of System Components

It has been indicated in Chapter 1 that for analysis and design of a system to give satisfactory dynamic behaviour it is necessary to obtain a suitable mathematical model to represent the system. The combination of a block diagram and the mathematical expressions relating the input and output of each block provides a pictorial and a quantitative representation of the cause-and-effect relationship between the variables of the system.

Although all systems with a single input and a single output may be denoted by a single block connecting the input and the output, the advantage of the block diagram concept lies in the fact that many systems are composed of several non-interacting elements whose output–input relationships can be determined independently. In this chapter it is shown how these relationships can be obtained for relatively simple components, and the form which the equations take. It is also shown how they can be combined to yield the overall output–input relationship for the system.

Section 2.1 considers the concept of linearity, and shows the way in which many non-linear systems can be linearized provided any perturbations from a datum are small. The Laplace transform technique is used widely in system analysis and synthesis, and for those unfamiliar with the method an introduction and an outline of the most important features are given in Section 2.2. This is followed by the definition of a transfer function, and the derivation of transfer functions for some physical components. To complete the picture, representation of a system by means of state equations is introduced in Section 2.6.

2.1 Linearity of systems

The expression relating input and output of a component of a system will in general be a differential equation. For ideal systems this is frequently linear and if it is possible to represent practical systems sufficiently closely by linear differential equations considerable analytical advantage is gained.

A system is said to be *linear* if it obeys the *principle of superposition*. This requires that if the separate application of time dependent inputs $u_1(t)$ and $u_2(t)$ produces outputs $c_1(t)$ and $c_2(t)$ respectively, then the simultaneous application of $u_1(t) + u_2(t)$ will produce the output $c_1(t) + c_2(t)$. The input $u_1(t)$ might be a step change, and $u_2(t)$ a ramp change where the input increases at a constant rate. Alternatively if $u_2(t) = u_1(t)$ the result would be that a doubling of the step size would double the output response curve, or increasing the step size by a factor of 10 would merely scale up the response by 10. A differential equation which is linear does not contain any terms which are products of or powers of the variable and its derivatives.

No real system component is completely linear, but often the range of operation is such that linearity can be assumed. This is the case, say, for a helical spring where the input is the force acting and the output is the spring length, provided the load does not exceed that which causes the spring to compress till the coils touch, and provided any tensile force does not cause material yield to occur. Similarly an electronic amplifier will saturate for very large inputs, but for inputs within the design range the gain should be substantially constant.

Many system elements are inherently governed by a non-linear relationship. The rate of flow of fluid through an orifice is proportional to the square root of the pressure difference across it; doubling the pressure difference does not double the flow rate, and the principle of superposition does not apply. With such elements the function relating the input and output variables does not have any linear region. If the system is operating about a nominal datum condition (say point A on Fig. 2.1), and if the range of operation is such that

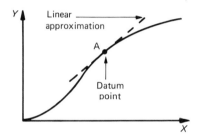

Fig. 2.1 Non-linear relationship

movement from this datum is small, then the departure from linearity is small. Replacing the curve by the tangent at the datum point would allow linear techniques of analysis to be used. If the range of operation is large, linear techniques intelligently used could still give a useful indication of the nature of the expected performance.

In analysing a system with such continuous types of non-linearity it is often useful to adopt a linear approach and carry out a *small perturbation analysis*. Linearization essentially consists of replacing the actual operating characteristic functions by tangents at the operating point.

Consider a non-linear relationship

$$Y = f(X_1, X_2, X_3 \ldots) \qquad 2.1$$

Differentiation gives

$$dY = \frac{\partial Y}{\partial X_1} dX_1 + \frac{\partial Y}{\partial X_2} dX_2 + \frac{\partial Y}{\partial X_3} dX_3 + \ldots \qquad 2.2$$

Let a subscript $_0$ be used to indicate conditions at a datum point. Considering

$\mathrm{d}Y$, $\mathrm{d}X_1$, $\mathrm{d}X_2$ ... to be incremental changes from the datum $[Y]_0$, $[X_1]_0$, $[X_2]_0$ ... the partial derivatives will be evaluated at that datum and will be constants. Let the changes from the datum be y, x_1, x_2, x_3 ... The linearized equation then becomes

$$y = C_1 x_1 + C_2 x_2 + C_3 x_3 + ... \qquad 2.3$$

$$\text{where } C_1 = \left[\frac{\partial Y}{\partial X_1}\right]_0, \ C_2 = \left[\frac{\partial Y}{\partial X_2}\right]_0, \text{ etc.}$$

Note that the variables are now not absolute variables but variables relative to a datum point. For this one section of the book absolute variables are represented by upper case letters and variables relative to the datum by lower case letters. The original non-linear relationship between the absolute variables has been replaced by a linear relationship involving the new variables.

Example 2.1. Consider a mechanical flyweight governor as shown schematically in Fig. 2.2. A reasonable assumption would be that the force F exerted by

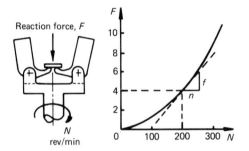

Fig. 2.2 Flyweight governor with force–speed relationship

the flyweights, arising from centrifugal action, will be proportional to the square of the rotational velocity N

i.e. $F = KN^2$ where K is a constant. This is a non-linear relationship.

$$\text{If } K = \frac{1}{10\,000}$$

the force–speed curve is as shown in Fig. 2.2.
    If the datum point is 200 rev/minute

$$\left[\frac{\mathrm{d}F}{\mathrm{d}N}\right]_0 = 2K\left[N\right]_0 = \frac{2 \times 200}{10\,000} = \frac{1}{25}$$

Hence the linearized equation is

$$f = \frac{1}{25} n$$

where force f and speed n are measured relative to the datum $F = 4$ and $N = 200$.

To assess the error arising from linearization choose $N = 250$ rev/minute

i.e. $n = 50$.

This gives $f = 2$ i.e. $F = 6$.

$$\text{The true value of } F = \frac{(250)^2}{10\,000} = 6.25$$

The smaller the change from the datum the smaller will be the percentage error. If the datum point is 100 rev/minute

$$\left[\frac{dF}{dN}\right]_0 = 2K\left[N\right]_0 = \frac{2 \times 100}{10\,000} = \frac{1}{50}$$

and the linearized equation is

$$f = \frac{1}{50}\,n$$

Example 2.2. Consider the equation for the flow of fluid through an orifice:

$$Q = C_d A \sqrt{\left(\frac{2\Delta P}{\rho}\right)}$$

where Q is the fluid flow rate, C_d the discharge coefficient, A the orifice area, ΔP the pressure difference across the orifice and ρ the density of the fluid.
If C_d, A and ρ are constant then this becomes

$$Q = C\sqrt{(\Delta P)} \quad \text{where } C = \text{constant}$$

In linearized form this is

$$q = C'\Delta p$$

where q and Δp are changes relative to a datum $[Q]_0, [\Delta P]_0$

$$\text{and } C' = \left[\frac{dQ}{d\Delta P}\right]_0 = \left[\frac{C}{2\sqrt{(\Delta P)}}\right]_0$$

If the area A is not constant, such as would be the case in a flow control valve, then the linearized equation would be

$$q = C_1 a + C_2 \Delta p$$

where

$$C_1 = \left[\frac{\partial Q}{\partial A}\right]_0 = \left[C_d \sqrt{\left(\frac{2\Delta P}{\rho}\right)}\right]_0$$

$$C_2 = \left[\frac{\partial Q}{\partial \Delta p}\right]_0 = \left[\frac{C_d A}{\sqrt{(2\rho\Delta P)}}\right]_0$$

If the density is also variable then the equation would be

$$q = C_1 a + C_2 \Delta p + C_3 \rho$$

Linearized equations can also be obtained directly from experimental curves. The constant coefficients are then obtained by measuring the slopes at the datum points directly from the plotted graphs.

It should be noted that certain types of non-linearity cannot be dealt with by linearization. Notable amongst these are effects such as hysteresis or backlash where decreasing the perturbation size causes the effect to be more prominent. Sometimes it is convenient to deal with such systems in a quasi-linear manner by writing down a set of linear equations for each distinct operating region.

Throughout the remainder of this book all variables will normally be considered to be relative to a datum; hence the need for maintaining a distinction between absolute and relative variables is not great. This allows use of the more usual convention that lower case letters are employed to denote functions of time and upper case letters the equivalent functions of the Laplace operator, as will be shown in the next section.

2.2 Laplace transforms and their significance

The Laplace transform technique is a very convenient method for assisting in the solution of differential equations. It is helpful at first to consider this technique as being somewhat analogous to the use of logarithms to simplify such mathematical operations as multiplication, division and raising numbers to powers. When carrying out such operations, the original numbers of the problems are transformed into the logarithmic domain by the use of log tables, the solution in the logarithmic domain is obtained by a simpler process (addition instead of multiplication, multiplication instead of raising to a power, etc.), and finally the result is transformed back into the normal number domain by use of the anti-log tables.

Similarly, when solving a differential equation using Laplace transforms, the equation is first transformed into the Laplace domain by changing the variable from time t to a new complex variable $s = \sigma + j\omega$, known as the Laplace operator. The solution of the differential equation is then effected by simple algebraic manipulations in the s domain yielding a solution which is a function of s. Finally, to obtain the desired time solution, it is necessary to invert the transform of the solution from the s domain back to the time domain. As with logarithms, tables exist and can be used to transform from one domain to another.

The Laplace transform of a function of time $f(t)$ is written as $F(s)$ and is defined as

$$F(s) = \mathscr{L}[f(t)] = \int_0^\infty f(t)e^{-st}\,dt \qquad 2.4$$

where $s = \sigma + j\omega$ is an arbitrary complex variable.

The transformation is thus an integration process applied to $f(t)$. $F(s)$ is finite even when $f(t)$ does not tend to zero, the only requirements being that the variable $f(t)$ must be defined for all values of time $t > 0$ and be zero for $t < 0$, and that s is sufficiently large to ensure that the integral converges. There is a unique value of $F(s)$ in spite of there being a large range of values of s which are suitable. By applying the above integration process the Laplace transform for any function $f(t)$ can be obtained, and once obtained it need not be derived again. Tables of Laplace transforms have thus been compiled, and appear in many control engineering and mathematics textbooks. Table 2.1 lists the Laplace transform pairs of most importance in control work, and which will be used in this book; the rather complicated $f(t)$ describes a damped sine wave whose significance will be made clear later.

Table 2.1 Common Laplace transform pairs

$f(t)$	$F(s)$	$f(t)$	$F(s)$
unit step	$\dfrac{1}{s}$	$\dfrac{df(t)}{dt}$	$sF(s) - f(0)$
unit ramp t	$\dfrac{1}{s^2}$	$\dfrac{df^n(t)}{dt^n}$	$s^n F(s) - s^{n-1} f(0) - \ldots f^{n-1}(0)$
unit impulse $\delta(t)$	1		where $f^n(0) = \left[\dfrac{d^n f(t)}{dt^n}\right]_{t=0}$
e^{-at}	$\dfrac{1}{s+a}$	$\dfrac{\omega_n}{\sqrt{(1-\zeta^2)}} e^{-\zeta\omega_n t} \sin \omega_n t \sqrt{(1-\zeta^2)}$	$\dfrac{\omega_n{}^2}{s^2 + 2\zeta\omega_n s + \omega_n{}^2}$
$\sin \omega t$	$\dfrac{\omega}{s^2 + \omega^2}$	$e^{-at} \sin \omega t$	$\dfrac{\omega}{(s+a)^2 + \omega^2}$
$\cos \omega t$	$\dfrac{s}{s^2 + \omega^2}$	$e^{-at} \cos \omega t$	$\dfrac{s+a}{(s+a)^2 + \omega^2}$

The following theorems are those of most frequent use:

(a) *Addition and subtraction:*

$$\mathscr{L}[f_1(t) \pm f_2(t)] = F_1(s) \pm F_2(s) \qquad 2.5$$
$$\text{where } \mathscr{L}[f_1(t)] = F_1(s), \; \mathscr{L}[f_2(t)] = F_2(s)$$

(b) *Multiplication by a constant:*

$$\mathscr{L}[Kf(t)] = KF(s) \qquad 2.6$$

(c) *Final value theorem:*

$$\lim_{t \to \infty} f(t) = \lim_{s \to 0} sF(s) \qquad 2.7$$

This is useful since it gives the final value of a time function (i.e. the steady state value) by determining the value of its Laplace transform as $s \to 0$. The theorem is not valid if the denominator of $sF(s)$ contains any root whose real part is zero or positive (which as will be seen later implies that the function tends to infinity as $t \to \infty$).

(d) *Shifting theorem:*

$$\text{If } \mathcal{L}[f(t)] = F(s) \quad \text{then } \mathcal{L}[f(t - T)] = e^{-sT}F(s) \qquad 2.8$$

It can be seen from the table that the Laplace transform of the *n*th derivative of a function is given by

$$\mathcal{L}\left[\frac{d^n f(t)}{dt^n}\right] = s^n F(s) - s^{n-1}f(0) - s^{n-2}f'(0) - \dots - sf^{n-2}(0) - f^{n-1}(0) \qquad 2.9$$

The second and subsequent terms are dependent on the initial conditions, the values of the function and its derivatives at $t = 0$. Hence, if all initial conditions are zero, transformation of a differential equation into the *s*-domain can be achieved by replacing $\dfrac{d}{dt}$ by s, $\dfrac{d^2}{dt^2}$ by s^2, $\dfrac{d^3}{dt^3}$ by s^3 etc. The linear differential equation thus becomes an algebraic equation in *s*.

Inverse Laplace transformation, $\mathcal{L}^{-1}[F(s)] = f(t)$, is required to obtain the time response. A transformed solution will in general be a ratio of polynomials:

$$F(s) = \frac{a_m s^m + a_{m-1}s^{m-1} + \dots a_0}{s^n + b_{n-1}s^{n-1} + \dots b_0}$$

When this is not in a form which can be found in the available tables it must be split by partial fraction expansion into a number of functions which are listed in the tables:

$$F(s) = F_1(s) + F_2(s) + \dots$$

$$\text{therefore } f(t) = \mathcal{L}^{-1}[F_1(s)] + \mathcal{L}^{-1}[F_2(s)] + \dots$$

The process of using the Laplace transform technique in this way to solve the differential equation for a given system input function is illustrated in Chapter 4. Often however in control system analysis, information in the *s*-plane suffices, and it is not necessary to carry out the final step of transforming the solution back into the time domain.

2.3 Transfer functions and the characteristic equation

The relationship between input and output of a dynamic system component will normally be described by a differential equation. For the purposes of system analysis the control engineer uses Laplace transform notation, and if the component is linear writes the equation in the form of a transfer function.

The *transfer function* of a linear system is defined as the ratio of the Laplace transform of the output to the Laplace transform of the input when all initial conditions are zero. Conventionally the symbol $G(s)$ is used, but if the element appears in a feedback loop the symbol would be $H(s)$ (see Fig. 2.3).

It is thus seen that the transfer function is a property of a system and describes the dynamic characteristics of the system but is not influenced by the state of the system. Since initial conditions are assumed to be zero for evaluating the transfer function it follows that the differential equation can be

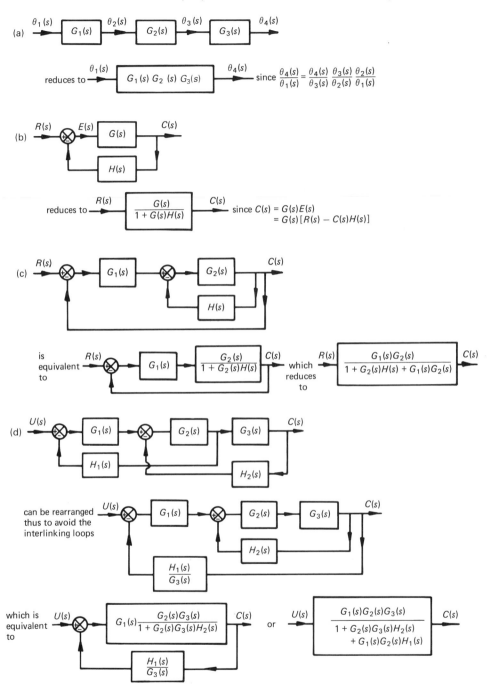

Fig. 2.3 Examples illustrating block diagram reduction

transformed into the Laplace domain by replacing $\dfrac{d}{dt}$ by s, $\dfrac{d^2}{dt^2}$ by s^2 etc. The resulting transfer function in the general case then takes the form

$$G(s) = \frac{P(s)}{Q(s)}$$

where $P(s)$ and $Q(s)$ are polynomials in s. For the system to be physically realizable the order of the numerator cannot exceed that of the denominator.

It will be seen in Chapter 4 that the form of the output response of a system when subjected to a changing input variable is determined by the values of the roots of the equation $Q(s) = 0$. This equation, obtained by equating the denominator of the overall transfer function to zero, is termed the *characteristic equation*. The roots of the characteristic equation are referred to as the *poles* of the overall system transfer function, since they are values of s which cause the transfer function magnitude to become infinite. The number of roots, and thus the order of the characteristic equation is termed the order of the system.

Where a complex system comprises many interconnected simple blocks the overall transfer function can be obtained by reduction of the block diagram to a simple one with a single block, which has however a complex transfer function. The process is one of simple algebraic manipulation, and is illustrated by Fig. 2.3. Where loops interlink as in Fig. 2.3d some additional manipulation is needed.

2.4 Transfer functions for some simple elements

Transfer functions will be obtained for six simple components to illustrate the form which they take and also the way in which they are derived analytically.

Example 2.3. Ideal spring. Consider a simple coil spring of negligible mass, to one end of which a force $f_s(t)$ is applied, the other end being fixed (Fig. 2.4).

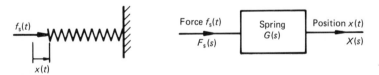

Fig. 2.4 Simple spring

There will be a deflection $x(t)$ from the unloaded position of the end of the spring. This component could be represented by a block with input $f_s(t)$ and output $x(t)$.

The equation relating input and output is

$f_s(t) = Kx(t)$, where K = spring stiffness

$$\therefore \quad \frac{x(t)}{f_s(t)} = \frac{1}{K}$$

Taking Laplace transforms yields the transfer function

$$G(s) = \frac{X(s)}{F_s(s)} = \frac{1}{K} \qquad 2.10$$

In this case there is no time dependence, and the transfer function is a pure gain term. This relationship assumes that the spring stiffness is constant, and is obviously valid only provided the force is not so large that the spring coils come together.

Example 2.4. Ideal hydraulic damper. Consider now a piston of negligible mass sliding with some clearance in an oil-filled cylinder under the action of a force $f_d(t)$ (Fig. 2.5). Again there will be a relationship between the position of the

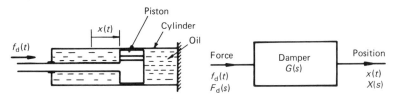

Fig. 2.5 Hydraulic damper

piston $x(t)$ and the applied force. This is obtained from the basic physical considerations which are that the viscous drag on the piston is proportional to the velocity of the piston in the cylinder.

$$f_d(t) = C \frac{dx(t)}{dt} \qquad 2.11$$

where C = viscous damping coefficient = force per unit velocity

Taking Laplace transforms gives, for zero $x(0)$

$$F_d(s) = CsX(s) \qquad 2.12$$

and hence the transfer function is

$$G(s) = \frac{X(s)}{F_d(s)} = \frac{1}{Cs} \qquad 2.13$$

Again no inertia has been included and it has been assumed that there is a free flow through the piston so that no pressure difference can arise across the piston. If either were not valid then the force balance equation (Eq. 2.11) would not be correct. Clearly these equations are only valid so long as the piston does not reach either limit of its stroke.

Example 2.5. Mass-spring-damper. A frequently occurring physical arrangement that can be represented by a force acting on a mass which is restrained by a spring and viscous damper is shown diagrammatically in Fig. 2.6. It is assumed that the mass is constrained to move in the direction of the applied force by friction-free guiding surfaces.

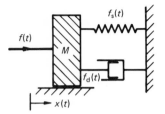

Fig. 2.6 Mass-spring-damper

The basic physical law relating the position of the mass to the force acting upon it is Newton's second law of motion i.e. the sum of the applied forces is equal to the rate of change of momentum.

$$\therefore \quad f(t) - f_s(t) - f_d(t) = M \frac{d^2x(t)}{dt^2}$$

$$\text{but } f_s(t) = Kx(t) \text{ and } f_d(t) = C \frac{dx(t)}{dt}$$

$$\therefore \quad f(t) = M \frac{d^2x(t)}{dt^2} + C \frac{dx(t)}{dt} + Kx(t) \qquad 2.14$$

For zero initial conditions the Laplace transform is

$$F(s) = Ms^2 X(s) + Cs X(s) + K X(s)$$

Hence the transfer function is

$$\frac{X(s)}{F(s)} = \frac{1}{Ms^2 + Cs + K} \qquad 2.15$$

The most general form of equation 2.14, using the dot notation for differentiation, is

$$\ddot{x}(t) + 2\zeta\omega_n \dot{x}(t) + \omega_n^2 x(t) = \omega_n^2 u(t) \qquad 2.16$$

where $u(t)$ is the forcing term, $\omega_n = \sqrt{(K/M)}$ is the system natural frequency, and the symbol ζ is known as the damping factor. The full significance of these terms will be considered in Section 4.2.

For zero initial conditions, the Laplace transform of Eq. 2.16 is

$$(s^2 + 2\zeta\omega_n s + \omega_n^2)X(s) = \omega_n^2 U(s)$$

and thus the transfer function is

$$\frac{X(s)}{U(s)} = \frac{\omega_n^2}{s^2 + 2\zeta\omega_n s + \omega_n^2} = G(s) \qquad 2.17$$

Example 2.6. Liquid in glass thermometer. For a simple thermometer (or equivalent temperature measurement device) there is a relationship between the indicated temperature and the temperature being measured. Let $\theta_i(t)$, the temperature of the fluid around the bulb, be the input and $\theta_0(t)$, the temperature of the fluid in the thermometer, be the system output. The thermometer fluid volume will vary in proportion to its temperature, and the stem is graduated accordingly. The temperatures are both time varying and hence functions of time t.

The rate of heat flow $q(t)$ into the thermometer fluid is proportional to the temperature difference across the walls

$$\therefore \quad q(t) = \frac{\theta_i(t) - \theta_0(t)}{k_1} \qquad 2.18$$

where k_1 is the thermal resistance and is determined by the coefficients of heat transfer from fluid to glass, through the glass, and from glass to inner fluid.

Also, the rate of heat flow $q(t)$ is proportional to the rate of temperature rise of the thermometer fluid

$$\therefore \quad q(t) = cm \frac{d\theta_0(t)}{dt} \qquad 2.19$$

where c is the specific heat and m is the mass of the thermometer fluid.

$$\therefore \quad \theta_i(t) - \theta_0(t) = k_2 \frac{d\theta_0(t)}{dt} \quad \text{where } k_2 = k_1 cm$$

Taking Laplace transforms yields the equation

$$\theta_i(s) - \theta_0(s) = k_2 s \theta_0(s)$$

$$\therefore \quad \frac{\theta_0(s)}{\theta_i(s)} = \frac{1}{1 + k_2 s} \qquad 2.20$$

Note that the thermal capacity of the glass has been assumed to be negligible, and the overall coefficient of heat transfer assumed to be constant.

Note also that the parameters have been considered to be *lumped*, which means that the thermometer fluid temperature has been assumed to be uniform in a spatial sense, as has the temperature of the fluid being measured. If the temperatures were to be considered as functions of both time and position, it would be necessary to describe the system by partial differential equations, and it would be termed a *distributed parameter system*.

Example 2.7. Resistance–capacitance network. Consider the circuit shown in Fig. 2.7 with input voltage $V_i(t)$ and output voltage $V_0(t)$. Assume that the output impedance is infinite.

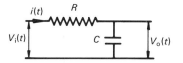

Fig. 2.7 *R C* network

$$i(t) = \frac{V_i(t) - V_0(t)}{R} = C\frac{dV_0(t)}{dt}$$

$$\therefore \quad V_i(s) - V_0(s) = RCsV_0(s)$$

$$\therefore \quad \frac{V_0(s)}{V_i(s)} = \frac{1}{1 + RCs} \qquad\qquad 2.21$$

Example 2.8. Hydraulic servomechanism. Fig. 2.8 shows schematically a hydraulic servomechanism, a feedback device commonly found in practice,

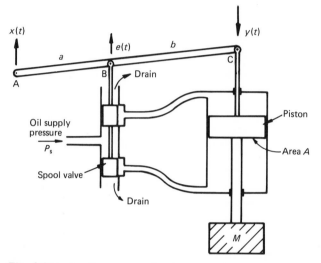

Fig. 2.8 Hydraulic servomechanism

whose function is to move a load of mass M to a position $y(t)$ in response to a command signal $x(t)$ using a hydraulic or pneumatic supply to provide the power. Let the input and output be positive in the direction of the arrows and let the position of the spool valve be given by $e(t)$. Note that x, y, and e are functions of time t. Increase of x, say, would cause the link AC (called a *walking beam*) to pivot about C, cause e to increase and the spool valve to move upwards thus allowing fluid to flow to the space above the piston and from the space below. The piston thus moves downward, so causing AC to pivot about A and thus e to decrease again. Ideally the whole system will come to rest when the valve is again in the central position.

What is the relationship between output $y(t)$ and input $x(t)$?

Ideally in the steady state, i.e. as $t\to\infty$, $e=0$ and $y=(b/a)x$. Transiently however this is not true.

By geometry $\qquad\qquad e(t) = \frac{b}{a + b}\, x(t) - \frac{a}{a + b}\, y(t)$

and if $a = b$, then $\qquad\quad e(t) = \frac{x(t) - y(t)}{2} \qquad\qquad 2.22$

Assuming that the pressure drop across the valve is constant, then the rate of flow through the valve $q(t)$ is proportional to the area of opening (see Example 2.2),

say
$$q(t) = Ce(t) \qquad \qquad 2.23$$

But also this flow rate must equal the rate of change of volume of the chamber into which it is flowing

$$\therefore \quad q(t) = A \frac{dy(t)}{dt} \qquad \qquad 2.24$$

$$\therefore \quad \frac{C[x(t) - y(t)]}{2} = A \frac{dy(t)}{dt}$$

Taking Laplace transforms

$$X(s) - Y(s) = \frac{2A}{C} sY(s)$$

$$\therefore \quad \frac{Y(s)}{X(s)} = \frac{1}{1 + \dfrac{2A}{C} s} \qquad \qquad 2.25$$

In addition to the assumption about constant pressure drop across the valve, many other gross assumptions have been made: no leakage, fluid is incompressible, no inertia, constant temperature, no clearance at pin joints etc. In the next section some of these other effects will be considered.

For each of the last three systems the transfer function has the same form, namely $\dfrac{1}{1 + \tau s}$. This form of relationship is called a *simple time lag*; the constant τ which is dependent on the system parameters is called the *time constant*. Although physically the systems are completely different, mathematically they are represented by the same form of model. They will thus all behave in a similar way and for analytical purposes can be considered to be identical. If the time constants are equal, and the excitation functions are of the same form, then the response functions will also be the same.

2.5 Effect of secondary factors on transfer functions

As has been shown above, in order to obtain the transfer function for a system element, it is necessary first to define clearly the boundaries of the system and the relevant signal variables. The relationships between these variables must then be determined by writing down the physical equations governing the system behaviour. Those variables which are not of direct interest must be eliminated leaving the relationship between input and output. The form of the resulting transfer function will be governed by what effects have been included. In a mechanical system, is the inertia of various parts significant? In a hydraulic system, are fluid leakage or compressibility effects of importance?

To illustrate the significance of secondary factors consider the effect of various factors on the transfer function of a simple hydraulic ram. Let the piston area be A, the system input be the input flow rate $q(t)$, the system output be the piston position $x(t)$, and the fluid pressure be $p(t)$ (Fig. 2.9).

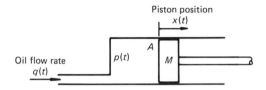

Fig. 2.9 Simple ram

(a) *Simplest representation of ram.* Neglect inertia and leakage; assume that the fluid is incompressible and the piping and cylinder are rigid. The governing equation is the flow continuity equation

$$q(t) = A \frac{dx(t)}{dt} \qquad\qquad 2.26$$

Laplace transformation and rearrangement gives the transfer function

$$\frac{X(s)}{Q(s)} = \frac{1}{As} \qquad\qquad 2.27$$

This is the relationship for an integrator, the integration occurring at rate $\dfrac{1}{A}$.

(b) *Ram with inertia.* Let the piston and whatever is connected to it have mass M.

If there is no leakage past the piston then the flow continuity equation, Eq. 2.26, is still valid and inertia has no effect.

If leakage does exist this is likely to be viscous in nature with a flow rate proportional to pressure difference. Let the leakage flow be $K_L p(t)$ where K_L is a leakage coefficient, $p(t)$ is the fluid gauge pressure, and the pressure at the other side of the piston is atmospheric. The flow continuity equation is now

$$q(t) = A \frac{dx(t)}{dt} + K_L p(t) \qquad\qquad 2.28$$

It is necessary to obtain another equation to allow $p(t)$ to be eliminated. In this case it is obtained by applying Newton's second law.

$$p(t)A = M \frac{d^2 x(t)}{dt^2} \qquad\qquad 2.29$$

$$\therefore \quad q(t) = A \frac{dx(t)}{dt} + \frac{K_L M}{A} \frac{d^2 x(t)}{dt^2} \qquad\qquad 2.30$$

Taking Laplace transforms for zero initial conditions gives

$$Q(s) = AsX(s) + \frac{K_L M}{A} s^2 X(s)$$

$$\therefore \quad \frac{X(s)}{Q(s)} = \frac{1}{\left(A + \frac{K_L M}{A} s\right)s} = \frac{1}{As\left(1 + \frac{K_L M}{A^2} s\right)} \qquad 2.31$$

It can be seen that the effect of including inertia and leakage is to introduce a simple lag of time constant $K_L M/A^2$ proportional both to the mass and the leakage coefficient.

(c) *Ram with viscous load.* If the resistance to motion arises not from inertia of the moving parts but from viscous drag forces then the following equations are relevant:

$$q(t) = A \frac{dx(t)}{dt} + K_L p(t)$$

and
$$p(t)A = \mu \frac{dx(t)}{dt} \quad \text{where } \mu = \text{constant}$$

$$\therefore \quad q(t) = A \frac{dx(t)}{dt} + \frac{K_L \mu}{A} \frac{dx(t)}{dt}$$

and hence
$$\frac{X(s)}{Q(s)} = \frac{1}{\left(A + \frac{K_L \mu}{A}\right)s} \qquad 2.32$$

In this case the effect is still one of integration, but at a slower rate.

(d) *Ram with inertia and viscous load.* The equations are

$$q(t) = A \frac{dx(t)}{dt} + K_L p(t)$$

and
$$p(t)A - \mu \frac{dx(t)}{dt} = M \frac{d^2 x(t)}{dt^2}$$

$$\therefore \quad q(t) = A \frac{dx(t)}{dt} + K_L \left\{ \frac{M}{A} \frac{d^2 x(t)}{dt^2} + \frac{\mu}{A} \frac{dx(t)}{dt} \right\}$$

and
$$\frac{X(s)}{Q(s)} = \frac{1}{\left(A + \frac{K_L \mu}{A}\right)s + \frac{K_L M}{A} s^2} = \frac{\dfrac{1}{A + \dfrac{K_L \mu}{A}}}{s\left(1 + \dfrac{K_L M}{A^2 + K_L \mu} s\right)} \qquad 2.33$$

(e) *Effect of compressibility.* In writing down the flow continuity equation above it has been assumed that the fluid is incompressible. In practice, even liquids are not completely incompressible, and so if the pressure rises the fluid volume decreases slightly. Hence some of the fluid entering goes to make up the decrease in volume due to compressibility of the fluid (and expansion of pipes, if the containing system is not completely rigid).

Compressibility is defined by the

$$\text{Bulk modulus } K_B = \frac{\text{change in pressure}}{\text{change in volume per unit volume}}$$

$$= \frac{\Delta p}{\dfrac{\Delta v}{v}} \quad \text{where } v = \text{volume of fluid under pressure}$$

$$\therefore \quad \Delta v = \frac{v}{K_B} \Delta p$$

and

$$\frac{dv}{dt} = \frac{v}{K_B} \frac{dp}{dt} = q_{\text{compressibility}} \qquad 2.34$$

The flow continuity equation is

$$q_{\text{in}} = q_{\text{velocity}} + q_{\text{leakage}} + q_{\text{compressibility}} \qquad 2.35$$

$$\therefore \quad q(t) = A \frac{dx(t)}{dt} + K_L p(t) + \frac{v}{K_B} \frac{dp(t)}{dt}$$

also

$$p(t)A - \mu \frac{dx(t)}{dt} = M \frac{d^2 x(t)}{dt^2}$$

$$\therefore \quad q(t) = A \frac{dx(t)}{dt} + K_L \left(\frac{M}{A} \frac{d^2 x(t)}{dt^2} + \frac{\mu}{A} \frac{dx(t)}{dt} \right)$$

$$+ \frac{v}{K_B} \left(\frac{M}{A} \frac{d^3 x(t)}{dt^3} + \frac{\mu}{A} \frac{d^2 x(t)}{dt^2} \right)$$

$$\therefore \quad q(t) = \frac{vM}{K_B A} \frac{d^3 x(t)}{dt^3} + \left(\frac{K_L M}{A} + \frac{\mu v}{K_B A} \right) \frac{d^2 x(t)}{dt^2} + \left(\frac{K_L \mu}{A} + A \right) \frac{dx(t)}{dt}$$

and

$$\frac{X(s)}{Q(s)} = \frac{1}{s \left\{ \dfrac{Mv}{K_B A} s^2 + \left(\dfrac{K_L M}{A} + \dfrac{\mu v}{K_B A} \right) s + \left(\dfrac{K_L \mu}{A} + A \right) \right\}} \qquad 2.36$$

It can be seen that the effect of inclusion of compressibility has been to raise by one the order of the polynomial in s in the denominator, and that the transfer function $G(s)$ is a property of the system elements only and is independent of excitation and initial conditions. Similarly, including compressibility, inertia and leakage for the hydraulic servo would give a third order equation.

2.6 State equations

An alternative method of system representation developed since about 1960 has been the characterization of dynamic systems by means of state equations instead of transfer functions. The state equation will be recognizable as no more than a set of differential equations which define the behaviour of a dynamic system in terms of the dependent variables, at least if these equations are written in a certain form.

As a simple example to show the form taken by state equations, consider again the mechanical system shown in Fig. 2.6.

The equation of motion, written in the general form of Eq. 2.16, is

$$\ddot{x}(t) + 2\zeta\omega_n\dot{x}(t) + \omega_n^2 x(t) = \omega_n^2 u(t) \qquad 2.37$$

where $x(t)$ is the horizontal motion (output) and $u(t)$ is the forcing (input) function. The equation may be solved by the application of the Laplace transform technique; this will indicate the variation of the dependent variable $x(t)$ with respect to the independent variable time.

Eq. 2.37 can be rewritten as a pair of first order differential equations:

$$\dot{x}_1(t) = x_2(t) \qquad 2.38$$

$$\dot{x}_2(t) = -2\zeta\omega_n x_2(t) - \omega_n^2 x_1(t) + \omega_n^2 u(t) \qquad 2.39$$

where $x_1(t) = x(t)$ (position) and $x_2(t) = \dot{x}(t)$ (velocity). The terms $x_1(t)$ and $x_2(t)$ are the dependent variables of a pair of differential equations, written in a certain form, which define the behaviour of a second order system and are known as *state variables*.

A two dimensional vector, having components $x(t)$ and $\dot{x}(t)$ also defines the *state* of the system and is known as the *state vector*. If the mass M is displaced a distance x_0 from its static equilibrium position and released, the solution trajectory could be as shown in Fig. 2.10. This form of trajectory represents an oscillation which is decreasing until the system comes to rest.

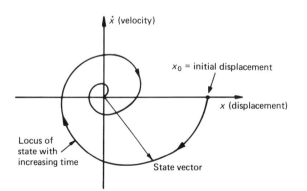

Fig. 2.10 Typical solution trajectory

The importance of the state vector is that all future system states are completely defined if the initial state and system inputs are known. To illustrate this, Eq. 2.38 and Eq. 2.39 are rewritten as a single vector matrix equation:

$$\begin{Bmatrix} \dot{x}_1(t) \\ \dot{x}_2(t) \end{Bmatrix} = \begin{bmatrix} 0 & 1 \\ -\omega_n{}^2 & -2\zeta\omega_n \end{bmatrix} \begin{Bmatrix} x_1(t) \\ x_2(t) \end{Bmatrix} + \begin{bmatrix} 0 \\ \omega_n{}^2 \end{bmatrix} u(t)$$

or more briefly as

$$\{\dot{x}(t)\} = A\{x(t)\} + Bu(t) \qquad\qquad 2.40$$

where $\{x(t)\}$ is the state vector, A is a 2×2 square matrix and B is a two element column vector. Equation 2.40 relates the rate of change of the state of the system to the present state of the system and the input signals. Some examples of the derivation of state equations will be given in Chapter 5.

The total space occupied by all possible values of the state vector is known as the *state space*. An nth order system will require a state vector having n components, and the equivalent state space will be n-dimensional.

3
Analogue Computers and System Simulation

It has been shown how a system can be represented schematically by a block diagram, each block having associated with it a transfer function describing the relevant output–input relationship. Also, a complex block diagram incorporating many elements with relatively simple transfer functions can be reduced to a single block with a high order transfer function relating the system output to the system input. In studying system behaviour it is desirable to be able to determine how the system would react to various input or disturbance functions. ‹

If the form of the input function and of the transfer function are simple, then the dynamic response can be determined analytically by solving the governing differential equation, as will be shown in Chapter 4. If the response is required for a number of different input functions, or for a number of different system parameters, then the equation solution time can be excessive. It is useful to be able to obtain time response traces quickly, particularly for complex systems, or where it is necessary to investigate the effect of parameter changes. This is most satisfactorily achieved by computer solution of the governing equations, a very convenient method being by simulating the system on an analogue computer, or on a digital computer using a high level simulation language.

3.1 Analogue and digital computers

An analogue computer is a machine in which various physical components can be selected and interconnected in such a way that the equations describing the resulting computer arrangement are the same as those describing the physical behaviour of the system to be studied. The computer arrangement is then analogous to the system. It is a continuous data device which operates in a real time parallel mode, making it particularly suitable for the solution of differential equations and hence for the simulation of dynamic systems. Almost the only type now in use is the electronic analogue computer, in which voltages at various points within the programmed computer circuit represent the variable quantities of the system being simulated. The ease of use, and the direct interactive control which the engineer has over the running of such a computer, allows full scope for engineering intuition and makes it an invaluable tool for the analysis of dynamic systems and the synthesis of any associated controllers. A facility which is frequently helpful is that of being able to slow down or speed up the problem solution. The accuracy of solution, since it is dependent on analogue devices, is generally only of the order of a few percent but, for the purposes of system analysis and design, higher accuracy is seldom necessary; also this accuracy often matches the quality of the available input data.

The digital computer, by contrast, is a discrete data machine which basically operates in a serial mode and with which real time operation is generally not possible. It is a highly sophisticated calculating machine which performs simple arithmetic operations sequentially at very high speed. It has extensive capacity for storage of information; this memory is a very important feature of the machine and makes it different from the simple calculating machine. Solution of system equations is effected by writing appropriate programs but, with the modern simulation languages which are now available, this can be a simple process very similar to programming for an analogue computer. The accuracy of solution can be made as high as required by selecting a small enough sampling interval for the discrete data being handled, but the penalty is one of long computation times, particularly with the relatively inefficient compilation associated with high level simulation languages. With the development of interactive systems utilizing visual display units the advantage of a close man–machine relationship is being extended to many digital computer installations.

Because of the ability of both digital and analogue computers to solve complicated mathematical equations at high speed, digital or analogue computational elements are often incorporated as part of the control system or as the complete control system.

A number of *hybrid* machines were developed to combine the two and enable a problem to be programmed in such a way that each machine is used for the computations which it performs most efficiently. Much of the cost of such a machine arises from the rather complicated interface equipment which is required to make the necessary conversions between analogue and digital signals, and vice versa. Specific computational needs arising with certain control problems have contributed significantly to the development of the hybrid computer as, in earlier years, they did with the analogue computer. The cost of an analogue or hybrid computer is now justified only for certain large simulations where fast computing speed attained by parallel operation is important.

3.2 Basic analogue computer elements (linear)

(a) *Summing amplifier.* The basic building block of the analogue computer is the *high gain d.c. amplifier*, represented schematically by Fig. 3.1. When the input voltage is $e_i(t)$ then the output voltage is given by

$$e_0(t) = -Ae_i(t) \qquad 3.1$$

where A, the amplifier voltage gain, is a large constant value.

Fig. 3.1 High gain d.c. amplifier

When this is used in conjunction with a resistance network, as shown in Fig. 3.2, then the resulting circuit can be used to add a number of voltages. Let V_1,

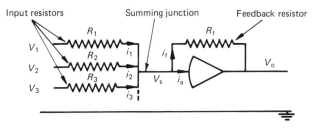

Fig. 3.2 Circuit for summing amplifier

V_2, V_3 ... be voltages, relative to some base potential, which can be functions of time; also let these be applied to resistors R_1, R_2, R_3 ... At any given instant, applying Kirchoff's 1st Law to the *summing junction*, the point where the outputs of these resistors are connected,

$$i_1 + i_2 + i_3 = i_f + i_a \qquad 3.2$$

where i_f is the current through the feedback resistor, and i_a is the input current into the high gain amplifier. If V_s and V_0 are the voltages at input and output of the amplifier respectively, then

$$\frac{V_1 - V_s}{R_1} + \frac{V_2 - V_s}{R_2} + \frac{V_3 - V_s}{R_3} = i_a + \frac{V_s - V_0}{R_f}$$

Now the amplifier voltage gain A will be of the order of 10^8 and the computer will have an operational range of ± 100 volts, or in some cases ± 10 volts. Hence, for V_0 to remain within this range, V_s must not exceed about 10^{-6} volts; it is then negligible compared to V_1, V_2, V_3 and V_0 and is virtually at earth potential. The summing junction is thus referred to as a virtual earth point.

Also, the input impedance of the amplifier will be of the order of 10^{10} ohms, compared to 10^6 ohms for the feedback resistor. Hence i_a can also be neglected.

$$\therefore \quad \frac{V_1}{R_1} + \frac{V_2}{R_2} + \frac{V_3}{R_3} = -\frac{V_0}{R_f}$$

$$\therefore \quad V_0 = -\left(\frac{R_f}{R_1} V_1 + \frac{R_f}{R_2} V_2 + \frac{R_f}{R_3} V_3 + ... \right) \qquad 3.3$$

If $R_1 = R_2 = R_3 = ... = R_f$ then

$$V_0 = -(V_1 + V_2 + V_3 + ...) \quad \text{addition of voltages.}$$

If there is only one voltage input

$$V_0 = -\frac{R_f}{R_1} V_1 \quad ... \text{ multiplication by a constant.}$$

It should be noted that in all cases there is a sign inversion. Usually the available ratios R_f/R_1 etc. are standardized to 1 and 10, the appropriate gain being selectable as required. The complete circuit comprising high gain amplifier, input resistors, and feedback element is termed an *operational amplifier*, and for it to act as a summing amplifier the feedback element must be a resistor. It is given a symbol as shown in Fig. 3.3.

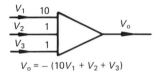

$$V_o = - (10V_1 + V_2 + V_3)$$

Fig. 3.3 Symbol for summing amplifier

(b) *Coefficient potentiometer.* In order to multiply a voltage by a constant other than 10, use is made of a grounded potentiometer (usually a 10-turn helical potentiometer), as shown in Fig. 3.4. This permits multiplication by a constant in the range 0 to 1. If larger values are required then one or more summing amplifiers with gain 10 must be used in series with the potentiometer.

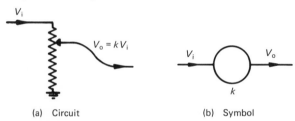

(a) Circuit   (b) Symbol

Fig. 3.4 Coefficient potentiometer

Coefficient potentiometers are generally set to the desired value when in circuit, as will be described in Section 3.4. Since the setting is affected by the loading, the load resistance should be constant, hence two potentiometers should not be placed in series but should be buffered by placing an amplifier between them.

(c) *Integrating amplifier.* The circuit for the integrating amplifier shown in Fig. 3.5a is similar to that for the summing amplifier, the difference being that there

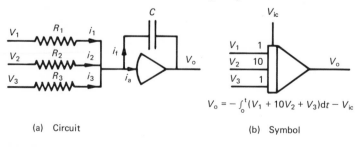

$$V_o = - \int_0^t (V_1 + 10V_2 + V_3)\,dt - V_{ic}$$

(a) Circuit   (b) Symbol

Fig. 3.5 Integrating amplifier

is a capacitor instead of a resistor in the feedback path. Again the summing junction is a virtual earth point and i_a is negligible.

$$\therefore \quad \frac{V_1}{R_1} + \frac{V_2}{R_2} + \frac{V_3}{R_3} = -C\frac{dV_0}{dt}$$

$$\therefore \quad V_0 = -\int_0^t \left(\frac{1}{R_1C}V_1 + \frac{1}{R_2C}V_2 + \ldots\right)dt \qquad 3.4$$

The values $\dfrac{1}{RC}$, the time constants of the integration, vary the integration rate, and again are generally standardized at 1 and 10. An initial condition voltage can be applied to the capacitance, and integration would then commence from this value. This involves the inclusion of two additional resistors as shown in Fig. 3.13. Fig. 3.5b shows the diagrammatic representation for the integrating amplifier with three inputs and an initial condition value applied. As with the summing amplifier there is always a sign inversion.

3.3 Production of circuit diagrams to solve differential equations

The three basic elements described in the section above are sufficient to simulate any linear system and hence to solve the corresponding differential equation. To illustrate the technique for deriving the computer circuit diagram consider a system with differential equation

$$A\ddot{c}(t) + B\dot{c}(t) + c(t) = u(t) \qquad 3.5$$

The transfer function corresponding to this is

$$\frac{C(s)}{U(s)} = \frac{1}{1 + Bs + As^2} \qquad 3.6$$

The following steps are carried out:

(a) The equation is rearranged so that the highest derivative term is on the left hand side and all other terms are on the right hand side of the equation:

$$\text{i.e.} \quad A\ddot{c}(t) = u(t) - c(t) - B\dot{c}(t) \qquad 3.7$$

(b) It is assumed that a voltage representing the highest derivative term is available, then lower derivative terms can be obtained by successive integrations. For a second order differential equation, as in this case, two integrators are required (Fig. 3.6).

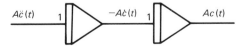

$A\ddot{c}(t)$ 1 $-A\dot{c}(t)$ 1 $Ac(t)$

Fig. 3.6 Successive integration

(c) Potentiometers and summing amplifiers are used to obtain the correct coefficients and signs of the lower derivative terms on the right hand side of the equation, and these signals are added to $u(t)$ in a summing amplifier to produce $A\ddot{c}(t)$ at the point where it was assumed to be available (Fig. 3.7).

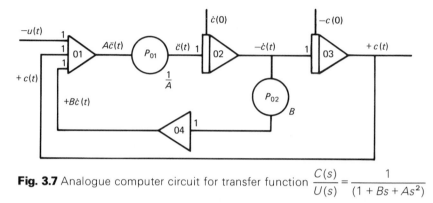

Fig. 3.7 Analogue computer circuit for transfer function $\dfrac{C(s)}{U(s)} = \dfrac{1}{(1 + Bs + As^2)}$

(d) For identification purposes, numbers are assigned to the amplifiers and potentiometers on the circuit diagram; the interconnections are then made externally on the patch panel of the computer by means of plugs and leads.

(e) The system can now be forced with any desired voltage waveform representing $u(t)$ and the resulting response $c(t)$ can be observed and recorded if required. Potentiometer values can be altered to represent variation of system parameters and the resulting system behaviour change noted. Other system quantities, in this case $-\dot{c}(t)$ and $\ddot{c}(t)$, can also be monitored if desired. If $c(t)$ and $\dot{c}(t)$ are required to have values other than zero at the start of computation then these initial condition values are applied as voltages to the initial condition inputs of amplifiers 03 and 02.

Normally the circuit diagrams might be modified for a number of reasons:

(i) The circuit can generally be rearranged slightly to reduce the number of amplifiers used. In this example if the signal $\ddot{c}(t)$ does not require to be monitored amplifiers 01 and 02 can be combined as in Fig. 3.8, reducing the number of amplifiers needed from four to three.

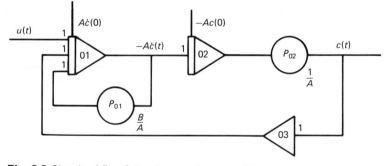

Fig. 3.8 Circuit of Fig. 3.7 using one less amplifier

(ii) The circuit may be rearranged so that each variable parameter is represented by a single potentiometer. Fig. 3.7 is better than Fig. 3.8 in this respect. Care must be taken to ensure that potentiometers are not placed in series, since alteration of one potentiometer setting would then affect the setting of the other.

(iii) It may be found necessary to adjust the scaling of the problem to avoid, in certain parts of the circuit, voltages which are either so large that they exceed the linear range of the amplifiers, or so small that the poor signal to noise ratio causes significant inaccuracies. Also it may be found desirable to adjust the time scale of the problem to slow down or speed up the solution. The principles of amplitude scaling and time scaling will be described in Section 3.7.

Example 3.1. For the block diagram of Fig. 3.9 consider the derivation of an analogue computer circuit diagram which could be used to investigate the

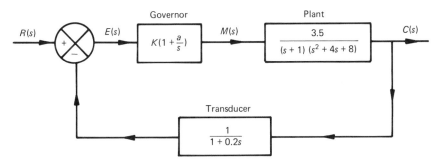

Fig. 3.9 Block diagram of feedback control system

effect on dynamic behaviour of the system of changes in settings of the proportional plus integral governor. Assume that the operational amplifiers available have gains of 1 or 10.

It would be possible to reduce this diagram by the methods illustrated in Fig. 2.3 to one single block with input $R(s)$, output $C(s)$, and transfer function which is of fifth order. The fifth order differential equation which this represents could then be simulated by following the above procedure and using 5 integrators in series, from which would be obtained the 5 signals proportional to $c(t)$, $\dot{c}(t)$, $\ddot{c}(t)$, etc. which must be summed with $r(t)$ to produce the highest order derivative term. (There would in this case be a difficulty, namely the need also to obtain derivatives of the input signal; the method of overcoming this is described in Section 3.6.) It is, however, much more useful and also simpler to draw a circuit diagram for each system component separately, and then to combine these in the appropriate way to obtain a circuit diagram for the overall system. This then gives a true simulation where all intermediate system variables can be easily identified and monitored.

Obtain first a circuit diagram for the plant, noting that it comprises a first and a second order component which are in series, as represented by Fig. 3.10a.

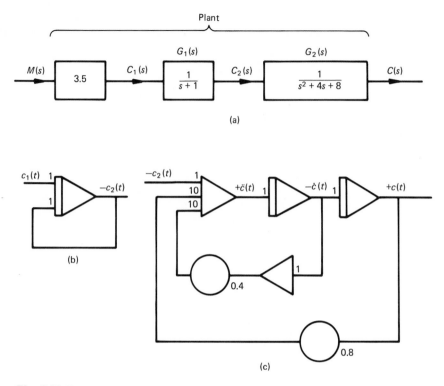

Fig. 3.10 Representation of plant

For block $G_1(s)$

$$\frac{C_2(s)}{C_1(s)} = \frac{1}{s+1}$$

$$\therefore \quad sC_2(s) = C_1(s) - C_2(s)$$

or

$$\dot{c}_2(t) = c_1(t) - c_2(t)$$

and this requires the circuit diagram of Fig. 3.10b.

For block $G_2(s)$

$$\frac{C(s)}{C_2(s)} = \frac{1}{s^2 + 4s + 8}$$

$$\therefore \quad s^2C(s) = C_2(s) - 4sC(s) - 8C(s)$$

or

$$\ddot{c}(t) = c_2(t) - 4\dot{c}(t) - 8c(t)$$

which can be simulated by the circuit of Fig. 3.10c. The summer and the first integrator can be combined requiring one amplifier less. The constant 3.5

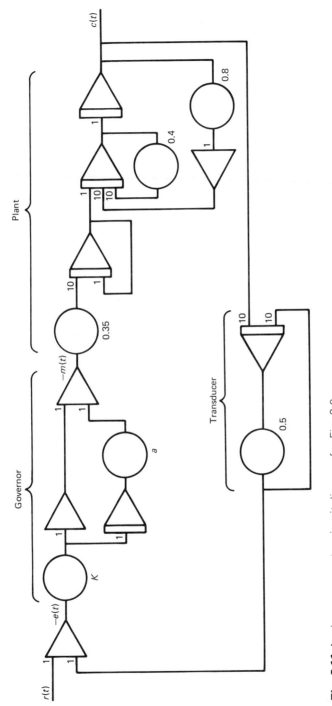

Fig. 3.11 Analogue computer circuit diagram for Fig. 3.9

requires a potentiometer set to 0.35 in conjunction with an input into an amplifier in the gain 10 position.

The circuit for the transducer is similar to that for $G_1(s)$, except that a potentiometer is required to give the time constant of 0.2 seconds. A summing amplifier enables $e(t)$ to be obtained from $r(t)$ and the transducer output. The governor output is obtained by addition of $e(t)$ and a constant a times $\int e(t)\,dt$, the whole being multiplied by the constant K. Combination of all of these parts, paying careful attention to ensure that the signs of signals are correct, yields the overall circuit diagram, Fig. 3.11.

3.4 Computer operating modes

If there is a voltage at the input of an integrating amplifier, then the output will increase continually until the amplifier saturates. It is necessary therefore to be able to control the operation of the amplifiers by starting and stopping the computation as required. Also it is necessary to be able to adjust potentiometers to their required settings, and to be able to set the circuit variables to the desired initial conditions. These are achieved by means of a mode control switch or push buttons which energize relays in the amplifier and potentiometer circuits in the way described below for the usual operating modes.

(a) *'POT SET'*. This mode enables each potentiometer to be set while in circuit, and loaded by the normal amplifier input resistance. Switching to this mode connects the reference voltage supply, $+100$ volts on many machines, to the input of all potentiometers and connects the summing junction (SJ) of all amplifiers to earth potential as shown in Fig. 3.12. By switching a digital

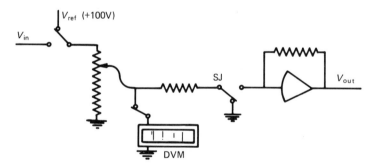

Fig. 3.12 Potentiometer and amplifier in 'POT SET' mode

voltmeter (DVM) to display a potentiometer output voltage, each potentiometer can in turn be adjusted to its required setting.

(b) *'RESET'* or *'IC'*. Two relays are actuated in each integrator circuit, as shown in Fig. 3.13, thus applying initial condition voltages to the feedback capacitors and setting each integrator output to the initial value of the vari-

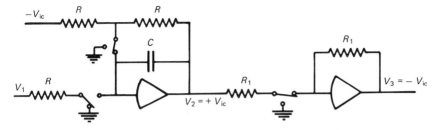

Fig. 3.13 Operational amplifiers in 'RESET' mode

able which it represents. (The voltage applied to the initial condition socket must be of opposite polarity to V_{ic}.) When no connection is made to the initial condition socket, the amplifier starts from an initial voltage of zero. The summing amplifiers remain in their normal operating state.

(c) *'COMPUTE', or 'OPERATE'*. The initial condition voltages are disconnected and the integrator inputs are connected, the integrators start, and the computation proceeds. Any variables of interest can be observed on an oscilloscope or can be recorded.

(d) *'HOLD'*. Switching the computer to *HOLD* causes the integrator inputs to be disconnected and the problem to be 'frozen', Fig. 3.14. The circuit voltages

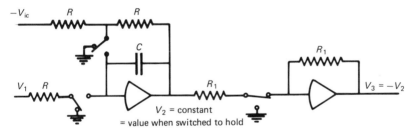

Fig. 3.14 Operational amplifiers in 'HOLD' mode

can thus be measured at a given instant of time. Returning to the *COMPUTE* mode allows the problem solution to continue from the point at which it was frozen.

(e) *'REP OP'*. Sometimes a repetitive operation mode is available allowing automatic and continuous cycling between *RESET* and *COMPUTE*.

On analogue computers intended for use in a hybrid installation, electronic switching controlled by logic signals replaces the mechanical switches in the amplifier circuits. With electronic mode control, there is usually available fast integration, achieved by using capacitors of about 1% or so of the normal values. In the *REP OP* mode the complete response can then be viewed as a persistent trace on an oscilloscope, and the effect of a gradually changing potentiometer setting is very clearly seen.

3.5 Non-linear analogue computer components

The analogue computer is particularly useful for simulating systems where non-linearities are present, analytical solution then generally being complex or impossible. To deal with non-linearities, several other computer elements are available, and these are described briefly below.

(a) *Multipliers.* These enable two variables to be multiplied together or divided by one another, or the square root of one obtained, and are available in three main forms. Servo multipliers operate by positioning a shaft, connected to the wiper of a potentiometer, to an angular position proportional to the first voltage, applying the second voltage to the potentiometer winding, and taking the product from the wiper. By having several potentiometers ganged together one variable can be multiplied by a number of others. Being electromechanical these are not suitable for rapidly varying signals. Quarter square multipliers make use of electronic squaring circuits to mechanize the relationship

$$\tfrac{1}{4}[(V_1 + V_2)^2 - (V_1 - V_2)^2] = V_1 V_2 \qquad 3.8$$

Time division multipliers alter the amplitude and mark/space ratio of a signal in proportion to the two signals and filter the resulting waveform to give a mean value representing the product.

(b) *Servo resolvers.* These are servo multipliers which have specially wound sine/cosine potentiometers and produce the functions sin V and cos V when the input variable is V. Their use is of importance where there is transformation between rectangular and polar coordinates.

(c) *Diode function generators.* The relationship $V_2 = f(V_1)$ can be simulated by approximating the curved relationship by a series of straight-line segments. The break points and the slopes of the segments must be set prior to running the simulation.

(d) *Comparator relays.* A relay which can be incorporated in the circuit is switched one way or the other according to whether the sign of the sum of two signals $(V_1 + V_2)$ is positive or negative. This allows different parts of circuit to be connected depending on the magnitude of a variable V_1 relative to a reference variable V_2. For high speed repetitive operation the mechanical relay is replaced by its electronic counterpart, a D to A switch.

In addition to these components which are built into the computer, effects such as saturation, deadband, and hysteresis can be simulated using external diodes and appropriate circuits. It is also possible to include a human being or items of physical equipment as part of the simulation.

3.6 Differentiation

The method of solving a differential equation by analogue computation, which has been described in Section 3.3, requires the equation to be written in such a form that a circuit diagram can be produced which involves integration of system variables rather than differentiation. Although differentiation could be achieved by means of a high gain amplifier with a capacitor at the input and a resistor in the feedback path, it is something to be avoided since differentiation is a noise amplifying process. An unwanted noise signal $A \sin \omega t$, say, with amplitude A and frequency ω, would become a noise signal of amplitude ωA after differentiation, or $\omega^2 A$ after two stages of differentiation. Further problems arise when step changes of variables occur. Wherever possible, therefore, the equations must be manipulated so that integrators can be employed.

A form of transfer function for which additional manipulation is required is one which has a polynomial in s on the numerator in addition to that on the denominator. The corresponding differential equation thus contains terms involving derivatives of the input function in addition to the derivatives of the output function. Consider the transfer function

$$\frac{C(s)}{U(s)} = \frac{2s^2 + s + 1}{s^3 + 5s^2 + 6s + 1} \qquad 3.9$$

which represents the differential equation

$$\dddot{c}(t) + 5\ddot{c}(t) + 6\dot{c}(t) + c(t) = 2\ddot{u}(t) + \dot{u}(t) + u(t) \qquad 3.10$$

To simulate Eq. 3.9 introduce a new variable $C_1(s)$ so that

$$\frac{C_1(s)}{U(s)} = \frac{1}{s^3 + 5s^2 + 6s + 1} \qquad 3.11$$

The output $C(s)$ is then given by

$$C(s) = (2s^2 + s + 1)C_1(s) \qquad 3.12$$

Equation 3.11 can be tackled by the methods of Section 3.3, and the output can then be obtained by addition of the appropriate derivative terms of the new variable as given by Eq. 3.12. The computer circuit which results is shown in Fig. 3.15.

Situations sometimes occur where differentiation cannot be avoided. Satisfactory results can then usually be obtained by the use of a circuit giving an approximation to differentiation, such as that shown in Fig. 3.16 with transfer function

$$\frac{C(s)}{U(s)} = \frac{s}{1 + (1 - k)s} \qquad 3.13$$

It can be seen that the differential term is modified by the presence of a simple lag term with time constant $(1 - k)$. It will be shown in Chapter 6 that this has the effect of attenuating high frequency components of signal input. In practice the potentiometer setting can be adjusted to be as close to unity as the noise permits.

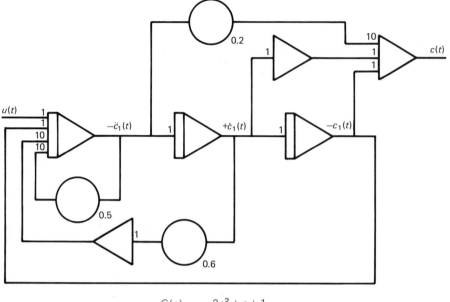

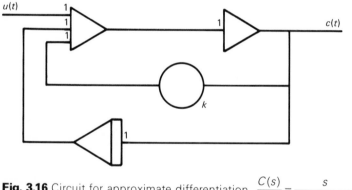

Fig. 3.15 Circuit diagram for $\dfrac{C(s)}{U(s)} = \dfrac{2s^2 + s + 1}{s^3 + 5s^2 + 6s + 1}$

Fig. 3.16 Circuit for approximate differentiation $\dfrac{C(s)}{U(s)} = \dfrac{s}{1 + (1-k)s}$

3.7 Problem scaling

Circuit diagrams obtained by the method described in Section 3.3 usually require some further modification, often of a minor nature, in order to obtain acceptable accuracy of solution by minimizing the effect of inherent physical limitations of the computer elements and of the recording device, and perhaps also to alter the speed of computation for reasons of convenience. For any given input signal the maximum values of the voltage signals within the circuit, which depend on the maximum values of each variable and its derivatives, must neither be so large that the linear range of one or more amplifiers is exceeded, with resulting errors in the solution, nor so small that poor signal-noise ratios cause unacceptable inaccuracy. An excessively slow solution is wasteful of computer and operator time and can introduce inaccuracy caused by integration of small voltage errors over a long period. At the other extreme a very short solution time can cause errors due to the limitations of the dynamic response of certain of the elements being used. Modification to a circuit diagram to minimize these problems takes two forms referred to as *time scaling*, where the solution time is altered, and *amplitude scaling*, where the variables are scaled to ensure that voltage levels throughout the circuit are as high as possible without exceeding the reference value.

Inspection of the coefficients of the system equations and the gain values in the circuit diagram often suggests whether or not scaling is likely to be needed; suitable modifications can then be determined in a number of ways. It is not inappropriate to tackle the problem by a practical trial and observation approach, first making any changes which suggest themselves by inspection of the circuit diagram, patching in the resulting circuit on the computer, observing the response of the output voltage and of the voltages elsewhere in the circuit to see whether further scaling is desirable, and then making additional modifications if required. For any circuit the computer variables are directly proportional to the problem variables in such a way that α volts, say, represent one unit of the corresponding variable. The magnitude of the forcing function voltage can be increased so that the operating voltages within the circuit become as large as possible, without anywhere exceeding the computer reference voltage, and preferably until the scaling constant α is a convenient number. Provided that the problem solution time is reasonable and that voltages are nowhere so small that unacceptable errors are likely to occur then no further action on scaling is required.

If the solution time must be increased or decreased then time scaling is required. This is effected by a change of time variable

$$t = \beta T$$

where t is the problem time, T is the computer or machine time, and β is a constant which is greater than unity if the solution is to be speeded up, and less than unity if it is to be slowed down. Hence 1 problem second $= \beta$ machine seconds, and when $\beta = 1$ the solution is referred to as a *real time simulation*. This change of variable causes a change in the magnitudes of the time derivatives of any problem variable such as $c(t)$, hence

$$\frac{dc(t)}{dt} = \frac{dc(T)}{dT}\frac{dT}{dt} = \frac{1}{\beta}\frac{dc(T)}{dT}, \quad \frac{d^2c(t)}{dt^2} = \frac{1}{\beta^2}\frac{d^2c(T)}{dT^2}, \quad \text{etc.}$$

The differential equation when written in terms of T is therefore the same as the original equation but with the coefficient of each derivative term multiplied by the appropriate power of $\dfrac{1}{\beta}$. The effect on the circuit diagram is to require the gain of each integrator to be changed by the factor β. As illustration consider the differential equation Eq. 3.5

$$A\ddot{c}(t) + B\dot{c}(t) + c(t) = u(t)$$

which in terms of machine time T becomes

$$\frac{A}{\beta^2}\ddot{c}(T) + \frac{B}{\beta}\dot{c}(T) + c(T) = u(T)$$

This has the circuit diagram shown in Fig. 3.17 where for ease of comparison with Fig. 3.7 the integrating amplifier gains have been shown as having the

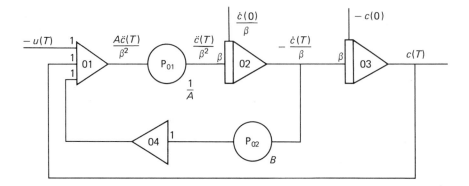

Fig. 3.17 Analogue computer circuit corresponding to Fig. 3.7 for solution speeded up by a factor β

value β. Since amplifier gains normally have values of 1 or 10 only, the time scaling would be straightforward for $\beta = 10$ but would require the introduction of additional potentiometers, and perhaps also summing amplifiers, to accommodate other values of β. If when first drawing a circuit diagram amplifier gains are consistently high, as occurs inherently in equations for fast systems, then it is likely that the solution time should be increased whilst, if potentiometer settings are consistently low, it is probable that the time scale should be altered to speed up the solution. On many machines the integrating amplifier gains and hence the time scale can be changed automatically by a switch on the operating console, enabling the system to be studied visually on an oscilloscope using repetitive operation and a fast solution time, and then slowed down to within the dynamic range of a pen recorder whenever a hard copy trace is required.

The need for amplitude scaling is indicated if gains are very high or very low in certain parts only of the circuit, since the accuracy decreases as the signal amplitude reduces. If somewhere in a loop there is a gain of 100 or an attenuation of 0.01, say, then there is at least one point in the circuit where the voltage can at most be 1% of the reference voltage, and consequently small absolute errors in this voltage could cause large percentage errors in the solution. The procedure for amplitude scaling is not easily learned by reading alone and can best be understood by practical application on a computer. It is a compromise between obtaining the highest possible accuracy of solution and having a simulation where interpretation is easy and where least confusion can arise. The procedure is as follows:

(i) estimate the maximum values of each of the variables $x_1(t)$, $x_2(t)$, $x_3(t)$ ... $x_r(t)$ ... for the forcing function of interest

(ii) determine scaling factors A_1, A_2, ... A_r, ... which are simple numbers and equal to or slightly less than the corresponding value of the ratio

$$\frac{\text{reference voltage}}{\text{maximum expected value of } x_r(t)}$$

(iii) rewrite the differential equations in terms of scaled variables $A_1 x_1(t)$, $A_2 x_2(t)$, ... $A_r x_r(t)$ ...

(iv) draw the circuit diagram by the method of Section 3.3

(v) try the circuit, observe maximum voltages throughout, and readjust where necessary.

The result is that instead of each variable being represented by the voltage at an appropriate point in the circuit multiplied by the common scaling factor α, the variables appear in a normalized form and effectively have different scaling factors. This procedure has the effect of levelling out the maximum voltages around the various loops of the circuit, avoiding high gains being followed by large attenuation or vice versa, and ensuring that each amplifier has a range of operating voltage which is as large as possible.

For many problems, where high accuracy of solution is not of prime importance, the above procedure for amplitude scaling need not be followed fully. The aim can be simply to arrange potentiometer positions and values, and amplifier gain settings, in a sensible manner when first drawing the circuit, and then to carry out the last step of the procedure, making adjustments if they appear necessary in a logical practical manner.

Example 3.2. To illustrate the features of time and amplitude scaling consider the differential equation Eq. 3.5 in which $A = 125$ and $B = 5$

i.e. $125\ddot{c}(t) + 5\dot{c}(t) + c(t) = u(t)$

and prepare a circuit diagram which could be used to investigate the response to a step change of input for varying values of A and B. Assume that the computer reference voltage is 100 volts, and that the available amplifier gains are 1 and 10.

The circuit diagram for $A = 125$ and $B = 5$ is that derived in section 3.3 (Fig. 3.7) which, with the potentiometers set to the appropriate values, is shown in Fig. 3.18a. It can be observed that the voltages at the circuit input and at the outputs of potentiometer P_{01} and amplifiers 02 and 03 are directly proportional to $-u(t)$, $\ddot{c}(t)$, $-\dot{c}(t)$ and $c(t)$ respectively. For the value $A = 125$ the setting of potentiometer P_{01} is very small, and hence to avoid errors which would arise from overloading of amplifier 01 the output voltage of P_{01} cannot be allowed to exceed 0.8 volt. The small magnitude of this voltage which is the input to the integrating amplifier 02 could lead to significant inaccuracy, and also suggests that the solution time may be long. Applying a step change of 50 volts at the input, and measuring the resulting peak voltages throughout the circuit, yields the approximate voltage values shown in the diagram. The large

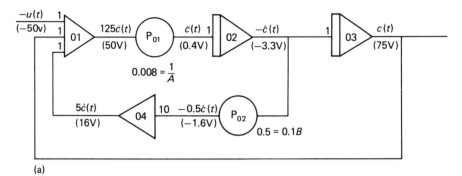

(a)

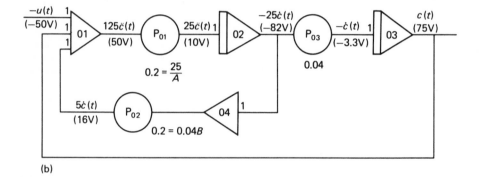

(b)

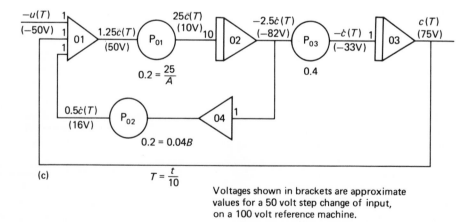

(c) $T = \dfrac{t}{10}$

Voltages shown in brackets are approximate values for a 50 volt step change of input, on a 100 volt reference machine.

Fig. 3.18 Analogue computer circuit diagrams for simulation of differential equation $A\ddot{c}(t) + B\dot{c}(t) + c(t) = u(t)$ for $A = 125$, $B = 5$ (a) basic circuit (b) circuit modified by amplitude scaling (c) circuit further modified to decrease solution time by factor of 10

range of values suggests that amplitude scaling is desirable and study of the diagram suggests where changes could be made to avoid very small voltages. Initial experimental tests also show that the settling time is of the order of 200 seconds which is inconveniently large; this confirms the desirability of time scaling the problem. Fig. 3.18b shows the circuit and the resulting peak voltages after carrying out amplitude scaling by simple trial and observation or by the method described above. The attenuation of 0.008 is carried out in two stages with the result that the voltage output of potentiometer P_{01} now represents the signal $25\ddot{c}(t)$ rather than the signal $\ddot{c}(t)$. The loop gains remain identical at 0.04 for the inner loop and 0.008 for the outer loop. Relatively small voltages at certain points (in this case the input to amplifier 03) cannot be avoided. The solution can be speeded up, say by a factor of 10, merely by altering the inputs of integrating amplifiers 02 and 03 to gain 10 (Fig. 3.18c). The voltage levels remain unchanged. For a complex simulation such a change is particularly convenient if push button time scaling is available. To decrease the solution time by a factor of 20 say, the settings of potentiometers P_{01} and P_{03} are also adjusted. With time scaling the loop gains are altered, in the case of Fig. 3.18c to 0.4 and 0.8 respectively. Study of the variations in the form of the transient response for changing values of coefficients A and B can now be carried out by altering the settings of potentiometers P_{01} and P_{02} to the appropriate values. This is a particularly simple simulation which, however, demonstrates the method of approach which would be used to obtain an actual simulation diagram for a more complex dynamic model.

3.8 Digital continuous system simulation

An analogue computer simultaneously solves all of the differential equations which form the model for a physical system, and continuous voltage signals represent the variables of interest. This enables the machine to operate in real time which permits the incorporation within the simulation of actual items of equipment or of human beings where these form part of the system to be studied. Significant disadvantages of analogue simulation are the high cost of the computer due to the multiplicity of elements with demanding performance specifications, difficulties of problem scaling to avoid overloading of amplifiers, and relatively limited accuracy and repeatability due in part to amplifier drift. As a consequence of the very rapid development of digital computer hardware and software giving ever greater capability and flexibility at decreasing cost, system simulation is inevitably being carried out more and more on the digital computer. There is effectively no problem of overloading so very wide ranges of parameter variation can readily be accommodated, any desirable accuracy can be attained, and with the aid of appropriate high level languages program writing is straightforward. With the availability of the 'on-line' computer facility a simulation can be run interactively in a closely similar manner to that of the analogue computer.

The solution of a differential equation involves the process of integration, and for the digital computer analytical integration must be replaced by some numerical method which yields an approximation to the true solution. A continuous signal $x(t)$ is represented by a series of numbers x_0, x_1, x_2, x_3, $\ldots x_n$, say, which define the signal amplitude at times t_0, t_1, t_2, t_3, ... t_n. These sample values are normally at equally spaced time intervals, and if the sampling interval is chosen to be small enough then no information about the signal is lost (see Section 7.5). With such discrete representation of continuous signals differential equations are converted to difference equations and integration is carried out in a stepwise fashion. Integration of a signal $x(t)$ of known form (where the sample values x_0, x_1, x_2, ... x_n are known at the outset) can be effected by means of the trapezoidal rule

$$\int x(t)\, dt = \left(\frac{x_0 + x_1}{2} + \frac{x_1 + x_2}{2} + \frac{x_2 + x_3}{2} + \ldots + \frac{x_{n-1} + x_n}{2} \right) \Delta t$$

The solution of a differential equation, however, requires integration of a signal $\dot{x}(t)$ which is itself a function of $x(t)$. Consider the first order differential equation

$$\dot{x}(t) = ax(t) + bu(t) \qquad 3.14$$

If the value of $x(t)$ at time t is known then the value at time $t + \Delta t$ is given by

$$x(t + \Delta t) = x(t) + \int_{t}^{t+\Delta t} \dot{x}(t)\, dt$$

but to evaluate the integral term it is necessary to know $x(t + \Delta t)$! Numerous *integration algorithms* are available to overcome this difficulty and enable the next value of $x(t)$ to be estimated. To solve a differential equation the unknown solution trajectory x_1, x_2, x_3, ... x_n is built up progressively, one integration time step at a time, starting from a known value x_0.

The simplest integration algorithm is the *Euler method* which assumes that the function to be integrated, the derivative function, remains unchanged from t to $t + \Delta t$ with the value which it has at time t, i.e. $\dot{x}(t)$. Hence

$$x(t + \Delta t) = x(t) + \Delta t \dot{x}(t) \qquad 3.15$$

which shows that the values $x(t)$ and $\dot{x}(t)$ are used to estimate $x(t + \Delta t)$. For any specified input function $u(t)$ starting from a known initial output value $x(0)$ equations 3.14 and 3.15 can be alternately and repeatedly applied to calculate successive values of the output function as follows:

$$x(\Delta t) \ \ = x(0) + \Delta t\{ax(0) + bu(0)\}$$
$$x(2\Delta t) = x(\Delta t) + \Delta t\{ax(\Delta t) + bu(\Delta t)\}$$
$$x(3\Delta t) = x(2\Delta t) + \Delta t\{ax(2\Delta t) + bu(2\Delta t)\}$$
$$\text{etc.}$$

To help visualize this computational procedure consider Eq. 3.14 in which $a = -5$ and $b = 1$

$$\text{i.e.} \quad \dot{x}(t) = u(t) - 5x(t) \qquad 3.16$$

This corresponds to the transfer function

$$\frac{X(s)}{U(s)} = \frac{1}{s + 5} = \frac{0.2}{1 + 0.2s}$$

which is a simple lag system with time constant 0.2 seconds and gain 0.2. For a unit step input function, $u(t) = 1$, an initial value $x(0) = 0$, and an integration step size of $\Delta t = 0.1$ seconds the output is given in discrete form by

$$x(t + 0.1) = x(t) + 0.1\{1 - 5x(t)\}$$
$$\text{i.e.} \quad x(t + 0.1) = 0.5x(t) + 0.1 \qquad\qquad 3.17$$

The successive output sample values are thus

$$
\begin{aligned}
x(0) \quad &= 0 &&= 0.0000 \\
x(0.1) &= 0.5(0.0000) + 0.1 &&= 0.1000 \\
x(0.2) &= 0.5(0.1000) + 0.1 &&= 0.1500 \\
x(0.3) &= 0.5(0.1500) + 0.1 &&= 0.1750 \\
x(0.4) &= 0.5(0.1750) + 0.1 &&= 0.1875 \\
&\text{etc.}
\end{aligned}
$$

For comparison these discrete values together with the true analytical solution $x(t) = 0.2(1 - e^{-5t})$ are plotted in Fig. 3.19 and it can be seen that there is a significant difference in the solution trajectories. Reduction of the integration time step size Δt improves the accuracy of the solution at the expense of an increase in computation time. If Δt is reduced by a factor of 2 then the discrete equation becomes

$$x(t + 0.05) = 0.75x(t) + 0.05 \qquad\qquad 3.18$$

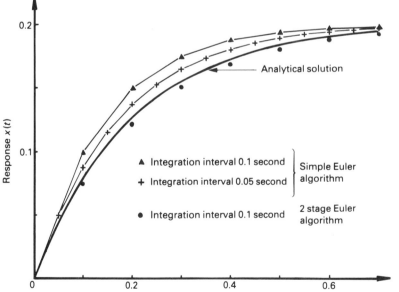

Fig. 3.19 Step response of 1st order system evaluated analytically and using discrete algorithms

from which $x(0.05) = 0.0500$, $x(0.1) = 0.0875$, $x(0.15) = 0.1156$, $x(0.2) = 0.1367$, ... There are twice as many computations, but the errors are approximately halved.

The Euler method is a helpful introduction for understanding the principles of integration algorithms but is not often used in practice since it employs a poor estimate of the mean value of the derivative function for the time interval Δt. Better accuracy for a given integration step size is achieved by making use of multistage algorithms. The *improved Euler method* is a two stage computation in which a first estimate of the next point is made using the Euler method, the derivative is calculated for this estimated point, the average of this derivative value and that at the beginning of the step is evaluated and this average value used to calculate the next point. As an illustration of the method, consider again the first order system of Eq. 3.16 with a unit step input and an integration step size of 0.1. As before

$$\dot{x}(t) = 1 - 5x(t)$$

A first estimate of $x(t + 0.1)$ is given by

$$x_e(t + 0.1) = x(t) + 0.1\{1 - 5x(t)\} = 0.5x(t) + 0.1$$

The derivative value at this point is

$$\dot{x}_e(t + 0.1) = 1 - 5\{0.5x(t) + 0.1\} = 0.5 - 2.5x(t)$$

The average derivative value is then

$$\tfrac{1}{2}\{\dot{x}(t) + \dot{x}_e(t + 0.1)\} = 0.75 - 3.75x(t)$$

which is used to obtain an improved and final estimate of $x(t + 0.1)$ as

$$x(t + 0.1) = x(t) + 0.1\{0.75 - 3.75x(t)\} = 0.625x(t) + 0.075 \qquad 3.19$$

The solution using Eq. 3.19 shows a marked improvement in accuracy. In this example the solution is particularly simple since $u(t)$ is a constant and thus $\dot{x}(t)$ is a function only of $x(t)$, resulting in one single equation to be repetitively solved. Normally $\dot{x}(t)$, $x_e(t + \Delta t)$, $\dot{x}_e(t + \Delta t)$, $\dot{x}_{mean}$, and $x(t + \Delta t)$ must all be computed in turn for each integration time interval Δt. A similar two stage method referred to as the modified Euler method makes a first estimate of the next point, evaluates the derivative at the estimated midpoint, and uses this as the derivative value to calculate the next point. A more complex and efficient algorithm which, like the above, uses only the current value to estimate the next value, but estimates three or more usually four derivative values to do so, is the *Runge–Kutta method*. A different class of integration algorithm is that of *predictor–corrector methods* which make use of both present and past values to predict the next value, and then correct the predicted value by an appropriate algorithm, the prediction and the correction sometimes being done iteratively. A complication is that at the start there are no past values, hence one of the Runge–Kutta class of algorithms must be used for the first one or two steps of integration. Many algorithms are available in standard software libraries and are documented in textbooks such as references 17 and 18.

The choice of value for the time interval Δt, referred to as the integration step size or integration interval, must clearly be a sensible one. Using the basic Euler method the above example suggests that the integration step size should be of the order of one tenth of the time constant or smaller (corresponding to a sampling frequency of approximately 60 times the bandwidth, a concept which is discussed in Section 6.5). If a large step size is chosen then quite erroneous results may be obtained since not only is the error significant but oscillations can occur, as illustrated in Fig. 3.20 for the above numerical example with an

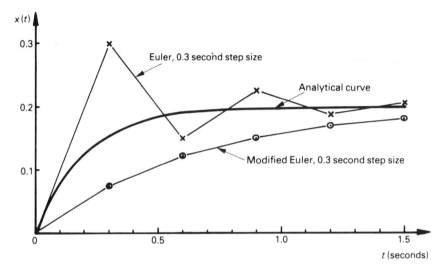

Fig. 3.20 Illustration of errors from use of large integration step

integration step size of 0.3 seconds. The integration step size can be larger, say one quarter of the time constant, if using a better algorithm. With some algorithms the integration time step is not fixed but is changed automatically so that it is increased in value when changes are slow and decreased when the variable changes more rapidly.

With the above background, together with some understanding of a scientific high level language such as Fortran or Pascal the reader will be able to write a digital computer program to evaluate the time response for any chosen simple system, and to output the results in an appropriate graphical or tabular form. A sample program is outlined in the next paragraph. A quicker and more convenient approach to simulation, if appropriate software is available, is to employ a simulation language, a special programming language for dynamic system simulation designed to require a minimum knowledge of computer programming and computer procedures. Simulation languages are discussed in Section 3.9.

Figure 3.21 lists a Fortran program which can be used to evaluate $c(t)$ for the second order differential equation, Eq. 3.5, with a unit step forcing function $u(t)$, and is thus a digital computer equivalent of the analogue computer circuit diagram of Fig. 3.7. The heart of the program which uses the Euler approach to integration is the iterative application of the following three statements:

```
CDDOTI = (1.0 - C(I) - B*CDOT(I))/A

CDOT(I + 1) = CDOT(I) + DT*CDDOTI

C(I + 1) = C(I) + DT*CDOT(I)
```

The similarity between these (which correspond to equations 3.14 and 3.15) and the analogue computer circuit will be evident. The initial part of the program is written in a form such that the system parameters A and B, the integration interval DT, the run time, and the time interval between the solution values which are to be printed out can be chosen at run time and entered

```
C SOLUTION OF SECOND ORDER DIFFERENTIAL EQUATION
C
        DIMENSION C(500),CDOT(500),PRTPLT(61)
        DATA BLANK/1H /,CROSS/1HX/,DASHV/1H-/,DASHH/1HI/
        DATA C0/0.0/,CDOT0/0.0/,CMAX/0.0/
C
C    REQUEST DATA INPUT FOR SIMULATION RUN
        WRITE(6,10)
10      FORMAT('0*** STEP RESPONSE OF SECOND ORDER SYSTEM ***'/
     1  '  A*CDDOT+B*CDOT+1=U   OR   C(S)/R(S)=1/(A*S**2+B*S+1)'/
     2  '0 (INSERT NUMBERS IN REAL FORM -I.E. WITH DEC POINT)'/
     3  '$COEFFICIENT "A" = ')
        READ(5,20)A
20      FORMAT(F10.4)
        WRITE(6,30)
30      FORMAT('$COEFFICIENT "B" = ')
        READ(5,20)B
        WRITE(6,40)
40      FORMAT('$INTEGRATION INTERVAL (SECONDS) = ')
        READ(5,20)DT
        WRITE(6,50)
50      FORMAT('$RUN TIME (MAXIMUM 500*DT, SECONDS) = ')
        READ(5,20)FINTIM
        WRITE(6,60)
60      FORMAT('$PRINT INTERVAL (SECONDS) = ')
        READ(5,20)PI
        IP=IFIX(PI/DT)
        N=IFIX(FINTIM/DT)
C
C    COMPUTE C(T)  USING EULER INTEGRATION
        CDDOTI=(1.0-C0-B*CDOT0)/A
        C(1)=C0+DT*CDOT0
        CDOT(1)=0.0+DT*CDDOTI
        DO 100 I=1,N-1
          CDDOTI=(1.0-C(I)-B*CDOT(I))/A
          C(I+1)=C(I)+DT*CDOT(I)
          CDOT(I+1)=CDOT(I)+DT*CDDOTI
100       IF(C(I+1).GT.CMAX)CMAX=C(I+1)
C
C    PRINT AND PLOT THE TIME RESPONSE
        WRITE(6,120)
120     FORMAT(3X,'TIME      OUTPUT')
        PRTPLT(1)=CROSS
        DO 130 K=2,61
130       PRTPLT(K)=DASHV
        TIME=0.0
        WRITE(6,150)TIME,C0,PRTPLT
        PRTPLT(1)=DASHH
        DO 140 K=2,61
140       PRTPLT(K)=BLANK
        DO 160 J=1,N/IP
          PRTPLT(1)=DASHH
          TIME=J*IP*DT
          K=60.0*C(J*IP)/CMAX+1
          PRTPLT(K)=CROSS
          WRITE(6,150)TIME,C(J*IP),PRTPLT
150       FORMAT(1X,F7.3,F10.4,2X,61A1)
          PRTPLT(K)=BLANK
160     CONTINUE
        STOP
        END
```

Fig. 3.21 Fortran program to solve Eq. 3.5

interactively. The initial values of C and CDOT are selected to be zero. The third part of the program produces a simple print and plot of the output response in the form shown in Fig. 3.22 which gives the results for A = 1.0,

```
TIME      OUTPUT
0.000     0.0000    X-----------------------------------------------------------
0.500     0.0976    I    X
1.000     0.3367    I              X
1.500     0.6155    I                        X
2.000     0.8631    I                              X
2.500     1.0426    I                                  X
3.000     1.1444    I                                     X
3.500     1.1783    I                                       X
4.000     1.1638    I                                       X
4.500     1.1223    I                                      X
5.000     1.0725    I                                    X
5.500     1.0275    I                                  X
6.000     0.9944    I                                 X
6.500     0.9752    I                               X
7.000     0.9683    I                               X
7.500     0.9703    I                               X
8.000     0.9775    I                               X
8.500     0.9864    I                                X
9.000     0.9945    I                                X
9.500     1.0006    I                                X
10.000    1.0043    I                                 X
10.500    1.0056    I                                 X
11.000    1.0054    I                                 X
11.500    1.0041    I                                 X
12.000    1.0026    I                                 X
12.500    1.0011    I                                X
```

Fig. 3.22 Typical output from program of Fig. 3.21; A = 1.0, B = 1.0, DT = 0.05

B = 1.0, and DT = 0.05. The integration interval must be small but not every output sample value calculated is (or need be) printed out. Values of CDOT(I) are also stored and with suitable addition to the third part of the program could also be printed or plotted. If initial values other than zero are to be investigated alterations can be made so that they, too, can be supplied at run time. Such an approach can be used for any other simple simulation. The experienced programmer will be able to incorporate more efficient integration algorithms and more comprehensive output, perhaps producing a family of curves to show the effect of variation of one of the parameters, with hard copy output produced on a graph plotter.

3.9 Simulation languages

A number of special programming languages referred to as continuous system simulation languages (CSSL) or simply as *simulation languages* have been developed as analytical tools which can be used to study the behaviour of a wide range of dynamic systems without the need for a detailed knowledge of computing procedures. The languages are designed to be simple to understand and use, and they minimize programming difficulty by allowing the program to be written as a sequence of relatively self-descriptive statements. The programs may not have very high computational efficiency, but learning and writing time is minimized which can make them cost effective in an engineering design situation and free the user to concentrate on interpretation of the results rather than on computational details. Familiarity with a high level programming language and an understanding of computer graphics may well be helpful but is not necessary. Numerous different languages with acronyms such as CSMP, CSSL, DYNAMO, DARE, MIMIC AND TELSIM have been developed by computer manufacturers, software companies, universities and others, some for specific families of machines and others for wider application. Many features have now been standardized and thus a number of the languages tend to be broadly similar. Symbolic names are used for the system variables (these names being required to follow certain conventions) and the main body of the program is written as a series of simple statements based either on the system equations or on a block diagram representation of the system. To these are added statements specifying initial parameter values and values of system constants, and simple command statements controlling the running of the program and specifying the form in which the output is required. The short user written program is then automatically translated into a Fortran (or other high level language) program which is then compiled, loaded and executed to produce a time history of the variables of interest in printed or plotted form. System constants and initial conditions can be altered and the program rerun without the need to retranslate and recompile. Many of the languages are designed to be run interactively from a graphics terminal and have the facility of displaying on the screen whichever outputs are of interest and, if the solution is not developing as desired, the capability of interrupting the program, changing parameters, and rerunning immediately.

To illustrate the general nature of a simulation language and the way in which it is used CSMP (Continuous System Modelling Program), a widely available Fortran based language developed by IBM will be described in outline. The aim is to show the contrast both with analogue computer simulation and with user written programs, and to give an appreciation of the facilities available. The ease of use, power and versatility can only be appreciated by actually using the software, and the reader is strongly recommended to seek access to a simulation language and to undertake some simulation studies. The self-descriptive nature of the program statements is evident in Fig. 3.23, a CSMP program for the feedback control system of Fig. 3.9. It can be seen that lines 7 to 12 describe almost directly the mathematical equations and physical variables of the system (the whole program is shorter than that of Fig. 3.21 which is for a much simpler system).

The basic elements which appear in the statements of such a program are (i) system variables (i.e. quantities which may change in magnitude during a program run) represented by appropriately descriptive symbolic names, (ii) numerical constants, (iii) the basic arithmetical operators $+$, $-$, $*$, $/$, $**$, and ( ), (iv) functions or functional blocks for more complex mathematical operations and (v) labels, which are key words at the start of certain statements to indicate the type of statement so that it is appropriately handled in the translation phase. A program is constructed from three classes of statement:

(a) *Structural statements:* These define the model by relating the system variables to one another by the appropriate mathematical relationships and form the heart of the program. They are similar to Fortran statements, make wide use of functions, in particular one specifying integration, and are executed repetitively during the running of the program. (Writing these statements is

```
* CSMP SIMULATION OF SYSTEM OF FIG 3.9
*   -EFFECT OF GAIN 'K' AND INTEGRAL ACTION SETTING
*    'A' ON RESPONSE TO A UNIT STEP CHANGE OF INPUT
*
CONSTANT A=0.5
PARAM K=(0.5,2.0,3.5,5.0)
E=R-F
M=K*(E+A*INTGRL(0.0,E))
C1=3.5*M
C2=REALPL(0.0,1.0,C1)
C=CMPXPL(0.0,0.0,2/SQRT(8.0),SQRT(8.0),C2)
F=REALPL(0.0,0.2,C)
R=STEP(0.0)
*
TIMER DELT=0.05,FINTIM=12.0,OUTDEL=0.2
OUTPUT C
LABEL   1 .... " SERVO RESPONSE FOR UNIT STEP INPUT "
PAGE MERGE
OUTPUT M
LABEL   2 .... " CONTROLLER OUTPUT "
PAGE MERGE
END
*
CONSTANT A=1.0
END
STOP
ENDJOB
```

Fig. 3.23 Typical CSMP program

equivalent to drawing the circuit diagram and connecting it up in analogue simulation.)

(b) *Data statements:* These assign numerical values to the system constants and to the initial values of system variables. (This is analogous to adjusting potentiometer settings and amplifier gains, and to setting integrator initial condition voltages.)

(c) *Control statements:* These specify the conditions under which the program is to run, in particular the integration step size and the finish time for the solution, and specify the form in which the output is to be presented. (The latter is equivalent to selecting analogue computer voltages for display on oscilloscope or plotter, and the finish time corresponds to the length of time in the 'Compute' mode). Control statements also determine what is to occur when the finish time is reached, whether to stop, or to alter a parameter value and repeat the computation.

CSMP has available an extensive range of *functions* which can be grouped into the categories listed below. Certain of the most important functions are included so that the reader can understand the program of Fig. 3.23 and can himself write comparable programs. For other than simple systems reference must clearly be made to a programming manual or to a descriptive textbook such as reference 19.

(i) *Standard mathematical functions:* All the standard Fortran mathematical functions such as sine, SIN(X), and square root, SQRT(X), are available for use within algebraic expressions.

(ii) *Integration function:* The main simulation language function is INTGRL (IC, X), where IC is the initial condition and X the variable to be integrated. CSMP offers a choice of 7 or more integration methods, the default being the Runge–Kutta method with variable step size, or the user may incorporate his own routine. The input variable X can be an algebraic expression, thus a typical statement could be

```
OUTPUT = INTGRL (YØ, ERROR * GAIN)
```

(iii) *Transfer functions:* To facilitate simulation of a system whose mathematical model is available in block diagram form functions are provided for a simple lag, REALPL (IC, τ, X), for a quadratic lag, CMPXPL (IC1, IC2, ζ, ω_n, X) and for a lead-lag or lag-lead element. Higher order transfer functions must be split into factors by redrawing the block diagram with primitive blocks each with named input and output.

(iv) *Non-linearities:* These are functions for common non-linearities such as time delay, saturation, and hysteresis, for arbitrary function generation, and for sampled data system elements.

(v) *Input functions:* A unit step at time T can be called for by the function STEP(T), and corresponding functions are available for ramp, impulse, pulse and sinusoidal inputs.

(vi) *User defined functions:* User written Fortran subroutines can be incorporated to define functions for specific features not already included, and groups of statements can be combined to form larger functional blocks which can be called whenever needed by a one-line statement.

The first word of a data statement or control statement is referred to as a *label* and specifies the form of action required. A data statement of the form

```
CONSTANT A = 1.Ø, C = 5.4, XDOT = Ø.Ø
```

is used to assign specific values to parameters which are constant for a program run and to initial conditions. By using variable names rather than numerical values in structural statements and assigning numbers with such a statement it is easy to alter parameter values at run time simply by a new CONSTANT statement. A statement of the form

```
PARAM B = (Ø.2, Ø.5, 1.Ø, 2.Ø)
```

calls for separate runs in which one named parameter takes the successive values listed.

```
TIMER DELT = Ø.Ø1, FINTIM = 1Ø.Ø, PRDEL = Ø.1, OUTDEL = Ø.1
```

is the form of the statement which is required to specify the variables which control the integration step size, the finish time for the run, the time increment for printed output, and the time increment for print-plotted output. The label PRINT followed by one or more variable names specifies which variables are to be printed out, and TITLE followed by an appropriate title allows the programmer to specify the heading for each page of printout. The label PRTPLT (or OUTPUT in CSMP III) followed by one or more variable names specifies for which variables a printer plot is required and LABEL indicates the heading for the output. CSMP III, an enhancement of earlier versions of CSMP, offers such facilities as multiple curves on the same plot (PAGE MERGE), contour plots and shaded plots. The statement END indicates the end of a run. If additional runs are required with changes of variables

```
OUTPUT VARIABLE RANGES FOR ALL RUNS IN CASE

VARIABLE      MINIMUM        MAXIMUM        VARIABLE     MINIMUM        MAXIMUM

  TIME        0.000000E+00   12.0000          C          0.000000E+00   1.41023
  M          -2.903968E-02   5.76765
1
1    1 .... " SERVO RESPONSE FOR UNIT STEP INPUT "
0 MERGED OUTPUT PRESENTATION FOR C
0 PARAMETER    RUN    1        RUN    2        RUN    3        RUN    4
    K          0.50000         2.0000          3.5000          5.0000

                              0.0000E+00                 'O'= RUN   4                    1.600
                              0.0000E+00                 'X'= RUN   3                    1.600
                              0.0000E+00                 '*'= RUN   2                    1.600
                              0.0000E+00                 '+'= RUN   1                    1.600
  TIME            RUN    1
0.00000E+00   0.00000E+00   0------------I-------------I-------------I-------------I-------------I
0.20000       1.85598E-03   0                 I              I              I              I
0.40000       1.17418E-02   +* X0             I              I              I              I
0.60000       3.12292E-02   I+   *    X   0    I              I              I              I
0.80000       5.82712E-02   I +        *      X        0     I              I              I
1.0000        8.96794E-02   I +          * I       X       I 0            I              I
1.2000        0.12248       I   +         I   *        X          0 I        I              I
1.4000        0.15447       I     +       I      *       I      X       I   0            I
1.6000        0.18432       I       +     I          *      I         X      I       0      I
1.8000        0.21147       I       +     I            * I             X I   0          I
2.0000        0.23584       I-------+-----I-------------I--------*----------*--------xX I----0---------I
2.2000        0.25768       I         +   I             I*              X   0    I              I
2.4000        0.27739       I           + I             I *           0X       I              I
2.6000        0.29539       I           + I             I *0         X        I              I
2.8000        0.31206       I           + I           0 I *    X              I              I
3.0000        0.32770       I          + I        0    I *X                  I              I
3.2000        0.34257       I          + I      0      IX                    I              I
3.4000        0.35683       I          + I      0      X*                    I              I
3.6000        0.37059       I         +I         0   X*                     I              I
3.8000        0.38394       I         +I        IX0                         I              I
4.0000        0.39693       I----------------------------I-X---X---0--------I-------------I
4.2000        0.40959       I           +      I *   X         0   I        I              I
4.4000        0.42194       I            I+    I *    X          0 I        I              I
4.6000        0.43399       I            I+    I *     X           0I        I              I
4.8000        0.44577       I            I+    I *      X         0         I              I
5.0000        0.45728       I            I +   I *       X        0 I        I              I
5.2000        0.46853       I            I +   I *        X    0    I        I              I
5.4000        0.47953       I            I  +  I *       0      I        I              I
5.6000        0.49029       I            I  +  I *   0   X      I        I              I
5.8000        0.50082       I            I   + I       0   X    I        I              I
6.0000        0.51113       I------------I---+----I-0---*-X-------I-------------I
6.2000        0.52121       I            I    +    I 0    *  X    I        I              I
6.4000        0.53108       I            I     +   I 0    *X      I        I              I
6.6000        0.54075       I            I     +   I    0*X       I        I              I
6.8000        0.55021       I            I     +   I    0X        I        I              I
7.0000        0.55947       I            I      +  I   *X0        I        I              I
7.2000        0.56855       I            I      +  I    X   0     I        I              I
7.4000        0.57743       I            I      +  I   *X   0     I        I              I
```

Fig. 3.24 Part of printer plot output from CSMP program of Fig. 3.23

this is called for by defining each change after the END statement and concluding it with another END statement. The final two statements are STOP and ENDJOB, and if there is any user defined subroutine this is interposed between the two. An asterisk at the start of any line indicates that what follows is comment.

The above outline should explain the CSMP program listed in Fig. 3.23. If there is a likelihood of wishing to change any parameters other than the two controller settings, say the plant parameters, then these would be best included as variables and assigned values in the constant statement. With A = 0.5 there will be 4 runs, each evaluating the response up to a finish time of 12 seconds for a different value of K, and then the whole will be repeated for A = 1.0. For each value of A there will be a printer plot of C and one of M, each with the 4 traces superimposed. Part of one of these is shown in Fig. 3.24 (with the

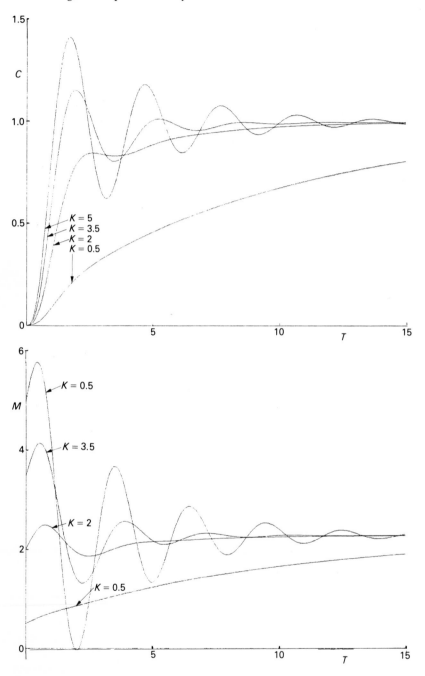

Fig. 3.25 Graph plotter output from CSMP program of Fig. 3.23

printed values for runs 2, 3 and 4 omitted for clarity). Due to the severe resolution limitations of a lineprinter the plots are rather uneven, and a much improved plot is obtained if a graphics display unit or graph plotter output is available (Fig. 3.25).

It is hoped that the above gives some idea of the nature of digital simulation languages and of the advantages that they offer: simple program writing, accuracy and reproducibility, cost effectiveness, and, where interactive facilities exist, keyboard entry of program and running, inspection of plots on graphics display screen, on-line modification and rerunning.

4
Transient Response of Systems

When concerned with dynamic systems it is of interest to know how the output of the system will change as a result of specific types of input change. On the basis of some appropriate criterion, an assessment can be made of whether or not the system behaviour is satisfactory and, if not, an attempt made to improve the response by a realizable modification to the system. With practical systems the exact form of the input excitation function may be known in advance, but most frequently the input will vary in a somewhat random and hence largely unpredictable manner (such would be the case where ambient temperature is a significant input variable for process plant or heating systems).

For analysis and design certain basic input functions are chosen, mainly to bring the analysis into regions of reasonably simple mathematics, but often they may also represent the most typical or the most severe form of disturbance to which the system is subjected. The forcing function giving the best insight for transient response studies is the unit step function—a sudden change in the input, conventionally normalized to unit magnitude and considered to occur at an arbitrarily chosen time datum $t = 0$ (Fig. 4.1). The step change is the most severe disturbance possible for any given signal amplitude and is a type of change which frequently occurs in practice; mathematically it is simple to handle and the resulting system response is easily assessed for practical suitability. A forcing function which is less severe and more relevant for some physical systems, such as those possessing high inertia input characteristics, is the ramp function, or step change in velocity. This would be applicable where a step function is undesirable or is not physically possible, or where a change in input velocity is the normal forcing function. A parabolic input function or step change of acceleration could be used in situations where even the ramp input is too severe.

A further type of input function which is of considerable analytical importance is the unit impulse function, the limiting case of a pulse of unit area where the pulse duration tends to zero (Fig. 4.1). Although physical systems can seldom be satisfactorily tested with an impulsive forcing function, because of the very large change in input variable required to introduce sufficient energy into the system, the concept is one of great convenience. The impulse response can be obtained indirectly using random inputs and correlation techniques as will be described in Chapter 7. Other important forms of input function are sinusoidal signals, and statistical signals such as white noise, described in Chapters 6 and 7 respectively.

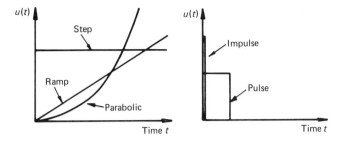

Fig. 4.1 Basic system forcing functions

In this chapter is considered the calculation of the time response of systems of known dynamic characteristics for step, ramp, and impulse forcing functions. The forcing function and system response are given the symbols $u(t)$ and $c(t)$ respectively. From the results can be seen the effect of variation of the form of the system equations and the magnitude of the equation coefficients on the nature of the resulting transient response. The ideas can also be applied to the identification of practical systems by experimental testing. It is shown how a physical system of unknown dynamic characteristics can be subjected to a disturbance of such a form, and the resulting response curve used to estimate the system transfer function. The chapter concludes by describing the convolution integral and its use in evaluating transient system response for a more complex form of input function.

4.1 Response of first order system to step, ramp, or impulse function

Consider any system, such as the thermometer or the simple hydraulic servo-mechanism of Section 2.4, which is described by the first order differential equation

$$c(t) + \tau \frac{dc(t)}{dt} = u(t) \qquad 4.1$$

If the initial value $c(0)$ of the output is zero then this can be transformed into the Laplace domain by replacing d/dt by s, $c(t)$ by $C(s)$ and $u(t)$ by $U(s)$ giving

$$C(s) + \tau s C(s) = U(s) \qquad 4.2$$

In transfer function form this would be written as

$$\frac{C(s)}{U(s)} = \frac{1}{1 + \tau s} \qquad 4.3$$

(a) *Unit step.* What would be the response $c(t)$ of this first order system to a step change of input? In other words, for the examples given, how does the mercury level rise when the thermometer is suddenly inserted in hot water, and how does the piston position vary as a function of time if the servomechanism input position is suddenly changed to a new desired value?

The Laplace transform of the output is, from Eq. 4.3,

$$C(s) = \frac{U(s)}{1 + \tau s}$$

and the Laplace transform of the input $U(s)$ for a unit step is $\frac{1}{s}$,

$$\therefore \quad C(s) = \frac{1}{s(1 + \tau s)} \qquad 4.4$$

The time response $c(t)$ can now be obtained by seeking the Laplace inverse of this expression from tables, or alternatively the expression can be split into partial fractions before inversion,

$$\text{i.e.} \quad C(s) = \frac{1}{s} - \frac{\tau}{1 + \tau s}$$

or
$$C(s) = \frac{1}{s} - \frac{1}{s + \dfrac{1}{\tau}} \qquad 4.5$$

Each of the terms on the right appears in Table 2.1 and so the solution can be written directly as

$$c(t) = 1 - e^{-t/\tau} \qquad 4.6$$

This is traditionally known as a *simple lag* or *exponential lag* and the constant τ is called the *time constant*. The form of the step response curve is shown in Fig. 4.2 and is such that

(i) $c(t) = 0.63$ when $t = \tau$.
(ii) a tangent to the curve at $t = 0$ meets the final value line at $t = \tau$.
(iii) a tangent drawn at any point on the curve meets the final value line τ seconds later.
(iv) $c(t)$ is within 2% of unity for $t > 4\tau$.

The response can be considered to be in two parts, the *transient response* $-e^{-t/\tau}$ which decays to zero as $t \to \infty$, and the *steady state response* 1 which

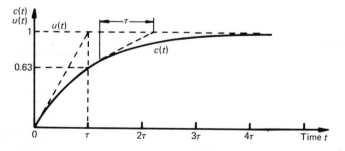

Fig. 4.2 Step response of first order system

implies that in the steady state the output is equal to the input. These are respectively the complementary function and the particular integral obtained by classical methods of solution of the differential equation. All physical systems represented by a first order transfer function will have this solution trajectory.

For a step of magnitude k the response is scaled accordingly,

$$\text{i.e.} \quad c(t) = k(1 - e^{-t/\tau}) \quad\quad\quad 4.7$$

(b) *Ramp.* What would be the response $c(t)$ of the first order system to an input which is changing at a fixed rate? How does the mercury level rise when the thermometer is placed in water whose temperature starts to rise uniformly, and how does the servomechanism respond to a velocity input?

The Laplace transform of a unit ramp is $\dfrac{1}{s^2}$

$$\therefore \quad C(s) = \frac{U(s)}{1 + \tau s} = \frac{1}{s^2(1 + \tau s)} \quad\quad\quad 4.8$$

As before, the time response $c(t)$ can be obtained directly from Laplace transform tables, or by Laplace inversion after separation into partial fractions.

$$\text{i.e.} \quad C(s) = \frac{1}{s^2} - \frac{\tau}{s} + \frac{\tau^2}{1 + \tau s} = \frac{1}{s^2} - \tau\left(\frac{1}{s}\right) + \tau\left(\frac{1}{s + 1/\tau}\right)$$

and hence from Table 2.1

$$c(t) = t - \tau + \tau e^{-t/\tau} \qu\quad\quad 4.9$$

The transient response is $\tau e^{-t/\tau}$ which decays to less than 2% of τ in time 4τ, and the steady state response is $t - \tau$. It can thus be seen that there is a *steady state error* of magnitude τ for a unit ramp input (Fig. 4.3). For large values of time t the output lags the input by a constant value τ.

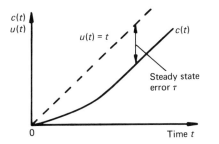

Fig. 4.3 Response of first order system to unit ramp function

For a ramp of magnitude k' i.e. for an input which increases steadily at k' units per second

$$c(t) = k'(t - \tau + \tau e^{-t/\tau}) \qu\quad\quad 4.10$$

and the steady state error is $k'\tau$.

(c) *Unit impulse.* The Laplace transform of the input is

$$U(s) = 1$$

$$\therefore \quad C(s) = \frac{1}{1 + \tau s} = \frac{\dfrac{1}{\tau}}{s + \dfrac{1}{\tau}} \tag{4.11}$$

and
$$c(t) = \frac{1}{\tau}\, e^{-t/\tau} \tag{4.12}$$

The response decays exponentially to a steady state value of zero after a sudden rise to $\dfrac{1}{\tau}$ at $t = 0$, the time of application of the impulse (Fig. 4.4).

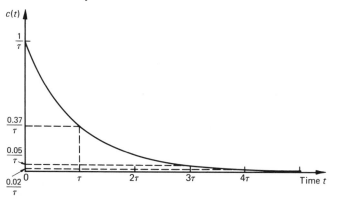

Fig. 4.4 Impulse response of first order system

4.2 Response of second order system to step, ramp, or impulse function

Many mechanical systems are characterized by the presence of inertia, stiffness, and viscous damping and are thus described by the second order transfer function (Eq. 2.17) derived in Section 2.4. How does such a mass-spring-damper system react to a suddenly applied force, or to a steadily increasing force, or to an impulsive force? What will be the response to these inputs of an electrical or other system with this same transfer function? All have the same form of transfer function and thus will have the same form of response.

The output response is given by

$$C(s) = \frac{U(s)\omega_n{}^2}{s^2 + 2\zeta\omega_n s + \omega_n{}^2} \tag{4.13}$$

(a) For a unit step $U(s) = \dfrac{1}{s}$

$$\therefore \quad C(s) = \frac{\omega_n^2}{s(s^2 + 2\zeta\omega_n s + \omega_n^2)} \qquad 4.14$$

$$= \frac{1}{s} + \frac{A_1}{s - p_1} + \frac{A_2}{s - p_2} \qquad 4.15$$

where A_1 and A_2 are constants, and p_1 and p_2 are the roots of the characteristic equation $s^2 + 2\zeta\omega_n s + \omega_n^2 = 0$

$$\therefore \quad c(t) = 1 + A_1 e^{p_1 t} + A_2 e^{p_2 t} \qquad 4.16$$

where $\qquad A_1 = -\tfrac{1}{2} - \dfrac{\zeta}{2\sqrt{(\zeta^2 - 1)}} \quad$ and $A_2 = -\tfrac{1}{2} + \dfrac{\zeta}{2\sqrt{(\zeta^2 - 1)}}$

$$p_1 = -\zeta\omega_n + \omega_n\sqrt{(\zeta^2 - 1)} \quad \text{and} \quad p_2 = -\zeta\omega_n - \omega_n\sqrt{(\zeta^2 - 1)}$$

Three distinct types of response are possible (Fig. 4.5) according to whether the roots p_1 and p_2 are real and unequal, real and equal, or complex, this being determined by the value of the damping factor ζ.

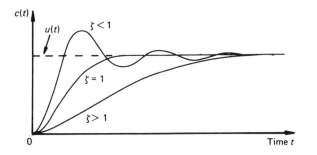

Fig. 4.5 Form of step response for second order system

(i) $\zeta > 1$: gives two negative real unequal roots, and an overdamped response where the coefficients A_1 and A_2 are also real.

(ii) $\zeta < 1$: gives a pair of complex conjugate roots and coefficients A_1 and A_2 which also form a complex conjugate pair. The expression for the system response can be rearranged to give

$$c(t) = 1 - \frac{e^{-\zeta\omega_n t}}{\sqrt{(1 - \zeta^2)}} \sin(\omega_n\sqrt{(1 - \zeta^2)}t + \varphi), \text{ where } \varphi = \cos^{-1}\zeta \qquad 4.17$$

This is an oscillatory or underdamped response.

(iii) $\zeta = 1$: gives two negative real equal roots, a critically damped system corresponding to the minimum value of damping factor for which there is no overshoot.

(b) For a unit ramp input $U(s) = \dfrac{1}{s^2}$

$$\therefore \quad C(s) = \frac{\omega_n^2}{s^2(s^2 + 2\zeta\omega_n s + \omega_n^2)} \tag{4.18}$$

$$= \frac{B_1}{s^2} + \frac{B_2}{s} + \frac{A_1}{s - p_1} + \frac{A_2}{s - p_2}$$

where B_1, B_2, A_1 and A_2 are constants which can be evaluated in terms of ζ and ω_n. Their values are given by

$$B_1 = 1, \ B_2 = -\frac{2\zeta}{\omega_n}, \ A_1 \text{ and } A_2 = \frac{\zeta}{\omega_n} \pm \frac{2\zeta^2 - 1}{2\omega_n\sqrt{(\zeta^2 - 1)}}$$

$$\therefore \quad c(t) = t - \frac{2\zeta}{\omega_n} + A_1 e^{p_1 t} + A_2 e^{p_2 t} \tag{4.19}$$

There is a steady state error of $-\dfrac{2\zeta}{\omega_n}$. The form of the transient part of the response described by the third and fourth terms is discussed below.

(c) For a unit impulse input $U(s) = 1$

$$\therefore \quad C(s) = \frac{\omega_n^2}{s^2 + 2\zeta\omega_n s + \omega_n^2} \tag{4.20}$$

and

$$c(t) = A_1 e^{p_1 t} + A_2 e^{p_2 t} \tag{4.21}$$

where

$$A_1 = -A_2 = \frac{\omega_n}{2\sqrt{(\zeta^2 - 1)}}$$

Whatever the type of input, whether a step ramp or impulse, it can be seen that the transient part of the solution has the form

$$A_1 e^{p_1 t} + A_2 e^{p_2 t}$$

where $\quad p_1$ and $p_2 = -\zeta\omega_n \pm \omega_n\sqrt{(\zeta^2 - 1)} = -\zeta\omega_n \pm j\omega_n\sqrt{(1 - \zeta^2)}$

are the roots of the characteristic equation. It is helpful to see how the values of these roots affect the transient portion of the response, in other words, how the position of the roots in the complex s-plane influences the time response.

Consider a second order system with fixed value of ω_n but with varying ζ. As ζ varies from zero to infinity the roots will trace the locus shown in Fig. 4.6.

(i) For $\zeta = 0$

$$p_1 \text{ and } p_2 = \pm j\omega_n$$

The roots are wholly imaginary, and the transient part of the solution is

$$A_1 e^{j\omega_n t} + A_2 e^{-j\omega_n t}$$

For a unit step input $A_1 = A_2 = -\frac{1}{2}$ and $c(t) = 1 - \cos \omega_n t$
For a unit ramp input $A_1 = -A_2 = -j/\omega_n$ and $c(t) = t + (2/\omega_n) \sin \omega_n t$
For a unit impulse input $A_1 = -A_2 = -j\omega_n/2$ and $c(t) = \omega_n \sin \omega_n t$
In each case the transient part of the solution is a sinusoidal oscillation of constant amplitude.

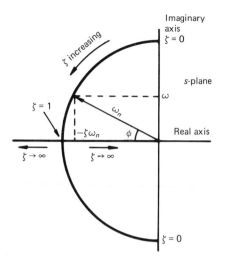

Fig. 4.6 Locus of roots of second order system with fixed w_n as ζ varies from 0 to ∞

(ii) For $0 < \zeta < 1$

p_1 and $p_2 = -\zeta\omega_n \pm j\omega_n\sqrt{(1 - \zeta^2)}$ and the locus of the roots is a semicircle of radius ω_n. If the angle subtended with the real axis at the origin is φ as shown in Fig. 4.6 then $\zeta\omega_n = \omega_n \cos \varphi$

$$\therefore \quad \zeta = \cos \varphi \qquad\qquad 4.22$$

$$\therefore \quad \varphi = \cos^{-1}\zeta \text{ or } \varphi = \tan^{-1} \frac{\sqrt{(1 - \zeta^2)}}{\zeta} \qquad\qquad 4.23$$

The value $\omega = \omega_n\sqrt{(1 - \zeta^2)}$ is often referred to as the *conditional frequency* or *damped natural frequency*. It is the frequency associated with the period of successive oscillations of the damped sinusoid. As $\zeta \to 0$ then $\omega \to \omega_n$.

(iii) For $\zeta \geq 1$ the two roots lie on the negative real axis. When $\zeta = 1$ the roots are real and equal, with value $-\omega_n$, and as ζ increases one root moves along the real axis towards the origin while the other moves towards $-\infty$. The effect of the former root on the time response becomes dominant, while the effect of the distant real root decreases, and when more than about six times as far from the origin as the dominant root its influence is negligible. Hence as the value of ζ becomes very large the response becomes very similar to that of a first order system.

The effect on the step and impulse response of a second order unity gain system with varying damping factor is shown in Fig. 4.7 for a few selected values of ζ. It can be clearly seen how as ζ decreases the response becomes more oscillatory and the damped natural frequency increases. The magnitude of the first overshoot is frequently of significance and can be found either from standard curves such as these or from Eq. 4.17 or Eq. 4.21 by finding the value of t for which $\dot{c}(t) = 0$ and then inserting this in the expression for $c(t)$.

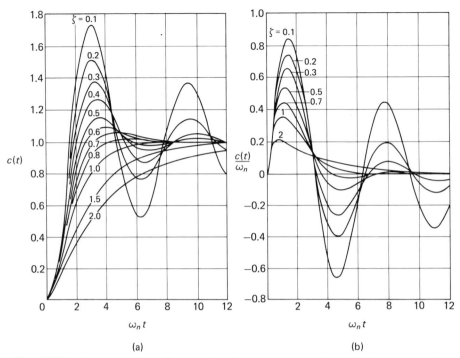

Fig. 4.7 Transient response of second order system to unit step and unit impulse forcing functions

4.3 Transient response of third and higher order systems

In the general case the transfer function can be written as

$$\frac{C(s)}{U(s)} = \frac{P(s)}{Q(s)} \qquad\qquad 4.24$$

where $P(s)$ and $Q(s)$ are polynomials in s. If $Q(s)$ is of order N then the characteristic equation defined as $Q(s) = 0$ will have N roots $p_1, p_2, p_3, \ldots p_N$, and $Q(s)$ can be factorized to give

$$\frac{C(s)}{U(s)} = \frac{P(s)}{(s - p_1)(s - p_2)(s - p_3) \ldots (s - p_N)} \qquad\qquad 4.25$$

Dividing this expression into partial fractions, and then taking the inverse Laplace transform gives for a unit step input

$$c(t) = 1 + A_1 e^{p_1 t} + A_2 e^{p_2 t} + A_3 e^{p_3 t} + \ldots A_N e^{p_N t}$$

or

$$c(t) = 1 + \sum_{n=1}^{N} A_n e^{p_n t} \qquad\qquad 4.26$$

where $A_1, A_2, \ldots A_N$ are constants.

The transient portion of the response is thus composed of a summation of terms of the form $A_n \exp p_n t$ where the values $p_1, p_2, \ldots p_n, \ldots p_N$ are the roots of the characteristic equation, which are at the same time the poles of the overall transfer function. The contribution which each term makes towards the overall response is dependent on the magnitude and sign of A_n, and on the position of the pole p_n in the complex s-plane, each pole generally having a real part σ and an imaginary part $j\omega$. The effect of pole position on the time response is shown schematically in Fig. 4.8, the magnitude A_n being assumed the same in all cases. It should be noted that complex roots always occur as conjugate pairs, and the responses shown arise from the pairs of roots.

It can be seen that the presence of any pole with a positive real part, which means any pole located in the right half of the complex s-plane, gives rise to a contribution to the time response which is increasing without limit. Thus if any pole lies in the right half plane the system will be unstable, where instability implies the fact that the output is unbounded for a bounded input. Of the poles in the left half plane, those farthest from the imaginary axis will have contributions to the transient response which decay most rapidly, and hence the system response will be influenced most by the poles closest to the imaginary axis, called the *dominant poles*. A convenient rule of thumb approximation for design purposes is to assume that the effect of any roots more than 5 or 6 times as far from the imaginary axis as the dominant roots can be neglected.

In addition to the transient response, the value of the steady state gain is generally of interest. This can be evaluated quickly and conveniently making use of the final value theorem of Laplace transform analysis (Section 2.2).

If
$$\frac{C(s)}{U(s)} = G(s)$$

then
$$\lim_{t \to \infty} c(t) = \lim_{s \to 0} sC(s) \quad \text{by the final value theorem}$$

$$= \lim_{s \to 0} G(s) \quad \text{for a steady unit input, } U(s) = \frac{1}{s}$$

e.g. if
$$\frac{C(s)}{U(s)} = \frac{50(1 + 5s)}{(s^2 + 3s + 16)(1 + s)}$$

then
$$[c(t)]_{t \to \infty} = \lim_{s \to 0} \frac{50(1 + 5s)}{(s^2 + 3s + 16)(1 + s)} = \frac{50}{16} \quad \text{for unit input}$$

4.4 Performance characteristics (time domain)

What is a 'good' type of transient response? How should the transient response of a practical system, or the type of response desired for a system be described? The algebraic equation is not very helpful since the form of the response is not readily apparent. A plot of the response is not satisfactory since a numerical description is required for analysis.

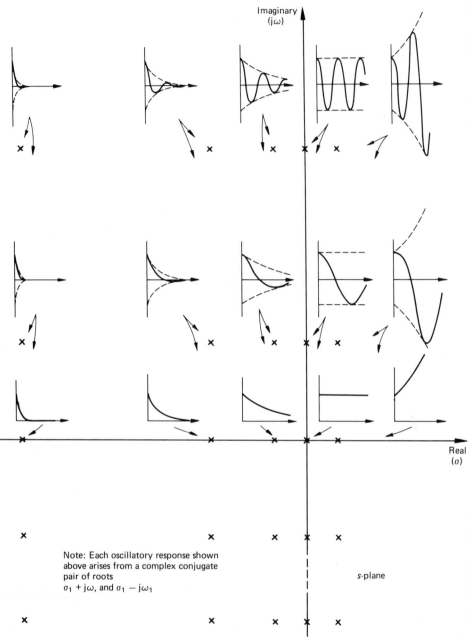

Fig. 4.8 Effect of pole position on contribution to transient response

A first order system can be completely described by specifying the value of the time constant. A second order system can be clearly described by specifying the two time constant values if overdamped, or the values of ζ and ω_n if underdamped. For a higher order system, values of ζ and ω_n cannot be specified since they do not exist—though values of these can be given for the dominant roots.

In general the following parameters, shown in Fig. 4.9, give an adequate description and are used to describe the step response of a system:

    (i) maximum overshoot—this is usually expressed as a percentage of the step size,

    (ii) number of oscillations,

    (iii) rise time—this is usually defined as the time taken to rise from 5% to 95% of the step size, or over some similar range; defining rise time thus avoids the practical difficulty of having to determine the exact start of the transient, and the finish, if overdamped,

    (iv) settling time—the time taken until the output falls within and remains within $\pm 5\%$, say, of the steady state value,

    (v) steady state error.

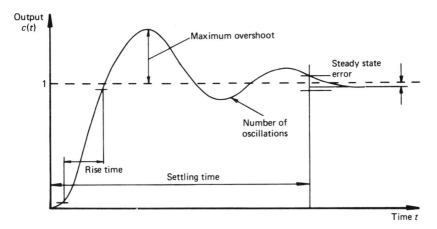

Fig. 4.9 Parameters describing unit step response

These parameters are interrelated, and requirements tend to conflict. The maximum overshoot can generally only be decreased at the expense of an increase in rise time, steady state error can generally only be reduced at the expense of making the transient more oscillatory.

It can be useful to be able to describe a complete transient response by a single numerical value. Such a requirement commonly exists in adaptive control where, to compensate for general system changes, a specific system parameter is caused to be adjusted to maintain sensibly constant dynamic performance. Several types of function have been used for this purpose, the chosen value being called the *performance index*. This generally involves integration of the transient response, some frequently used functions being

$$\int_0^\infty |e(t)| \, dt$$ integral of absolute error (IAE)

$$\int_0^\infty e^2(t) \, dt$$ integral of error squared (IES)

$$\int_0^\infty t |e(t)| \, dt$$ integral of time × absolute error (ITAE)

In general, the value of these functions will be large if the transient is either very sluggish or very oscillatory and, as a system parameter is changed to give a resulting response which varies from one to the other, there will be a value of parameter for which the performance index is a minimum. This would be the 'best' transient response for the chosen performance index.

The IES function accentuates large errors. The ITAE function, by introducing time weighting of the error signal, has the effect of placing small emphasis on the largely unavoidable large initial errors but great emphasis on long duration transients. In addition the ITAE criterion generally gives a more sharply defined minimum and it is thus the most selective. For a second order system with fixed ω_n and varying ζ the optimum is achieved for $\zeta = 0.7$ (ITAE), $\zeta = 0.5$ (IES), $\zeta = 0.7$ (IAE). For many purposes a damping factor of 0.7 is taken to be the ideal for a second order response.

4.5 Step response testing of practical systems

Whenever an existing design requires modification or forms a basis for a future design an appropriate mathematical model must be obtained for the practical system. The system may be one whose internal structure is not understood sufficiently to allow analytical formulation of equations, a so-called *black-box* system. In this case, the dynamic characteristics would have to be obtained by practical testing of the system itself, and the information used to determine a representative mathematical model. On the other hand, by making certain assumptions it may be possible to write down governing equations for the system, in which case the equipment could be tested practically to confirm the form of the theoretically obtained dynamic relationship, and to confirm or determine the parameter values for this model.

Step response testing will usefully and relatively easily give a first idea of the general form of the transfer function and its parameters, and can also give some indication of how linear the system is. A step change of input can usually be applied fairly easily, and inspection of the resulting response for various magnitudes of step size and for step changes in a positive and a negative direction relative to the datum condition will indicate whether a linear model can realistically be assumed. If not, some idea of the type of non-linearity may be forthcoming. If a large transportation lag or dead time is present then this is generally detectable from the transient response curve.

The dynamic information may be suitably presented in the form of the actual transient response curves—a non-parametric model—but usually a parametric model is required and it becomes necessary to fit a transfer function or state space model to the response curve. To do this it is necessary to select some error criterion to quantify the goodness of fit, and then to adjust the model and its parameter values to minimize the chosen error index.

(a) *Response apparently of first order.* If the step response apparently rises exponentially to the new steady state it is likely that the system is predominantly of first order. The dominant time constant can be found by any of the three measurements described in Section 4.1(a) and Fig. 4.2. Each should give the same value.

Superimposing the curve $1 - e^{-t/\tau}$ will show qualitatively whether this is a reasonable model, or whether it is necessary to use a higher order model.

(b) *Response apparently lightly damped second order.* A mathematical relationship between ζ and the relative magnitudes of overshoots and undershoots can be found for the second order system with damping low enough to give more than one oscillation. This can be used to estimate ζ from an oscillatory step response.

From Eq. 4.17 and Eq. 4.23

$$c(t) = 1 - \frac{\exp(-\zeta\omega_n t)}{\sqrt{(1-\zeta^2)}} \sin\left(\omega_n\sqrt{(1-\zeta^2)}t + \tan^{-1}\frac{\sqrt{(1-\zeta^2)}}{\zeta}\right) \qquad 4.27$$

$$\therefore \quad \frac{dc(t)}{dt} = -\frac{1}{\sqrt{(1-\zeta^2)}}\{\exp(-\zeta\omega_n t)\cos[\omega_n\sqrt{(1-\zeta^2)}t + \varphi]\omega_n\sqrt{(1-\zeta^2)}$$

$$+ \exp(-\zeta\omega_n t)(-\zeta\omega_n)\sin[\omega_n\sqrt{(1-\zeta^2)}t + \varphi]\}$$

$$= \frac{\exp(-\zeta\omega_n t)}{\sqrt{(1-\zeta^2)}}\{\zeta\omega_n\sin[\omega_n\sqrt{(1-\zeta^2)}t + \varphi]$$

$$- \omega_n\sqrt{(1-\zeta^2)}\cos[\omega_n\sqrt{(1-\zeta^2)}t + \varphi]\}$$

$$= 0 \quad \text{when } \tan[\omega_n\sqrt{(1-\zeta^2)}t + \varphi] = \frac{\sqrt{(1-\zeta^2)}}{\zeta}$$

But $\varphi = \tan^{-1}\dfrac{\sqrt{(1-\zeta^2)}}{\zeta}$

Hence peaks and troughs occur when $\omega_n\sqrt{(1-\zeta^2)}t = n\pi$

$$\text{i.e.} \quad \text{when } t = \frac{n\pi}{\omega_n\sqrt{(1-\zeta^2)}} = t_n \quad \text{where } n = 1, 2, 3 \ldots$$

$n = 1$ gives the 1st overshoot: $c(t_1) =$

$$1 - \frac{\exp\left(-\dfrac{\zeta\pi}{\sqrt{(1-\zeta^2)}}\right)}{\sqrt{(1-\zeta^2)}} \sin\left(\pi + \tan^{-1}\frac{\sqrt{(1-\zeta^2)}}{\zeta}\right)$$

$$= 1 + \exp\left(-\frac{\zeta\pi}{\sqrt{(1-\zeta^2)}}\right)$$

$n = 2$ gives the 1st undershoot: $c(t_2) = 1 - \exp\left(-\dfrac{2\zeta\pi}{\sqrt{(1-\zeta^2)}}\right)$

$n = 3$ gives the 2nd overshoot: $c(t_3) = 1 + \exp\left(-\dfrac{3\zeta\pi}{\sqrt{(1-\zeta^2)}}\right)$

Hence if x_1 and x_3 are the magnitudes of the 1st and 2nd overshoots (Fig. 4.10) the ratio of these overshoot values is:

$$\frac{x_1}{x_3} = \frac{\exp\left(-\dfrac{\zeta\pi}{\sqrt{(1-\zeta^2)}}\right)}{\exp\left(-\dfrac{3\zeta\pi}{\sqrt{(1-\zeta^2)}}\right)}$$

$$\therefore \quad \log_e\left(\frac{x_1}{x_3}\right) = \frac{2\pi\zeta}{\sqrt{(1-\zeta^2)}} \qquad\qquad 4.28$$

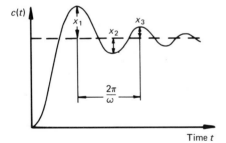

Fig. 4.10 Step response of oscillatory system

Practically it is more often possible to obtain ζ using the first overshoot and first undershoot

$$\log_e\left(\frac{x_1}{x_2}\right) = \frac{\pi\zeta}{\sqrt{(1-\zeta^2)}}$$

Also, the interval between successive overshoots is $\dfrac{2\pi}{\omega}$ where $\omega = \omega_n \sqrt{(1-\zeta^2)}$

Hence for an experimentally obtained transient response which appears to be of a lightly damped second order system it is possible to quickly obtain estimates of ζ and ω_n. Again, comparison of the actual response with the second order response for the calculated values of ζ and ω_n, and taking into account the use to which the model will be put, will show whether or not it is necessary to attempt to fit a higher order model to the response.

(c) *Overdamped second order response.* For a second order system with damping factor greater than unity

$$c(t) = 1 + A_1 e^{p_1 t} + A_2 e^{p_2 t}$$

where p_1 and p_2 are negative real numbers.

There are two separate time constants. If these are an order of magnitude different, then the effect of the smaller time constant is only evident in the first part of the response, and the approximate value of the dominant time constant can be found from the slope of the later portion of the response curve (Fig. 4.11). For more accurate values a curve fitting procedure is needed.

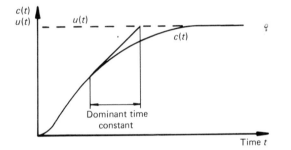

Fig. 4.11 Step response of overdamped second order system

(d) *Higher order overdamped system.* In the general case of an overdamped system the response is of the form

$$c(t) = 1 - \sum_{n=1}^{N} A_n e^{-t/\tau_n}$$

where $\tau_1 > \tau_2 > \tau_3 > \ldots > \tau_N$ are the time constants of the system.

$$\therefore \quad 1 - c(t) = A_1 e^{-t/\tau_1} + A_2 e^{-t/\tau_2} + A_3 e^{-t/\tau_3} + \ldots$$
$$\simeq A_1 e^{-t/\tau_1} \qquad \text{for large } t$$

$$\therefore \quad \log_e [1 - c(t)] = \log_e A_1 - \frac{t}{\tau_1} \qquad \text{for large } t$$

By plotting $\log_e[1 - c(t)]$ against t (Fig. 4.12), and looking for a linear relationship at large values of t, the values of A_1 and τ_1 can be estimated. The coefficient A_1 is the value of the intercept of the straight line with the $t = 0$ axis. The dominant time constant τ_1 is obtained from the slope of the line.

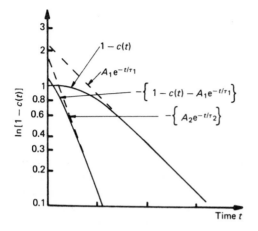

Fig. 4.12 Evaluation of time constants and equation coefficients

$$\text{i.e.}\quad \tau_1 = \frac{t_2 - t_1}{\log_e[1 - c(t_2)] - \log_e[1 - c(t_1)]}$$

Now
$$1 - c(t) - A_1 e^{-t/\tau_1} = A_2 e^{-t/\tau_2} + A_3 e^{-t/\tau_3} + \dots$$

$$\simeq A_2 e^{-t/\tau_2} \quad \text{for large } t$$

The procedure is then to subtract the $A_1 e^{-t/\tau_2}$ line from the curve $1 - c(t)$ to obtain a second curve, attempt to draw a straight line to fit this for large values of t and hence find values for A_2 and τ_2. It may then be possible to repeat this once more.

This method gives values of the time constants fairly quickly providing they differ in magnitude by, say, more than a factor of 2 or 3. The accuracies of the results for a second order system would then be about 10% and 25% for the primary and secondary time constants respectively. If the values of the time constants are closer together than this, the method fails, as it becomes impossible to detect linear portions of the curves. A severe constraint is always the value of the noise–signal ratio pertaining when making practical measurements.

4.6 Comparison of transient forcing functions

The main advantages of the step function as a test signal for a practical system are that step changes are physically easy to apply, and that the resulting response curves very readily give an idea of the general dynamic characteristics of the system. Simple observation shows whether a system is oscillatory or not, and hence by simple measurement can be determined the order of magnitude of the dominant time constant, or of the damping factor and undamped natural frequency. One can look for the presence of a transportation lag and, with different magnitudes of steps, look for signs of non-linearity.

There are, however, several important disadvantages:

  (i) the size of step required to give a transient response of the system which is detectable in the presence of the inherent noise may result in an unacceptably large disturbance to the system,
  (ii) the steady state point of the system changes,
  (iii) very small variations in the shape of the time response curve have a large effect on the higher order terms of the transfer function.

An impulse forcing function does avoid the second problem above in that the steady state point before and after applying the disturbance is the same. The disturbance to the system is however even larger than for a step change, and is almost always unacceptable in the presence of noise. It is difficult to apply a true impulse with enough energy to give a transient which is detectable in the presence of noise, without saturating part of the system. A representation of the impulse response curve can, however, be obtained using correlation techniques, as will be shown in Chapter 7.

With some practical systems a step change which implies a substantially instantaneous change of a variable is physically impossible. In such cases it may be more relevant to consider a ramp input function, or a step change in velocity. An example might be an item of process plant where a motorized valve can only close at some finite rate.

4.7 The convolution integral

It has been shown above how, knowing a system transfer function, the response of the system to inputs of certain simple analytical forms can be calculated. Sometimes the response must be evaluated when the input is more complex and perhaps not even expressible in a deterministic manner. A procedure based on the convolution integral enables this to be done. In such situations the input can be considered as being made up of a series of pulses of varying amplitude, and the principle of superposition can be used to obtain an expression for the system output.

For the linear system shown in Fig. 4.13, the output response is given by

$$Y(s) = X(s)G(s)$$

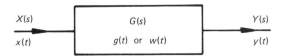

Fig. 4.13 Single-input–single-output linear system

If the input is a unit impulse $\delta(t)$

then $X(s) = \mathscr{L}[\delta(t)] = 1$

and $Y(s) = G(s)$

       $\therefore$ $y(t) = \mathscr{L}^{-1}[G(s)] = g(t)$ or $w(t)$, the unit impulse response.

If the input is now an arbitrary function $x(t)$, consider it as being made up of an infinite number of impulses of width $\delta\lambda$ and height $x(t)$, Fig. 4.14.

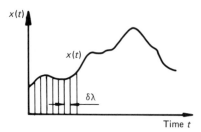

Fig. 4.14 Representation of time function by a series of pulses

The contribution $\Delta y(t)$ to the output at time t due to an inpulse applied λ seconds earlier (i.e. at time $t - \lambda$) will be the value of the impulse response at time λ times the magnitude of the impulse which was applied at time $t - \lambda$.

$$\therefore \quad \Delta y(t) = w(\lambda)x(t - \lambda)\delta\lambda$$

The impulse response function is frequently called the *weighting function* because it specifies by how much the input applied λ seconds in the past has decayed.

The total system output is the sum of terms due to all impulses which have occurred in the past prior to time t, the summation being performed in the limit by the integral

$$y(t) = \int_{-\infty}^{t} w(\lambda)x(t - \lambda)\,\mathrm{d}\lambda$$

Now $w(t) = 0$ for $t < 0$ for any real system

$$\therefore \quad y(t) = \int_{0}^{t} w(\lambda)x(t - \lambda)\,\mathrm{d}\lambda$$

This is called the *convolution integral* or *superposition integral* and is sometimes written as

$$y(t) = w(t) * x(t)$$

where the symbol * implies convolution. This has a similar form to the equivalent Laplace domain relationship

$$Y(s) = G(s)X(s)$$

Physically the process of convolution can be illustrated by Fig. 4.15.

If the system weighting function is as shown in Fig. 4.15a, and the input function as in Fig. 4.15b, then $x(t - \lambda)$ will be as Fig. 4.15d and the product for this value of t will be as Fig. 4.15e; $y(t)$ is the area under this curve.

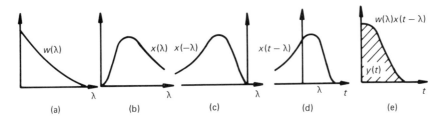

Fig. 4.15 Illustration of process of convolution

It can be seen that the convolution integral can be evaluated by time shifting $w(\lambda)$ rather than $x(\lambda)$ giving the alternative expression

$$y(t) = \int_0^t x(\lambda)w(t - \lambda)\, \mathrm{d}\lambda$$

Also, provided the signal is bounded, i.e. $x(t) = 0$ for $t < 0$, the upper limit of integration can be extended to infinity since $x(t - \lambda) = 0$ for $\lambda > t$, or $w(t - \lambda) = 0$ for $\lambda > t$. Such extension of the limits from $-\infty$ to $+\infty$ can simplify certain manipulations.

5
State Space Representation and Analysis

Transfer function representation, described in Chapter 2, is one of two established methods employed in the modelling and analysis of linear control system elements. The approach is based implicitly on the use of Laplace transforms, and associated design procedures for use with this method are described in Chapter 10. These design methods enable system performance to be predicted without actually solving to find the roots of the characteristic equation. It is against a design background requiring the use of trial and observation procedures, and with impetus given by the rapid development of the high speed digital computer, that the second approach to control system modelling has been developed. This method does not use a transfer function description, but replaces it by a state space representation, as introduced and described briefly in Section 2.6. The state space model representation makes possible the use of mathematical techniques that lead to a more systematic design process than is directly possible with a transfer function representation. Extensive use of the digital computer in design makes it necessary to be able to replace differential equations by difference equations, and to this end the first order state equations are easier to handle than the high-order equations associated with the transfer function.

The state space procedure basically involves transforming a single nth order differential equation into a set of n first order simultaneous differential equations, employing matrix notation as a form of technical shorthand. This requires the introduction of additional variables, the state variables; the number of state variables required to define a system completely is equal to the order of the system. These variables are not unique and several different methods of choosing them are presented to illustrate this. The actual state variables used may be chosen to suit the particular problem and an appropriate choice of variable at an early stage may well facilitate later solution.

For example, the second order differential equation which describes mathematically an electrical circuit consisting of a resistor, a capacitor, and an inductor in series, requires a two-state-variable description. The pair of variables could be the current flowing to the capacitor and the voltage across the capacitor, or alternatively the current from and voltage across the inductor. However, any other two variables such as the voltage across the resistor and the rate of change with respect to time of this voltage would be equally valid as state variables for this simple system.

The use of matrices can simplify the computational manipulations since two matrices A and B, defined later in this chapter, specify the dynamic characteristics of a particular linear system and so the dynamic properties of the system can be studied by investigating the properties of these matrices. An additional advantage of the state space method is that the restriction to single-input single-output models, which is implicit throughout the preceding chapters, disappears and the state equation can be used directly to describe a multi-variable dynamic system with many inputs and outputs.

Section 5.1 describes three methods of obtaining the state equations and writes them both as a set of first order differential equations and also more compactly in matrix equation form. The section which follows extends the thinking to multi-input multi-output systems by defining the generalized state equations, and deriving them for an illustrative 2-input–3-output system. Section 5.3 investigates the *s*-domain representation of the state equations and derives a matrix transfer function, a set of transfer functions, each of which relates one output to one input. Section 5.4 shows how in principle the state equations can be solved analytically to find the time response, although in practice only simple situations are amenable to such solution. The section following gives an insight into the principles of handling a discrete time model in computer solution of the state equations.

A useful background for this chapter for those not familiar with simple matrix methods is given in Appendix C.

5.1 State variable diagrams

A convenient method for deriving state equations is based on analogue computing techniques. A circuit diagram is constructed for the system equations in the manner illustrated in Chapter 3, and the integrator output signals are defined as the state variables. The integrator inputs then become the derivatives of the state variables and the state equations can be written down immediately by inspection of the circuit diagram.

The basic elements most frequently used in such diagrams are similar to those described in Section 3.2 and consist of the ideal integrator, ideal amplifier and ideal adder as shown in Fig. 5.1. These differ from the practical

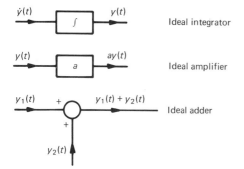

Fig. 5.1 Symbols used in state variable diagrams

analogue computer symbols because the integrator and adder do not incorporate a sign change, and the amplifier achieves multiplication by any constant within the range $\pm \infty$.

To illustrate the construction of state variable diagrams for the derivation of state equations, and to give an insight into the structure of a state variable expression, consider the transfer function relationship

$$\frac{Y(s)}{U(s)} = \frac{s^2 + 3s + 1}{s(s^2 + 6s + 8)} \qquad 5.1$$

By expansion of Eq. 5.1 into partial fraction form the transfer function can be written in an alternative way as

$$\frac{Y(s)}{U(s)} = \frac{1}{8s} + \frac{5}{8(s + 4)} + \frac{2}{8(s + 2)} \qquad 5.2$$

or it can be written in factored form as

$$\frac{Y(s)}{U(s)} = \frac{(s + 2.62)(s + 0.38)}{s(s + 4)(s + 2)} \qquad 5.3$$

and by programming each of these equations separately three different state variable diagrams can be produced. From each diagram a different set of state variables results, which clearly indicates that no single set is unique to a particular dynamic system.

To avoid confusion later in this chapter, the symbol $Y(s)$ or $y(t)$ is used to define the output response, instead of the symbol $C(s)$ or $c(t)$ used elsewhere in the text.

(a) *State variable diagram for Eq. 5.1.* Since a transfer function can be treated as an algebraic expression, the numerator and denominator of Eq. 5.1 can each be divided by the highest power of s to replace all differentiating terms by integrating terms. Eq. 5.1 can thus be written as

$$\frac{Y(s)}{U(s)} = \frac{s^{-1} + 3s^{-2} + s^{-3}}{1 + 6s^{-1} + 8s^{-2}}$$

or

$$Y(s) = (s^{-1} + 3s^{-2} + s^{-3})V(s) \qquad 5.4$$

where

$$V(s) = \frac{U(s)}{1 + 6s^{-1} + 8s^{-2}}$$

which transposes to

$$V(s) = U(s) - 6s^{-1}V(s) - 8s^{-2}V(s) \qquad 5.5$$

The variable $V(s)$ must be introduced to avoid the need for differentiation, as in Section 3.6. The state variable diagram, shown in Fig. 5.2, follows from Eq. 5.4 and Eq. 5.5 by integrating $V(s)$ three times and combining signals as required.

By designating the integrator outputs to be the system state variables, it can readily be seen by inspection of Fig. 5.2 that the state equations are:

$$\dot{x}_1(t) = x_2(t)$$
$$\dot{x}_2(t) = x_3(t) \qquad 5.6$$
$$\dot{x}_3(t) = u(t) - 6x_3(t) - 8x_2(t)$$

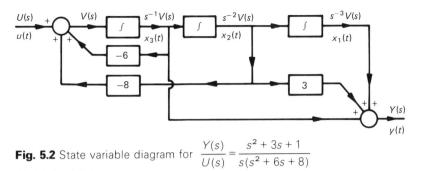

Fig. 5.2 State variable diagram for $\dfrac{Y(s)}{U(s)} = \dfrac{s^2 + 3s + 1}{s(s^2 + 6s + 8)}$

When written using matrix notation Eqns. 5.6 become

$$\left\{\begin{matrix} \dot{x}_1(t) \\ \dot{x}_2(t) \\ \dot{x}_3(t) \end{matrix}\right\} = \begin{bmatrix} 0 & 1 & 0 \\ 0 & 0 & 1 \\ 0 & -8 & -6 \end{bmatrix} \left\{\begin{matrix} x_1(t) \\ x_2(t) \\ x_3(t) \end{matrix}\right\} + \begin{bmatrix} 0 \\ 0 \\ 1 \end{bmatrix} u(t) \qquad 5.7$$

or more concisely

$$\{\dot{x}(t)\} = A\{x(t)\} + Bu(t) \qquad 5.8$$

where

$$\{x(t)\} = \left\{\begin{matrix} x_1(t) \\ x_2(t) \\ x_3(t) \end{matrix}\right\}, \quad A = \begin{bmatrix} 0 & 1 & 0 \\ 0 & 0 & 1 \\ 0 & -8 & -6 \end{bmatrix}, \quad B = \begin{bmatrix} 0 \\ 0 \\ 1 \end{bmatrix}$$

The important points about this notation are:

(i) $\{x(t)\}$ is the state vector and has n components $x_1(t)$, $x_2(t)$, ... $x_n(t)$, where n is the order of the dynamic system. The brackets { } are used to represent a column matrix indicating a system vector.

(ii) A and B are matrices of order $n \times n$ and $n \times 1$ respectively. The brackets [ ] are used to indicate a matrix representing the coefficient parameters of a system.

Also, from inspection of Fig. 5.2 the system output $y(t)$ can be seen to be

$$y(t) = x_1(t) + 3x_2(t) + x_3(t)$$

or

$$y(t) = C\{x(t)\} = [1\ 3\ 1]\{x(t)\} \qquad 5.9$$

(b) *Alternative state variable diagram, using Eq. 5.2.* The second and third terms on the right-hand side of Eq. 5.2 which have the form $\dfrac{b}{s + a}$ can be expressed as $Y(s) = \dfrac{b}{s}\left(U(s) - \dfrac{a}{b}\,Y(s)\right)$, enabling the ideas of Chapter 3 to be used. The circuit diagram for such an equation is shown in Fig. 5.3a and the state variable diagram Fig. 5.3b for Eq. 5.2 follows immediately.

The integrator outputs are, as before, chosen to be the state variables; the set of simultaneous first-order dynamic equations can be written down by inspection of Fig. 5.3b.

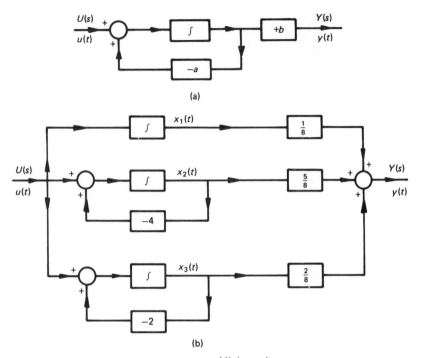

(a)

(b)

Fig. 5.3 State variable diagram for (a) $\dfrac{Y(s)}{U(s)} = \dfrac{b}{s+a}$

(b) $\dfrac{Y(s)}{U(s)} = \dfrac{1}{8s} + \dfrac{5}{8(s+4)} + \dfrac{2}{8(s+2)}$

$$\dot{x}_1(t) = u(t)$$
$$\dot{x}_2(t) = u(t) - 4x_2(t) \qquad\qquad 5.10$$
$$\dot{x}_3(t) = u(t) - 2x_3(t)$$

or $\qquad \{\dot{x}(t)\} = \begin{bmatrix} 0 & 0 & 0 \\ 0 & -4 & 0 \\ 0 & 0 & -2 \end{bmatrix} \{x(t)\} + \begin{bmatrix} 1 \\ 1 \\ 1 \end{bmatrix} u(t) \qquad 5.11$

and the output is given by

$$y(t) = \tfrac{1}{8}x_1(t) + \tfrac{5}{8}x_2(t) + \tfrac{2}{8}x_3(t)$$
or $\qquad\qquad y(t) = \begin{bmatrix} \tfrac{1}{8} & \tfrac{5}{8} & \tfrac{2}{8} \end{bmatrix} \{x(t)\} \qquad\qquad 5.12$

It can be clearly seen that these are not the same state equations or variables as those obtained by method (*a*).

(c) *Second alternative state variable diagram, using Eq. 5.3.* Consider first a general transfer function

$$\frac{Y(s)}{U(s)} = \frac{s+b}{s+a}$$

As shown in case (a), this can be written

$$\frac{Y(s)}{U(s)} = \frac{1 + bs^{-1}}{1 + as^{-1}}$$

and introducing a variable $V(s)$ to avoid the operation of differentiation yields the pair of equations

$$Y(s) = (1 + bs^{-1})V(s)$$

and
$$V(s) = U(s) - as^{-1}V(s)$$

The diagram for these equations is shown in Fig. 5.4a; using this the state diagram for Eq. 5.3 can now be drawn, Fig. 5.4b.

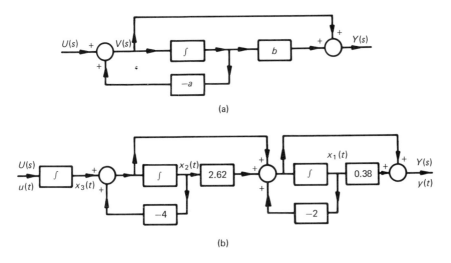

(a)

(b)

Fig. 5.4 State variable diagram for (a) $\dfrac{Y(s)}{U(s)} = \dfrac{s + b}{s + a}$

(b) $\dfrac{Y(s)}{U(s)} = \dfrac{(s + 2.62)}{s(s + 4)} \dfrac{(s + 0.38)}{(s + 2)}$

The state equations follow from Fig. 5.4b after some simple algebraic manipulations:

$$\dot{x}_1(t) = -2x_1(t) - 1.38\,x_2(t) + x_3(t)$$
$$\dot{x}_2(t) = -4x_2(t) + x_3(t) \qquad\qquad 5.13$$
$$\dot{x}_3(t) = u(t)$$

or
$$\{\dot{x}(t)\} = \begin{bmatrix} -2 & -1.38 & 1 \\ 0 & -4 & 1 \\ 0 & 0 & 0 \end{bmatrix}\{x(t)\} + \begin{bmatrix} 0 \\ 0 \\ 1 \end{bmatrix} u(t) \qquad 5.14$$

The output is

$$y(t) = -1.62 \, x_1(t) - 1.38 \, x_2(t) + x_3(t)$$

or $\quad\quad\quad y(t) = [-1.62 \ -1.38 \ 1]\{x(t)\}$ $\quad\quad\quad$ 5.15

The above example demonstrates very clearly that it is possible to characterize the same system by different sets of state variable equations. So far as the authors are aware there is no rigorous method for determining which set is likely to prove the most useful analytically and the choice is largely dictated by the form in which the dynamic equations appear.

5.2 Generalized state equations

Up to this point only nth order systems having a single input and a single output have been considered. The state equations may be generalized to include the multi-input–multi-output case by writing them in the form

$$\{\dot{x}(t)\} = A\{x(t)\} + B\{u(t)\} \quad\quad\quad 5.16$$
$$\{y(t)\} = C\{x(t)\} + D\{u(t)\} \quad\quad\quad 5.17$$

The additional term $D\{u(t)\}$ introduced in Eq. 5.17 allows for possible interaction between system inputs and outputs. The terms in Eq. 5.16 and Eq. 5.17 are referred to in the literature by the following names:

$\{x(t)\}$ is the state vector
$\{y(t)\}$ is the response or output vector
$\{u(t)\}$ is the control or input vector
A $\quad$ is the coefficient matrix of the process
B $\quad$ is the driving matrix
C $\quad$ is the output matrix
D $\quad$ is the transmission matrix.

If a system has p inputs and q outputs, then $\{u(t)\}$ is an input column vector containing the p elements $u_1(t)$, $u_2(t)$, ... $u_j(t)$ ... $u_p(t)$, and $\{y(t)\}$ is an output column vector containing the q elements $y_1(t)$, $y_2(t)$, ... $y_i(t)$, ..., $y_q(t)$. Consequently the B matrix must be of order $(n \times p)$, the C matrix of order $(q \times n)$ and the D matrix of order $(q \times p)$ to satisfy the rules of matrix multiplication (Appendix C). No standard notation has yet been accepted for Eq. 5.16 and Eq. 5.17 and other symbols will be found in the published literature, $\{c(t)\}$ in place of $\{y(t)\}$ and $\{r(t)\}$ in place of $\{u(t)\}$ being the most common.

Example 5.1. As an illustration of the form of the state equations for a system with more than one input and output, consider the multi-tank system shown in Fig. 5.5. The input liquid flow rates are labelled $q_1(t)$ and $q_2(t)$ and the output variables, or system response, will be assumed to be the liquid heads in the 3 tanks, designated $h_1(t)$, $h_2(t)$ and $h_3(t)$.

For simplicity of modelling, the interconnecting and outlet pipes are assumed to have a linear head-flow relationship, so that the flow through each constriction is related to the liquid head difference across the constriction by the relationship

$$q(t) = \frac{\Delta h(t)}{R}$$

where $\Delta h(t)$ is the liquid head difference and the constant R is the linear flow resistance. The rate of change of fluid volume within a tank can be described by $a \dfrac{\mathrm{d}}{\mathrm{d}t} h(t)$ where a is the cross-sectional area of a tank.

For each tank a flow continuity equation can be written in which the rate of change of fluid volume is equated to the rate of inflow of fluid. By inspection

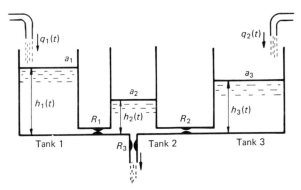

Fig. 5.5 Multi-tank flow system

of Fig. 5.5, and using the symbols shown, the flow continuity equations for tanks 1, 2, and 3 are respectively

$$a_1 \frac{\mathrm{d}}{\mathrm{d}t} h_1(t) = q_1(t) - \frac{1}{R_1} (h_1(t) - h_2(t))$$

$$a_2 \frac{\mathrm{d}}{\mathrm{d}t} h_2(t) = \frac{1}{R_1} (h_1(t) - h_2(t)) - \frac{1}{R_2} (h_2(t) - h_3(t)) - \frac{1}{R_3} h_2(t) \qquad 5.18$$

and $\quad a_3 \dfrac{\mathrm{d}}{\mathrm{d}t} h_3(t) = q_2(t) + \dfrac{1}{R_2} (h_2(t) - h_3(t))$

Rearranging equations 5.18 gives

$$\dot h_1(t) = \left(-\frac{1}{a_1 R_1} \right) h_1(t) + \left(\frac{1}{a_1 R_1} \right) h_2(t) + \left(\frac{1}{a_1} \right) q_1(t)$$

$$\dot h_2(t) = \left(\frac{1}{a_2 R_1} \right) h_1(t) - \left(\frac{1}{a_2 R_1} + \frac{1}{a_2 R_2} + \frac{1}{a_2 R_3} \right) h_2(t) + \left(\frac{1}{a_2 R_2} \right) h_3(t) \qquad 5.19$$

$$\dot h_3(t) = \left(\frac{1}{a_3 R_2} \right) h_2(t) - \left(\frac{1}{a_3 R_2} \right) h_3(t) + \left(\frac{1}{a_3} \right) q_2(t)$$

The three expressions in $\dot{h}(t)$ which constitute Eqns. 5.19 are equivalent to the matrix equation 5.16, if corresponding terms are equated; i.e.

$$\{\dot{x}(t)\} = A\{x(t)\} + B\{u(t)\}$$

where $\{x(t)\} = \begin{Bmatrix} h_1(t) \\ h_2(t) \\ h_3(t) \end{Bmatrix}$, $A = \begin{bmatrix} -\dfrac{1}{a_1 R_1} & \dfrac{1}{a_1 R_1} & 0 \\[2ex] \dfrac{1}{a_2 R_1} & -\dfrac{1}{a_2}\left(\dfrac{1}{R_1} + \dfrac{1}{R_2} + \dfrac{1}{R_3}\right) & \dfrac{1}{a_2 R_2} \\[2ex] 0 & \dfrac{1}{a_3 R_2} & -\dfrac{1}{a_3 R_2} \end{bmatrix}$

$\{u(t)\} = \begin{Bmatrix} q_1(t) \\ q_2(t) \end{Bmatrix}$, $B = \begin{bmatrix} \dfrac{1}{a_1} & 0 \\[2ex] 0 & 0 \\[2ex] 0 & \dfrac{1}{a_3} \end{bmatrix}$

The system output is given by the matrix equation Eq. 5.17

$$\{y(t)\} = C\{x(t)\} + D\{u(t)\}$$

The outputs are $h_1(t)$, $h_2(t)$ and $h_3(t)$ which in this example are also the state variables.

Hence

$$\{y(t)\} = \{h(t)\} = \{x(t)\}$$
$$\therefore \quad D = 0$$

and

$$C = \begin{bmatrix} 1 & 0 & 0 \\ 0 & 1 & 0 \\ 0 & 0 & 1 \end{bmatrix}$$

Such a matrix with coefficients of 1 on the principal diagonal and zero elsewhere is called a *unit matrix* and is given the symbol I.

5.3 State relations in the *s*-domain

It may be desirable to develop a transfer function representation from a state model since, in engineering work, it is often necessary to confirm a mathematical model experimentally. A well established experimental modelling procedure is given in Chapter 6 and it will be seen that this is based on frequency response data, making direct comparison with a state model extremely difficult. In this section the relationship between the two model representations is derived.

Ordinary differential equations are transformed into algebraic equations by using Laplace transformation to change from the time domain to the *s*-domain. Since Laplace transformation is a scalar operation, it can be applied to the generalized state equations (Eq. 5.16 and Eq. 5.17) to obtain the following s-domain equations:

$$s\{X(s)\} - \{x(0)\} = A\{X(s)\} + B\{U(s)\} \qquad 5.20$$

$$\{Y(s)\} = C\{X(s)\} + D\{U(s)\} \qquad 5.21$$

where $\{x(0)\} = \lim_{t \to 0} \{x(t)\}$ is the initial condition vector.

Eq. 5.20 can be written as

$$s\{X(s)\} - A\{X(s)\} = \{x(0)\} + B\{U(s)\} \qquad 5.22$$

To combine the terms on the left-hand side of Eq. 5.22, the rules for matrix addition and subtraction must be observed, namely that such an arithmetic operation can be performed only if the two matrices have the same order. Thus, since s is a scalar quantity, the unit matrix I must be introduced and Eq. 5.22 written as

$$sI\{X(s)\} - A\{X(s)\} = \{x(0)\} + B\{U(s)\}$$

and the Laplace transformed state variable can now be expressed as

$$\{X(s)\} = (sI - A)^{-1}(\{x(0)\} + B\{U(s)\}) \qquad 5.23$$

Substitution of Eq. 5.23 into Eq. 5.21, yields the system response equation in algebraic form, i.e.

$$\{Y(s)\} = C(sI - A)^{-1}(\{x(0)\} + B\{U(s)\}) + D\{U(s)\} \qquad 5.24$$

The transfer function representation as defined in Chapter 2 can be used to describe multivariable systems if the scalar variables and transfer functions are replaced by vector variables and matrix transfer functions respectively. Therefore, using vector notation, the transfer function $G(s)$ is given by

$$G(s) = \frac{\{Y(s)\}}{\{U(s)\}} \qquad 5.25$$

Substituting Eq. 5.24 into Eq. 5.25, for zero initial conditions, gives

$$G(s) = C(sI - A)^{-1}B + D \qquad 5.26$$

$G(s)$ is a *matrix transfer function*, and each element represents one component of the single variable output–input relationship

$$G_{ij}(s) = \frac{Y_i(s)}{U_j(s)} \qquad 5.27$$

Examination of Eq. 5.26 shows that the inverse matrix $(sI - A)^{-1}$ plays an important role in the solution of the system equations and in determining the transfer function. It is shown in Appendix C that $(sI - A)^{-1}$ can be evaluated as

$$(sI - A)^{-1} = \frac{\text{adj}(sI - A)}{|sI - A|}$$

Expansion of the determinant $|s\boldsymbol{I} - \boldsymbol{A}|$ yields an nth order polynomial in s. This determinant appears as the denominator of the transfer function, therefore the characteristic equation is given by

$$|s\boldsymbol{I} - \boldsymbol{A}| = 0$$

and the roots of this nth order polynomial are the poles of the transfer function.

Example 5.2. To demonstrate the use of Eq. 5.26, the transfer function relating the input $u(t)$ and the output response $y(t) = x_1(t)$ is derived for the second order system shown in Fig. 2.6. For a natural frequency of 2 rad/second and a damping factor of 0.5, it can be shown from Eq. 2.40 that the state equation is

$$\begin{Bmatrix} \dot{x}_1(t) \\ \dot{x}_2(t) \end{Bmatrix} = \begin{bmatrix} 0 & 1 \\ -4 & -2 \end{bmatrix} \begin{Bmatrix} x_1(t) \\ x_2(t) \end{Bmatrix} + \begin{bmatrix} 0 \\ 4 \end{bmatrix} u(t)$$

In matrix form the system response is

$$\{y(t)\} = [1 \quad 0]\{x(t)\}$$

hence from Eq. 5.26

$$G(s) = \boldsymbol{C}(s\boldsymbol{I} - \boldsymbol{A})^{-1}\boldsymbol{B} + \boldsymbol{D} = [1 \quad 0] \begin{bmatrix} s & -1 \\ 4 & s+2 \end{bmatrix}^{-1} \begin{bmatrix} 0 \\ 4 \end{bmatrix}$$

Now $$\text{adj}(s\boldsymbol{I} - \boldsymbol{A}) = \begin{bmatrix} s+2 & 1 \\ -4 & s \end{bmatrix} \text{ and } |s\boldsymbol{I} - \boldsymbol{A}| = s^2 + 2s + 4$$

$$\therefore \quad (s^2 + 2s + 4)G(s) = [1 \quad 0] \begin{bmatrix} s+2 & 1 \\ -4 & s \end{bmatrix} \begin{bmatrix} 0 \\ 4 \end{bmatrix}$$

$$= [1 \quad 0] \begin{bmatrix} 4 \\ 4s \end{bmatrix} = 4$$

i.e. $$G(s) = \frac{4}{s^2 + 2s + 4}$$

The result is verified by the results from the conventional Laplace transform technique in Chapter 2, Eq. 2.17.

5.4 Solution of the state vector differential equation

As explained earlier in this chapter, one of the benefits to be gained from use of state space representation is that it enables system performance in the time domain to be more readily computed. The aim of this section is to develop a general solution for the vector differential equation, Eq. 5.16, from which a system time response can be predicted. To simplify the mathematical development of the general solution, first consider the solution of a simple one-dimensional differential equation representing the dynamic behaviour of a first-order system,

$$\text{i.e.}\quad \dot{x}(t) = ax(t) + bu(t) \qquad\qquad 5.28$$

This was solved in Section 4.1 for certain specific functions $u(t)$.

To determine the general solution of Eq. 5.28, the law of superposition is used, an inherent and unique property of a linear system. Consider $x(t)$ to comprise two motions, a free component $x_i(t)$ with $u(t) = 0$ and initial condition $x(0)$, and a forced component $x_j(t)$ for the actual input $u(t)$ but with zero initial state, $x(0) = 0$.

(i) *Free motion $x_i(t)$*

The equation is

$$\dot{x}_i(t) - ax_i(t) = 0, \text{ with } x_i(t) = x(0) \text{ at time } t = 0$$

The Laplace transform of this equation is

$$(s - a)X_i(s) = x(0)$$

and from the Laplace transform table given in Section 2.2, the solution is

$$x_i(t) = x(0)e^{at} \qquad\qquad 5.29$$

(ii) *Forced motion $x_j(t)$*

The equation is

$$\dot{x}_j(t) - ax_j(t) = bu(t), \text{ with } x_j(t) = 0 \text{ at time } t = 0,$$

and its Laplace transform is

$$(s - a)X_j(s) = bU(s) \qquad\qquad 5.30$$

The most obvious choice for a solution for $x_j(t)$ is one of similar form to that of $x_i(t)$

$$\text{i.e.}\quad e^{at}x_p(t) = x_j(t) \qquad\qquad 5.31$$

where $x_p(t)$ is an unknown function.

Now
$$\frac{d}{dt}[e^{at}x_p(t)] = ae^{at}x_p(t) + e^{at}\dot{x}_p(t)$$

Converting this to an algebraic form by use of the Laplace transform gives, since initial conditions are zero,

$$s\mathscr{L}[e^{at}x_p(t)] = a\mathscr{L}[e^{at}x_p(t)] + \mathscr{L}[e^{at}\dot{x}_p(t)]$$

or
$$(s - a)\mathscr{L}[e^{at}x_p(t)] = \mathscr{L}[e^{at}\dot{x}_p(t)]$$

Substituting for $e^{at}x_p(t)$ from Eq. 5.31 gives

$$(s - a)X_j(s) = \mathscr{L}[e^{at}\dot{x}_p(t)]$$

and on substituting $bU(s)$ for the left-hand side (Eq. 5.30), taking the Laplace inverse yields

$$bu(t) = e^{at}\dot{x}_p(t)$$

or
$$x_p(t) = \int_0^t e^{-a\tau}bu(\tau)\,d\tau$$

where τ is a dummy variable of integration that will vanish when the integration limits are inserted.

Thus
$$x_j(t) = e^{at} \int_0^t e^{-a\tau} bu(\tau) \, d\tau$$

$$= \int_0^t e^{a(t-\tau)} bu(\tau) \, d\tau \qquad 5.32$$

and the total solution to Eq. 5.28 is

$$x(t) = x(0)e^{at} + \int_0^t e^{a(t-\tau)} bu(\tau) \, d\tau \qquad 5.33$$

An integral of a product of two functions of this form, Eq. 5.32, is called a convolution integral as was explained in Section 4.7.

Since the vector equation, Eq. 5.16, is simply a collection of first order differential equations which must be solved simultaneously, then for the general case involving n independent state variables

$$\{x(t)\} = e^{At}\{x(0)\} + \int_0^t e^{A(t-\tau)} B\{u(\tau)\} \, d\tau \qquad 5.34$$

The exponential term e^{At} which is an $n \times n$ matrix that appears in both the free and forced motion portions of the solution is called the *solution matrix* or *transition matrix* $\varphi(t)$. The final solution to the vector differential equation is written

$$\{x(t)\} = \varphi(t)\{x(0)\} + \int_0^t \varphi(t - \tau) B\{u(\tau)\} \, d\tau \qquad 5.35$$

The evaluation of the solution matrix $\varphi(t)$ is possible by a series expansion of e^{At}, but this is impractical manually for all but the simplest problems. The most direct method is by taking the inverse Laplace transform of Eq. 5.23, that is

$$\{x(t)\} = \{x(0)\}\mathscr{L}^{-1}[(sI - A)^{-1}] + \mathscr{L}^{-1}[(sI - A)^{-1}B\{U(s)\}] \qquad 5.36$$

Thus, to obtain $\varphi(t) = e^{At} = \mathscr{L}^{-1}[(sI - A)^{-1}]$, the inverse of the $(sI - A)$ matrix is found and the inverse transform of the resulting matrix is evaluated term by term.

From the definition of the inverse matrix

$$\mathscr{L}[\varphi(t)] = \frac{\text{adj}(sI - A)}{|sI - A|} \qquad 5.37$$

Example 5.3. It will be illustrated in this example how Eq. 5.37 can be used to find all the elements of the solution matrix $\varphi(t)$.

Consider a second order system (with coefficients different to those in Example 5.2 for arithmetic simplicity) described by the transfer function

$$\frac{X(s)}{U(s)} = \frac{2}{s^2 + 3s + 2}$$

which in state vector form is

$$\{\dot{x}(t)\} = \begin{bmatrix} 0 & 1 \\ -2 & -3 \end{bmatrix} \{x(t)\} + \begin{bmatrix} 0 \\ 2 \end{bmatrix} u(t)$$

The characteristic equation is $|s\boldsymbol{I} - \boldsymbol{A}| = 0$ and expansion of this determinant yields

$$\left| \begin{bmatrix} s & 0 \\ 0 & s \end{bmatrix} - \begin{bmatrix} 0 & 1 \\ -2 & -3 \end{bmatrix} \right| = 0$$

$$\therefore \quad \left| \begin{bmatrix} s & -1 \\ 2 & s+3 \end{bmatrix} \right| = 0$$

$$\therefore \quad s^2 + 3s + 2 = 0$$

or

$$(s + 1)(s + 2) = 0$$

and from Eq. 5.37

$$\mathscr{L}[\varphi(t)] = \frac{1}{(s + 1)(s + 2)} \begin{bmatrix} s + 3 & 1 \\ -2 & s \end{bmatrix}$$

$$\therefore \quad \varphi(t) = \mathscr{L}^{-1} \begin{bmatrix} \dfrac{s + 3}{(s + 1)(s + 2)} & \dfrac{1}{(s + 1)(s + 2)} \\ \dfrac{-2}{(s + 1)(s + 2)} & \dfrac{s}{(s + 1)(s + 2)} \end{bmatrix}$$

According to matrix theory, the inverse Laplace transform of a matrix is a matrix whose elements are the inverse transforms of the corresponding elements of the original matrix.

Now $\mathscr{L}^{-1}\left(\dfrac{s + 3}{(s + 1)(s + 2)}\right) = \mathscr{L}^{-1}\left(\dfrac{2}{s + 1} - \dfrac{1}{s + 2}\right) = (2\mathrm{e}^{-t} - \mathrm{e}^{-2t})$

$\mathscr{L}^{-1}\left(\dfrac{1}{(s + 1)(s + 2)}\right) = \mathscr{L}^{-1}\left(\dfrac{1}{s + 1} - \dfrac{1}{s + 2}\right) = (\mathrm{e}^{-t} - \mathrm{e}^{-2t})$

$\mathscr{L}^{-1}\left(\dfrac{-2}{(s + 1)(s + 2)}\right) = \mathscr{L}^{-1}\left(\dfrac{2}{s + 2} - \dfrac{2}{s + 1}\right) = (-2\mathrm{e}^{-t} + 2\mathrm{e}^{-2t})$

$\mathscr{L}^{-1}\left(\dfrac{s}{(s + 1)(s + 2)}\right) = \mathscr{L}^{-1}\left(\dfrac{2}{s + 2} - \dfrac{1}{s + 1}\right) = (-\mathrm{e}^{-t} + 2\mathrm{e}^{-2t})$

and hence

$$\varphi(t) = \begin{bmatrix} (2e^{-t} - e^{-2t}) & (e^{-t} - e^{-2t}) \\ (-2e^{-t} + 2e^{-2t}) & (-e^{-t} + 2e^{-2t}) \end{bmatrix}$$

Note that the numerical values -1 and -2 in the exponential terms are the roots of the characteristic equation defined by $|sI - A| = 0$.

To apply this solution matrix, consider first the case $u(t) = 0$, $x_1(0) = 1$ and $x_2(0) = 0$. This would mean, for a simple spring mass system, that the mass is released with zero initial velocity and finite initial displacement in the absence of a forcing function.

From Eq. 5.35

$$\{x(t)\} = \varphi(t)\{x(0)\}$$

$$= \varphi(t)\begin{bmatrix} 1 \\ 0 \end{bmatrix}$$

$$\therefore \quad x_1(t) = 2e^{-t} - e^{-2t}$$

and

$$x_2(t) = -2e^{-t} + 2e^{-2t}$$

Secondly, consider the response to a unit step input. If the system is initially at rest with zero displacement, $\{x(0)\} = 0$. For this particular example $B = \begin{bmatrix} 0 \\ 2 \end{bmatrix}$ and $u(\tau) = 1$ for $\tau > 0$; hence from Eq. 5.35

$$x_1(t) = 2\int_0^t (e^{-(t-\tau)} - e^{-2(t-\tau)})\, d\tau$$

$$= 1 - 2e^{-t} + e^{-2t}$$

and

$$x_2(t) = 2\int_0^t (-e^{-(t-\tau)} + 2e^{-2(t-\tau)})\, d\tau$$

$$= 2e^{-t} - 2e^{-2t}$$

This example demonstrates that from a knowledge of a system A matrix, the solution matrix, $\varphi(t)$, can be found and hence the time response evaluated for a given set of conditions. Thus the evolution of an excited system from one state to another through time may be visualized as a process of state transition.

5.5 Discrete time model

If a system response or forcing function can be observed at discrete intervals of time only, that system is termed a discrete or sampled-data system and is mathematically modelled by difference equations rather than by differential equations. A digital computer solution must use a discrete-time model of the continuous time system. In formulating the discrete-time model a sequence of numerical and logical operations, known as a computer algorithm, is devised and programmed for digital computer solution.

The use of state model formulation avoids the need for the introduction of z-transform theory, a technique which extends the transfer function model into the realms of discrete data systems. Although striking similarities exist between Laplace and z-transform representation, the step from continuous to discrete system representation is more direct using the state model, and is more readily understood.

The solution of the state equations, Eq. 5.16 and Eq. 5.17, has been derived, Eq. 5.34 or Eq. 5.35, and consists of a set of solutions of the form of Eq. 5.33.

$$x(t) = x(0)e^{at} + \int_0^t e^{a(t-\tau)}bu(\tau)\,d\tau \qquad (5.33)$$

In order to carry out the integration digitally, the signals must be considered in sampled form, and the input function $u(\tau)$ must be represented by a suitable approximation. If the sampling interval is T it is convenient to approximate $u(\tau)$ by a series of steps forming a staircase, Fig. 5.6; the choice of the value of

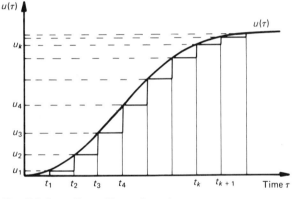

Fig. 5.6 Sampling of input function

T dictates the resolution accuracy possible in the evaluation of $x(t)$, but also dictates the computing time necessary to achieve the solution. Therefore in practical engineering situations a compromise between accuracy and computing time is always necessary. If $t_k = kT$, where k is a positive integer, it will be assumed that for the time interval $t_k < t < t_{k+1}$, $u(\tau)$ is a constant u_k, and hence Eq. 5.33 can be written as

$$x(t_{k+1}) = x(t_k)e^{aT} + \int_0^T e^{a(T-\tau)}bu_k\,d\tau \qquad 5.38$$

$$= x(t_k)e^{aT} + bu_k\left[-\frac{1}{a}e^{a(T-\tau)}\right]_0^T$$

$$\therefore \quad x(t_{k+1}) = e^{aT}x(t_k) + (e^{aT} - 1)\frac{b}{a}u_k \qquad 5.39$$

To illustrate the application of Eq. 5.39 consider a unit ramp input, $u(\tau) = t$, and for arithmetic simplicity let $a = -1$ and $b = 1$ which is equivalent to a time constant of 1 second. The continuous response, obtained by analytical solution of Eq. 5.33 or from Eq. 4.9, for zero initial conditions, is

$$x(t) = t - 1 + e^{-t}$$

which is plotted in Fig. 5.7. The discrete time solution is evaluated from Eq. 5.39, and for a value of $T = 0.5$ seconds, since in this case $u_k = kT$, the equation becomes

$$x(t_{k+1}) = e^{-0.5}x(t_k) - (e^{-0.5} - 1)0.5\ k$$
$$= 0.6065x(t_k) + 0.1967\ k$$

Successive values of the discrete time solution are thus

$$x(t_0) = x(0) = 0$$
$$x(t_1) = x(0.5) = 0 + 0 = 0$$
$$x(t_2) = x(1.0) = 0 + 0.1967 = 0.1967$$
$$x(t_3) = x(1.5) = (0.6065)(0.1967) + 0.1967(2) = 0.5127$$
etc.

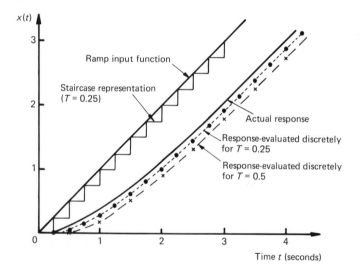

Fig. 5.7 Response of first order system to unit ramp evaluated discretely

The resulting response is shown in Fig. 5.7 together with the corresponding results obtained for $T = 0.25$. As is to be expected, as the sampling interval is decreased the resulting response tends closer to the true continuous curve. It should be noted that reasonable accuracy has been achieved with a sampling interval of 0.25 seconds; this is relatively large compared to the time constant of 1 second.

By inspection of Eq. 5.33 and Eq. 5.39, the general solution to Eq. 5.34, making use of the staircase approximation $\{u(\tau)\} = \{u_k\}$, yields

$$\{x(t_{k+1})\} = e^{AT}\{x(t_k)\} + [-e^{A(T-\tau)}]_0^T A^{-1}B\{u_k\}$$
$$= e^{AT}\{x(t_k)\} + [e^{AT} - I]A^{-1}B\{u_k\}$$

or $\qquad \{x(t_{k+1})\} = \varphi(T)\{x(t_k)\} + [\varphi(T) - I]A^{-1}B\{u_k\}$ $\qquad$ 5.40

If the substitution $A_1 = \varphi(T)$ and $B_1 = [\varphi(T) - I]A^{-1}B$ is made in Eq. 5.40

$$\{x(t_{k+1})\} = A_1\{x(t_k)\} + B_1\{u_k\} \qquad 5.41$$

The response $\{x(t_k)\}$ at time $t_k = kT$ is computed by repeated application of Eq. 5.41:

$$\{x(t_1)\} = A_1\{x(0)\} + B_1\{u(0)\}$$
$$\{x(t_2)\} = A_1\{x(t_1)\} + B_1\{u_1\}$$
$$= A_1^2\{x(0)\} + A_1B_1\{u(0)\} + B_1\{u_1\}$$
$$\{x(t_3)\} = \dots\dots\dots\dots\dots\dots\dots\dots$$
$$\dots = \dots\dots\dots\dots\dots\dots\dots\dots$$
$$\dots = \dots\dots\dots\dots\dots\dots\dots\dots$$
$$\{x(t_k)\} = A_1^k\{x(0)\} + \sum_{i=0}^{k-1} A_1^{k-1-i}B_1\{u_i\} \qquad 5.42$$

The sampling interval T, involved in evaluating A_1 and B_1, must be chosen to give the desired accuracy in the calculated time response. The most direct way to evaluate A_1 and B_1 is to use the series expansion of e^{AT}:

$$e^{AT} = I + AT + \frac{1}{2!}(AT)^2 + \dots = A_1$$

and $\quad [e^{AT} - I]A^{-1}B = \left[\left[I + AT + \frac{1}{2!}(AT)^2 + \dots\right] - I\right]A^{-1}B$ $\qquad$ 5.43

$$= T\left[I + \frac{1}{2!}AT + \frac{1}{3!}(AT)^2 + \dots\right]B = B_1$$

The matrix inversion, A^{-1}, is avoided in Eqs. 5.43 and the series expansion of A_1 and B_1 can be truncated to any desired accuracy.

It has been shown in this chapter that the transfer function and state matrix constitute alternative methods for the mathematical representation of a linear dynamic system. It is now recognized that in general the theoretical results needed in system design can be obtained equally well either by vector-space methods or by algebraic methods using Laplace transforms.

The area in which the state concept is most effective is that of discrete and multivariable system studies. The state concept makes possible a systematic formulation for all systems, including those with arbitrary sampling patterns and non-linear operation. However, frequency response methods give an unrivalled engineering insight into system behaviour.

It must be emphasized that despite the unified approach that is possible by use of state description, the Laplace formulation of system equations remains significant with practising engineers. The particular problem to be studied, however, should always determine the preference of one approach to the other.

6
Frequency Response of Systems

Chapter 4 has described how for specific forcing functions the time response of a system of known transfer function can be evaluated, and in what ways the form of the response is dependent on the form of the transfer function. In this chapter the equivalent response in the frequency domain is presented. Frequency response methods of analysis have been very popular since the early stages of development of control theory, and are still of importance largely because of the physical understanding which they help the engineer to acquire. The methods are easy to apply, they are graphical, and they offer a good basis for synthesizing systems, in that they indicate clearly the type of change that is required to improve system dynamic behaviour.

The description of a system in the frequency domain is given in terms of the response to a sinusoidally varying input signal after all initial transients have died out. Provided the system is linear this steady state output, which is the particular integral term of the solution of the governing differential equation, is a sinusoid of the same frequency as the input, but with a shift of phase and a change of amplitude. The ratio of the amplitude of the output sine wave to the amplitude of the input sine wave is usually referred to as the *magnitude* (or sometimes as the magnitude ratio, amplitude ratio, or gain); the shift of phase of the output sine wave relative to the input is termed simply the *phase*. The magnitude and phase are dependent both on the system transfer function and on the forcing frequency but not, with a linear system, on the amplitude. The variation of magnitude and phase with frequency is traditionally known as the *frequency response* or the *harmonic response* of the system. Any non-linearity which is present in the system introduces signal components at higher frequencies, with the result that the output then contains the basic forcing frequency plus certain of its harmonics.

The main part of the chapter shows how the harmonic response information can be found from the transfer function $G(s)$ by letting $s = j\omega$, and how it can be presented graphically by means of either a polar diagram or a Bode diagram. The physical significance of plots of various shapes is discussed to illustrate the understanding that can be obtained from a knowledge of the harmonic response characteristics of a system. Frequency response testing of practical systems, and the estimation of transfer functions from the measured frequency response, is then discussed. The chapter concludes by describing the criteria which are used to describe performance in the frequency domain.

6.1 The transfer function in the frequency domain

The object of this section is to show that the magnitude and phase, the ratio of the amplitude of the steady state output to the amplitude of the input sine wave, and the phase shift between the output and input sinusoids, are given respectively by the modulus and argument of $G(j\omega)$, the transfer function with s replaced by $j\omega$.

For a linear system, the transfer function $G(s)$ has been shown to be a ratio of two polynomials in s, each of which can be factorized to give

$$G(s) = \frac{C(s)}{U(s)} = \frac{K(s - z_1)(s - z_2) \dots (s - z_m)}{(s - p_1)(s - p_2)(s - p_3) \dots (s - p_n)} \qquad 6.1$$

$z_1, z_2, \dots z_m$ are defined as the *zeros* of $G(s)$, values of s which make the function zero, while $p_1, p_2, p_3, \dots p_n$ are the *poles* of $G(s)$, values which make the function infinite.

If the input to this system is

$$u(t) = \sin \omega t$$

a sine wave of unit amplitude and of frequency ω rad/second, then the Laplace transform of the input (Table 2.1) is

$$U(s) = \frac{\omega}{s^2 + \omega^2}$$

$$\therefore \quad C(s) = G(s)U(s) = \frac{K\omega(s - z_1)(s - z_2) \dots (s - z_m)}{(s^2 + \omega^2)(s - p_1)(s - p_2) \dots (s - p_n)} \qquad 6.2$$

This expression can be rewritten by a partial fraction expansion to give

$$C(s) = \frac{G(s)\omega}{s^2 + \omega^2} = \frac{A_1}{s - j\omega} + \frac{A_2}{s + j\omega} + \frac{B_1}{s - p_1} + \frac{B_2}{s - p_2} + \dots + \frac{B_n}{s - p_n} \qquad 6.3$$

where $A_1, A_2, B_1, B_2, \dots B_n$ are constants. Taking the Laplace inverse (using the fourth transform pair of Table 2.1) gives the time response as

$$c(t) = A_1 e^{j\omega t} + A_2 e^{-j\omega t} + B_1 e^{p_1 t} + B_2 e^{p_2 t} + \dots + B_n e^{p_n t} \qquad 6.4$$

The first two terms describe the particular integral component of the solution, frequently referred to as the steady state response, while the remaining terms describe the complementary function, the transient response. Provided the system is stable and linear the poles $p_1, p_2, \dots p_n$ all have negative real parts and hence all of the modes in Eq. 6.4 decay to zero with increasing time t except the first two.

Hence
$$[c(t)]_{t \to \infty} = A_1 e^{j\omega t} + A_2 e^{-j\omega t}$$

To determine the coefficient A_1 multiply both sides of equation 6.3 by $(s - j\omega)$, and then let $s = j\omega$:

$$A_1 = \left[\frac{(s - j\omega)G(s)\omega}{s^2 + \omega^2} \right]_{s=j\omega} = \left[\frac{G(s)\omega}{s + j\omega} \right]_{s=j\omega} = \frac{G(j\omega)}{2j} = \frac{1}{2j} |G(j\omega)| e^{j\angle G(j\omega)}$$

Similarly to obtain A_2 multiply by $(s + j\omega)$ and let $s = -j\omega$:

$$A_2 = \left[\frac{(s + j\omega)G(s)\omega}{s^2 + \omega^2} \right]_{s = -j\omega} = \frac{G(-j\omega)}{-2j} = -\frac{1}{2j} |G(j\omega)| e^{-j\angle G(j\omega)}$$

$$\therefore \quad [c(t)]_{t \to \infty} = |G(j\omega)| \frac{1}{2j} \{ e^{j\omega t + j\angle G(j\omega)} - e^{-j\omega t - j\angle G(j\omega)} \}$$

i.e. $[c(t)]_{t \to \infty} = |G(j\omega)| \sin (\omega t + \angle G(j\omega))$ \hfill 6.5

The magnitude and phase as functions of frequency can thus be obtained from the transfer function $G(s)$ by replacing s by $j\omega$ and determining the modulus and argument of $G(j\omega)$, which for any particular frequency is generally a complex number. In the next section the magnitude and phase characteristics are evaluated for different forms of $G(s)$.

6.2 Polar plots

The frequency response information for a system can conveniently be displayed on an Argand diagram and is then referred to by the control engineer as a polar plot. The input sinusoid is considered to be represented by a unit vector lying along the positive real axis, and for any given frequency the magnitude and phase of the output can then be defined by a corresponding output vector. By convention a phase lag is represented by rotation of the vector in a clockwise direction; the quadrants are also numbered in this direction relative to the real axis as datum.

A polar plot is a plot showing the variation of magnitude and phase of the output on polar coordinates, for a constant amplitude input, as the frequency ω is varied from zero to infinity. The curve drawn is the locus of the termini of the system output vectors, and a typical plot is shown in Fig. 6.1. The harmonic information is evaluated discretely for specific values of ω, and thus numerical values of frequency should be marked against points on this locus. The plot shown in the figure represents a third order system with a steady

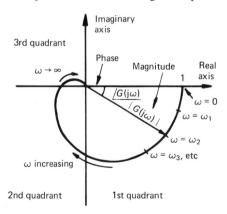

Fig. 6.1 Typical polar plot

state gain of unity. At frequencies tending to zero the output has the same amplitude as the input and is in phase with it; as frequency increases the output amplitude is seen to decrease, tending towards zero for high frequencies, while the output lags the input by an ever increasing amount tending towards 270° maximum for a third order system (180° for a second order system, etc. as will be shown later in this section).

The harmonic information for such a plot can be calculated if the transfer function is known, or if an actual system is available for test it can be determined experimentally, provided that frequency response testing is feasible.

Consider, first, plots obtained analytically for systems of known transfer function.

(a) *First order system, or simple lag.* Examples of some physical systems having first order transfer functions have been given in Section 2.4 and their transient response characteristics have been studied in Section 4.1. The transfer function for unity steady state gain is

$$G(s) = \frac{1}{1 + \tau s}$$

To obtain the frequency response characteristics replace s by $j\omega$:

$$\therefore \quad G(j\omega) = \frac{1}{1 + j\omega\tau} = \frac{1 - j\omega\tau}{1 + \omega^2\tau^2} = \left(\frac{1}{1 + \omega^2\tau^2}\right) - j\left(\frac{\omega\tau}{1 + \omega^2\tau^2}\right) \qquad 6.6$$

This gives the real and imaginary coordinates of the harmonic locus, and can be rewritten in terms of magnitude and phase as

$$G(j\omega) = |G(j\omega)| \angle\, G(j\omega) = \frac{1}{\sqrt{(1 + \omega^2\tau^2)}} \angle (-\tan^{-1} \omega\tau) \qquad 6.7$$

For $\omega = 0 \quad |G(j\omega)| = 1$ and $\angle\, G(j\omega) = 0$

As $\omega \to \infty \quad |G(j\omega)| \to 0$ and $\angle\, G(j\omega) \to -90°$

The locus can be shown to be a semicircle as follows. In Eq. 6.6 let the real and imaginary coordinates for $G(j\omega)$ at frequency ω be x and y respectively

$$\therefore \quad x = \frac{1}{1 + \omega^2\tau^2}$$

and

$$y = -\frac{\omega\tau}{1 + \omega^2\tau^2} = -x\omega\tau$$

Eliminating ω

$$y^2 = x^2\omega^2\tau^2 = x^2\left(\frac{1 - x}{x}\right) = x - x^2$$

$$\therefore \quad (x - \tfrac{1}{2})^2 + y^2 = (\tfrac{1}{2})^2 \qquad 6.8$$

The harmonic locus for a simple lag is thus a semi-circle with centre (0.5, 0) and radius 0.5 as shown in Fig. 6.2. Frequency points can be marked on this locus by determining the phase lag $\varphi = \tan^{-1} \omega\tau$.

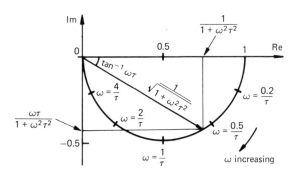

Fig. 6.2 Polar plot for first order system, $G(j\omega) = \dfrac{1}{1 + j\omega\tau}$

When $\omega = 1/\tau$, $\varphi = -45°$ which corresponds to the mid-point of the semi-circular locus. For a frequency $1/\tau$ rad/second the phase lag is $45°$; for higher frequencies the lag increases but it never exceeds $90°$. It must be realized that this single semi-circle represents all unity gain first order systems, irrespective of the value of the time constant, but that any single point on the locus represents different frequencies for systems with different time constants.

(b) *Second order system, or quadratic lag.* The transfer function of this, Eq. 2.17, is, for unity gain,

$$G(s) = \frac{\omega_n^{\,2}}{s^2 + 2\zeta\omega_n s + \omega_n^{\,2}}$$

$$\therefore \quad G(j\omega) = \frac{\omega_n^{\,2}}{\omega_n^{\,2} - \omega^2 + j2\zeta\omega\omega_n} = \frac{1}{1 - \left(\dfrac{\omega}{\omega_n}\right)^2 + j\left(2\zeta\,\dfrac{\omega}{\omega_n}\right)} \qquad 6.9$$

By inserting a range of values of $\dfrac{\omega}{\omega_n}$ and evaluating the real and imaginary parts of Eq. 6.9 (or alternatively the magnitude and phase) the location of points on the polar plot can be calculated and the harmonic locus drawn to join them.

e.g. for $\omega = 0 \quad G(j\omega) = 1 = 1\angle 0°$

$$\omega = \infty \quad G(j\omega) = -\frac{\omega_n^{\,2}}{\omega^2} = 0\angle -180°$$

$$\omega = \omega_n \quad G(j\omega) = \frac{1}{j2\zeta} = \frac{1}{2\zeta}\angle -90°$$

$$\omega = 2\omega_n \quad G(j\omega) = \frac{1}{-3 + j4\zeta} = \frac{-3 - j4\zeta}{9 + 16\zeta^2}$$

$$= \frac{1}{\sqrt{(9 + 16\zeta^2)}} \angle \left(\tan^{-1} \frac{4\zeta}{3} - 180° \right)$$

etc.

The completed locus is one member of a family of curves of which three are shown in Fig. 6.3, the shape of the curve being dependent on the value of the

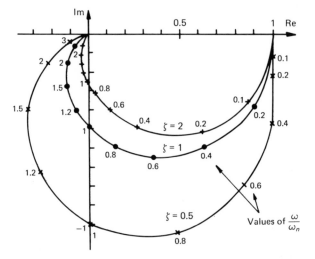

Fig. 6.3 Polar plots for second order system, $G(j\omega) = \dfrac{\omega_n{}^2}{\omega_n{}^2 - \omega^2 + j2\zeta\omega\omega_n}$

damping factor. For $\zeta > 1$ the magnitude is 1 for zero frequency, and decreases continuously with increase in frequency, while the phase lag increases to a maximum of 180°. For $\zeta < 1$ there is a range of frequency for which the magnitude exceeds unity, and when $\zeta \ll 1$, as illustrated by the curve for $\zeta = 0.5$, the phase lag increases very rapidly over a small range of frequency around ω_n.

It should be noted that for a second order system, for all values of damping factor ζ, when $\omega = \omega_n$ the phase lag is 90° and the magnitude is $\dfrac{1}{2\zeta}$.

(c) *Integrator.* Consider now a device such as an electric motor or a hydraulic ram which integrates the input signal at a constant rate. Let this rate be one unit per second.

$$G(s) = \frac{1}{s}$$

$$\therefore \quad G(j\omega) = \frac{1}{j\omega} = -\frac{j}{\omega} = \frac{1}{\omega} \angle -90° \qquad \qquad 6.10$$

The harmonic locus thus lies wholly on the imaginary axis (Fig. 6.4). The phase lag is 90° for all frequencies, and the magnitude is the reciprocal of the

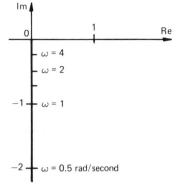

Fig. 6.4 Polar plot for integrator, $G(j\omega) = \dfrac{1}{j\omega}$

frequency in rad/second. Hence as $\omega \to 0$ the magnitude becomes infinite, and as $\omega \to \infty$ the magnitude tends to zero.

(d) *Higher order systems.* The harmonic information and hence polar plot for any higher order transfer function can be obtained similarly by writing down $G(j\omega)$, rationalizing, and inserting in turn different values of frequency ω. If the transfer function appears in factorized form the magnitude and phase information is likely to be more easily obtained by thinking of the system as a number of elements in series. The overall phase for any given frequency is then obtained by adding the individual phase components, and the overall magnitude is obtained by multiplying together the individual values of magnitude.

Example 6.1. Obtain a polar plot for a system with transfer function

$$G(s) = \frac{1}{(1 + 2s)(s^2 + s + 1)}$$

Letting $s = j\omega$

$$G(j\omega) = \frac{1}{(1 + j2\omega)(1 - \omega^2 + j\omega)}$$

$$= \frac{1}{1 - 3\omega^2 + j(3\omega - 2\omega^3)}$$

$$= \frac{(1 - 3\omega^2) - j\omega(3 - 2\omega^2)}{1 + 3\omega^2 - 3\omega^4 + 4\omega^6}$$

Now insert a range of numerical values of frequency ω rad/second

$$\text{e.g.} \quad \text{for } \omega = 1 \quad G(j\omega) = -0.4 - j0.2$$
$$\omega = 0.5 \quad G(j\omega) = +0.154 - j0.77$$
$$\text{etc.}$$

Such calculation is rather tedious and errors easily occur, particularly with high order transfer functions. Considering $G(s)$ as two factors multiplied together, curves for the first and second order factors can be drawn with the relevant frequencies marked on (as Fig. 6.2 and Fig. 6.3) and for corresponding frequency points the vectors can be combined graphically. Easiest, however, is to use the graphical method as an aid to understanding, but to do the multiplication of magnitudes and addition of phase angles in tabular form, obtaining the component magnitudes and phases by calculation, or from standard curves or tables (Table 6.1, Fig. 6.5).

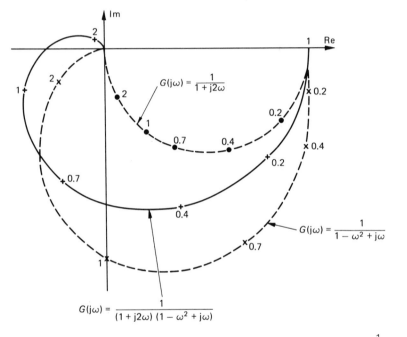

Fig. 6.5 Polar plot for system with transfer function $G(s) = \dfrac{1}{(1 + 2s)(s^2 + s + 1)}$

6.3 Bode plots

An alternative method for obtaining and presenting system frequency response data which is particularly useful where the transfer function is available in factorized form is the Bode plot. This consists of two plots normally drawn on semi-logarithmic graph paper: a magnitude plot, $\log |G(j\omega)|$, and a phase plot, $\angle G(j\omega)$, both on a linear scale, against frequency ω plotted on a logarithmic scale. The magnitude is most commonly plotted in decibels i.e. $20 \log_{10} |G(j\omega)|$. One reason for this choice of graph is that, since the magnitude is plotted in logarithmic form, the overall magnitude and phase information can both be obtained from the component parts by graphical addition. A second important advantage of such a plot is that certain approximations

Table 6.1. Tabular evaluation of harmonic response (Example 6.1)

Frequency (rad/second)	0	0.2	0.4	0.7	1	2
$\left\|\dfrac{1}{1+j2\omega}\right\| = \dfrac{1}{\sqrt{(1+4\omega^2)}}$	1	0.928	0.781	0.581	0.447	0.243
$\left\|\dfrac{1}{1-\omega^2+j\omega}\right\| = \dfrac{1}{\sqrt{\{(1-\omega^2)^2+\omega^2\}}}$	1	1.020	1.075	1.155	1.000	0.277
$\|G(j\omega)\|$	1	0.947	0.840	0.671	0.447	0.067
$\angle\left(\dfrac{1}{1+j2\omega}\right) = \tan^{-1} 2\omega$ (degrees lag)	0	21.8	38.7	54.5	63.4	76.0
$\angle\left(\dfrac{1}{1-\omega^2+j\omega}\right) = \tan^{-1}\dfrac{\omega}{1-\omega^2}$ (degrees lag)	0	11.8	25.5	53.9	90.0	146.3
$\angle G(j\omega)$ (degrees lag)	0	33.6	64.2	108.4	153.4	222.3

etc.

using straight line constructions can be quickly drawn and often suffice for accuracy.

It has been shown in Section 6.1 that any transfer function can be factorized into the form

$$G(s) = \frac{K(s - z_1)(s - z_2) \dots (s - z_m)}{(s - p_1)(s - p_2) \dots (s - p_n)}$$

The zeros $z_1, z_2 \dots z_m$ and the poles $p_1, p_2, \dots p_n$ will each be either zero, real, or complex, and thus in general $G(s)$ can be considered to be composed entirely of terms of the four following types appearing on the numerator or the denominator:

$$K, s, 1 + \tau s, \frac{s^2 + 2\zeta\omega_n s + \omega_n^2}{\omega_n^2} \quad .$$

Hence $G(j\omega)$ is composed of multiples or quotients of terms of the form

$$K, j\omega, 1 + j\omega\tau, \frac{\omega_n^2 - \omega^2 + j2\zeta\omega\omega_n}{\omega_n^2}$$

Consider now the Bode plots for these types of component term, and the way in which they can be added to produce a plot for a known transfer function.

(a) *Constant term* (gain term)

$$G(s) = K, \qquad \therefore \quad G(j\omega) = K$$

The magnitude is $20 \log_{10} K$ dB; the argument is zero (Fig. 6.6). Hence a gain term has a constant multiplying effect irrespective of frequency, and thus merely shifts the overall magnitude plot up or down by a certain number of dB. There is no effect on phase.

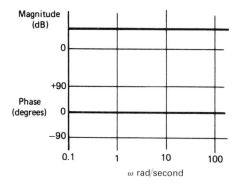

Fig. 6.6 Bode plot for constant term

(b) *Integral term or derivative term* (pole or zero at origin)
(i) Pole at origin:

$$G(s) = \frac{1}{s}$$

$$\therefore \quad G(j\omega) = \frac{1}{j\omega} = -\frac{j}{\omega}$$

The magnitude is $\frac{1}{\omega}$, or $-20 \log_{10} \omega$ dB, which has value 0 dB when the frequency is 1 rad/second and decreases by 20 dB for a tenfold increase in frequency. With ω plotted on a logarithmic scale the magnitude is represented by a straight line of slope -20 dB per decade of frequency and passing through 0 dB for $\omega = 1$ rad/second (Fig. 6.7). The phase is $-90°$, a constant

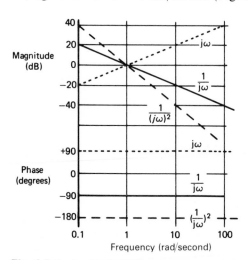

Fig. 6.7 Bode plot for poles or zeros at origin

lag, which does not vary with frequency. If a double pole is present, $G(s) = \dfrac{1}{s^2}$, the magnitude line has twice the slope, and the phase is a constant $-180°$.

(ii) Zero at origin:

$$G(s) = s$$

$$\therefore \quad G(j\omega) = j\omega$$

The magnitude is $20 \log_{10} \omega$ dB, a straight line of slope $+20$ dB per decade passing through 0 dB at $\omega = 1$ rad/second. The phase is $90°$, which means that the output would lead the input by $90°$ irrespective of frequency.

(c) *Simple lag or lead* (real pole or zero)
(i) Real pole:

$$G(s) = \frac{1}{1 + \tau s}$$

$$\therefore \quad G(j\omega) = \frac{1}{1 + j\omega\tau}$$

The magnitude is $|G(j\omega)| = \dfrac{1}{\sqrt{(1 + \omega^2\tau^2)}}$

$$= -20 \log_{10}\sqrt{(1 + \omega^2\tau^2)} \text{ dB}$$

A linear asymptotic approximation is frequently used, making use of the following:

for $\omega\tau \ll 1$ $|G(j\omega)|\,\mathrm{dB} \simeq -20 \log_{10} 1 = 0$

for $\omega\tau \gg 1$ $|G(j\omega)|\,\mathrm{dB} \simeq -20 \log_{10} \omega\tau$

The latter is a straight line of slope -20 dB per decade of frequency, which intersects the zero dB line when $\omega\tau = 1$ i.e. at $\omega = 1/\tau$. This is termed the *break point* or *corner frequency*. The true plot rounds off the junction as shown in Fig. 6.8, the maximum error being 3 dB at the break point. On either side of this the errors are 1 dB at ± 1 octave of frequency $\left(\dfrac{2}{\tau} \text{ and } \dfrac{0.5}{\tau}\right)$ and 0.3 dB at ± 1 decade of frequency $\left(\dfrac{10}{\tau} \text{ and } \dfrac{0.1}{\tau}\right)$. The rounding if required can generally be done sufficiently accurately by hand through these points.

The phase is $\angle G(j\omega) = -\tan^{-1} \omega\tau$

A linear approximation can also be used for phase, as shown in Fig. 6.8, namely $0°$ for $\omega \leq 0.1/\tau$, $-90°$ for $\omega \geq 10/\tau$, and a linear variation between. The true curve is gently curving, the error being approximately $5\frac{1}{2}°$ at ω equal to $0.1/\tau$, $0.4/\tau$, $2.5/\tau$, and $10/\tau$. The error is zero at the break point frequency since the lag is exactly $45°$ when $\omega = 1/\tau$.

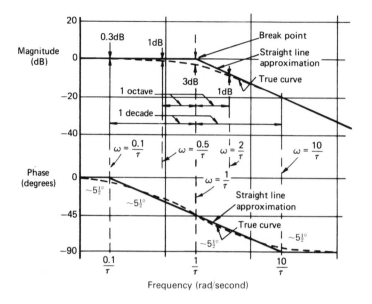

Fig. 6.8 Bode plot for a simple lag

(ii) Real zero

$$G(s) = 1 + \tau s$$
$$\therefore \quad G(j\omega) = 1 + j\omega\tau$$

The expressions for magnitude and phase are identical to those for a real pole except that they have the opposite sign. The curves on the Bode plot are thus mirror images about the 0 dB and 0 degree lines. The magnitude and phase therefore both increase with frequency, the latter tending towards 90° (a phase lead) for frequencies in excess of $\dfrac{10}{\tau}$.

For different values of τ the curves are merely shifted along the frequency axis. If curves are to be drawn frequently, templates can be produced to enable the true curves to be drawn quickly and easily.

(d) *Quadratic lag or lead* (pairs of complex conjugate poles or zeros)
    (i) Pair of conjugate poles:

$$G(s) = \frac{\omega_n^2}{s^2 + 2\zeta\omega_n s + \omega_n^2}$$

$$\therefore \quad G(j\omega) = \frac{1}{\left(1 - \dfrac{\omega^2}{\omega_n^2}\right) + j\left(2\zeta\dfrac{\omega}{\omega_n}\right)}$$

The magnitude is $-20\log_{10}\sqrt{\left\{\left(1-\dfrac{\omega^2}{\omega_n^{\,2}}\right)^2+\left(\dfrac{2\zeta\omega}{\omega_n}\right)^2\right\}}$ dB

and the phase is $\qquad -\tan^{-1}\left(\dfrac{2\zeta\dfrac{\omega}{\omega_n}}{1-\dfrac{\omega^2}{\omega_n^{\,2}}}\right)$

For $\dfrac{\omega}{\omega_n}\ll 1$ $\qquad |G(j\omega)|\simeq -20\log_{10}1=0$ dB

and for $\dfrac{\omega}{\omega_n}\gg 1$ $\qquad |G(j\omega)|\simeq -20\log_{10}\left(\dfrac{\omega^2}{\omega_n^{\,2}}\right)=-40\log_{10}\left(\dfrac{\omega}{\omega_n}\right)$

The straight line approximation for magnitude is thus a line at 0 dB for low frequencies, changing to a line of slope -40 dB per decade at the break point given by $\omega=\omega_n$, the undamped natural frequency. The shape of the true curve depends on the value of ζ, the error being least for $\zeta\simeq 0.5$. Curves for a range of values of ζ are shown in Fig. 6.9. (For $0.35<\zeta<0.7$, the error <3 dB.)

The phase curve varies from $0°$ for $\dfrac{\omega}{\omega_n}\ll 1$ to $-180°$ for $\dfrac{\omega}{\omega_n}\gg 1$, and passes through the $-90°$ point at $\omega=\omega_n$. There is no convenient straight line approximation, the transition again being a function of ζ, and being most rapid for very small values of ζ, as shown in Fig. 6.9.

(ii) Pair of conjugate zeros:

$$G(s)=\frac{s^2+2\zeta\omega_n s+\omega_n^{\,2}}{\omega_n^{\,2}}$$

$$\therefore\quad G(j\omega)=\left(1-\frac{\omega^2}{\omega_n^{\,2}}\right)+j\left(2\zeta\frac{\omega}{\omega_n}\right)$$

The magnitude and phase are numerically the same as for a pair of poles but of opposite sign, and are thus represented on the Bode plot by families of curves which are the mirror images of those of Fig. 6.9 reflected about the 0 dB and the 0 degree lines.

Here, even more than with the simple lag, templates can prove useful. The curves for the calculated value of ζ can be quickly drawn at the position along the frequency scale corresponding to the appropriate ω_n.

Example 6.2. Using straight line approximations draw a Bode diagram for a system with transfer function

$$G(s)=\frac{10}{s(1+0.5s)(1+0.1s)}$$

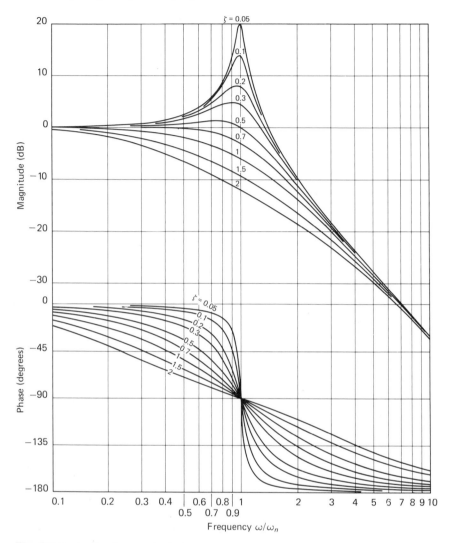

Fig. 6.9 Bode plot for quadratic lag

This transfer function can be seen to be made up of 4 constituent components:

(a) a constant gain term of 10
(b) an integrating term $1/s$
(c) a simple lag of time constant 0.5 second
(d) a simple lag of time constant 0.1 second

Using straight line approximations the contributions of these terms to the overall magnitude are respectively:

(a) a constant of $20 \log_{10} 10 = 20$ dB for all frequencies

(b) a line of slope -20 dB/decade, passing through 0 dB at the frequency 1 rad/second

(c) a magnitude of 0 dB up to a break point at $\dfrac{1}{0.5} = 2$ rad/second, and thereafter a line of slope -20 dB/decade

(d) a magnitude of 0 dB up to a break point at $\dfrac{1}{0.1} = 10$ rad/second, and thereafter a line of slope -20 dB/decade

These magnitude contributions are shown in Fig. 6.10 together with the overall magnitude curve which results from summing them. The overall curve

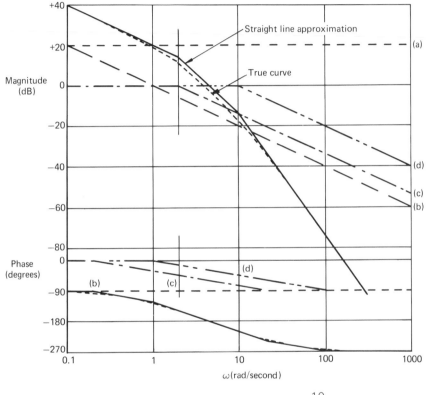

Fig. 6.10 Bode plot for transfer function $G(s) = \dfrac{10}{s(1 + 0.5s)(1 + 0.1s)}$

is in error particularly in the region of the break points. The true curves for (c) and (d) and hence for the overall curve can be drawn in with sufficient accuracy for most purposes by interpolating by eye, using the guide points of error being 3 dB at the corner frequency, 1 dB at ± 1 octave, 0.3 dB at ± 1 decade. It can be seen that the result is a rounding of the corners.

The contributions of these four components to the overall phase are respectively:

(a) no effect.

(b) a constant phase lag of 90° for all frequencies.

(c) zero lag to $\omega = 0.2$ rad/second, 90° lag for $\omega > 20$ rad/second, and a linear variation between, with a lag of 45° at $\omega = 2$ rad/second, the corner frequency.

(d) a similar curve to (c), but centred about $\omega = 10$ rad/second.

The true curves for phase vary from these straight line approximations by a maximum of $5\frac{1}{2}°$, as described earlier in this section, and they can be drawn in by eye very easily.

Example 6.3. Draw a Bode diagram for the transfer function

$$G(s) = \frac{5}{(1 + 2s)(s^2 + 3s + 25)}$$

This transfer function is made up of three components for which the Bode plots can readily be drawn:

(a) a constant gain term of $\dfrac{5}{25} = 0.2$. This contributes a constant magnitude of $20 \log_{10} 0.2 = -14$ dB at all frequencies, and has no effect on phase.

(b) a simple lag of time constant 2 second. This gives magnitude and phase contributions as in the previous example, but centred on a break point at 0.5 rad/second.

(c) a quadratic lag with $\omega_n = \sqrt{25} = 5$ and $\zeta = \dfrac{3}{2\omega_n} = 0.3$. The straight line approximation is 0 dB to the corner frequency 5 rad/second, and falling at 40 dB per decade beyond this. With a value of $\zeta = 0.3$ the true curve peaks very close to 5 rad/second and can be drawn from Fig. 6.9. The phase curve passes steeply through 90° at $\omega = \omega_n = 5$ rad/second and can also be drawn from Fig. 6.9.

The overall magnitude and phase can now be obtained by addition, Fig. 6.11. It should be noted that the effect of the quadratic lag is felt at high frequencies where the amplitude has already been markedly attenuated by the simple lag. This is consistent with the fact that the poles at $-1.5 \pm j4.77$ are three times as far from the imaginary axis in the s-plane as the dominant root at -0.5 (see Section 4.3).

6.4 Frequency response testing of practical systems

Methods have been described in the earlier part of this chapter by means of which the frequency response information for a system can be calculated, provided that the transfer function is known. In the derivation of the transfer function from the basic physical laws certain assumptions have been made, and the validity of these should be confirmed by experimental testing of the actual system, provided that this is possible. With some physical components theoretical derivation of a transfer function is impossible and in such cases experimental testing can provide a means of determining a transfer function for the component. The form of the testing is dependent on various factors e.g.

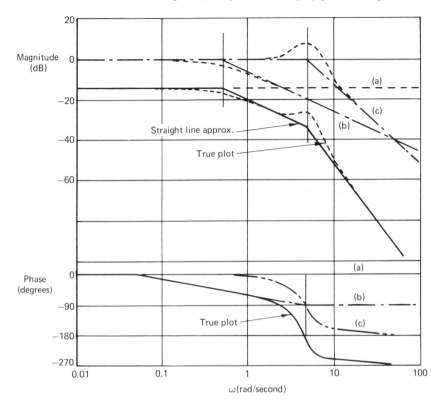

Fig. 6.11 Bode plot for transfer function $G(s) = \dfrac{5}{(1 + 2s)(s^2 + 3s + 25)}$

Can the system be tested off-line? What types of forcing function are physically realizable? How much disturbance to the system can be tolerated, and what is the noise level present? These aspects will be discussed further in the next chapter, particularly considerations of signal level and noise.

Clearly, provided that the input can be varied in a sinusoidal manner then the output or some variable representing it can be monitored, and its amplitude and phase measured for a range of frequencies. Any distortion of the waveform would suggest the presence of non-linearities in the system. The magnitude and phase information can be obtained in a number of ways, a convenient one being by using a transfer function analyser, a special purpose instrument which generates a sinusoidal forcing voltage for use as the system input, and which compares the system output voltage with this as reference to produce a direct readout of the harmonic information. Less accurate measurements can, however, be made in other ways not involving specialized equipment, such as by the use of an XY oscilloscope and a waveform generator. A sine wave from the signal generator is used to force the system input, the voltage from the transducer which measures the system output is applied to the Y input of the oscilloscope, and an auxiliary triangular waveform from the signal generator in phase with the forcing sine wave is applied to the X input of the oscilloscope. The amplitude and phase shift can be measured directly from the resulting trace.

The harmonic information would normally be presented on a polar or Bode plot. The polar plot gives by inspection a good idea of the likely form of the transfer function and, if the system approximates to one of first or second order, the values of τ or ζ and ω_n can be estimated. In principle, on the magnitude against frequency Bode plot it should be possible to draw straight lines whose slopes are multiples of 20 dB/decade and from the intersection of the asymptotes determine time constants; where complex lags are present ζ and ω_n can be estimated by comparison with standard curves. In practice, where time constants are close together it is difficult to decide where to draw asymptotes; hence prior knowledge of the theoretically expected form of the transfer function is of considerable help.

It will be clear from Section 6.3 that for a linear system there is a unique phase relationship associated with any given magnitude relationship. Study of the phase curve can assist significantly in the attempt to fit asymptotes to the magnitude curve with a view to determining factors of the transfer function. Lack of correspondence between experimentally obtained magnitude and phase curves would suggest the existence within the system of some non-linear effect. Any non-linearity increases the phase lag from that expected for a given magnitude curve, and is thus frequently referred to as a *non-minimum phase* effect.

Once an approximate transfer function has been determined an estimate of its accuracy may be made by evaluating its frequency response and comparing with the experimental data. A common criterion for 'goodness of fit' is the integral squared error

$$\frac{1}{\pi} \int\limits_{0}^{\infty} | G_{\text{calc}}(j\omega) - G_{\text{exp}}(j\omega)|^2 \, d\omega$$

At this stage of curve fitting a digital computer program can clearly be of great assistance when attempting to minimize this function.

Certain difficulties arise in practice indicating that harmonic testing has distinct limitations. If the input variable is not a voltage, current, position, or other easily controlled variable then variation of the input in a sinusoidal fashion of known amplitude may be very difficult or impossible. If the system is relatively slow, a long period of testing is required since each frequency in a wide range must be used in turn, and the system allowed to settle to a steady state each time before amplitude and phase measurements can be averaged over a number of cycles. The system characteristics may well change during the test period, especially when considering process or boiler plant, where ambient conditions have a significant influence. Finally, for perturbations of an amplitude that are relevant and tolerable, the response of the system may be masked by uncontrollable disturbances collectively referred to as *noise*.

6.5 Frequency domain performance criteria

Having described how to determine the harmonic characteristics of a system of known transfer function, or of a physical system which can be practically tested, it is necessary to decide what form of response is likely to be most acceptable. Consider the case where the system in question is a positional control, a measuring system, or other system where the output is intended to be equal to the input, or directly proportional to it. Ideally, the overall magnitude which in such cases is generally referred to as the *magnification* would be specified to be unity (or a constant) for all frequencies from zero to the maximum frequency component of interest in the input signal, and zero for higher frequencies which can be thought of as unwanted noise. Ideally also there should be no phase shift for the frequencies of interest. The input signal of interest would then be handled in an undistorted way and any noise at higher frequencies would be filtered out.

Such an ideal characteristic cannot be achieved in practice, but the form of curve which is typical is shown in Fig. 6.12 where the overall magnification M

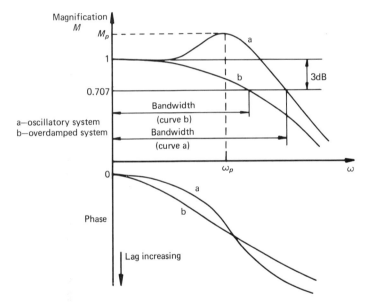

Fig. 6.12 Typical frequency response characteristics for unity gain systems

has been normalized to unity for low frequencies. It can be seen that there is no sharp cut-off. The response characteristics are often described by the following parameters:

(a) bandwidth—defined as the frequency beyond which the magnification drops more than 3 dB from the low frequency value; i.e. below 0.707 for the unity gain system. All frequency components of interest should lie within the bandwidth.

(b) peak magnification M_p—the height of the peak, which should ideally be in the range 1.1 to 1.5 for good transient behaviour. For an overdamped system there will be no peak.

(c) ω_p—the frequency at which the peak magnification occurs. In the case of an underdamped second order system this is close to the undamped natural frequency.

(d) cut-off rate—the rate at which the magnification curve falls beyond the peak, and is thus a measure of the selectiveness of the filter characteristics.

For accurate measurement, say recording of a dynamic trace, it is important that the gain and phase are as close as possible to a constant and zero respectively for the frequency range being covered. Transducers not infrequently have very low damping ratio and thus a very large value of M_p; in this case the flat region must be used otherwise there is likely to be severe distortion of the signal. In such instances the transducer chosen should have a value of ω_n which is some ten times larger than the maximum frequency of interest.

7
Statistical Methods for System Identification

System identification is the process of determining by means of practical testing the transfer function or some equivalent mathematical description for the dynamic characteristics of a system component. This of necessity requires the application to the component of some specific input signal since it relies on the analysis of input and output signals to identify the relationship between them. Traditional experimental procedures involve subjecting the system to step, ramp, pulse or sinusoidal input variations, and then carrying out relatively simple analysis of the output response curves, as outlined in Chapters 4 and 6. The advantages of these test inputs, which are typical of many normally occurring system inputs, have already been described from the point of view of the relative ease of signal generation and ease of analysis, and the physical understanding of system response which results. Unfortunately, response testing with these input functions is not always practical because of limitations imposed by the existence of system noise. Consider a component of process plant whose transfer function is to be determined, and which normally operates in a nominally steady state condition. With such a practical system component the output often varies randomly with time, even with a constant input, this variation arising from disturbances to the system component and being referred to as *noise*. The amplitude of the forcing functions when response testing must then be large enough to avoid the resulting output response being swamped by the noise signal, and this often requires input signals much larger than the normally occurring input variations. The results may not then be representative, as they are likely to include non-linearities and make small perturbation analysis invalid. Also, for large plant components the input variations would often need to be larger than the plant or the management can tolerate, so these methods find somewhat limited application where the component can be isolated for off-line testing.

This chapter describes a statistical method of identification applicable to the determination of transfer functions by on-line testing during normal plant operation with minimum disturbance to that operation. The method uses a non-deterministic forcing function which has random characteristics, unlike the above deterministic signals which are explicit functions of time, and which must thus be described by means of an appropriate statistical function. It can be considered as a wanted noise signal, and its amplitude can be small enough, if necessary, for it to be almost indistinguishable from the normal input signal. The effect of this forcing function on the output is not obviously noticeable from the plant operating records since it is buried in the inherent natural noise. Nevertheless, when the appropriate statistical procedure is used to analyse the signals, the effect of the inherent noise is largely eliminated and the response characteristics can be determined. The penalty of using a small amplitude forcing signal is that it must be applied for a long time period, of the order of 10 to 100 times the largest time constant of the plant but, because the effect of the test disturbance is not obviously detectable in the output, normal operation need not be interrupted. Occasionally it may be necessary to try to extract information from the inherent noise on the input and output signals, but the bandwidth of the input noise is seldom wide enough to yield adequate information by this means.

The primary purpose of this chapter is to describe this method and its advantages. As a background to understanding the method it also introduces the general ideas of correlation and spectral analysis, mathematical techniques employed widely in the handling of non-deterministic signals. The chapter can be omitted at a first reading since an understanding of the contents is not essential to the later chapters of the book.

The first section introduces the concept of correlation and defines the auto-correlation function, one of the ways available for describing a nondeterministic signal which is of particular use to the engineer. The autocorrelation functions for certain signals are given to illustrate the forms they can take; their main properties are also outlined. The section concludes by defining the cross correlation function which is used to describe the dependence of one signal upon another; in system identification these signals are the system input and output responses. Section 7.2 describes how correlation can be used to determine the impulse response of a practical system when the forcing function is chosen to be a signal which is equivalent to an ideal random signal known as *white noise*. Section 7.3 defines and gives examples of power spectral density, the frequency domain description of a signal and Section 7.4 discusses the determination of the harmonic response of a system by means of spectral analysis. This explanation of correlation functions and power spectral density functions and their use is followed by guidance on how they can be estimated for a given continuous signal by sampling and digital computation. Section 7.6 describes the pseudo random binary sequence, or PRBS signal, which is the forcing function most frequently used for the statistical testing of systems. The chapter concludes by illustrating graphically the forms of the various functions involved in the identification of a noisy second order system.

7.1 Correlation functions

A non-deterministic signal cannot be defined by means of an explicit function of time but must instead be described in some probabilistic manner. When undertaking system identification with non-deterministic forcing functions and carrying out the analysis in the time domain the appropriate statistical descriptions for the signals are termed correlation functions. The concept of *correlation* is a familiar one, there being for example an obvious correlation between a flash of lightning and the thunder which follows, and between the depth of water in a river or reservoir and the variation over a period of time of the rate of rainfall. Mathematically, the correlation of two random variables is the expected value of their product; it shows whether one variable depends in any way on the other. If the variables have non-zero means, it is sometimes preferable to subtract the mean values before determining the correlation; the result is usually known as the *covariance*, by analogy to the variance of a single variable. If the two variables are values of a random signal at two different time instants then the expected value of the product depends on how rapidly the signal can change. A high correlation might be expected when the two time instants are very close together, but much less correlation when the time instants are widely separated. It thus becomes appropriate to define a *correlation function* or *covariance function* in which the independent variable is the time separation of the two random variables. If the random variables come from the same signal the function is called an *autocorrelation function*, if from different signals a *cross correlation function*.

The autocorrelation function (or ACF) of a signal $x(t)$ is given the symbol $\varphi_{xx}(\tau)$ and is defined as

$$\varphi_{xx}(\tau) = \frac{\lim}{T \to \infty} \frac{1}{2T} \int_{-T}^{T} x(t)x(t + \tau)\, \mathrm{d}t \qquad 7.1$$

or
$$\varphi_{xx}(\tau) = \frac{\lim}{T \to \infty} \frac{1}{2T} \int_{-T}^{T} x(t - \tau)x(t)\, \mathrm{d}t \qquad 7.2$$

i.e. it is the time average of the product of the values of the function τ seconds apart as τ is allowed to vary from zero to some large value, the averaging being carried out over a long period $2T$. The process is shown graphically in Fig. 7.1 and consists of operations of displacement of the signal $x(t)$ through a

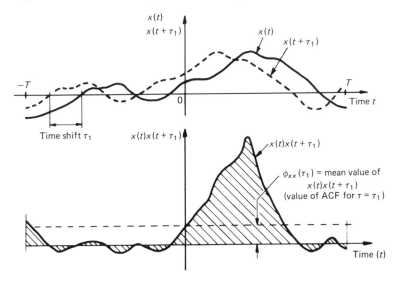

Fig. 7.1 Calculation of ACF of $x(t)$ for one value of time shift

time τ, multiplication of $x(t)$ by $x(t + \tau)$, integration of the product, and division by the integration time to give the value of $\varphi_{xx}(\tau)$ for that single value of τ. This process is repeated for other values of τ to yield φ_{xx} as a function of τ. The autocorrelation function is a measure of the predictability of the signal at some future time based on knowledge of the present value of the signal. If the value τ seconds from now is closely dependent on the present value then $\varphi_{xx}(\tau)$ will generally be large.

Consider first the forms which the autocorrelation function could have by evaluating it for certain signals which are functions of time.

Example 7.1. Sine wave. Consider the deterministic signal $f_1(t) = A \sin{(\omega t + \psi)}$, a sine wave with amplitude A, frequency ω, and phase ψ relative to the zero time datum (Fig. 7.2).

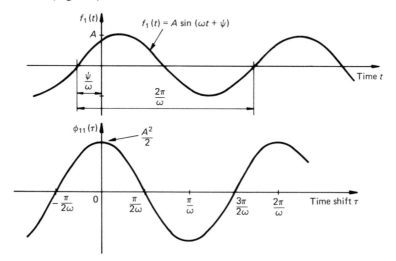

Fig. 7.2 Sine wave and its ACF

Using the above definition (Eq. 7.1) the ACF is given by

$$\varphi_{11}(\tau) = \lim_{T \to \infty} \frac{1}{2T} \int_{-T}^{T} A \sin{(\omega t + \psi)} A \sin{(\omega t + \omega \tau + \psi)} \, dt$$

Since the signal is periodic it is theoretically only necessary to average over one period, the time $\dfrac{2\pi}{\omega}$, where ω is the frequency in rad/second.

$$\therefore \quad \varphi_{11}(\tau) = \frac{\omega}{2\pi} A^2 \int_{0}^{2\pi/\omega} \sin{(\omega t + \psi)} \sin{(\omega t + \omega \tau + \psi)} \, dt$$

This integration can be carried out most conveniently by means of a change of variable.

Let $u = \omega t + \psi$

$$\therefore \quad du = \omega \, dt \text{ or } dt = \frac{du}{\omega}, \text{ since } \psi \text{ is a constant.}$$

$$\therefore \quad \varphi_{11}(\tau) = \frac{A^2}{2\pi} \int\limits_{\psi}^{2\pi + \psi} \sin u \sin (u + \omega\tau) \, du$$

$$= \frac{A^2}{2\pi} \int\limits_{\psi}^{2\pi + \psi} [\sin^2 u \cos \omega\tau + \sin u \cos u \sin \omega\tau] \, du$$

$$= \frac{A^2}{2\pi} \int\limits_{\psi}^{2\pi + \psi} \left[\cos \omega\tau \left(\frac{1 - \cos 2u}{2} \right) + \sin \omega\tau \left(\frac{\sin 2u}{2} \right) \right] du$$

$$= \frac{A^2}{2\pi} \left[\cos \omega\tau \left(\frac{u}{2} - \frac{\sin 2u}{4} \right) + \sin \omega\tau \left(- \frac{\cos 2u}{4} \right) \right]_{\psi}^{2\pi + \psi}$$

$$\therefore \quad \varphi_{11}(\tau) = \frac{A^2}{2} \cos \omega\tau \qquad\qquad 7.3$$

Although a sine wave is not a random function many non-deterministic signals contain sinusoidal components and it is important to know what their effect would be on the overall autocorrelation function. This will be discussed later in this section. Note that the amplitude A and frequency ω appear in the autocorrelation function, but the phase angle ψ is absent, so movement of the sine wave function relative to the time axis has no effect on the autocorrelation function.

Example 7.2. Random binary function. Consider now a signal $f_2(t)$ which has the general form shown in the upper part of Fig. 7.3. (It will be seen in Section 7.6 that a deterministic and hence repeatable function of this form, termed a pseudo random binary sequence, is a very suitable input disturbance for the statistical testing of systems.) The signal has zero mean, only two possible values $\pm a$, and is able to change from one to the other only every Δt seconds, there being an equal probability of the signal being $+a$ or $-a$ in each interval Δt. What is the autocorrelation function of this signal?

Let the function $f_2(t)$ be shifted τ seconds along the time axis, and evaluate the ACF by determining the time average of the product of $f_2(t)$ and $f_2(t + \tau)$ as a function of τ. When $|\tau| > \Delta t$, then any time instant t_1 and the subsequent $t_1 + \tau$ cannot lie in the same Δt interval, hence $f_2(t_1)$ and $f_2(t_1 + \tau)$ are statistically independent; the value of the product is thus equally likely to be $+a^2$ or $-a^2$, and the time average is zero. When $|\tau| < \Delta t$, then the probability that

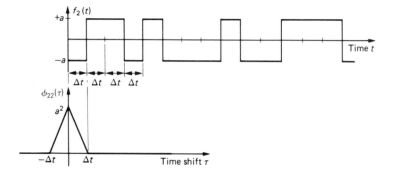

Fig. 7.3 Random binary function and its ACF

t_1 and $t_1 + \tau$ lie in the same interval is $\dfrac{\Delta t - |\tau|}{\Delta t}$, i.e. 1 for $\tau = 0$, 0 for $\tau = \pm \Delta t$, and a linear variation between. When they are in the same interval the product $f_2(t_1) f_2(t_1 + \tau)$ is $+a^2$, when they are not in the same interval the average value of the product is again zero.

Hence the ACF is given by

$$\varphi_{22}(\tau) = \begin{cases} a^2 \left(1 - \dfrac{|\tau|}{\Delta t} \right) & \text{for } |\tau| \le \Delta t \\ 0 & \text{for } |\tau| > \Delta t \end{cases} \qquad 7.4$$

This same autocorrelation function results also from certain other random time functions, such as one where the magnitude can take a random value to be held constant for each of the time intervals Δt.

Example 7.3. White noise. This is a completely random signal with defined properties which will be described in terms of its frequency characteristics in Section 7.3. Let it be referred to as the signal $f_3(t)$.

The correlation is zero for all time shifts τ except $\tau = 0$.
For $\tau = 0$

$$\varphi_{33}(\tau) = \lim_{T \to \infty} \frac{1}{2T} \int_{-T}^{T} f_3{}^2(t)\, dt = \text{mean square value} \qquad 7.5$$

The autocorrelation function thus consists of an impulse of magnitude equal to the mean square value occurring at $\tau = 0$, and is zero elsewhere. It can be seen that such a function results from letting $\Delta t \to 0$ in Example 7.2.

These examples illustrate certain important properties of autocorrelation functions and, to give a more complete understanding of the nature of the autocorrelation function $\varphi_{xx}(\tau)$ of a signal $x(t)$, some of these properties are outlined below.

(i) the ACF is an even function of τ, i.e. $\varphi_{xx}(\tau) = \varphi_{xx}(-\tau)$, because the same set of product values is averaged regardless of the direction of translation in time.

(ii) $\varphi_{xx}(0)$ is the mean square value, or average power of $x(t)$.

(iii) $\varphi_{xx}(0)$ is the largest value of the ACF, but if $x(t)$ is periodic, then $\varphi_{xx}(\tau)$ will have the same maximum value when τ is an integer multiple of the period.

(iv) if $x(t)$ has a d.c. component or mean value, then $\varphi_{xx}(\tau)$ also has a d.c. component, the square of the mean value.

(v) if $x(t)$ has a periodic component, then $\varphi_{xx}(\tau)$ also has a component with the same period, but with a distorted shape resulting from the lack of discrimination between differing phase relationships of the constituent sinusoidal components.

(vi) if $x(t)$ has only random components, $\varphi_{xx}(\tau) \rightarrow 0$ as $\tau \rightarrow \infty$.

(vii) a given ACF may correspond to many time functions, but any one time function has only one ACF.

A consequence of (iv), (v), and (vi) is that examination of the autocorrelation function for large values of τ shows whether any d.c. level or any periodic component is present in the signal.

Frequently there exist two signals $x(t)$ and $y(t)$ which are not completely independent (in system identification these would be an input and an output); a measure of the dependence of one signal on the other is given by the *cross correlation function* (CCF) which is defined as

$$\varphi_{xy}(\tau) = \lim_{T \rightarrow \infty} \frac{1}{2T} \int_{-T}^{T} x(t)y(t + \tau)\, \mathrm{d}t \qquad 7.6$$

or

$$\varphi_{yx}(\tau) = \lim_{T \rightarrow \infty} \frac{1}{2T} \int_{-T}^{T} y(t)x(t + \tau)\, \mathrm{d}t \qquad 7.7$$

Two analytical functions are defined, since time shifting $y(t)$ yields a different result to that obtained by shifting $x(t)$. If the two signals are from independent sources, and if they have zero mean values, then the cross correlation function is zero and the signals are said to be uncorrelated. If the mean values $\bar{x}$ and $\bar{y}$ are both non-zero, then the cross correlation function has a d.c. value equal to the product $\bar{x}\,\bar{y}$. The CCF is not an even function, though there is a type of symmetry because $\varphi_{xy}(\tau) = \varphi_{yx}(-\tau)$, since shifting one function forwards gives the same result as shifting the other backwards. $\varphi_{xy}(0)$ and $\varphi_{yx}(0)$ have no particular significance and the CCF generally does not have a maximum at $\tau = 0$. Examples of cross correlation functions are given in Fig. 7.18.

The ACF of the sum of two signals, say a sine wave plus noise, can be expressed in terms of the ACF and CCF of the individual signals thus:

$$\varphi_{(x+y)(x+y)}(\tau) = \lim_{T \to \infty} \frac{1}{2T} \int_{-T}^{T} [x(t) + y(t)][x(t + \tau) + y(t + \tau)] \, dt$$

$$= \lim_{T \to \infty} \frac{1}{2T} \int_{-T}^{T} [x(t)x(t + \tau) + y(t)y(t + \tau) + x(t)y(t + \tau)$$

$$+ y(t)x(t + \tau)] \, dt$$

$$\therefore \quad \varphi_{(x+y)(x+y)}(\tau) = \varphi_{xx}(\tau) + \varphi_{yy}(\tau) + \varphi_{xy}(\tau) + \varphi_{yx}(\tau) \qquad 7.8$$

Provided that $x(t)$ and $y(t)$ are uncorrelated then the third and fourth terms each have the value $\bar{x} \, \bar{y}$, and hence

$$\varphi_{(x+y)(x+y)}(\tau) = \varphi_{xx}(\tau) + \varphi_{yy}(\tau) + 2\bar{x} \, \bar{y} \qquad 7.9$$

A noisy sine wave would thus have an ACF as in Fig. 7.2 but rising to a peak at $\tau = 0$.

The general nature of correlation functions has been explained in this section, together with the principle of evaluation using the three operations of time shifting, multiplication, and averaging. Evaluation of the correlation functions of continuous signals by analogue methods using electronic circuits, tape recorders and analogue computers has almost completely been superseded by digital methods operating on discrete data representations of the signals. Digital evaluation of correlation functions is described in Section 7.5. This principle can perhaps be best understood by hand calculation for a signal with a small number of sample values, though normally the equations are programmed for digital computer solution.

7.2 Dynamic testing using correlation techniques

First the analytical background will be considered and then the method of implementation. Assume the system to be tested is as in Fig. 7.4a with transfer function $G(s)$, and impulse response or weighting function $w(t)$. It has been shown in Section 4.7 that for an input $x(t)$ the output $y(t)$ is given by the convolution integral

$$y(t) = \int_{0}^{t} w(\lambda)x(t - \lambda) \, d\lambda$$

or

$$y(t) = \int_{-\infty}^{\infty} w(\lambda)x(t - \lambda) \, d\lambda \qquad 7.10$$

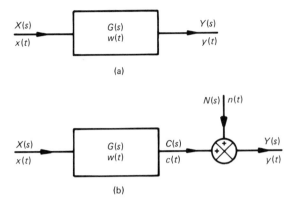

Fig. 7.4 Single-input–single-output system (a) without noise (b) with noise

Also, the cross correlation function between $x(t)$ and $y(t)$ is given (Eq. 7.6) by

$$\varphi_{xy}(\tau) = \frac{\lim}{T \to \infty} \frac{1}{2T} \int_{-T}^{T} x(t)y(t + \tau) \, dt$$

$$\therefore \quad \varphi_{xy}(\tau) = \frac{\lim}{T \to \infty} \frac{1}{2T} \int_{-T}^{T} x(t)\left(\int_{-\infty}^{\infty} w(\lambda)x(t + \tau - \lambda) \, d\lambda \right) dt$$

Interchanging the order of integration gives

$$\varphi_{xy}(\tau) = \int_{-\infty}^{\infty} w(\lambda)\left(\frac{\lim}{T \to \infty} \frac{1}{2T} \int_{-T}^{T} x(t)x(t + \tau - \lambda) \, dt \right) d\lambda$$

$$\therefore \quad \varphi_{xy}(\tau) = \int_{-\infty}^{\infty} w(\lambda)\varphi_{xx}(\tau - \lambda) \, d\lambda \qquad\qquad 7.11$$

It should be noted that this equation is very similar to Eq. 7.10 above. Comparing the two, it can be seen that if a signal $x(t)$ whose autocorrelation function is $\varphi_{xx}(\tau)$ is applied to a system with weighting function $w(t)$, then the cross correlation function of the input and output signals is equivalent to the time response of the system when subjected to an input signal $\varphi_{xx}(\tau)$. In particular if the input signal $x(t)$ is chosen to be the idealized signal called white noise then, as has been seen in Example 7.3, the autocorrelation function $\varphi_{xx}(\tau)$ is an impulse; hence $\varphi_{xy}(\tau)$ is proportional to the impulse response or weighting function. This is the basis for statistical testing methods. A true white noise signal is not physically realizable but approximations to it, in particular a form of the random binary function of Example 7.2 (to be described more fully in Section 7.6), can be used as system forcing functions and can yield close approximations to the system impulse response.

This testing technique is at its most useful where noise is present in the system output, since the process of cross correlation extracts from the output only that part which is correlated with the test input. The noise disturbance $n(t)$ is conventionally represented as an additive signal as shown in Fig. 7.4b; $c(t)$ is assumed to be the system output which would exist in the absence of this noise. The cross correlation function between $x(t)$ and $y(t)$ is given as above by

$$\varphi_{xy}(\tau) = \lim_{T \to \infty} \frac{1}{2T} \int_{-T}^{T} x(t)y(t + \tau) \, dt$$

But $y(t) = c(t) + n(t)$

$$\therefore \quad \varphi_{xy}(\tau) = \lim_{T \to \infty} \frac{1}{2T} \int_{-T}^{T} x(t)c(t + \tau) \, dt + \lim_{T \to \infty} \frac{1}{2T} \int_{-T}^{T} x(t)n(t + \tau) \, dt$$

$$= \varphi_{xc}(\tau) + \varphi_{xn}(\tau)$$

Normally, the noise disturbance is not correlated with the test input signal, hence $\varphi_{xn}(\tau) = 0$ and then

$$\varphi_{xy}(\tau) = \varphi_{xc}(\tau)$$

This relationship shows that the cross correlation of the output and input signals is the same whether or not there is any noise present, provided the noise is uncorrelated.

The test signal, which for convenience is usually referred to as white noise, although not physically realizable and hence in practice replaced by an approximation to white noise, is added to the normal system input and cross correlation is carried out between the system output and the test signal. The configuration required for obtaining one point on the impulse response curve by analogue methods is shown in Fig. 7.5. The output $y(t)$ of the system under test, corrupted by additive noise, is multiplied by $x(t + \tau_1)$, the test signal delayed τ_1 seconds. The multiplier output $z_1(t)$ is then integrated for a given period of time to obtain an estimate of $w(\tau_1)$, the value of the impulse response for time τ_1. When the system component has a large bandwidth the integrator may be replaced by an averaging filter. Additional points can be obtained by adding more delay-multiplier-integrator paths and/or repeating the testing with different values of time delay. It is much more common now to use a digital computer either on-line or off-line to carry out the correlation, and in either case the signals $x(t)$ and $y(t)$ must be sampled to obtain time series representations as input data for the correlation program. If a special purpose correlator is available the signals are fed directly to the instrument and the resulting correlation functions are usually displayed on a screen; a choice of algorithm for averaging is common, whereby the picture may gradually be built up over a selected time period, or an approximation may appear almost immediately and then be gradually improved by continual updating as

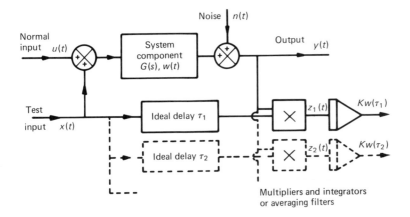

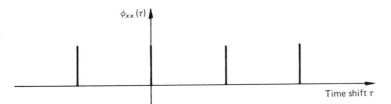

Fig. 7.5 Configuration for determining impulse response by statistical testing using analogue methods.

more data becomes available. Typical traces obtained from a correlator are shown in Figs. 7.17 and 7.18.

A disadvantage of using a white noise signal is that a long averaging time is required to obtain an accurate and consistent estimate of its autocorrelation function, necessary to ensure that changes in the autocorrelation function of the input are not affecting the cross correlation function; also, if the period of testing is too long, the system characteristics may not remain constant. It is thus generally preferable to attempt to generate a white noise signal which is periodic and which has an autocorrelation function as shown in Fig. 7.6, in

$\phi_{xx}(\tau)$

Time shift τ

Fig. 7.6 ACF of periodic white noise

which case the autocorrelation function can theoretically be computed to its full accuracy by correlation over one period of the input signal. With a noise free system the cross correlation function and hence impulse response could then theoretically be obtained to its full accuracy by correlation for one period. In a real system where noise is present correlation must be carried out for an integral number of periods of the input signal; the smaller the signal–noise ratio the longer the correlation time required to integrate out the inherent system noise. Results can be obtained with signal–noise ratios significantly less than unity.

7.3 Power spectral density

The autocorrelation function describes the statistical properties of a signal in the time domain but for many purposes it is convenient to describe the signal in terms of frequency domain characteristics. This particularly applies where artificial inputs are not possible and where information must be obtained from naturally occurring signals. The function used is the *power density spectrum* or *power spectral density* $\Phi_{xx}(\omega)$ which is the Fourier transform of the autocorrelation function:

$$\Phi_{xx}(\omega) = \int_{-\infty}^{\infty} \varphi_{xx}(\tau)e^{-j\omega\tau}\, d\tau \qquad 7.12$$

The transformation can be seen to be similar to Laplace transformation, though in this case the real part of the power of e is zero and the integration extends from $-\infty$ to $+\infty$.

Now
$$e^{-j\omega\tau} = \cos\omega\tau - j\sin\omega\tau$$

$$\therefore\ \Phi_{xx}(\omega) = \int_{-\infty}^{\infty} \varphi_{xx}(\tau)(\cos\omega\tau - j\sin\omega\tau)\, d\tau$$

Also, $\varphi_{xx}(\tau)$ has been shown to be always an even function, hence the product $\varphi_{xx}(\tau)\sin\omega\tau$ integrates to zero

$$\therefore\ \Phi_{xx}(\omega) = \int_{-\infty}^{\infty} \varphi_{xx}(\tau)\cos\omega\tau\, d\tau \qquad 7.13$$

It can be seen that the power spectral density is a real and even function. Applying the inverse Fourier transformation gives

$$\varphi_{xx}(\tau) = \frac{1}{2\pi} \int_{-\infty}^{\infty} \Phi_{xx}(\omega)e^{j\omega\tau}\, d\omega$$

or, since $\Phi_{xx}(\omega)$ has in Eq. 7.13 been shown to be an even function of ω,

$$\varphi_{xx}(\tau) = \frac{1}{2\pi} \int_{-\infty}^{\infty} \Phi_{xx}(\omega)\cos\omega\tau\, d\omega \qquad 7.14$$

Letting $\tau = 0$ gives

$$\varphi_{xx}(0) = \frac{1}{2\pi} \int_{-\infty}^{\infty} \Phi_{xx}(\omega)\, d\omega = \lim_{T\to\infty} \frac{1}{2T} \int_{-T}^{T} x^2(t)\, dt = \overline{x^2(t)}$$

If $x(t)$ were a voltage or current for a 1 ohm load, then the mean square value would be the mean power taken by the load; by borrowing this terminology $\varphi_{xx}(0)$ is termed the *mean power* of the signal $x(t)$.

Hence
$$\int_{-\infty}^{\infty} \Phi_{xx}(\omega)\, d\omega = 2\pi \times \text{mean power}$$
7.15

and the power spectral density is a measure of the energy distribution of the signal within the frequency spectrum. It is never negative, and extends over a frequency range from $-\infty$ to $+\infty$, thus being defined also for a hypothetical negative frequency region.

As with the ACF, the relative phase of the various frequency components is lost, and a given power density spectrum can correspond to a large number of different time functions. If the input signal has a periodic component such that the Fourier series for this component contains terms at frequencies ω_1, ω_2, ... then $\Phi_{xx}(\omega)$ will have discrete values at $\pm\omega_1$, $\pm\omega_2$, ...

The cross power spectral density $\Phi_{xy}(\omega)$ bears the same transform relationship to the cross correlation function $\varphi_{xy}(\tau)$ as does the power spectral density to the autocorrelation function.

Example 7.4. White noise. This is defined as a signal having uniform power content at all frequencies

i.e. $\Phi_{11}(\omega) = \text{constant, for } -\infty < \omega < \infty$

The ACF, given by the inverse transform of a constant, is an impulse at $\tau = 0$. It can now be seen why this is only a convenient theoretical function, since it implies that the mean power (Eq. 7.15) is infinite.

Example 7.5. Band limited white noise. Here, the power spectral density is constant for all frequencies less than some given frequency ω_1, and zero for all higher frequencies.

i.e. $\Phi_{11}(\omega) = \begin{cases} A \text{ for } -\omega_1 \leq \omega \leq \omega_1 \\ 0 \text{ for } \omega > \omega_1 \text{ and } \omega < -\omega_1 \end{cases}$

Hence
$$\varphi_{11}(\tau) = \frac{1}{2\pi} \int_{-\infty}^{\infty} \Phi_{11}(\omega) \cos \omega\tau \, d\omega$$

$$= \frac{A}{\pi} \int_{0}^{\omega_1} \cos \omega\tau \, d\omega$$

$$= \frac{A}{\pi} \frac{\sin \omega_1 \tau}{\tau}$$

This has the form shown in Fig. 7.7; it can be seen that as $\omega_1 \to \infty$ the ACF will tend towards an impulse. Provided that ω_1 is an order of magnitude larger than the bandwidth of a system being tested, then such a signal is an adequate approximation to true white noise.

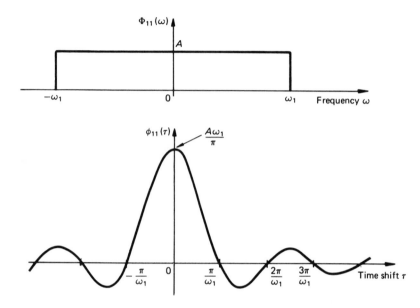

Fig. 7.7 Power spectral density and ACF of a band limited white noise signal $f_1(t)$

Example 7.6. Random binary function. Consider the random binary function of Example 7.2.

$$\varphi_{22}(\tau) = \begin{cases} a^2\left(1 - \dfrac{|\tau|}{\Delta t}\right) & \text{for } |\tau| < \Delta t \\ 0 & \text{for } |\tau| \geq \Delta t \end{cases}$$

Now

$$\Phi_{22}(\omega) = \int_{-\infty}^{\infty} \varphi_{22}(\tau)\, \cos \omega\tau \; d\tau$$

$$\therefore \quad \Phi_{22}(\omega) = \int_{-\Delta t}^{\Delta t} a^2\left(1 - \frac{|\tau|}{\Delta t}\right) \cos \omega\tau \; d\tau$$

$$= 2a^2 \int_{0}^{\Delta t} \left(\cos \omega\tau - \frac{\tau \cos \omega\tau}{\Delta \tau}\right) d\tau$$

$$= 2a^2 \left[\frac{\sin \omega\tau}{\omega} - \frac{1}{\Delta t} \left(\frac{\tau \sin \omega\tau}{\omega} + \frac{\cos \omega\tau}{\omega^2} \right) \right]_0^{\Delta t}$$

$$= \frac{2a^2}{\omega^2 \Delta t} (1 - \cos \omega\Delta t)$$

$$= a^2 \Delta t \left(\frac{\sin \omega\Delta t/2}{\omega\Delta t/2} \right)^2$$

The form of this is shown in Fig. 7.8.

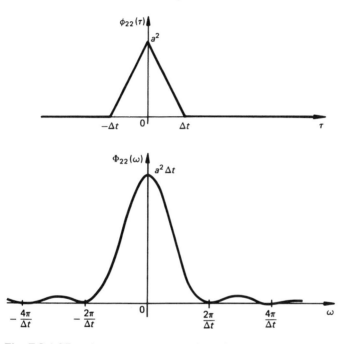

Fig. 7.8 ACF and power spectral density of random binary function

Fourier analysis allows any continuous signal $x(t)$ which is periodic with period T to be represented by the summation of a number of sine and cosine waves of varying amplitudes with frequencies ω, 2ω, 3ω, ..., $n\omega$ where $\omega = 2\pi/T$ radians per second,

i.e. $x(t) = a_0 + a_1 \cos \omega t + a_2 \cos 2\omega t + a_3 \cos 3\omega t$

$$+ \ldots + a_n \cos n\omega t + b_1 \sin \omega t + b_2 \sin 2\omega t + \ldots + b_n \sin n\omega t$$

By combining cosine and sine terms of like frequency the Fourier series representation of $x(t)$ can be written as

$$x(t) = a_0 + c_1 \cos (\omega t + \varphi_1) + c_2 \cos (2\omega t + \varphi_2)$$

$$+ c_3 \cos (3\omega t + \varphi_3) + \ldots + c_n \cos (n\omega t + \varphi_n)$$

The signal can thus be seen to have a mean value a_0, and to have its energy at specific discrete frequencies ω, 2ω, 3ω, ... $n\omega$ (the fundamental frequency ω and integer multiples of it), the energy contained in the respective constituents being given by $c_1{}^2$, $c_2{}^2$, $c_3{}^2$, ... $c_n{}^2$. The energy or power in the signal can be represented by lines of appropriate length spaced ω apart on a plot of power against frequency (as in Fig. 7.12 say). As the period T increases ω decreases and the discrete frequency values come closer together. In the limit for a non-periodic signal ($T \rightarrow \infty$) the discrete line spectrum tends towards a continuous spectrum. This is the power density spectrum. The power spectral density for a signal can thus be evaluated by first obtaining the autocorrelation function and then carrying out Fourier transformation, as in the above definition, or directly from the signal itself by Fourier transformation of the signal.

The approach adopted for evaluating power spectral density is dictated by the nature of the signal of interest and the equipment available. If the signal is a continuous voltage waveform of large bandwidth, a good estimate of the power spectral density can be obtained by means of a wave analyser. This is an instrument which utilizes a tuneable bandpass filter and measures the signal power contained in narrow bands of frequency, usually scanning automatically through a wide frequency range. Many signals from industrial processes have a bandwidth which is low in comparison to the smallest frequency that can be discriminated, allowing only a very approximate estimate of the power spectral density curve to be obtained by this method. A more flexible approach to determination of spectral density is by digital computation, operating on a sampled representation of the signal as outlined in Section 7.5. Direct computation of the Fourier coefficients and hence power density spectrum of a signal by means of a digital computer involves the handling of a vast amount of data, and the computation time increases very rapidly as the number of sample values increases. Prior to the development of computer algorithms known as *Fast Fourier Transforms* the power spectral density function was evaluated from the autocorrelation function. Now, however, the spectrum is usually evaluated directly using one of these algorithms and their computational efficiency is such that the correlation function is often evaluated from the density spectrum rather than directly from the time series data.

7.4 System identification using spectral density functions

The preceding section has shown that the power spectral density is a function of frequency and that it describes quantitatively how the energy in a signal is distributed over the frequency spectrum. From Chapter 6 it should be clear that a system affects the magnitude and phase of input signal components of different frequencies by different amounts. The amplitude of the output of a system with transfer function $G(s)$, for a frequency ω_1, is the input amplitude multiplied by $|G(j\omega_1)|$, while the phase of the output relative to the input is $\angle G(j\omega_1)$. For a statistical input signal it should thus be possible to determine the transfer function from a knowledge of the power density spectra of the input and output signals and the appropriate cross spectra. Consider now the form of the relationships between these for the system of Fig. 7.4.

The output of the system can be described by the convolution integral, Eq. 7.10, in the form

$$y(t) = \int_{-\infty}^{\infty} w(\lambda_1)x(t - \lambda_1)\, d\lambda_1$$

and for time $t + \tau$ the output is

$$y(t + \tau) = \int_{-\infty}^{\infty} w(\lambda_2)x(t + \tau - \lambda_2)\, d\lambda_2$$

The dummy variable λ_2 has been introduced in place of λ_1 so that the two integrals can be kept distinct later in the analysis.

From the definition, Eq. 7.1, the autocorrelation function of the output is

$$\varphi_{yy}(\tau) = \lim_{T \to \infty} \frac{1}{2T} \int_{-T}^{T} y(t)y(t + \tau)\, dt$$

Substitution for $y(t)$ and $y(t + \tau)$ from above gives

$$\varphi_{yy}(\tau) = \lim_{T \to \infty} \frac{1}{2T} \int_{-T}^{T} dt \int_{-\infty}^{\infty} w(\lambda_1)x(t - \lambda_1)\, d\lambda_1 \int_{-\infty}^{\infty} w(\lambda_2)x(t + \tau - \lambda_2)\, d\lambda_2$$

Interchanging the order of the limit process and the integration enables this to be written as

$$\varphi_{yy}(\tau) = \int_{-\infty}^{\infty} w(\lambda_1)\, d\lambda_1 \int_{-\infty}^{\infty} w(\lambda_2)\, d\lambda_2 \left\{ \lim_{T \to \infty} \frac{1}{2T} \int_{-T}^{T} x(t - \lambda_1)x(t + \tau - \lambda_2)\, dt \right\}$$

where the expression in brackets { } is, by definition, Eq. 7.1, the input autocorrelation function $\varphi_{xx}(\tau + \lambda_1 - \lambda_2)$

$$\therefore \quad \varphi_{yy}(\tau) = \int_{-\infty}^{\infty} w(\lambda_1)\, d\lambda_1 \int_{-\infty}^{\infty} \varphi_{xx}(\tau + \lambda_1 - \lambda_2)w(\lambda_2)\, d\lambda_2 \qquad 7.16$$

Now the power spectral density of the output signal is the Fourier transform of the autocorrelation function of the output, hence

$$\Phi_{yy}(\omega) = \int_{-\infty}^{\infty} \varphi_{yy}(\tau)e^{-j\omega\tau}\, d\tau$$

$$= \int_{-\infty}^{\infty} e^{-j\omega\tau} \left\{ \int_{-\infty}^{\infty} w(\lambda_1)\, d\lambda_1 \int_{-\infty}^{\infty} \varphi_{xx}(\tau + \lambda_1 - \lambda_2)w(\lambda_2)\, d\lambda_2 \right\} d\tau$$

$$= \int_{-\infty}^{\infty} w(\lambda_1) e^{j\omega\lambda_1} \, d\lambda_1 \int_{-\infty}^{\infty} w(\lambda_2) e^{-j\omega\lambda_2} \, d\lambda_2 \int_{-\infty}^{\infty} \varphi_{xx}(\tau + \lambda_1 - \lambda_2)$$

$$\times e^{-j\omega(\tau + \lambda_1 - \lambda_2)} \, d\tau \qquad \qquad 7.17$$

From the Laplace transform relationship between $w(t)$ and $G(s)$

$$G(s) = \int_0^{\infty} w(t) e^{-st} \, dt$$

and letting $s = j\omega$, since only frequency domain information is of interest

$$G(j\omega) = \int_0^{\infty} w(t) e^{-j\omega t} \, dt.$$

Hence, since $w(t) = 0$ for $t < 0$

$$G(j\omega) = \int_{-\infty}^{\infty} w(t) e^{-j\omega t} \, dt \qquad \qquad 7.18$$

Now also

$$\int_{-\infty}^{\infty} \varphi_{xx}(\tau + \lambda_1 - \lambda_2) e^{-j\omega(\tau + \lambda_1 - \lambda_2)} \, d\tau = \int_{-\infty}^{\infty} \varphi_{xx}(\tau) e^{-j\omega\tau} \, d\tau = \Phi_{xx}(\omega) \quad 7.19$$

Using Eq. 7.18 and Eq. 7.19 to simplify Eq. 7.17

$$\Phi_{yy}(\omega) = G(-j\omega) G(j\omega) \Phi_{xx}(\omega)$$

But $G(j\omega)$ is the conjugate of $G(-j\omega)$

$$\therefore \quad \Phi_{yy}(\omega) = |G(j\omega)|^2 \Phi_{xx}(\omega) \qquad \qquad 7.20$$

Hence the output spectral density is obtained from the input spectral density by multiplying by the square of $|G(j\omega)|$. This is to be expected since the spectral density represents signal power, or amplitude squared. For system identification purposes, knowing $\Phi_{xx}(\omega)$ and $\Phi_{yy}(\omega)$, $|G(j\omega)|$ can be found, and thus the magnitude curve of the Bode plot can be drawn.

The derivation of the corresponding phase relationship is somewhat lengthy; hence it will be stated without proof:

$$\frac{\Phi_{xy}(\omega)}{\Phi_{yx}(\omega)} = \frac{G(j\omega)}{G(-j\omega)} = \exp\left(-j2 \angle G(j\omega)\right) \qquad 7.21$$

Using this the phase curve of the Bode plot can be obtained.

In principle this is a useful method for determining experimentally the transfer function of a system component. It has the advantage that provided the normally occurring input signal has a wide enough frequency spectrum then an estimate of the transfer function can be made using only the information contained in the normal operating data. The value of the method, however, decreases rapidly as the level of internally generated system noise increases. If this inherent noise $n(t)$ affects the recorded system output as shown in Fig. 7.4b then the power spectrum of the noise contaminated output is that of the clean system output added to that of the noise; i.e.

$$\Phi_{yy}(\omega) = \Phi_{cc}(\omega) + \Phi_{nn}(\omega)$$

which means that Eq. 7.20 must be written as

$$\Phi_{yy}(\omega) = |G(j\omega)|^2 \Phi_{xx}(\omega) + \Phi_{nn}(\omega) \qquad 7.22$$

Unfortunately, the noise power spectrum $\Phi_{nn}(\omega)$ cannot be measured directly. However, an expression called the *coherence function* can be evaluated to estimate the degree of distortion of the clean output caused by the presence of noise. The coherence function is defined as

$$\gamma^2{}_{xy}(\omega) = \frac{|\Phi_{xy}(\omega)|^2}{\Phi_{xx}(\omega)\Phi_{yy}(\omega)} \qquad 7.23$$

and has a value of unity for a noise-free output. It is common practice to accept the data of the spectral analysis if the coherence function has a value greater than 0.8.

7.5 Digital evaluation of correlation functions and power spectral density

The present approach to signal analysis is to convert the continuous function $x(t)$ to a discrete *time series representation* $x_1, x_2, x_3, \ldots x_r, \ldots x_N$ by sampling at regular intervals Δt (Fig. 7.9a) and then to obtain an estimate of the correlation function or spectral density by digital computation. The choice of the sampling frequency and the length of the sample record to be analysed must be made with care since poor selection of either adversely affects the accuracy of the results, and both directly influence the computation time required. Intuitively one can see that in Fig. 7.9b the sampling interval is too large, detail is missing and results will be lacking in reliable data for the high frequency content of the signal, and conversely in Fig. 7.9c no information would be lost and computation time decreased if the sampling interval were increased significantly.

For the samples to be truly representative of the original signal it must be possible to recreate the signal accurately from the samples. It is well known in communication theory that this is possible only when the sampling frequency is at least twice the highest frequency component present in the signal. To be able to determine the dynamic characteristics of a process it is necessary that the time series shall contain all components of the signal at frequencies up to one or two orders of magnitude greater than the reciprocal of the smallest significant time constant of the process. This will determine the value of the minimum acceptable sampling rate. In practice the signal from the process almost always contains components extending to much higher frequencies

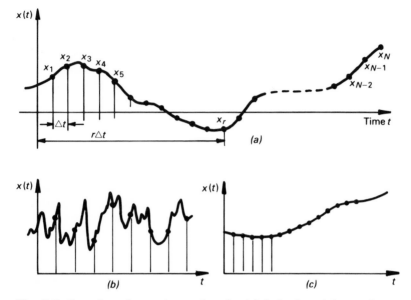

Fig. 7.9 Sampling of a continuous function (a) derivation of time series representation (b) Δt too large (c) $\Delta'' t$ unnecessarily small

than the wanted data because of noise pick-up, and this noise must be taken into consideration. It would be computationally wasteful to process the excessively large amount of data resulting from sampling at a rate sufficiently high to record the noise accurately. Merely reducing the sampling rate can give misleading results since the high frequency components then appear as though they are of lower frequency. This phenomenon, known as *aliasing*, is illustrated in Fig. 7.10, where a signal of constant magnitude but contaminated by noise at 50 Hz would appear to have a 2 Hz oscillation if sampled at 16 samples/second. The normal way to avoid this is to use an analogue filter to remove

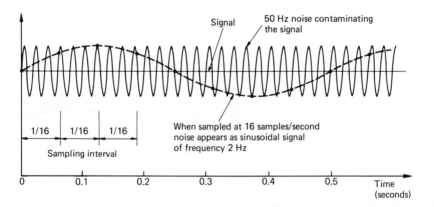

Fig. 7.10 Illustration of phenomenon of aliasing

the high frequency noise before sampling. It is not possible to remove aliased components after sampling since they are indistinguishable from signal components at the aliased frequencies.

Consider a continuous signal $x(t)$ which has been sampled at regular intervals Δt to yield a time series $x_1, x_2, x_3, \ldots x_N$ as in Fig. 7.9a. An *estimate of the autocorrelation function* of $x(t)$ can be obtained from the N sample values by time shifting, multiplying and averaging as follows:

$$\varphi_{xx}(0) \quad = \frac{1}{N} (x_1{}^2 + x_2{}^2 + x_3{}^2 + \ldots x_{N-1}{}^2 + x_N{}^2)$$

$$\varphi_{xx}(\Delta t) \quad = \frac{1}{N-1} (x_1 x_2 + x_2 x_3 + x_3 x_4 + \ldots x_{N-2} x_{N-1} + x_{N-1} x_N)$$

$$\varphi_{xx}(2\Delta t) = \frac{1}{N-2} (x_1 x_3 + x_2 x_4 + x_3 x_5 + \ldots x_{N-3} x_{N-1} + x_{N-2} x_N)$$

etc

Values are estimated for $\tau = 0$, $\tau = \Delta t$, $\tau = 2\Delta t$, $\tau = 3\Delta t$ etc., but there is no information about intermediate values of τ. It is clear that N should be large and that the estimates of $\varphi_{xx}(\tau)$ can only be realistic if $\tau \ll N\Delta t$. It may be that the signal is periodic such that $x_{N+1} = x_1$, $x_{N+2} = x_2$, etc. in which case each value of $\varphi_{xx}(\tau)$ can be evaluated from N products rather than from a decreasing number of products as above, the computations then being of the form

$$\varphi_{xx}(2\Delta t) = \frac{1}{N} (x_1 x_3 + x_2 x_4 + \ldots x_{N-2} x_N + x_{N-1} x_1 + x_N x_2)$$

and only one complete cycle need be considered. The resulting plot of $\varphi_{xx}(\tau)$ against τ is often referred to as a *correlogram*. In practice a smooth curve is often drawn through the points, or alternatively they are joined by straight lines, to highlight more clearly the general form of $\varphi_{xx}(\tau)$. For a signal which is not periodic an increase in the number of samples N should yield a better estimate of $\varphi_{xx}(\tau)$ at the expense of increased computation time. Increasing the number of samples N and simultaneously decreasing the sampling interval Δt gives a correlogram with more closely spaced points, which is desirable when the correlation function changes rapidly in magnitude from one value to the next.

As was stated in Section 7.3 the power spectral density of a signal is now usually determined digitally from a discrete time series representation of the signal, and generally by utilizing a Fast Fourier Transform (FFT) algorithm since it is very much faster than normal Fourier transformation on a digital computer. Spectral density plots for analogue signals can be most easily obtained if a proprietary spectrum analyser can be used, or if special software is available on a general purpose digital computer with analogue-to-digital converter. Failing this a program can be written incorporating the FFT algorithm from a software library, or the FFT routine can be obtained from a textbook. Any reader interested in the operation of the algorithm is referred to a textbook such as reference 29 in Appendix B which gives a clear description.

An appreciation of the artefacts associated with spectral density evaluation is essential, and the main object of the next few paragraphs is to explain some of these with the aid of simple pictorial representation so that spectral analysis can be undertaken sensibly and results interpreted correctly.

The FFT algorithm requires a number of samples which is a power of 2, i.e. $N = 2^n$ (say 2048, 4096, 8192, or 16384) and yields a discrete spectrum with 2^{n-1} frequency lines. The length of data record analysed is therefore $N\Delta t$, and spectral information is evaluated for the frequencies $1/N\Delta t$, $2/N\Delta t$, $3/N\Delta t$, ... $1/2\Delta t$, but not for any intermediate frequencies or higher frequencies. (Points can be joined by straight lines or by a smooth curve to highlight the trend.) The sample function of the signal or the autocorrelation function is thus truncated to a specific finite length prior to processing and this introduces some distortion in the spectral density curve estimated from the data. The signal $x(t)$ to be transformed is viewed through a *window* or *gate*, normally a *rectangular window function* hence

$$x_T(t) = x(t)W(t) \quad \text{where} \quad W(t) = \begin{cases} 1 \text{ for } |t| \le \dfrac{T}{2} \\ 0 \text{ for } |t| > \dfrac{T}{2} \end{cases}$$

The window function and its effect on the signal $x(t)$ are shown in Fig. 7.11a together with the Fourier transform of the window function

$$F(\omega) = T\left(\frac{\sin \omega T/2}{\omega T/2}\right)$$

The finite width of the window with its sharp edges and discontinuity between the ends introduces spurious harmonic information and thus a pure sine wave would be seen to have side lobes. The amplitude spectrum of a sine wave would then have the form shown in Fig. 7.11a instead of being a single line, and the power spectrum would be the square of this function.

Consider in a little more detail the effect of evaluating the power spectral density of a portion of sine wave using the FFT algorithm. If $N\Delta t$, the width of the window, corresponds to an integer number of cycles of the sine wave then the spectral line spacing is $2\pi/N\Delta t = 2\pi/T$ radians per second and one of these frequency values will correspond exactly with the frequency of the sine wave. In this case a single spectral line results, all other values being zero—if say there are 5 complete cycles then the 5th spectral line will have amplitude A, power A^2 and all others will be zero. Almost invariably, however, since N must be a power of 2 and Δt is a rounded time interval such as 10 ms or 0.05 ms, say, the product $N\Delta t$ will not correspond to an integer number of cycles. None of the frequencies for which spectral information is obtained will then coincide with the frequency of the sine wave, and the signal power will be shared across a number of frequencies, with the highest value corresponding to the frequency closest to that of the sine wave. Fig. 7.12 illustrates the effect. The shape and the peak amplitude change markedly with change in frequency. Note that an increase in N for the same Δt increases T and hence compresses

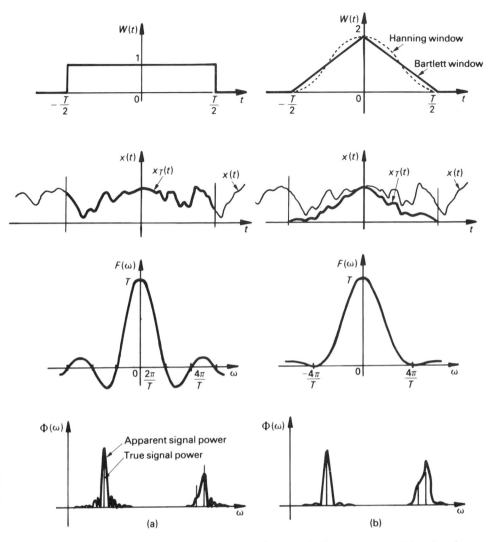

Fig. 7.11 Window function, its Fourier transform, and effect on spectral density of a signal (a) rectangular window (b) triangular (Bartlett) window (and Hanning window, shown dotted)

the effect to a narrower range of frequency but does not eliminate it. A square wave can be represented by the Fourier series

$$x(t) = \frac{4}{\pi} (\cos \omega t - \tfrac{1}{3} \cos 3\omega t + \tfrac{1}{5} \cos 5\omega t - \tfrac{1}{7} \cos 7\omega t + \ldots)$$

Hence there should be spectral lines for odd multiples of the fundamental frequency, and the successive power spectral values will be in the ratios $1, \tfrac{1}{9}, \tfrac{1}{25}$,

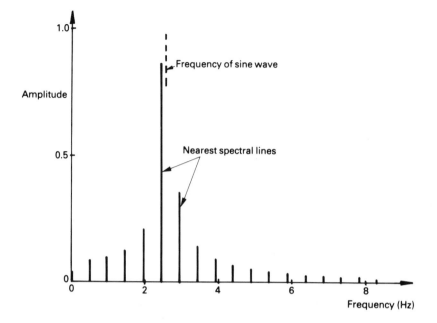

Fig. 7.12 Line spectrum for truncated sine wave (5.3 cycles, unit amplitude)

$\frac{1}{49}$, $\frac{1}{81}$, $\frac{1}{121}$ etc. or 0, -9.5, -14.0, -16.9, $-19.1 \ldots$ on a decibel scale. If an integer number of cycles of the square wave fills the window $N\Delta t$ then these lines and only these will appear on the spectral plot. Normally, however, each shows the windowing effect (Fig. 7.13) in which case there is a leakage of power to adjacent frequencies.

If a signal contains frequency components which are close together then the spectra tend to merge blurring the distinction between them (Fig. 7.11a). The resolvability is improved with a wider window (longer length of sample function analysed). Other window shapes, such as the triangular or Bartlett window and the raised cosine Hanning window, which reduce the emphasis on parts of the function towards the ends are sometimes used especially where a smoother spectrum is desired. The Fourier transform of the Bartlett window,

$$F(\omega) = T\left(\frac{\sin \omega T/4}{\omega T/4}\right)^2$$

is shown with its effect on a pure sine wave in Fig. 7.11b. The rectangular window is simple but suffers from large amplitude side lobes and poor amplitude accuracy. At the expense of an increase in bandwidth both the Bartlett and the widely used Hanning window have smaller side lobes and better amplitude accuracy.

7.6 Pseudo random binary sequences (PRBS)

These are very useful approximations to periodic white noise and are the

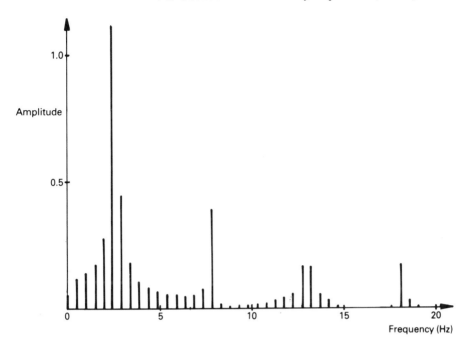

Fig. 7.13 Discrete spectrum for truncated square wave (5.3 cycles, unit amplitude)

forcing functions most widely used in statistical system testing. Their general form is shown in Fig. 7.3 since they are special cases of the random binary function of Example 7.2. They are signals which can take on only two possible states, say $+a$ and $-a$, the state can change only at discrete intervals of time Δt, the change occurs in a deterministic pseudo random manner, and the sequence is periodic with period $T = N\Delta t$ where N is an integer.

These deterministic repeatable signals all satisfy a set of 'conditions of randomness':

(i) Balance property: in any period of the sequence the number of logic ones $(+a)$ should not differ from the number of logic zeros $(-a)$ by more than one.

(ii) Run property: among the runs of one, two, three etc. in the period half should be of length 1, a quarter of length 2, an eighth of length 3 etc. and there should be as many of each run of logic one as logic zero state (these requirements cannot be satisfied exactly since sequence lengths are not powers of 2).

(iii) Correlation property: if a period of the sequence is compared term by term with any cyclic shift of itself then the number of agreements and disagreements should not differ by more than one.

When these conditions are satisfied the sequence can be thought of as being as random as is possible for any given length.

The most commonly used type of PRBS is the *maximum length sequence*, which is of length $N = 2^n - 1$, where n is an integer (i.e. $N = 15, 31, 63, 127, 255 \ldots$). This can be generated by an n stage shift register with the first stage determined by feedback of the appropriate modulo two sum of the last stage and one or two earlier stages (Fig. 7.14). Modulo 2 addition is the logic function 'exclusive or' i.e. if the inputs are the same the output is logic 0; if the

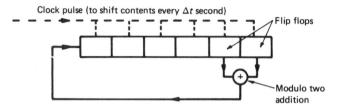

Fig. 7.14 Generation of PRBS by shift register

inputs are different the output is logic 1; alternatively it can be thought of as binary addition where only the least significant digit is recorded. The logic contents of the shift register are moved one stage to the right every Δt seconds by simultaneous triggering by a clock pulse. All possible states of the shift register are passed through except that of all zeros. The output can be taken from any stage and is a serial sequence of logic states having cyclic period $N\Delta t$. If feedback is taken from the modulo 2 sum of the wrong register stages then the resulting cyclic sequence has a length less than the maximum length, and will not be suitable. The correct stages for the most commonly used lengths are:

n	4	5	6	7	8	9
N	15	31	63	127	255	511
Feedback from modulo two addition of stages:	3 & 4	3 & 5	5 & 6	4 & 7	2, 3, 4 & 8	5 & 9

Delayed versions of the sequence can easily be obtained by modulo 2 addition of appropriate stages making use of a shift and add property which states that 'if a binary maximum length sequence is added modulo two to the same sequence delayed from the original then the resulting sequence is also a delayed version'.

Example 7.7. Consider as illustration of the above a 4 stage shift register with feedback from stages 3 & 4. Successive states of the shift register, starting all ones, are:

Stage
```
1   1 0 0 0 1 0 0 1 1 0 1 0 1 1 1 1
2   1 1 0 0 0 1 0 0 1 1 0 1 0 1 1 1   and the pattern
3   1 1 1 0 0 0 1 0 0 1 1 0 1 0 1 1   repeats
4   1 1 1 1 0 0 0 1 0 0 1 1 0 1 0 1
```

Hence the sequence length is 15, which is $2^n - 1$ with $n = 4$. With feedback from stages 2 and 4 the states would be:

Stage
1	1	0	0	1	1	1	1	
2	1	1	0	0	1	1	1	
3	1	1	1	0	0	1	1	
4	1	1	1	1	0	0	1	

and the pattern repeats, after only 6 states.

Investigate now the three properties of randomness when applied to the full 15 bit sequence:

(1) Balance property:
  Number of ones $= 8$
  Number of zeros $= 7$ $\therefore$ difference $= 1$
(2) Run property:

Length of run	1	2	3	4	
Number of runs	4	2	1	1	Total $= 8$
Actual ratio	4/8	2/8	1/8	1/8	
Ideal ratio	1/2	1/4	1/8	1/16	

There are equal numbers of runs of 1 and 0 except 3 and 4.
(3) Correlation property:
  Compare stages 1 and 4, say.
  Number of agreements $= 7$
  Number of disagreements $= 8$ $\therefore$ difference $= 1$.

If the output is from stage 1 then stages 2–4 give delays 1–3
$4 \oplus 1$ gives 0 1 1 1 1 0 0 0 1 0 0 1 1 0 1 i.e. delay 4
$(4 \oplus 1) \oplus 3$ gives 1 0 0 1 1 0 1 0 1 1 1 1 0 0 0 i.e. delay 11, etc.

There also exist other **PRBS** sequences e.g. *quadratic residue codes* which exist for $N = 4k - 1$ bit sequences, where k is an integer and N is a prime number (i.e. 11, 19, 23, 31, 43, 47, ...). These are difficult to generate using logic circuitry, but the sequences can be precomputed and read from paper tape, say, for slower applications. An advantage is that successive sequence lengths are much closer together.

Autocorrelation function and power spectral density of **PRBS**. Consider, first, values at $\tau = k\Delta t$ where k is an integer. Let values of the sequence for successive intervals Δt be $x(1), x(2), x(3), \ldots x(N)$. The ACF is

$$\varphi_{xx}(k) = \frac{1}{N} \sum_{j=1}^{N} x(j)x(j+k)$$

$$= \frac{a^2}{N} \times (\text{Number of matching digits} - \text{number of differing digits})$$

$$\therefore \quad \varphi_{xx}(k) = \begin{cases} -\dfrac{a^2}{N} \text{ if } k \neq 0 \\[2mm] +a^2 \text{ if } k = 0 \end{cases}$$

7.24

It can be shown by considering area changes that the ACF is linear between these points. Hence the form of the ACF is as shown in Fig. 7.15. As $\Delta t \to 0$ and N becomes large the ACF tends closer to that of true periodic white noise (Fig. 7.6).

The power spectral density, also shown in Fig. 7.15, differs from Fig. 7.8 in one respect—it is a line spectrum and not a continuous spectrum. This occurs

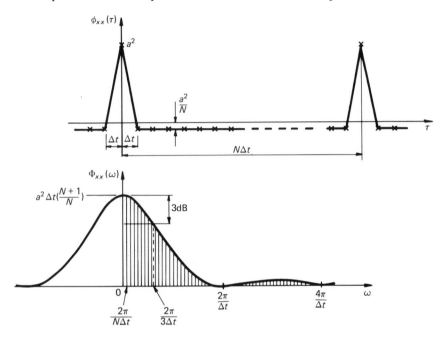

Fig. 7.15 Autocorrelation function and power spectral density of PRBS

because the lowest frequency component in the PRBS signal is that corresponding to the period, i.e. $2\pi/N\Delta t$ radians/second, and all other frequencies present are integer multiples of this value.

Advantages of PRBS and practical considerations

(a) The binary nature of the signal simplifies the cross correlation calculation since the multiplication can be replaced by simple gating of the output time function and its inverse.

(b) The binary signal is easy to generate and introduce into a system (using say a solenoid), and the constant Δt avoids the distortion which can occur with attempting too rapid switching which can be required with a completely random binary signal.

(c) The signal intensity is low, with energy spread over a wide frequency range, hence it is a suitable forcing function for a plant operating normally as it causes little disturbance from the operating condition.

(d) The power of the noise can be arranged to be in the band of frequencies of interest by appropriate choice of Δt and N. Choose $\Delta t \ll$ smallest system time constant, and $N\Delta t >$ settling time (some prior knowledge of the order of magnitude of system parameters is helpful).

(e) The input ACF is calculated to its full accuracy by correlation over one period; hence, to average out the effects of system noise, the cross correlation should be carried out for an integral number of input sequences. The smaller the PRBS amplitude relative to system noise, the longer the averaging time required. One sequence must be input to set the initial conditions correctly.

7.7 Illustrative example

To conclude the chapter, and to highlight the significance of its contents, this section presents and discusses briefly a typical set of graphs of the various

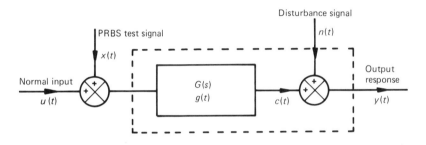

Fig. 7.16 Block diagram of system being identified

functions described earlier. The curves have been obtained from tests on a simulated second order system in the presence of noise, using a PRBS signal as forcing function. The system has been arbitrarily chosen to have $\omega_n = 6$ rad/ second and $\zeta = 0.3$; the results of statistical testing should therefore confirm these values. It is assumed that the normal input may include a noise component, and that a disturbance signal introduces further noise within the system, both contributing to give a noisy output signal $y(t)$, in the manner depicted schematically in Fig. 7.16.

In the absence of noise, the system can be subjected to an input change in the form of a step or an impulse function, and the resulting response recorded. Fig. 7.17 shows the response curves for a step of magnitude unity and an impulse of magnitude 1/4. Comparison of these curves with those of Fig. 4.7 would enable values to be estimated for ω_n and ζ, and the closeness of fit of each experimental response curve and the appropriate standard curve would indicate how well the system can be represented by a second order transfer function. In the presence of noise on the system output, these waveforms would be masked unless the input changes were of very large amplitude; with a real system a large enough step change to allow even an approximate estimate to be made would probably be unacceptable, and an impulse change would certainly not be acceptable. In this situation statistical testing can yield an impulse response curve with minimum disturbance to the system.

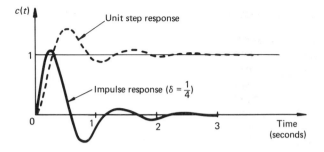

Fig. 7.17 Step response and impulse response of noise free system

Fig. 7.18b shows a typical sample trace of the output response of the system in the presence of noise for a nominally constant input (the noise characteristics have been arbitrarily chosen). A 63 bit PRBS signal of bit interval 0.1 second is used as input excitation for system identification; Fig. 7.18a shows the form of the PRBS input and the resulting system output in the absence of noise. The bit interval and the sequence length can be chosen on the basis of a preliminary estimate of the order of magnitude of the dominant roots of a system, and later can be confirmed as being satisfactory by inspection of the correlation functions. The chosen PRBS amplitude value gives a response amplitude which is of the same order of magnitude as the noise amplitude, although it can be seen to have quite different harmonic characteristics. The

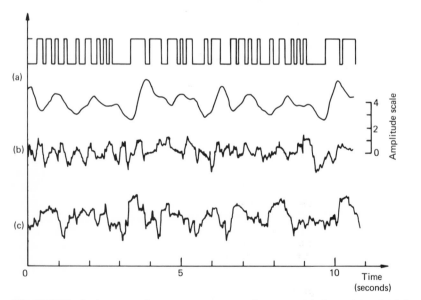

Fig. 7.18 Typical traces of output response of system (a) forced by PRBS in the absence of noise (b) without PRBS in the presence of noise (c) forced by PRBS in the presence of noise

response of the system to the PRBS signal in the presence of noise is shown in
Fig. 7.18c and, although a clear difference can be seen between this and the
normal noise output of Fig. 7.18b, the difference is not very marked. Smaller
PRBS amplitudes could be used resulting in a less obvious effect on the output
response, but a longer period of correlation would be required, and for very
low signal–noise ratios results would tend to be poor.

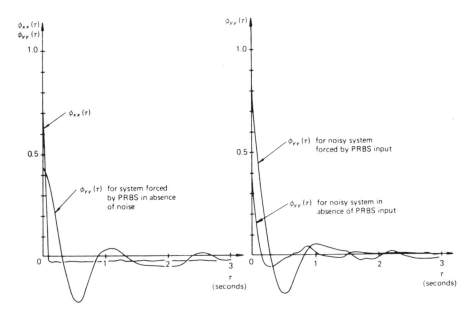

Fig. 7.19 Autocorrelation functions of input and output signals

The autocorrelation functions of these input and output signals are shown
in Fig. 7.19. The ACF of the PRBS signal has the form theoretically expected,
whilst that of the system output in the absence of noise shows a reduction in
signal power to somewhat less than half of the input power, and a marked
tendency in the short term towards harmonic change at about 1 Hz. The ACF
of the noise signal shows that there is a significant component of the signal
which approximates to white noise with, in addition, some increase in power
at frequencies around 1 to 1.5 Hz. The system is linear and hence the ACF of
the noisy output is broadly the sum of the previous two. Such information
from interpretation of the ACF curves confirms and quantifies trends predict-
able in this case from visual inspection of the response traces, and can be
supplemented by information obtained from the corresponding power spectral
density curves. Correlation for each curve shown was carried out for a time
duration of about 130 seconds, which corresponds to about 20 periods of the
PRBS; a longer period of correlation would help to smooth out the curves at
the larger values of time shift τ, provided the dynamic characteristics of the
system being tested remained unchanged over the longer time span involved.

Cross correlation of the system output signal with the PRBS input should yield a good approximation to the impulse response of the system, provided that the bit interval and sequence length are wisely chosen. Fig. 7.20 shows

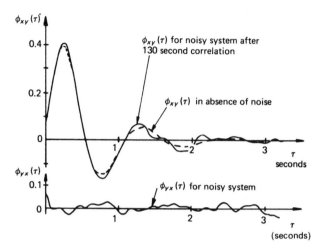

Fig. 7.20 Cross correlation functions

typical traces for the CCF with and without system noise; the former curve approaches the latter more closely when the correlation is carried out for longer time durations. The chosen bit interval of $\Delta t = 0.1$ second can now be seen to be a value which gives an adequate approximation to white noise for this system, and the period of 6.3 seconds correctly exceeds the system settling time (a sequence of length 31 bits could have been used instead). $\varphi_{xy}(\tau)$ can be seen to start from a small positive value for $\tau = 0$, consistent with the curve

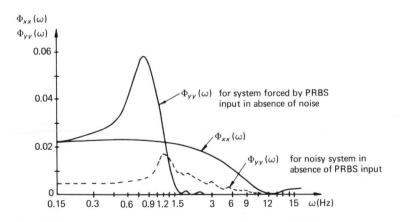

Fig. 7.21 Power spectral density curves of input and output curves

being the response to a narrow triangular pulse starting at time $-\Delta t$, and not a true impulse. This is confirmed by noting the form of $\varphi_{yx}(\tau)$, where the output response curve is shifted in the opposite direction when correlating and which thus gives values of $\phi_{xy}(\tau)$ for negative values of τ.

The power spectral density curves for the input and output signals, plotted against a logarithmic frequency scale, are shown in Fig. 7.21. It can be seen that with a PRBS input almost the entire power of the output signal is contained in the frequency range 0 to 2 Hz, and the curve for $\Phi_{xx}(\omega)$ shows that over this frequency range the input PRBS signal has a substantially constant

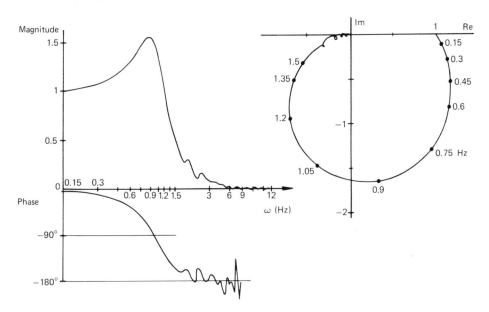

Fig. 7.22 Bode plot and polar plot obtained from CCF

power spectral density. This confirms that the bit interval used gives an excitation signal which is a good approximation to true white noise for the system tested. In the absence of noise the magnitude of the transfer function can be calculated from the input and output power spectral densities using Eq. 7.20. The power spectrum of the noise signal shows it to have a bandwidth of about 5 Hz, and confirms that it has white noise characteristics with additional power at frequencies around 1.2 Hz. The presence of this noise in the system output would clearly introduce large errors if Eq. 7.20 were to be used to determine $|G(j\omega)|$. The final figure, Fig. 7.22, shows the Bode and polar plots for the system obtained by evaluating the cross spectrum from the cross correlation function for the noisy system shown in Fig. 7.20. The results are clearly consistent with those expected for a second order system with $\omega_n = 6$ rad/second and $\zeta = 0.3$. The main evidence of errors arising from the presence of the noise shows up in the poor results for frequencies beyond about 3 Hz.

8
Feedback Systems—Accuracy and Stability

The earlier chapters of this book have been primarily concerned with describing how a dynamic physical system can be represented in certain convenient mathematical ways, and with showing how different types of system react to certain forms of forcing function. The main aim has been to present a clear picture of the nature of the dynamic behaviour of linear systems. This chapter and those following discuss the way in which the principle of feedback can be used to achieve a desired performance specification; some of the design methods available for synthesizing closed loop control systems are described.

Section 8.1 considers some general characteristics of systems incorporating a single feedback loop. It is shown that requirements for high accuracy of control and for fast well damped behaviour conflict, and that often a compromise must be made. Section 8.2 discusses the nature of steady state error and shows how it is a function both of the type of input and of the dynamic characteristics of the system. Sections 8.3 and 8.4 outline two widely used methods available for stability analysis, which are respectively relevant to time domain and frequency domain analysis; Section 8.5 defines gain and phase margins which are used to describe the degree of stability. The chapter concludes by considering the relationship between open loop and closed loop frequency response, and the graphical presentation of this information on a Nichols chart.

8.1 Closed loop or feedback control

An *open loop* or *scheduling control*, of which some everyday examples were given in Chapter 1, takes the form represented by Fig. 8.1. There is no comparison between the actual output variable of the system, usually referred to as the system response or controlled output $c(t)$, and the desired output of the system which would be some function of the input variable, usually referred to

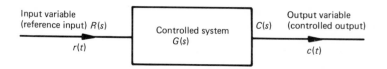

Fig. 8.1 Block diagram of open loop control system

as the reference input $r(t)$. The output, using Laplace transform notation, is given by the relationship

$$C(s) = R(s)\ G(s) \qquad\qquad 8.1$$

and is thus determined by both the input $R(s)$ and the transfer function $G(s)$ of the system. External disturbances or deterioration with increasing age may well cause changes in the parameters of $G(s)$; hence even in the steady state the system will only give the desired value of output at the design point.

Introduction of a negative feedback path allows the actual system output to be compared with the desired value, as shown in Fig. 8.2a, and an error signal

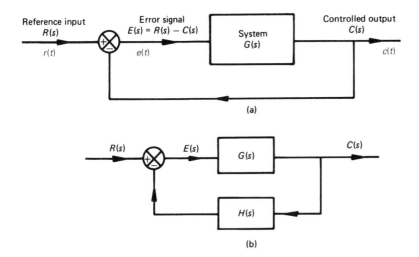

Fig. 8.2 Block diagram of simple feedback system (a) with unity feedback (b) with elements in the feedback loop

to be generated, this then forming the system input. This is termed *closed loop control* or *feedback control*. By inspection it can be seen that

$$C(s) = G(s)\ E(s)$$

and

$$E(s) = R(s) - C(s)$$

Elimination of $E(s)$ from these equations gives the output as

$$C(s) = \frac{G(s)}{1 + G(s)}\ R(s) \qquad\qquad 8.2$$

Again the output is dependent on the system transfer function and on the input function, but the effect of a change in $G(s)$ is less than for the open loop system, and by appropriate choice of $G(s)$ the error can be made small and the effects of external disturbances can be largely cancelled out.

If there is an element with transfer function $H(s)$ in the feedback path, representing perhaps the dynamic characteristics of the transducer measuring the output signal and converting it to the same form as the reference input signal, Fig. 8.2b, then

$$C(s) = G(s)\ E(s)$$

$$= G(s)[R(s) - C(s)\ H(s)]$$

$$\therefore \quad \frac{C(s)}{R(s)} = \frac{G(s)}{1 + G(s)\ H(s)} \qquad\qquad 8.3$$

The characteristic equation as defined in Section 2.3 is the denominator of the transfer function equated to zero, and is thus

$$1 + G(s)\ H(s) = 0 \qquad\qquad 8.4$$

Although closing the loop allows the steady state error to be reduced or eliminated completely, the system can become very oscillatory or even unstable. This arises as a result of the lags that occur within the loop; these lags cause a delayed response to the corrective action and often also a delayed sensing of the error signal. In an extreme case this results in pronounced overcorrection leading to large overshoots and undershoots. The requirements of accuracy and stability conflict; the engineer must be aware of this and must be able to design the feedback system to achieve a satisfactory compromise. Basically, design can be regarded as a problem of arranging the location in the *s*-plane of the roots of the characteristic equation in such a way that the corresponding system performs according to prescribed specifications.

Figure 8.3 shows the general form taken by a feedback control system. Most commonly the error signal obtained from the error detector is amplified and

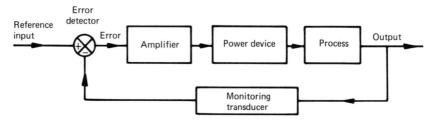

Fig. 8.3 General form of feedback control system

then fed to a power device which effects the necessary changes to the system, as shown in the figure. Often there are also compensating elements, auxiliary feedback loops, or other modifications designed to achieve the desired system performance. Some of these features will be illustrated in Chapter 10.

Servomechanisms or *servos* are, strictly speaking, a special group of feedback control systems where the output is a position or velocity. The term is, however, used much more widely and in many cases synonymously with feedback control systems. The input (or desired value) will in general be varying, and the output is designed to follow the input.

Regulators form another group of feedback control systems in which the reference input, although adjustable, is held constant for long periods of time (e.g. as in most temperature controllers). The output is maintained approximately constant at the value corresponding to the reference input, irrespective of external disturbances to the system. In process control, where regulating systems are widely used, the reference input is generally referred to as the *set point*.

Closed loop control action is frequently achieved in everyday life and in industrial situations by incorporating a human being within the feedback loop. Consider the action of moving to switch on a light, in relation to the generalized diagram, Fig. 8.3. The location of the switch can be thought of as the reference input, the position of the hand as the controlled output; there is no monitoring transducer, and the eyes act as the error detector. The eyes and brain generate the error signal and amplify it to give inputs to the muscles, the power device, which move the body and hand towards the switch and cause the hand to actuate the switch in the required manner. The importance of the feedback path can be seen by considering what occurs when it is broken by blindfolding or by complete darkness. It is worth noting that other feedback systems are also involved in this apparently simple action; for example, servo-mechanism action positions the pupil of the eye to focus on the hand and the switch, and regulator action alters the size of the iris to make adjustment for varying light intensity. The human being, although having a number of physical limitations and bringing with him problems of reliability, can act as a very sophisticated controller.

8.2 Steady state error

The prime reason for using feedback is to minimize the error between the actual system output and the desired system output. The magnitude of the steady state error, the value to which the error signal tends as the transient disturbance from any input change dies out, is of importance since it is a measure of system accuracy. To demonstrate what factors affect the value of the steady state error consider first the unity feedback system of Fig. 8.2a. The error signal $e(t)$ is the difference between the reference input and the controlled output:

$$e(t) = r(t) - c(t)$$

The reference input signal can thus be thought of as the desired output. The steady state error e_{ss} is the limiting value of the error $e(t)$ as time t becomes very large:

$$\text{steady state error} = e_{ss} = \lim_{t \to \infty} e(t) = \lim_{s \to 0} sE(s) \qquad 8.5$$

by the final value theorem of Laplace transform analysis.

But
$$E(s) = R(s) - C(s)$$
$$= R(s) - G(s) E(s)$$

$$\therefore \quad E(s) = \frac{R(s)}{1 + G(s)}$$

Hence the steady state error is

$$e_{ss} = \lim_{s \to 0} \left(\frac{sR(s)}{1 + G(s)} \right) \qquad 8.6$$

This equation shows that the steady state error is a function both of the type of system as described by the transfer function $G(s)$ and of the type of input $R(s)$. Consider in turn three types of input.

(a) *Step input function.* i.e. a constant input for values of time $t > 0$. Let the magnitude of the step be k. The Laplace transform of the input is then

$$R(s) = \frac{k}{s}$$

Inserting this in Eq. 8.6 gives

$$e_{ss} = \lim_{s \to 0} \left(\frac{k}{1 + G(s)} \right) = \frac{k}{1 + \lim\limits_{s \to 0} G(s)} = \frac{k}{1 + K_p}$$

where $K_p = \lim\limits_{s \to 0} G(s)$ is called the *positional error coefficient*, or *positional error constant*. Rearranging the expression for e_{ss} gives

$$K_p = \frac{k - e_{ss}}{e_{ss}}$$

Hence $\quad K_p = \lim\limits_{s \to 0} G(s) = \dfrac{\text{desired output} - \text{allowable steady state error}}{\text{allowable steady state error}} \qquad 8.7$

Thus for the steady state error to be zero it is necessary that $K_p = \lim\limits_{s \to 0} G(s) = \infty$, which requires $G(s)$ to have included in it a factor s in the denominator, an integral term. If no integral term is present then, for example, for an allowable steady state error of 1% of the step size, K_p must be at least $\dfrac{1 - 0.01}{0.01} = 99$; for an error of 5% it must be at least 19. Hence, if an allowable steady state error is specified for a constant input, a restriction is placed on the system transfer function $G(s)$ by requiring the gain to have a certain minimum value. In the field of process control this steady state error is termed the *offset*.

(b) *Ramp input function.* i.e. input changing at a constant rate. Let the input be a ramp increasing at k' units/second

$$\text{i.e.} \quad r(t) = k't$$

The Laplace transform of the input is then

$$R(s) = \frac{k'}{s^2}$$

$$\therefore \quad e_{ss} = \lim_{s \to 0} \left(\frac{k'}{s + sG(s)} \right) = \frac{k'}{\lim\limits_{s \to 0} sG(s)} = \frac{k'}{K_v}$$

where K_v is called the *velocity error coefficient* or *velocity error*.

$$K_v = \frac{\lim}{s \to 0} sG(s) = \frac{\text{desired output velocity}}{\text{allowable steady state error}} \qquad 8.8$$

It should be noted that this does not refer to an error in velocity, but rather a positional error in following a velocity input. K_v has units of seconds^{-1}.

For the steady state error to be zero with a ramp input, K_v must be infinite; this requires $G(s)$ to have a factor s^2 on the denominator. If the error must be kept within 1% of k', then $K_v = 100$, but if an error of 5% is allowable then the gain can be reduced until $K_v = 20$.

(c) *Acceleration input function.* In this case

$$K_a = \text{acceleration error coefficient} = \frac{\lim}{s \to 0} s^2 G(s)$$

$$= \frac{\text{desired output acceleration}}{\text{allowable steady state error}} (\text{seconds}^{-2}) \qquad 8.9$$

The analysis of these three types of input function shows that whether or not there is a steady state error for a given type of input depends on α, the power of s in the factored denominator of the open loop transfer function

$$G(s) = \frac{K(s - z_1)(s - z_2) \cdots}{s^\alpha (s - p_1)(s - p_2)(s - p_3) \cdots} \qquad 8.10$$

Systems are classified as being Type 0, 1, or 2, where the type number is the value of α, which corresponds to the number of open loop poles at the origin. The values of the steady state error for these system types are summarized in Table 8.1.

Table 8.1 Steady state error for type 0, 1, and 2 systems

System	Steady state error with:		
	steady input	ramp input	acceleration input
Type 0	finite	infinite	infinite
Type 1	0	finite	infinite
Type 2	0	0	finite

When there is an element with transfer function $H(s)$ in the feedback loop the error signal must be defined as $E(s) = R(s) - C(s) H(s)$. This causes certain differences in the above evaluation of steady state errors.

8.3 Routh–Hurwitz stability criterion

It has been shown in Section 4.3 that the form of the transient response of a dynamic system is largely dependent on the location in the s-plane of the roots of the characteristic equation. For a system to be useful it must clearly be stable at all times, where, considered in simple terms, it is defined as being stable if the output response to any bounded input function is finite. This implies that no roots of the characteristic equation can lie in the right half of the complex s-plane. A complex conjugate pair of roots with positive real part would give rise to an oscillation with amplitude increasing progressively and limited only by physical failure or saturation in part of the system. With a positive real root the output would increase exponentially and be limited for the same reasons. The problem of determining the stability of a linear system can thus be viewed as one of finding the roots of the characteristic equation.

If the characteristic equation is of high order then the task of determining the values of the roots can be tedious and time consuming. It is desirable to be able to determine more quickly and easily whether a system of known transfer function is stable or not. Around 1880 Routh and Hurwitz independently developed somewhat similar methods of determining whether any roots of a linear equation in the complex variable s have positive real parts, without having to solve the equation to find the values of the roots. The procedure is now used primarily as a rapid check on stability when all system parameters are fixed, and as a means of determining the limiting value for a variable parameter beyond which the system would become unstable.

Consider the general form of the characteristic equation, a polynomial in s:

$$1 + G(s)\,H(s) = a_0 s^n + a_1 s^{n-1} + a_2 s^{n-2} + \ldots a_{n-1}s + a_n = 0 \qquad 8.11$$

This has n roots, and these may be located anywhere in the complex s-plane.

For there to be no roots with positive real parts there is a necessary but not sufficient condition that all coefficients have the same sign and that none are zero. Hence, provided coefficient a_0 is positive, if inspection shows that one or more coefficients is negative or that one of the powers of s is absent, the equation is known to have at least one root in the right half of the s-plane. The system represented by that characteristic equation can then be said to be unstable without any further analysis being required. This can give a useful warning if an error of sign has been made in the theoretical derivation of a transfer function for a physical arrangement which is intuitively expected to be stable.

If this condition is satisfied then the necessary and sufficient condition that none of the roots has positive real parts is that the Hurwitz determinants of the polynomial must all be positive, where the determinants are given by

$$D_1 = a_1,\ D_2 = \begin{vmatrix} a_1 & a_3 \\ a_0 & a_2 \end{vmatrix},\ D_3 = \begin{vmatrix} a_1 & a_3 & a_5 \\ a_0 & a_2 & a_4 \\ 0 & a_1 & a_3 \end{vmatrix},\ D_4 = \begin{vmatrix} a_1 & a_3 & a_5 & a_7 \\ a_0 & a_2 & a_4 & a_6 \\ 0 & a_1 & a_3 & a_5 \\ 0 & 0 & a_2 & a_4 \end{vmatrix},\ \text{etc.}$$

The arithmetic involved in evaluating these determinants can largely be avoided since the Routh technique effectively does this more simply. An array of the following form is produced:

$$
\begin{array}{c|cccccc}
s^n & a_0 & a_2 & a_4 & a_6 & .. \\
s^{n-1} & a_1 & a_3 & a_5 & a_7 & .. \\
s^{n-2} & b_1 & b_2 & b_3 & .. \\
s^{n-3} & c_1 & c_2 & c_3 & .. \\
s^{n-4} & d_1 & d_2 & .. \\
... & .. & .. \\
... & .. & .. \\
s^0 & ..
\end{array}
$$

The first two rows are formed by writing down alternate coefficients of the polynomial equation. Each value in the subsequent rows is calculated from four of the previous values according to the following pattern

$$
b_1 = a_2 - \frac{a_0 a_3}{a_1}, \quad b_2 = a_4 - \frac{a_0 a_5}{a_1}, \quad b_3 = a_6 - \frac{a_0 a_7}{a_1}
$$

$$
c_1 = a_3 - \frac{a_1 b_2}{b_1}, \quad c_2 = a_5 - \frac{a_1 b_3}{b_1},
$$

$$
d_1 = b_2 - \frac{b_1 c_2}{c_1}, \quad \text{etc.}
$$

Coefficients are calculated until only zeros are obtained, the rows shortening until the s^0 row contains only one value.

Every change of sign in the first column of this array signifies the presence of a root with positive real part. For stability, therefore, all values in the first column of this array must be positive.

Example 8.1. Consider the characteristic equation

$$
s^4 + 2s^3 + s^2 + 4s + 2 = 0
$$

All coefficients are present and positive; hence, to determine whether the system is stable, form the Routh array by writing down these coefficients in the first two rows, and then evaluating from them the subsequent rows.

$$
\begin{array}{c|ccc}
s^4 & 1 & 1 & 2 \\
s^3 & 2 & 4 \\
s^2 & -1 & 2 \\
s^1 & 8 & 0 \\
s^0 & 2
\end{array}
$$

$$
b_1 = 1 - \frac{(1)(4)}{2} = -1 \qquad b_2 = 2 - \frac{(1)(0)}{2} = 2
$$

$$
c_1 = 4 - \frac{(2)(2)}{(-1)} = 8, \quad \text{etc.}
$$

There are two sign changes in the first column, hence there are 2 roots with positive real parts and the system represented by this characteristic equation is unstable. Note that the method does not give the value of these roots.

Special cases. Two kinds of difficulty can occur as a result of zeros in the array.

(a) If a zero appears in the first column and the remaining terms in the same row are not all zero, then the terms in the subsequent row would all be infinite. The procedure for applying the Routh criterion is then to replace s by a new variable $1/\sigma$ and thus obtain a new equation where the order of the coefficients has been reversed. If this equation has no roots with positive real parts then neither will the original equation have any.

Example 8.2

$$s^5 + s^4 + 4s^3 + 4s^2 + 2s + 1 = 0$$

The Routh array is:

s^5	1	4	2
s^4	1	4	1
s^3	0	1	0
s^2	$-\infty$		
s^1			

... and the table cannot be completed.

Letting $s = \dfrac{1}{\sigma}$, the equation becomes

$$\sigma^5 + 2\sigma^4 + 4\sigma^3 + 4\sigma^2 + \sigma + 1 = 0$$

and the array is:

σ^5	1	4	1
σ^4	2	4	1
σ^3	2	0.5	
σ^2	3.5	1	
σ^1	-0.07		
σ^0	1		

There are two changes of sign; hence each equation has two roots with positive real parts.

(b) If a complete row of zeros occurs then again the table cannot be completed. This condition indicates that one or more pairs of roots (real, imaginary, or complex) are an equal radial distance from the origin but diametrically opposite. The condition where one pair of conjugate roots lies on the imaginary axis is of most interest, since then the system will oscillate with constant amplitude, a condition of marginal stability. The equation corresponding to the coefficients just above the row of zeros is called the *auxiliary equation,* and has as its highest order term the power of s indicated in the reference column to the left of the row. The order is always even and indicates the number of root pairs, e.g. second order indicates presence of two equal and opposite roots. The value of these roots can be obtained by solving the auxiliary equation, and these roots are roots of the characteristic equation.

   To complete the Routh array, differentiate the auxiliary equation with respect to s, insert the coefficients of the resulting equation in place of the row of zeros, and then calculate the remaining coefficients as before.

Example 8.3

$$s^3 + 10s^2 + 16s + 160 = 0$$

The table begins:

$$\begin{array}{c|cc} s^3 & 1 & 16 \\ s^2 & 10 & 160 \\ s^1 & 0 & 0 \end{array}$$ and cannot be completed.

The auxiliary equation is: $10s^2 + 160 = 0$
Differentiate: $20s \qquad = 0$

This coefficient is inserted as the s^1 row, and the table completed

$$\begin{array}{c|cc} s^3 & 1 & 16 \\ s^2 & 10 & 160 \\ s^1 & 20 & 0 \\ s^0 & 160 \end{array}$$

There are no sign changes in the first column, hence there are no roots in the right half of the s-plane. The pair of roots is obtained from the auxiliary equation $10s^2 + 160 = 0$, or $s = \pm j4$, i.e. a pair of conjugate imaginary roots, indicating undamped oscillations of constant amplitude at a natural frequency of 4 rad/second.

Note: When analysing practical systems the coefficients often vary greatly in order of magnitude, in which case a substitution of the form $\sigma = 10s$ can help to ease the arithmetic.

8.4 Nyquist stability criterion

The Routh–Hurwitz criterion determines stability only in a binary sense (i.e. either stable, or unstable) and gives no information about the degree of stability; even although a system may be theoretically stable, oscillations may take too long to die out. Consider now the frequency domain. On the closed loop magnitude frequency plot (see Fig. 6.12) the absolutely unstable condition theoretically appears as a discontinuity, with amplitude tending to infinity at the frequency of instability. In practice, however, the amplitude is either limited to a steady value due to non-linearities, such as saturation within system components, or oscillation builds up to a point at which failure occurs. With sustained oscillations energy is transferred back and forth between two energy storage media (e.g. inertia and spring, or inductance and capacitance) and the external energy source only needs to make up the losses.

The *Nyquist diagram*, defined as an open loop polar plot, a polar plot of the system with the loop opened and hence a plot of $G(j\omega)\,H(j\omega)$, enables one to find whether any roots have positive real parts, without actually evaluating them. It also shows how near to instability that a system is, and thus can be used as one way of determining how best to improve the system stability.

Harmonic information experimentally obtained can also be used, without any need to determine the transfer functions.

In general the characteristic function will have the form

$$1 + G(s)H(s) = \frac{K(s - z_1)(s - z_2) \dots}{s^{\alpha}(s - p_1)(s - p_2)(s - p_3) \dots}$$ 8.12

For stability, none of the zeros of the characteristic function (roots of the characteristic equation) can have positive real parts. There is no particular restriction on the poles of $1 + G(s)H(s)$, which are also the poles of $G(s)H(s)$. If any of the poles of $G(s)H(s)$ lie in the right half of the s-plane (as can occur if there is a secondary feedback loop within the forward path) then the open loop system will be unstable, but the closed loop system can nevertheless still be stable.

The Nyquist stability criterion in its most comprehensive form is somewhat complex, and to understand it requires familiarity with the mathematical process of conformal mapping. For most practical systems, those in which the open loop system is itself stable, a simplified form of the criterion can be applied; the full criterion is only needed when the open loop system is unstable.

The simplified Nyquist stability criterion states that if an open loop system is stable then the system with the loop closed is also stable provided that the $G(j\omega)H(j\omega)$ locus on the polar plot does not enclose the $(-1, j0)$ point. This is illustrated by Fig. 8.4. If the locus passes through the critical $(-1, j0)$ point,

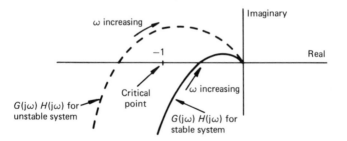

Fig. 8.4 Open loop polar plots of stable and unstable systems

this corresponds to a system of marginal stability, one with a pair of wholly imaginary roots.

The simplified Nyquist criterion can be described in an alternative way: a system is unstable if the open loop magnitude exceeds unity when the open loop phase lag is 180°. Physically, the condition of instability can be visualized as follows. If the reference input to a closed loop system is a sine wave, then the signal returning to the error detector will have a different amplitude and phase. If the phase lag is 180°, then the returning signal, when inverted and added to the reference input, will reinforce the signal. If the amplitude of the returning signal is less than that of the input signal at this phase lag, a steady condition will be reached, but if the amplitude is greater then the amplitude will build up continuously until the system saturates. Even if the input signal is removed the system continues to oscillate.

8.5 Gain margin and phase margin

The previous section makes it clear that the position of the $G(j\omega)H(j\omega)$ open loop polar plot relative to the $(-1, j0)$ point has great significance when considering system stability. It is desirable to be able to quantify the degree of stability or relative stability of a system, and this can be done by indicating how close the Nyquist plot passes to the critical point. The measures used are the *gain margin* and the *phase margin*; these are defined below and illustrated in Fig. 8.5.

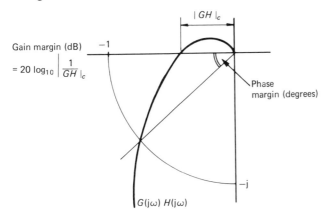

Fig. 8.5 Definition of gain margin and phase margin

The gain margin is defined as the amount by which the system gain can be increased before instability occurs, and is normally quoted in decibels.

Hence
$$\text{gain margin} = 20 \log_{10} \frac{1}{|GH|_c} \text{ dB} \qquad 8.13$$

where $|GH|_c$ is the open loop magnitude at the crossover point on the negative real axis, the magnitude corresponding to a phase lag of $180°$. Thus for the plot of Fig. 8.5 which crosses at around the value 0.4 the gain margin would be $20 \log_{10} 2.5 = 8$ dB. For first and second order systems the plot never crosses the negative real axis, and hence the gain margin is infinite. If the plot passes through the critical point the gain margin is zero, while if it encloses the critical point the gain margin is negative and gain must be reduced to attain stability of the feedback system. The gain margin by itself may not be sufficient to indicate relative stability, as can be seen from Fig. 8.6a where two plots each have an infinite gain margin although one passes very much closer to the critical point than the other, and Fig. 8.6b where the plot with the larger gain margin passes closer to the critical point.

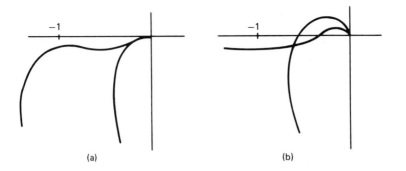

(a)   (b)

Fig. 8.6 Polar plots illustrating limitation of gain margin on its own as a measure of relative stability

The phase margin is defined as the angle through which the Nyquist locus must be rotated in order that the unity magnitude point on the locus passes through the critical point. It is thus the amount by which the open loop lag falls short of 180° at the frequency where the open loop magnitude is unity. It is particularly significant when investigating the effect on stability of system changes which primarily affect the phase of $G(j\omega)H(j\omega)$.

The gain and phase margins can be read directly from a Bode plot (Fig. 8.7). The gain margin is the attenuation at the *phase crossover frequency*, while the phase margin is the phase lag at the *gain crossover frequency* deducted from 180°. When a numerical value is specified for the minimum acceptable gain margin or phase margin, then the required value of loop gain can be determined by shifting the magnitude plot up or down on the graph until the

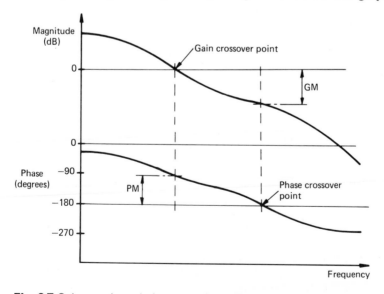

Fig. 8.7 Gain margin and phase margin on Bode plot of $G(j\omega)H(\omega)$

specified value is achieved, and then calculating the corresponding value of gain. This frequently results in a value of gain which is satisfactory for stability but too low to give an acceptable steady state error. Where this is the case it is, in principle, possible to increase the gain to satisfy the accuracy requirements, and then to improve the correspondingly low stability margin by introducing additional components into the loop to reshape the harmonic locus in the vicinity of the gain and phase crossover points in such a way as to increase the gain and phase margins. This process of system compensation is outlined in Chapter 11.

It must be stressed that when investigating the stability of a closed loop system by frequency domain methods it is the open loop polar diagram which is studied, and it is this plot of $G(j\omega)H(j\omega)$, referred to as a Nyquist plot, which must not pass too close to the critical $(-1, j0)$ point. It is, however, the closed loop and not the open loop which is potentially unstable. As a consequence, a practical system can be response tested with the feedback loop left open, and the margin of stability can be determined and any necessary alterations made before the loop is first closed.

8.6 Loci of constant closed loop magnitude and phase

The values of gain margin and phase margin form only one aspect of the description of the dynamic response of a feedback system, and there will frequently be a requirement to determine completely the variation of overall magnitude and phase with frequency, the closed loop frequency response. This can readily be evaluated from the open loop frequency response, whether obtained experimentally or analytically, with a small amount of calculation, and can be presented as a polar plot or as separate curves of closed loop magnitude and phase plotted against frequency.

Consider a unity feedback system. The overall transfer function is given by Eq. 8.2 and is

$$\frac{C(s)}{R(s)} = \frac{G(s)}{1 + G(s)}$$

or, in the frequency domain,

$$\frac{C(j\omega)}{R(j\omega)} = \frac{G(j\omega)}{1 + G(j\omega)}$$

Hence the closed loop magnitude, by convention given the symbol M and often referred to as the *magnification*, is

$$M = \frac{|C(j\omega)|}{|R(j\omega)|} = \left|\frac{C(j\omega)}{R(j\omega)}\right| = \frac{|G(j\omega)|}{|1 + G(j\omega)|} \qquad 8.14$$

For any given frequency the magnitudes $|G(j\omega)|$ and $|1 + G(j\omega)|$ can be measured from the plot as illustrated in Fig. 8.8, and the value of M calculated by dividing one by the other. It is clear that if the open loop plot approaches close to the $(-1, j0)$ point, then for a certain range of ω, $|1 + G(j\omega)| \ll |G(j\omega)|$

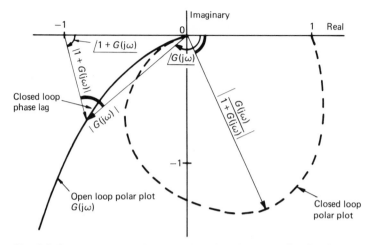

Fig. 8.8 Open and closed loop polar plots for unity feedback system with $G(s)$ of the form $\dfrac{1}{s(1 + \tau s)}$

and the closed loop magnification M rises to a maximum in the vicinity of one particular frequency. This is the peak value M_p occurring at frequency ω_p (see Section 6.5), and at the limiting point of stability M_p becomes infinite. The closed loop phase is given by

$$\angle C(j\omega) - \angle R(j\omega) = \angle [C(j\omega)/R(j\omega)] = \angle G(j\omega) - \angle [1 + G(j\omega)] \quad 8.15$$

and this angle can be measured directly from the plot.

Since every point in the complex plane of a Nyquist diagram has associated with it a value of closed loop magnitude and one of phase, then points with the same value of one or the other can be joined to form loci of constant closed loop magnitude and phase. These are referred to as M *contours* and N *contours* respectively, and can be shown to be two families of circles.

Let the coordinates of a point on the plot $G(j\omega)$ be represented by $x + jy$.

Then
$$M = \left| \frac{C(j\omega)}{R(j\omega)} \right| = \left| \frac{G(j\omega)}{1 + G(j\omega)} \right| = \left| \frac{x + jy}{1 + x + jy} \right| = \frac{\sqrt{(x^2 + y^2)}}{\sqrt{\{(1 + x)^2 + y^2\}}}$$

$$\therefore \quad M^2[(1 + x)^2 + y^2] = x^2 + y^2$$

$$\therefore \quad (1 - M^2)x^2 - 2M^2x + (1 - M^2)y^2 = M^2$$

Dividing through by $(1 - M^2)$, and adding the common term $\left(\dfrac{M^2}{1 - M^2}\right)^2$ to both sides gives

$$x^2 - \left(\frac{2M^2}{1 - M^2}\right)x + \left(\frac{M^2}{1 - M^2}\right)^2 + y^2 = \frac{M^2}{1 - M^2} + \left(\frac{M^2}{1 - M^2}\right)^2$$

or
$$\left(x - \frac{M^2}{1 - M^2}\right)^2 + y^2 = \left(\frac{M}{1 - M^2}\right)^2 \quad 8.16$$

This is the equation of a circle with centre $\left(\dfrac{M^2}{1-M^2}, j0\right)$ and radius $\left|\dfrac{M}{1-M^2}\right|$. A family of circles can thus be drawn on the Nyquist diagram; these circles are loci of constant M, as shown in Fig. 8.9. $M = 1$ is a special

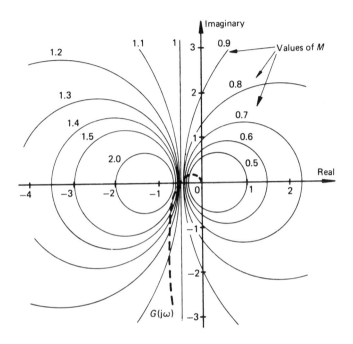

Fig. 8.9 M contours on polar diagram

case giving a locus which is a straight line at $x = -0.5$; as M becomes very large the circles become small and tend towards the critical $(-1, j0)$ point. When an open loop polar plot for a unity feedback system is superimposed on this, each intersection with an M circle gives a point on the M against ω plot, the value of ω being obtained by interpolation on the $G(j\omega)$ locus. The M circle which is just tangential to the $G(j\omega)$ locus gives the value of M_p, and ω_p is read off at the tangent point.

In a similar way it can be shown that contours of constant phase shift, the N loci, also form a family of circles. These loci have centres at $\left(-0.5, -j\dfrac{0.5}{N}\right)$ and have radii $0.5\sqrt{\left(\dfrac{N^2+1}{N^2}\right)}$ where N is the tangent of the phase angle; they thus take the form shown in Fig. 8.10.

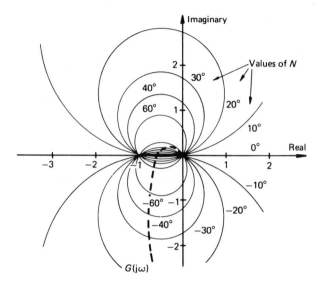

Fig. 8.10 *N* contours on polar diagram

For analysis and design it is more convenient to have the M and N loci plotted in the gain-phase plane rather than the polar plane. Such a plot is called a *Nichols chart* and is shown in Fig. 8.11 for the region of most interest to the engineer. The co-ordinates are open loop magnitude (in decibels) and open loop phase (in degrees), and the M and N circles when transferred to this plot take the form respectively of one set of contours encircling and another set radiating from the critical 0 dB, -180 degree point. When the open loop frequency response information is plotted on a Nichols chart, then the closed loop harmonic response information can be read off directly from the intersections of the locus with the M and N contours. Gain margin, phase margin, M_p, ω_p, and bandwidth can be determined as shown in Fig. 8.12. To find the required value of gain to meet a specified value of any of these parameters the $G(j\omega)$ locus is drawn for unity gain say, and the resulting locus shifted as required in the direction of the lines of constant open loop phase, the amount of shift then giving the value of open loop gain needed.

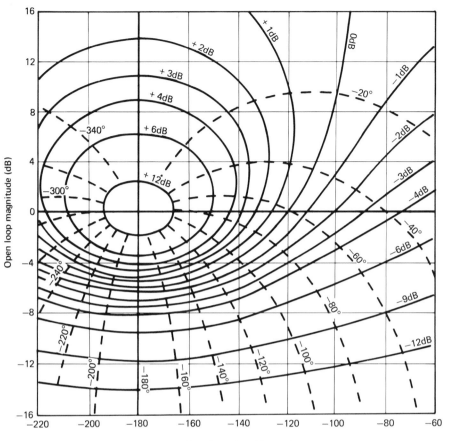

Fig. 8.11 Nichols chart

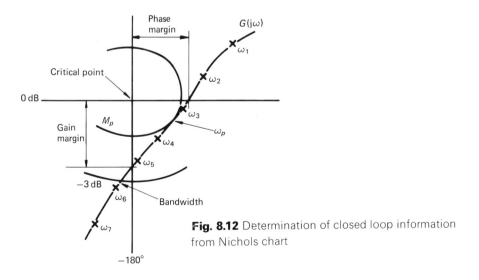

Fig. 8.12 Determination of closed loop information from Nichols chart

9
The Root Locus Method

The transient response of a linear system to deterministic forcing functions has been shown to be dependent on the roots of the characteristic equation. The *root locus method* is a graphical procedure which was devised for determining the changing values of the roots of a characteristic equation for variation in a given system parameter. This parameter, often a simple multiplying factor proportional to the loop gain and normally labelled K, can be considered an independent variable and all roots of the characteristic equation become dependent on the parameter K. A set of loci drawn in the s-plane, showing how the root positions move in the plane as functions of the parameter K, is called a *root locus plot*.

Appropriate digital computer programs are available for root evaluation, for plotting of the loci, and for Laplace inversion if time responses are required, and these programs ease the computational effort required. However, plots showing the approximate form of the root loci can be produced manually in a comparatively short time; frequently these will suffice to give a useful qualitative understanding of system behaviour and of the influence of parameter and system variations. For example, if a system has several roots, then those which move towards the imaginary axis with an increasing value of K will become more dominant, while those moving away have progressively less influence on the transient behaviour. The influence of root position on the transient response has been described in Section 4.3. A value of K that gives a negative real root close to the origin can result in a sluggish exponential type of response. Roots lying along the same horizontal line have the same damped natural frequency of oscillation, while roots lying along a particular vertical line constrain the amplitude of the decaying response to the same exponential envelope $\exp(-\zeta\omega_n t)$. Every pair of complex roots yields an oscillatory term in the response but the pair nearest the origin dominates the response.

After defining in detail what is meant by a root locus plot and showing how one can be produced, Sections 9.1 and 9.2, a number of aids to construction which simplify the manual plotting of a diagram are listed and explained in Section 9.3. Examples are given to illustrate the use of these aids, then Section 9.4 discusses the information obtainable from completed plots and the way in which such plots can be used. Finally, to cater for variations in more than one parameter, and to include situations where the independent variable is not a simple multiplying factor, the technique is generalized, Section 9.5, and the term *root contours* is then used to represent the loci of the roots of the characteristic equation.

9.1 Root locus plots

Consider a simple design situation in which the response of the mass-spring-damper system shown in Fig. 2.6 is to be investigated for a range of spring stiffness constants K. Variations in the numerical value of this parameter cause changes in the values of the roots of the characteristic equation, and thus an alteration in the position of the roots in the s-plane.

For arithmetic simplicity, let $M = C = 1$; the transfer function, Eq. 2.15, then reduces to

$$\frac{X(s)}{F(s)} = \frac{1}{s^2 + s + K} \qquad\qquad 9.1$$

The roots of the characteristic equation

$$s^2 + s + K = 0 \qquad\qquad 9.2$$

can in this case be evaluated algebraically as

$$p_{1,2} = \tfrac{1}{2}\{-1 \pm \sqrt{(1 - 4K)}\}$$

When $K = 0$ the two roots are both real, $p_1 = 0$ and $p_2 = -1$. If K is gradually increased through the range $0 < K < 0.25$, the two roots move towards each other along the negative real axis, starting from $p_1 = 0$ and $p_2 = -1$ until they coincide for $K = 0.25$ resulting in a double root at $s = -0.5$. Further increase in the value of K results in the roots becoming a complex conjugate pair, i.e.

$$p_{1,2} = \tfrac{1}{2}\{-1 \pm j\sqrt{(4K - 1)}\}$$

and the response then becomes oscillatory in nature. For $K = \infty$ the values of these roots are

$$p_{1,2} = -\tfrac{1}{2} \pm j\infty$$

which corresponds to an oscillatory response with infinite natural frequency, but nevertheless constrained within an amplitude decay envelope of $\exp -t/2$.

The loci of the two roots, when K varies from 0 to ∞, can now be drawn as shown in Fig. 9.1a. The step responses in Fig. 9.1b demonstrate how the system response changes with changing root position and how dependent the damped sinusoidal responses are on the parameter K. This result, of course, is not unexpected since for the second order transfer function, Eq. 9.1, the undamped natural frequency has the value $\sqrt{K}$ and the damping factor has the value $1/(2\sqrt{K})$. Both the transfer function and the nature of the physical system lead one to expect the change of steady state value with K as shown.

It will be appreciated that although theoretically such a system is inherently stable for all values of K, an acceptable engineering response is likely to require a value of K of the order of unity. A value of $K = 10$ is likely to be unacceptable because of the large initial overshoot which in certain situations would lead to mechanical failure.

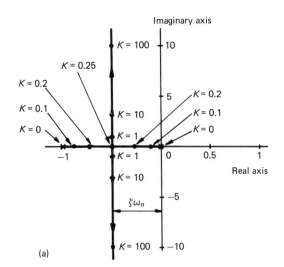

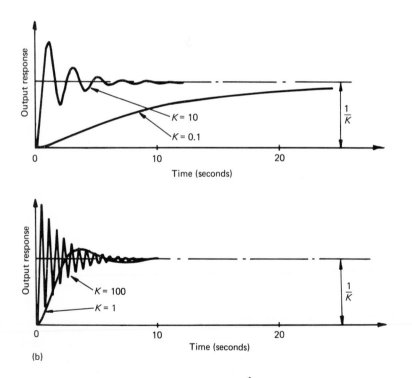

Fig. 9.1 Second order system $G(s) = \dfrac{1}{s^2 + s + K}$ (a) root locus diagram (b) step response for variation in K

By inspection of the root locus plot, the following information about the transient and frequency response is obtained for the system of Fig. 2.6 with transfer function given by Eq. 9.1.

(i) Stability: The system is inherently stable for all values of stiffness K, no roots appearing in the right half of the s-plane.

(ii) Transient response: For all values $0 < K < 0.25$, the system is over-damped, as there is no imaginary part contributing to the time solution. For $0.25 < K < \infty$, the system is under-damped, critical damping occurring at $K = 0.25$. The undamped natural frequency ω_n increases and the damping factor ζ decreases with increase in K, but the amplitude of the decaying response is constrained to the same exponential envelope.

(iii) Frequency response: For any given value of K the roots p_1 and p_2 are directly available from the root locus plot enabling the transfer function, Eq. 9.1, to be written as

$$\frac{X(s)}{F(s)} = \frac{1}{(s - p_1)(s - p_2)} \qquad 9.3$$

The Bode diagram can now be constructed by the methods of Section 6.3, enabling frequency response studies to be made.

To illustrate these ideas further consider a simple control engineering situation where feedback is used to maintain near constant speed of an internal combustion engine under varying load conditions. The arrangement assumed is that shown in block diagram form in Fig. 9.2a. The governor is a simple one with proportional gain term k_1 only, the actual engine speed is sensed by an electrical tachometer with a first order transfer function, and a reciprocating engine can for such a general study be adequately described by a second order transfer function (Eq. 2.17). At the design stage, one problem would be to evaluate the variation in dynamic performance resulting from changes in governor gain setting k_1. If, for this example, the numerical values of the system parameters are arbitrarily chosen to be $\tau = 1$ second, $\omega_n = 5$ rad/second, and $\zeta = 0.9$, then the open loop transfer function can be written as

$$G(s)H(s) = \frac{C(s)}{E(s)} = \frac{K}{(s + 1)(s^2 + 9s + 25)} \qquad 9.4$$

where $K = k_1 k_2 k_3$, and $H(s) = 1$, as it is a unity feedback system. The closed loop transfer function is then

$$\frac{C(s)}{R(s)} = \frac{K}{(s + 1)(s^2 + 9s + 25) + K} \qquad 9.5$$

from which the characteristic equation is

$$(s + 1)(s^2 + 9s + 25) + K = 0 \qquad 9.6$$

For $K = 0$, it can be seen that the roots of Eq. 9.6 are the poles of the transfer function $G(s)H(s)$, Eq. 9.4, and these poles are the starting points for the separate loci. For the numerical values selected there is one real root at -1 and a complex conjugate pair at $-4.5 \pm j2.18$. As K increases the values of these roots alter and the roots trace out the paths shown in Fig. 9.2b.

Transient response curves for varying values of K can be obtained by simulation of the system represented by the block diagram. Inspection of the measured engine speed response, Fig. 9.2c, obtained from simulation, to a unit step change in set point for a value of K near zero, shows a response similar to that of a first order system indicating that the real root close to $s = -1$ is dominant. As K increases the position of the real root moves to the left along the real axis while the complex roots move towards the right half of the s-plane and thus become more dominant. For a value of $K = 315$ the complex roots lie on the imaginary axis, the condition of marginal stability. As K increases from zero to infinity the system response varies from a rather sluggish overdamped response for small values of K, through what might be considered a 'good' response at a value of around $K = 35$ when the damping factor of the dominant roots is 0.7, to the unstable condition which exists for $K > 315$.

It is seen from Fig. 9.1a and Fig. 9.2b that a root locus plot consists of distinct loci each plotting the variation in the value of one root as the independent variable K is changed in value from zero to infinity. The number of root loci is equal to the order of the characteristic equation, and the plot is symmetrical with respect to the real axis, since complex roots must always occur in conjugate pairs for linear rational functions. Each locus starts $(K = 0)$ at an open loop pole and finishes $(K = \infty)$ at an open loop zero or else moves off to infinity.

9.2 Construction of root loci

The most general form of the characteristic equation for a feedback system is (Section 8.1)

$$1 + G(s)H(s) = 0 \qquad 9.7$$

Since $G(s)H(s)$ is generally derived from the grouping of several system elements, each with relatively simple transfer function, it normally appears in factored form

$$G(s)H(s) = \frac{K(s - z_1)(s - z_2) \ldots (s - z_m)}{(s - p_1)(s - p_2) \ldots (s - p_n)} \qquad 9.8$$

where K is a constant. Any point s in the s-plane which satisfies Eq. 9.7 is a point on the root locus plot; the procedure for finding such points is the basis of the root locus method.

The test to determine whether any point s lies on a locus is developed from Eq. 9.7 by substitution of Eq. 9.8, resulting in the equation

$$\frac{K(s - z_1)(s - z_2) \ldots (s - z_m)}{(s - p_1)(s - p_2) \ldots (s - p_n)} = -1 \qquad 9.9$$

As explained earlier, the standard terminology used in the literature is to

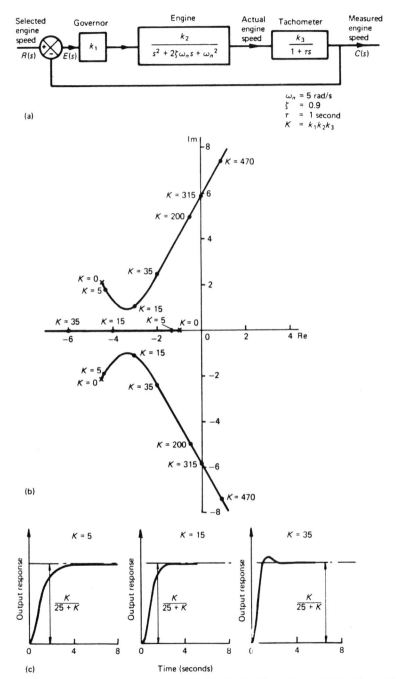

Fig. 9.2 Engine speed regulating system (a) block diagram representation (b) root locus diagram (c) measured engine speed responses to unit step input for variation in *K*

define the roots of the numerator labelled z as zeros, since they are the values of s that make the value of $G(s)H(s)$ zero, while the roots of the denominator labelled p are known as poles since they make $G(s)H(s)$ infinite in value. The left-hand side of Eq. 9.9 is a complex expression, therefore the equation is fully defined if the modulus and phase angle conditions are both satisfied. Writing Eq. 9.9 in modulus and angle form yields the equations

$$\frac{K\,|s-z_1|\,|s-z_2|\ldots|s-z_m|}{|s-p_1|\,|s-p_2|\ldots|s-p_n|} = 1 \qquad\qquad 9.10$$

$$[\angle(s-z_1) + \angle(s-z_2)\ldots\angle(s-z_m)] - [\angle(s-p_1) + \angle(s-p_2)\ldots$$
$$\angle(s-p_n)] = \text{odd multiple of } \pi \quad 9.11$$

The terms $|s-z|$ and $|s-p|$ will be recognized as the lengths of vectors drawn from either a zero or a pole to a point s, whilst $\angle(s-z)$ and $\angle(s-p)$ are the arguments of these vectors measured relative to the positive real axis in the s-plane. By repeated application of Eq. 9.10 and Eq. 9.11 a root locus diagram can be drawn. The *angle condition*, Eq. 9.11, is used to locate points which are on the loci and hence determine the shape of the root locus plot. The *magnitude condition*, Eq. 9.10, then enables values of K to be assigned to specific points on each locus.

As an illustration of the application of Eq. 9.10 and Eq. 9.11, consider the open loop transfer function

$$G(s)H(s) = \frac{K(s+1)(s+2)}{s(s^2+2s+5)}$$

which has poles marked $\times$, and zeros marked o at the locations shown in Fig. 9.3. If an arbitrary point s_1 in the s-plane is chosen and vectors a, b, c, d and e are drawn to the zeros and poles, Fig. 9.3, then s_1 is a point on a root locus if, and only if, the angle condition defined by Eq. 9.11 is satisfied. Using the symbols given in the figure, this requires that

$$(\beta_1 + \beta_2) - (\alpha_1 + \alpha_2 + \alpha_3) = \text{odd multiple of } \pi$$

If this is so, then the point s_1 lies on one of the loci and the value of K at this s_1 location can be evaluated from the magnitude condition, Eq. 9.10,

$$\frac{Kab}{cde} = 1 \qquad \therefore \quad K = \frac{cde}{ab}$$

Given the pole-zero configuration of the open loop transfer function $G(s)H(s)$, the construction procedure for manual plotting of a root locus diagram can be summarized as follows:

(i) find, by trial and error, points in the s-plane that satisfy the angle condition given by Eq. 9.11, and join them to form the root loci.
(ii) calculate the K values at points on the root loci by using the magnitude condition, Eq. 9.10.

It can now be seen that the root locus technique enables the position of the roots of the characteristic equation in the s-plane to be determined without

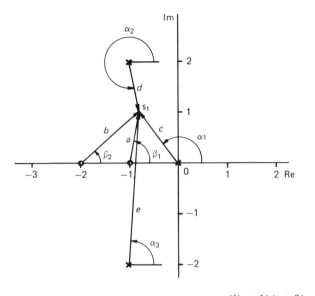

Fig. 9.3 Poles and zeros for $G(s)H(s) = \dfrac{K(s+1)(s+2)}{s(s^2+2s+5)}$

actually solving analytically for the roots of the characteristic equation for varying values of an independent variable. At first sight the application of (i) would appear to be a most impractical procedure to implement manually for all but the simplest of systems. However, with the aid of a series of rules which are described in the next section, the field of search can be reduced markedly and a root locus diagram can be drawn more readily.

9.3 Aids to construction of root locus diagram

A number of rules developed from Eq. 9.10 and Eq. 9.11 significantly aid the manual plotting of a root locus diagram and are of real value since, when methodically applied, they give a very good idea of the shape of the loci. The rules are given without rigorous proofs, but simple justification for each rule is provided whenever possible.

1. Starting point of loci: The loci start, $K = 0$, at the n poles of the open loop transfer function $G(s)H(s)$.

Using the relationship $G(s)H(s) = \dfrac{KP(s)}{Q(s)}$, then the characteristic equation is $Q(s) + KP(s) = 0$. From this equation it can be seen that the values of s that satisfy this equation when $K = 0$ are the factors of $Q(s)$, the poles of the open loop transfer function.

2. Number of loci: The number of loci is equal to the order of the characteristic equation.

Each root traces out a locus as K varies from 0 to infinity. The loci are continuous curves and, since complex roots must occur in conjugate pairs, the plot is symmetrical about the real axis.

3. Termini of loci: The root loci end at the m zeros of $G(s)H(s)$, and if $m < n$ as is usually the case the remaining $(n - m)$ loci end at infinity.

The loci terminate as $K \to \infty$, and the magnitude condition, Eq. 9.10, can then only be satisfied either if one of the terms $|s - z|$ is zero or one of the terms $|s - p|$ is infinite.

4. Loci on real axis: Portions of the real axis are sections of root locus if the number of poles and zeros lying on the axis to the right is odd.

Consider a trial point on the real axis. The angle contribution from any pair of complex conjugate poles is 2π (in Fig. 9.4 when s_1 is on the real axis then

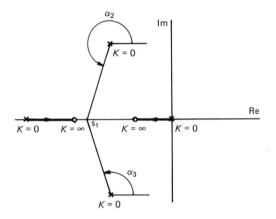

Fig. 9.4 Root loci on real axis

$\alpha_2 + \alpha_3 = 360°$), the angle contribution from a real pole or zero to the right is $-\pi$ or $+\pi$ respectively, while that from a real pole or zero to the left is 0. Hence the total angle is an odd multiple of π only if there is an odd number of poles and zeros lying on the real axis to the right of the trial point.

5. Angles of asymptotes: Those loci terminating at infinity tend towards asymptotes at angles relative to the positive real axis given by

$$\frac{\pi}{n - m}, \frac{3\pi}{n - m}, \frac{5\pi}{n - m}, \dots, \frac{\{2(n - m) - 1\}\pi}{n - m}.$$

This can be shown by considering the angle condition as applied to a point far from the group of open loop poles and zeros. The angle contribution from each pole and zero is then numerically equal. The effect of each zero is cancelled by that of a pole, and the sum of the angles for the remaining $(n - m)$ poles is then an odd multiple of π, provided points lie along lines at the above angles. If one locus goes to infinity it does so at 180°, i.e. along the negative real axis, if two loci go to infinity they approach asymptotes at angles 90° and 270°, if three at 60°, 180°, and 300° etc.

6. Intersection of asymptotes on real axis: This occurs at the 'centre of

gravity' of the $G(s)H(s)$ pole zero configuration, where the centre of gravity is determined from the following expression:

$$\frac{\sum(\text{numerical values of } G(s)H(s) \text{ poles}) - \sum(\text{numerical values of } G(s)H(s) \text{ zeros})}{n - m}$$

7. Intersection of root loci with imaginary axis: This is the limiting condition for stability; the value ω on the imaginary axis at intersection, together with the value of K, can be determined by application of the Routh–Hurwitz criterion as presented in Section 8.3.

8. Breakaway from real axis: A point in the s-plane where multiple roots exist is called a breakaway point; it occurs when two or more loci meet at the point and subsequently break away again along separate paths. The location of breakaway points can be found analytically by solving the equation $dK/ds = 0$.

Practical computational difficulties limit the ease of application of this rule, and it should be noted that not all of the roots of the equation $dK/ds = 0$ correspond to breakaway points. The actual breakaway points are those roots of the equation at which the root locus angle condition is satisfied. If the polynomial is of high order it may be easier to find the breakaway points graphically by use of the angle condition than by solution of this equation. In many engineering situations the poles and zeros of $G(s)H(s)$ all lie on the real axis, making it possible to use a graphical approach to find the breakaway point. Consider a case where there are three real poles at $s = 0$, $s = -1$, and $s = -2$ respectively, Fig. 9.5. A breakaway point must exist on the real axis

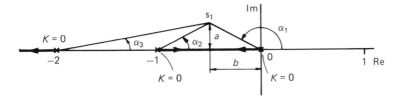

Fig. 9.5 Breakaway from real axis—multiple root condition

somewhere between $s = 0$ and $s = -1$ (rules 2 and 4). Choose a trial point which is very close to the axis and whose distance along the negative real axis is b, then application of Eq. 9.11 requires that

$$-(\alpha_1 + \alpha_2 + \alpha_3) = \text{odd multiple of } \pi$$

or

$$-\left[\left(\pi - \frac{a}{b}\right) + \left(\frac{a}{1-b}\right) + \left(\frac{a}{2-b}\right)\right] = -\pi$$

hence

$$3b^2 - 6b + 2 = 0$$

∴ $b = 0.42$ (or 1.58 which does not represent a breakaway point)

This procedure of constructing an algebraic equation by use of the angle condition and solving to find the breakaway point is a more direct and practical method. The root loci leave such a breakaway point in a direction normal to the real axis.

9. Angle of departure from complex pole: An indication of the initial direction in which a locus leaves a complex pole can be determined by applying Eq. 9.11 to a point very close to the pole of interest.

To illustrate, consider a situation in which a pair of complex poles is situated at $-1 \pm j$ with a third pole at the origin as shown in Fig. 9.6. Let s_1 be the trial point of interest, then

$$-(\alpha_1 + \alpha_2 + \alpha_3) = \text{odd multiple of } \pi$$

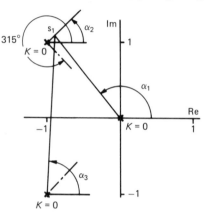

Fig. 9.6 Angle of departure of locus from complex pole

Since s_1 is very close to the pole, $\alpha_1 = 135°$ and $\alpha_3 = 90°$ irrespective of the value of α_2,

hence

$$-(135 + \alpha_2 + 90) = -540°$$

and

$$\alpha_2 = 540 - 225 = 315°$$

which indicates that the locus will initially leave the complex poles in the direction of the origin. This approach is also useful for finding the angle of arrival at complex zeros.

By application of these nine simple rules a good approximation to the shape of each locus can be found, enabling the general form of a root locus diagram to be sketched. If a more accurate location of certain intermediate points is desired, then these sketched locus paths will give guidance as to the location in which the search to satisfy the angle condition, Eq. 9.11, should be conducted. Finally, numerical values of K are then directly obtained by application of the magnitude condition, Eq. 9.10.

Example 9.1. As an exercise to illustrate the use of these rules, consider the speed regulating system shown in Fig. 9.2a which has the characteristic equation defined by Eq. 9.6, i.e.

$$(s + 1)(s^2 + 9s + 25) + K = 0 \qquad\qquad 9.12$$

Details are inserted on the *s*-plane (Fig. 9.7) as they are determined from the aids:

1. Starting point of loci: The loci start at the poles of $G(s)H(s)$, i.e. the roots of Eq. 9.12 when $K = 0$. These are

$$s = -1, s = -4.5 \pm j2.18$$

2. Number of loci: The number of loci is equal to the order of the characteristic equation, and Eq. 9.12 is of order 3.

3. Termini of loci: There are no zeros of $G(s)H(s)$, hence all loci move towards infinity as K becomes very large.

4. Loci on real axis: There will be a section of root locus between $s = -1$ and $s = -\infty$, since along this section of the real axis the total number of poles and zeros to the right is one, and hence is odd. The remainder of the real axis does not form part of a root locus.

5. Angles of asymptotes: Since all 3 loci move to infinity, they approach asymptotes at 60°, 180°, and 300° to the positive real axis.

6. Intersection of asymptotes on real axis: The position of this point is at the centre of gravity of the 3 poles, which is given by

$$s = \frac{(-1 - 4.5 + j2.18 - 4.5 - j2.18)}{3} = -3.33$$

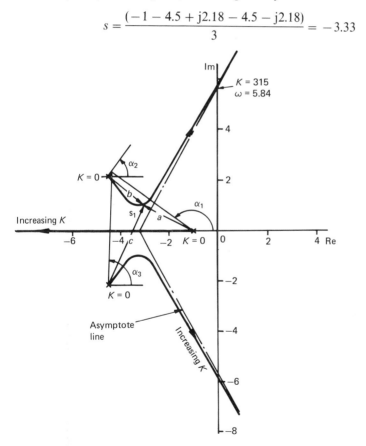

Fig. 9.7 Sketch of root locus diagram for speed regulating system of Fig. 9.2

7. Intersection of root loci with imaginary axis: This is found by construction of the Routh array for the characteristic equation, Eq. 9.12, viz
$$s^3 + 10s^2 + 34s + 25 + K = 0$$

$$
\begin{array}{lll}
s^3 & 1 & 34 \\
s^2 & 10 & 25 + K \\
s^1 & 34 - \left(\dfrac{25 + K}{10}\right) & 0 \\
s^0 & 25 + K &
\end{array}
$$

The limiting condition for a positive value of K is 315, and the frequency value is found from solution of the auxiliary equation

$$10s^2 + 25 + K = 0$$

On the imaginary axis $s = j\omega$, which yields

$$\omega = \sqrt{\left(\frac{25 + K}{10}\right)} = \sqrt{34} = 5.84 \text{ rad/second}$$

8. Breakaway from real axis: There is a single locus on the real axis moving from the pole at -1 to $-\infty$ and no multiple roots occur on the real axis.

9. Angle of departure from complex poles: Use of the angle condition, Eq. 9.11, and measuring angles from the diagram, yields

$$-(\alpha_1 + \alpha_2 + \alpha_3) = \text{odd multiple of } \pi$$
$$\therefore \quad -(149 + \alpha_2 + 90) = -540$$
$$\therefore \quad \alpha_2 = 540 - 239 = 301 \text{ degrees}$$

The exact location of a number of intermediate points on the dominant locus can now be found graphically by application of Eq. 9.11. The magnitude condition, Eq. 9.10, can be applied to find values of K at specific points on the loci. For example for the point s_1, Fig. 9.7, $a = 2.3$, $b = 1.9$, and $c = 3.5$, obtained by measurement, hence

$$K = 2.3 \times 1.9 \times 3.5 = 15.3$$

In many engineering design situations this approximate root locus diagram would be adequate for preliminary design purposes.

9.4 Interpretation of the root locus diagram

To help understand the significance of the root locus technique, and to use it as a design tool, it is necessary to know what effect altering the position of poles and zeros or introducing new poles and zeros has on a root locus plot and hence on the system dynamic behaviour. A control engineer must build up a background of knowledge that enables him to relate root position to transient behaviour if he wishes to use the root locus approach as a guide for better system design. For example, he must be fully aware that introduction of an additional pole or moving a pole towards the right pushes the dominant complex loci towards the imaginary axis and by so doing reduces the system relative stability. Conversely, the introduction of a zero pulls the dominant loci away from the imaginary axis, shortens the dominant portion of real locus and thus tends to make the response more sluggish for a given value of system gain. The root locus diagram shows where a dominant branch comes from and how it is affected by open loop poles and zeros; a designer's attention is usually focused on the specific aspect of how close this dominant branch runs to the imaginary axis rather than on the overall pattern of the loci. A final choice of root position, however, can only be made with the aid of physical understanding of the system and sound engineering judgement and skill.

To highlight some of the more important points of interpretation, the performance changes occurring in a system with a second order process and three different controllers will be studied. The system is shown in block diagram form in Fig. 9.8a for a controller with the simple transfer function of unity, and a process with a pair of complex poles $-2 \pm j2$, which are the factors of $s^2 + 4s + 8$. Fig. 9.8b, the root locus diagram for the overall system, shows that the closed loop system is always stable for all positive values of K. The inherent weakness of a system having these controller/process characteristics can be seen from Fig. 9.8c, in that although the system exhibits a typical second order step response of acceptable form when $K = 10$, it also shows a steady state error from the set point of 45%. This magnitude of set point error normally would not be acceptable in engineering practice, making it necessary to modify the controller characteristics. A steady state error can be avoided by the introduction of a pole at $s = 0$, which is achieved by using an integral action controller, as shown in the block diagram Fig. 9.9a. The root locus diagram is shown in Fig. 9.9b. For small values of K the response would be sluggish, as can be seen from Fig. 9.9c for a value of $K = 1$, and hence unacceptable in engineering practice. For values of K in excess of 32, instability occurs. Again a value of $K = 10$ gives a transient response that would be acceptable, still resembling the response of a second order system with damping factor 0.4, but with this controller the steady state positional error is now zero.

Guaranteed absolute stability can be restored for all positive values of K by the introduction of an open loop zero which pulls the complex loci of Fig. 9.9b away from the imaginary axis. An open loop zero results if the characteristics of each controller are added to create the controller shown in Fig. 9.10a. This type of controller is referred to as a proportional plus integral (P + I) controller and finds extensive use in engineering. There are still three loci but one now terminates at the zero at -1, and two move to ∞ as shown in Fig. 9.10b. The asymptotes are at 90° and 270° and they intersect the real axis at -1.5; on the real axis there is a portion of locus only between 0 and -1. This demonstrates that the introduction of the lead term $(1 + s)$, in the numerator of $G(s)H(s)$, has made the system stable for all values of K but has changed the system characteristics in such a way that the slow exponential decay term is more prominent for any given value of K. This undesirable condition must be minimized during design by appropriate positioning of the zero achieved by

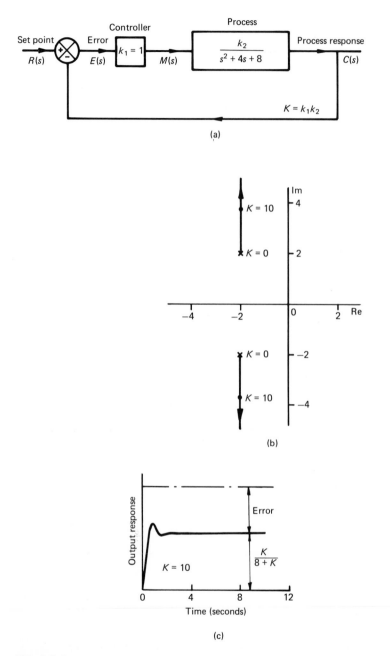

Fig. 9.8 System with proportional control action (a) block diagram (b) root locus diagram (c) step response of system

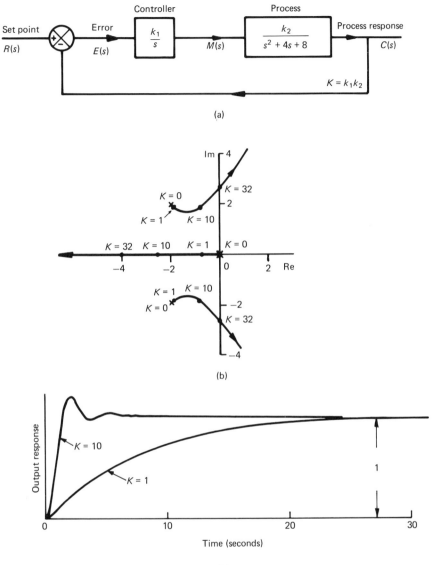

Fig. 9.9 System with integral control action (a) block diagram (b) root locus diagram (c) step response with variation in K

introducing a second controlled variable into the controller equations, i.e.
$M(s) = k_1 \left(1 + \dfrac{1}{T_i s} \right) E(s)$, a design situation discussed in Chapter 10. Transient
responses for $K = 10$, 20, and 100 are shown in Fig. 9.10c, indicating that the
best value of K would be in the region of 20, an increase of a factor of 2 over

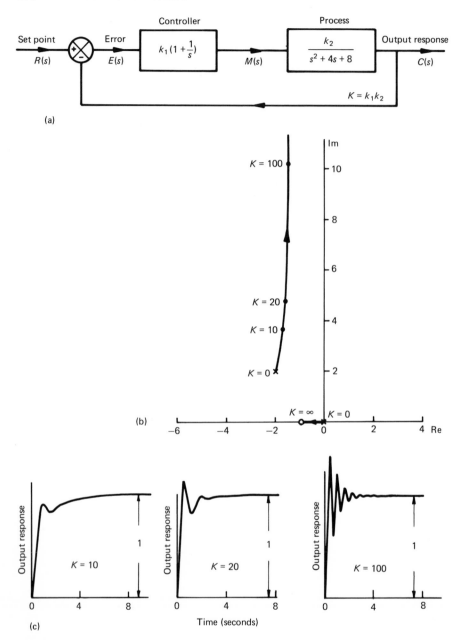

(a)

(b)

(c)

Fig. 9.10 System with proportional + integral control action (a) block diagram (b) upper half root locus diagram (c) step response with variation in K

the previous two controllers, resulting from the need to partially counteract the effect of the root on the shortened locus on the real axis.

The value of studying changes in the root locus pattern resulting from changes in the controller characteristics, and the design ideas that might emerge from consideration of these, are limited by the fact that there is no generally known acceptable specification for the optimum location of the roots of $1 + G(s)H(s) = 0$. Were this not so, the problem would be reduced to adjusting loop parameters or changing components in the loop to obtain the desired root positions.

It must be emphasized that the root locus plot shows the locus of the roots of the system characteristic equation only, and for the general case, Section 2.3, the transient response is also influenced by any closed loop zeros which are present. Therefore, when attempting to predict the transient response from a root locus pattern, the influence of both closed loop poles and zeros must be taken into account either by use of simulation studies or by direct solution of the equations. Having obtained a root locus plot, extension of the ideas presented in Section 4.3 enables an analytical expression for a closed loop transient response curve to be derived for any given value of K. The method is illustrated in the next example.

Example 9.2. For the system shown in block diagram form in Fig. 9.10a, find an analytical expression for the output response $c(t)$ for a unit step change in the set point $r(t)$.

The closed loop transfer function for this unity feedback system is

$$\frac{C(s)}{R(s)} = \frac{G(s)}{1 + G(s)}$$

where $\qquad G(s) =$ forward path transfer function.

Hence $\qquad \dfrac{C(s)}{R(s)} = \dfrac{k_1 k_2 (s + 1)}{s^3 + 4s^2 + 8s + k_1 k_2 (s + 1)}$

$$= \frac{K(s + 1)}{s^3 + 4s^2 + (8 + K)s + K} \qquad 9.13$$

where $\qquad K = k_1 k_2$

Examination of the root locus diagram, Fig. 9.10b, might suggest that a value of $K = 20$ is likely to give an acceptable transient response. The roots of the denominator of Eq. 9.13 for this value of K can be found from the plot or analytically and, with the root values rounded off to one decimal place, the equation can then be written in factored form as

$$\frac{C(s)}{R(s)} = \frac{20(s + 1)}{(s + 0.8)(s + 1.6 + 4.8j)(s + 1.6 - 4.8j)} \qquad 9.14$$

Letting $R(s) = \dfrac{1}{s}$, a unit step input, and expanding $C(s)$ into partial fractions, as in Section 4.3, enables the output response to be written as

$$c(t) = \mathcal{L}^{-1}\left\{\frac{A}{s} + \frac{B}{(s + 0.8)} + \frac{Ds + E}{s^2 + 3.2s + 25.6}\right\}$$

Solving for the constants A, B, D, and E gives $A = 1$, $B = -0.24$, $D = -0.76$, and $E = -2.64$, hence

$$c(t) = \mathcal{L}^{-1}\left\{\frac{1}{s} - \frac{0.24}{(s + 0.8)} - \frac{0.76s + 2.64}{(s^2 + 3.2s + 25.6)}\right\}$$

Expressing $c(t)$ in a form that enables the Laplace inverse of each term to be found from Table 2.1 gives

$$c(t) = \mathcal{L}^{-1}\left\{\frac{1}{s} - \frac{0.24}{(s + 0.8)} - \frac{0.76(s + 1.6)}{(s + 1.6)^2 + (4.8)^2} - \frac{0.30 \times 4.8}{(s + 1.6)^2 + (4.8)^2}\right\}$$

$$= 1 - 0.24e^{-0.8t} - 0.76e^{-1.6t}\cos(4.8t) - 0.30e^{-1.6t}\sin(4.8t)$$

$$= 1 - 0.24e^{-0.8t} - 0.82e^{-1.6t}\sin(4.8t + \tan^{-1} 2.54)$$

By inserting discrete values of t, output values can be calculated and the step response curve drawn.

If the open loop zero had appeared in the feedback path instead of the forward path

i.e.
$$G(s) = \frac{K}{s(s^2 + 4s + 8)}, \quad H(s) = s + 1$$

then the characteristic equation and the root locus plot would have been identical to the above. There would, however, be no zero in the closed loop transfer function, Eq. 9.14, and the resulting step response would be given by

$$c(t) = 1 - 1.08e^{-0.8t} - 0.17e^{-1.6t}\sin(4.8t - \tan^{-1} 0.53)$$

which is clearly not the same as that evaluated above. This demonstrates the importance of not overlooking closed loop zeros, as can happen when using a root locus diagram alone for design purposes.

Evaluation of a transient response equation can be a lengthy procedure for systems with high order characteristic equations. However, some simplification to the characteristic equation can be made by neglecting any root whose distance from the origin is more than 5 to 6 times that of the dominant roots, the resulting error being very small. It is more convenient to simulate a system on a computer, either analogue or digital, to obtain data on transient behaviour, and to use the root locus plot as a guide to the importance of, and likely changes resulting from, variation in system parameters. This approach has the advantage of avoiding the need for lengthy computer trial and observation periods.

9.5 Root contours

To enable the root locus technique to be applied to engineering design problems in which a number of independent variables are to be chosen, the technique was extended to allow additional loci to be added to a root locus diagram. Such loci representing variation of roots with a second independent variable, and each corresponding to a given value of the first independent variable (K), are known as *root contours*. The approach also enables a root locus diagram to be plotted for an independent variable which is not normally a simple multiplying factor. The method employed to construct root contours necessitates the rearrangement of the system equations to form an equivalent transfer function in which the independent variable does in fact appear as a simple multiplying factor; after this the plot can be drawn as described in Sections 9.2 and 9.3 above.

To illustrate the method of approach, consider the block diagram shown in Fig. 9.11a, where T is taken as the independent variable of interest, and the system gain constant K on this occasion has been previously specified. A root locus diagram is required to show the variation in the roots of the characteristic equation as T increases in value from 0 to ∞ for certain fixed values of K. To be able to study this effect of a variable amount of derivative action in the feedback loop on the roots of the characteristic equation, the closed loop transfer function must be rearranged as follows. The closed loop transfer function for the system shown in Fig. 9.11a can be written as

$$\frac{C(s)}{R(s)} = \frac{K}{s^3 + 4s^2 + 8s + KTs + K} \qquad 9.15$$

Divide through by terms not containing the independent variable T to yield

$$\frac{C(s)}{R(s)} = \frac{\dfrac{K}{s^3 + 4s^2 + 8s + K}}{1 + \dfrac{KTs}{s^3 + 4s^2 + 8s + K}} \qquad 9.16$$

The transfer function written in this form corresponds to an equivalent system with different values of $G(s)$ and $H(s)$ but with the same characteristic equation. By inspection it can be seen that

$$[G(s)H(s)]_{\text{equiv}} = \frac{KTs}{s^3 + 4s^2 + 8s + K} \qquad 9.17$$

where the independent variable T is now a simple multiplying factor and hence a root locus diagram can be plotted in the normal way. If a family of curves is constructed from Eq. 9.17 for a range of values of K, then the root contours begin at the poles of $[G(s)H(s)]_{\text{equiv}}$ and end at its zeros. A closer inspection of Eq. 9.17 reveals that the poles in this equation are the roots of the characteristic equation of Eq. 9.15 when $T = 0$. Hence the starting points of the root contours are points on the root loci for $G(s) = \dfrac{K}{s(s^2 + 4s + 8)}$ for

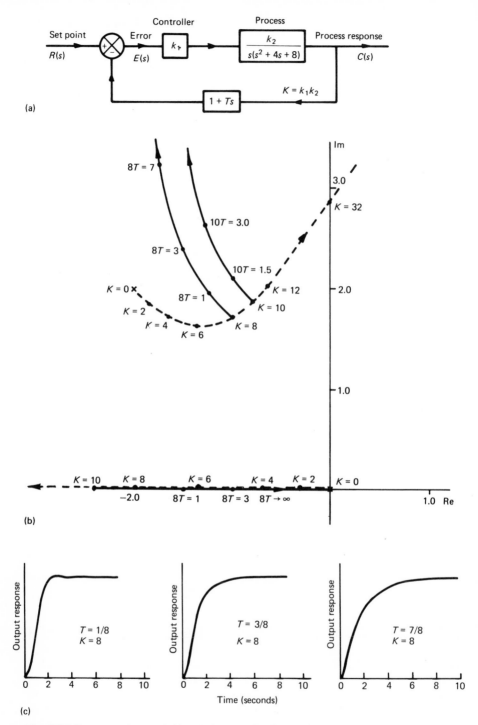

Fig. 9.11 System with variable derivative feedback (a) block diagram (b) root locus diagram (upper half) (c) step responses with variation in T

specific values of K. This is shown in Fig. 9.11b for a pair of values of K, and the independent parameter T. The introduction within the feedback loop of the transfer function $H(s) = 1 + Ts$ has made the system inherently stable but, for increasing values of T the response becomes sluggish, as can be seen from Fig. 9.11c, and these responses would, in general, not be satisfactory in an engineering situation.

The dynamic behaviour of this system would be affected by the presence of a simple time constant τ in the feedback loop, as shown in Fig. 9.12a. In a practical system this simple time constant could represent the dynamic characteristics of a monitoring transducer. Alternatively the combined feedback blocks can be viewed as a compensation network introduced into the system loop in an attempt to achieve a specific change in the system dynamic behaviour. Part of any design task would be to study the effect on system performance of variation in this parameter.

The approach is again to find from the actual closed loop transfer function an analytically equivalent open loop transfer function which enables the root locus diagram to be constructed. From inspection of Fig. 9.12a the closed loop transfer function is

$$\frac{C(s)}{R(s)} = \frac{K(\tau s + 1)}{s(s^2 + 4s + 8)(\tau s + 1) + K(1 + Ts)} \qquad 9.18$$

Choosing a value of $K = 8$

$$\frac{C(s)}{R(s)} = \frac{8(\tau s + 1)}{s^3 + 4s^2 + 8s + 8Ts + 8 + \tau(s^4 + 4s^3 + 8s^2)}$$

$$= \frac{\dfrac{8(\tau s + 1)}{s^3 + 4s^2 + (8 + 8T)s + 8}}{1 + \dfrac{\tau s^2(s^2 + 4s + 8)}{s^3 + 4s^2 + (8 + 8T)s + 8}}$$

which yields an equivalent open loop transfer function

$$[G(s)H(s)]_{\text{equiv}} = \frac{\tau s^2(s^2 + 4s + 8)}{s^3 + 4s^2 + 8(1 + T)s + 8} \qquad 9.19$$

For any chosen value of T, the root locus is plotted in the normal way, Fig. 9.12b. The loci start at the roots of the characteristic equation defined in Eq. 9.15 and end at the zeros $-2 \pm 2j$, 0 and 0 of Eq. 9.19. It will be noticed that since the order of the numerator of Eq. 9.19 is greater than that of the denominator, one of the three loci starts at infinity. In this case the portion of the real axis to the left of -1.5 forms part of a root locus; this is a necessary condition to satisfy Rule 4 of Section 9.3, and there will be a breakaway point to the left of the -1.5 point.

A most interesting result has emerged for the value of $T = \frac{1}{8}$; a fast response system has resulted with guaranteed stability as can be seen from inspection of Fig. 9.12b and Fig. 9.12c.

This illustration demonstrates clearly that the simple rules employed for

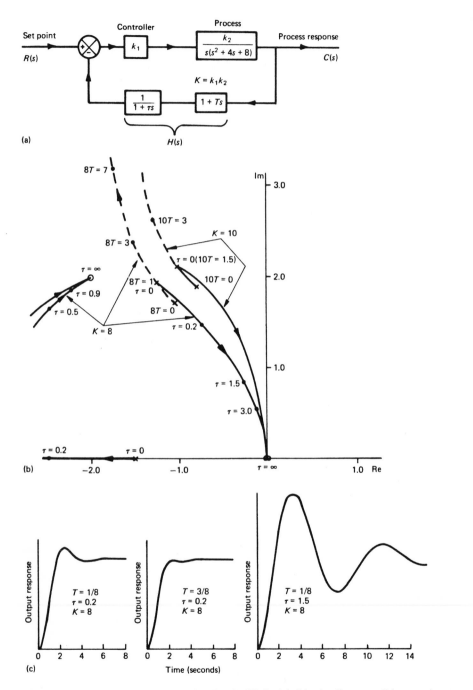

Fig. 9.12 System with variable feedback $H(s)$ (a) block diagram (b) root locus diagram (upper half) (c) step responses with variation in $H(s)$

constructing a root locus diagram can be extended to root contours for variation of any poles or zeros. If a pole and zero are both to be varied, then two sets of root contours are necessary, the poles of the second being roots on the first. This makes possible the design of compensation networks of the type shown in the feedback loop of Fig. 9.12a, via a root locus plot. Further illustration of the use of the method for design purposes is given in the concluding chapter.

10
The Sampled-Data Process

Comparisons are made in this chapter between the discrete data and the continuous data system. These are used to illustrate the impact on system performance resulting from the introduction into the closed loop control scheme of a *sampler*, a device that converts continuous data into a discrete data form. Typically this might simply be to replace an analogue control device by its digital equivalent. However, the wider use of computer control resulting from increased availability of micro-electronic devices does extend the range of control algorithms that can be physically realized by the design engineer without significantly increasing equipment cost. Expanding the number of control algorithms readily available will enable more efficient 'start-up' and 'shut-down' procedures to be designed and so ensure less product waste. The improvement possible in servomechanism and regulator system performance will lead to better process dynamics and the manufacture of higher quality product, particularly when frequent quality changes are necessary on the same plant.

In its most basic form the sampled-data scheme can be defined as one in which the error signal is intermittently sampled at a constant rate. The error signal is then transformed into a sequence of pulses which are amplitude modulated in accordance with the continuous function of the signal from which the samples are taken. This basic form of sampled-data system is illustrated in Fig. 10.1. The symbols $r(t)$, $c(t)$ and $e(t)$ represent the set-point disturbance (reference input for servo system), the output response and the

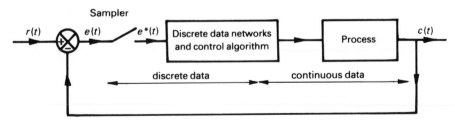

Fig. 10.1 Block diagram of sampled-data controller and process

actuating error signal respectively and each is a continuous time function. A starred symbol is used to indicate that a time function is in sampled form, thus the error variable denoted $e*(t)$ is the discontinuous time function which is the input disturbance to the controller.

10.1 Mathematical description of sampling process

Although the process of sampling can be performed at a constant rate, at a variable rate, or at random, in the following analysis and in most practical applications constant rate periodic sampling is used. The sampling device permits the input disturbance to be sensed only during the short interval (Δ) of a sampling period and ignores this disturbance during the much longer time interval ($T - \Delta$) until the next sampling instant, Fig. 10.2. In most engineering

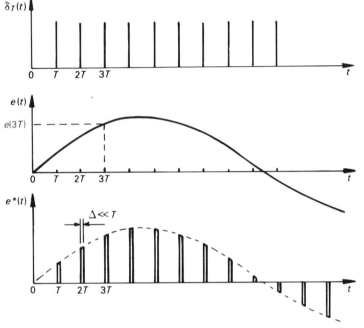

Fig. 10.2 The process of sampling a continuous signal, Eq. 10.1

applications the width Δ of the sampled pulse is small in comparison with the dominant process time constant and hence the sampler output can be represented without serious loss of accuracy as a train of rectangular pulses. The information from the continuous error signal is then contained in the amplitude variations that occur in the pulse train. The assumption of rectangular pulses of negligible width simplifies significantly the synthesis and analysis of sampled-data control schemes.

With $e(t)$ as the continuous input disturbance and $e^*(t)$ as the sampler output, the input and output variables for the sampler can be related by

$$e^*(t) = \delta_T(t)e(t) \qquad\qquad 10.1$$

where $\delta_T(t)$ is the *ideal sampling function* which is a train of unit strength impulses described by

$$\delta_T(t) = \sum_{n=0}^{\infty} \delta(t - nT)$$

The nomenclature $\delta(t - nT)$ by convention implies a unit impulse at time nT. To aid the understanding of the fundamental concept of sampling, each of the terms used in Eq. 10.1 is shown in Fig. 10.2.

Thus, Eq. 10.1 can be written as:

$$e^*(t) = e(t) \sum_{n=0}^{\infty} \delta(t - nT)$$

$$= \sum_{n=0}^{\infty} e(nT)\, \delta(t - nT) \qquad 10.2$$

where $e(nT)$ is the amplitude of $e(t)$ when $t = nT$. Applying Laplace transformation gives

$$E^*(s) = \mathscr{L}[e^*(t)] = \mathscr{L} \sum_{n=0}^{\infty} e(nT)\, \delta(t - nT)$$

$$= \mathscr{L}[e(0)\, \delta(t) + e(T)\, \delta(t - T) + e(2T)\, \delta(t - 2T) + \ldots]$$

Using Eq. 2.8 and Table 2.1 yields

$$E^*(s) = e(0) + e(T)e^{-Ts} + e(2T)e^{-2Ts} + \ldots$$

i.e. $\qquad E^*(s) = \sum_{n=0}^{\infty} e(nT)e^{-nTs} \qquad 10.3$

Jury (reference 24) shows that an equivalent harmonic representation is

$$E^*(s) = \frac{1}{T} \sum_{n=-\infty}^{\infty} E(s + jn\omega_s) \qquad 10.4$$

where ω_s denotes the sampling frequency $2\pi/T$.

The first of these two equations (Eq. 10.3) is a convenient representation for analysis in the time domain and allows the introduction of z-transform theory which is the discrete counterpart to the Laplace transform of continuous data system analysis. The second equation (Eq. 10.4) is a theoretical basis for the extension of the basic frequency analysis methods to sampled-data systems.

10.2 Transfer function of sampled-data element

In the sampler and process arrangement of Fig. 10.3 the response $c(t)$ is sampled synchronously with the manipulated variable $m(t)$ to yield the pulsed time responses $c^*(t)$ and $m^*(t)$; the function $g(t)$ is the impulse response function of a linear process with transfer function $G(s)$.

The process input disturbance $m^*(t)$ is a train of ideal narrow pulses of

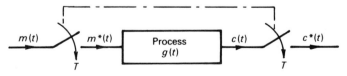

Fig. 10.3 Process with synchronized samplers

varying amplitude and for the linear process the output will be the sum of the individual impulse responses appropriately displaced in time. That is, for the time period $0 \leq t \leq nT$

$$c(t) = g(t)m(0) + g(t - T)m(T) + g(t - 2T)m(2T) + \ldots \qquad 10.5$$

Taking the Laplace transform of Eq. 10.5 and using Eq. 2.8 gives

$$C(s) = G(s)m(0) + G(s)m(T)e^{-Ts} + G(s)m(2T)e^{-2Ts} + \ldots$$

$$= G(s) \sum_{n=0}^{\infty} m(nT)e^{-nTs}$$

$$\therefore \quad C(s) = G(s)M^*(s) \qquad 10.6$$

Equation 10.6 implies that the Laplace transform of the output variable $c(t)$ is equal to the product of the Laplace transform of the pulsed input variable and the transfer function of the process. Note the similarity between Eq. 10.6 and that for the same arrangement but without the samplers given as Eq. 8.1.

By a similar argument it can be demonstrated that

$$C^*(s) = G^*(s)M^*(s) \qquad 10.7$$

where $G^*(s)$ is the overall transfer function of the sampled-data process and is defined (Eq. 10.4) as

$$G^*(s) = \frac{1}{T} \sum_{n=-\infty}^{\infty} G(s + jn\omega_s)$$

It should be noted that the sampled-data transfer function gives information only at sampling instants.

10.3 Closed-loop transfer function

Drawing an analogy with Fig. 8.2b, the basic sampled-data system would be as shown in Fig. 10.4a. To help in the development of the transfer function relationships, Eq. 10.3 allows $E^*(s)$ to be written as

$$E^*(s) = \sum_{n=0}^{\infty} [r(nT) - b(nT)]e^{-nTs}$$

$$= R^*(s) - B^*(s)$$

and hence the equivalent circuit shown in Fig. 10.4b can be introduced for analytical purposes.

Inspection of Fig. 10.4b reveals that

$$C(s) = G(s)E^*(s) \qquad 10.8$$

$$E^*(s) = R^*(s) - B^*(s) \qquad 10.9$$

$$B^*(s) = GH^*(s)E^*(s) \qquad 10.10$$

where $GH^*(s)$ is the pulsed transfer relationship of the product $G(s)H(s)$. These

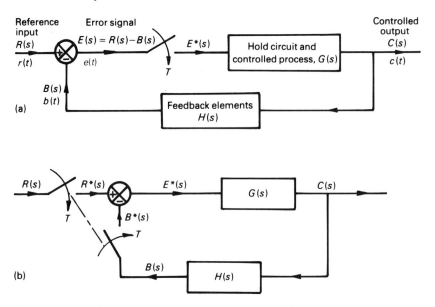

Fig. 10.4 Block diagram of sampled-data system (a) basic diagram (b) equivalent representation

expressions can be treated as algebraic equations in an identical manner to those in Sections 2.3 and 8.1.

Substituting for $B^*(s)$ from Eq. 10.10 into Eq. 10.9 gives

$$E^*(s) = \frac{R^*(s)}{1 + GH^*(s)} \qquad\qquad 10.11$$

Inserting Eq. 10.11 into Eq. 10.8 yields the Laplace transform for the output variable $c(t)$ of the sampled-data system

$$C(s) = \frac{G(s)R^*(s)}{1 + GH^*(s)} \qquad\qquad 10.12$$

Using Eq. 10.4 to replace the starred terms in Eq. 10.12 and substituting $s = j\omega$ yields the frequency function

$$C(j\omega) = \frac{G(j\omega)T^{-1} \sum_{n=-\infty}^{\infty} R(j\omega + jn\omega_s)}{1 + T^{-1} \sum_{n=-\infty}^{\infty} GH(j\omega + jn\omega_s)} \qquad\qquad 10.13$$

The function $GH^*(s)$ is defined as the open-loop transfer function of the sampled-data control system.

10.4 Polar plots

Graphical representation of the frequency response information for $GH^*(s)$ can be obtained from the Argand diagram as described in Section 6.2 if the frequency response function is written as

$$GH^*(j\omega) = T^{-1} \sum_{n=-\infty}^{\infty} GH[j(\omega + n\omega_s)]$$

$$= T^{-1}\left\{GH[j\omega] + \sum_{n=1}^{\infty} GH[j(\omega + n\omega_s)] + \sum_{n=1}^{\infty} GH[j(\omega - n\omega_s)]\right\}$$

$$= T^{-1}\{GH[j\omega] + GH[j(\omega + \omega_s)] + GH[j(\omega - \omega_s)]$$
$$+ GH[j(\omega + 2\omega_s)] + GH[j(\omega - 2\omega_s)] + \ldots\} \qquad 10.14$$

and then the vectors for the component functions in this expression are combined graphically or numerically. Since the sampling frequency is usually chosen to be at least 4 or 5 times the system bandwidth, Eq. 10.14 can be approximated by the first three terms without serious loss of accuracy in the polar plot, i.e.

$$GH^*(j\omega) \simeq T^{-1}GH[j\omega] + T^{-1}GH[j(\omega + \omega_s)] + T^{-1}GH[j(\omega - \omega_s)] \qquad 10.15$$

The contribution made by the second term with increasing values of ω becomes less significant and can often be omitted from Eq. 10.15. The

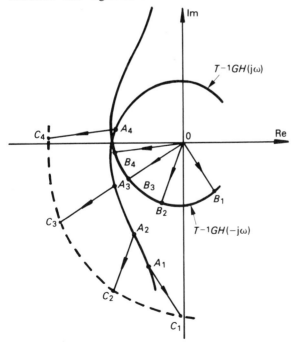

Fig. 10.5 Approximate polar plot for sampled-data system

sequence of events for the construction of $GH^*(j\omega)$ using the remaining two terms, illustrated in Fig. 10.5, is:

1. Draw the polar plots for both positive and negative frequency values, as described in Section 6.2.

2. Label the points for specific frequency values ω_1, ω_2, ..., ω_n, as A_1, A_2, ..., A_n on the positive plot and the points corresponding to $(\omega_1 - \omega_s)$, $(\omega_2 - \omega_s)$, ..., $(\omega_n - \omega_s)$ as B_1, B_2, ..., B_n on the negative plot.

3. Add graphically the vectors OB_1, OB_2, ..., OB_n to the vectors OA_1, OA_2, ..., OA_n respectively to give points labelled C_1, C_2, ..., C_n.

4. The line trajectory through these points is a first approximation to the sampled-data polar plot, as shown by the broken line in Fig. 10.5.

5. A better estimate would result if the vector $T^{-1}GH[j(\omega + \omega_s)]$ were included, particularly at low values of ω.

Example 10.1. To demonstrate the application of this procedure, consider the second order transfer function represented graphically by Fig. 6.3. For the largest of the polar plots shown, with $\omega_n = 1$ rad/second and $\zeta = 0.5$, the equation is:

$$G(j\omega) = \frac{1}{(1 - \omega^2) + j\omega}$$

Using the three terms of Eq. 10.15 the pulsed polar plot is described by

$$TG^*(j\omega) = G[j\omega] + G[j(\omega - \omega_s)] + G[j(\omega + \omega_s)]$$

$$= \frac{1}{(1 - \omega^2) + j\omega} + \frac{1}{[1 - (\omega - \omega_s)^2] + j(\omega - \omega_s)}$$

$$+ \frac{1}{[1 - (\omega + \omega_s)^2] + j(\omega + \omega_s)}$$

The continuous process has a natural frequency of 1 rad/second and Fig. 6.9 indicates the process bandwidth to be approximately 1.5 rad/second. A sampling frequency of 6 rad/second will be adequate to obtain representative process data. This corresponds to a sample interval of $\pi/3$ seconds ($\simeq 1$), hence

$$G^*(j\omega) = \frac{1}{(1 - \omega^2) + j\omega} + \frac{1}{[1 - (\omega - 6)^2] + j(\omega - 6)}$$

$$+ \frac{1}{[1 - (\omega + 6)^2] + j(\omega + 6)}$$

Values obtained from this equation are plotted in Fig. 10.6 for $0 \le \omega \le 4$, and show the contribution of each term of Eq. 10.15 to the shape and size of the polar plot. The most significant point to observe is that whilst the locus of $G(j\omega)$ indicates a process which is stable for any value of gain, the introduction of the sampler destroys this property (the simplified Nyquist criterion of Section 8.4 can still be applied). For frequencies in excess of $\omega_s/2$, 3 rad/second in this example, the polar plot becomes a mirror image of itself about the real

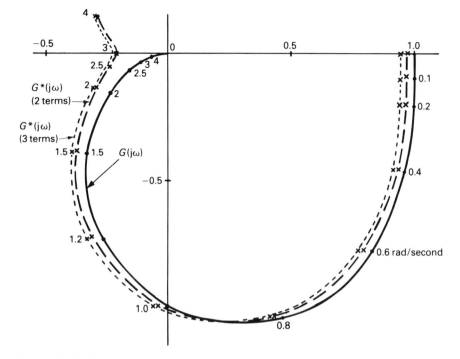

Fig. 10.6 Effect of sampler on polar plot · of second order system $G(s) = 1/(s^2 + s + 1)$, $\omega_s = 6\,\text{rad/second}$

axis, a consequence of the harmonic distortion introduced by the process of sampling (described in Section 7.5).

This illustrates that the sampling operation undermines system stability and that the harmonic characteristics as given by the shape and size of the polar plot are a function of both process gain and sampling frequency. Therefore, in system design, variation in the parameter T (sample interval) must be included when dynamic behaviour is investigated.

10.5 Pulse transfer function

The requirement to evaluate the infinite series specified by Eq. 10.3 can be avoided by the introduction of a new variable z defined by

$$z = e^{sT}$$

Application of this transformation to Eq. 10.3 yields

$$E^*\left(\frac{1}{T}\ln z\right) = E(z) = \sum_{n=0}^{\infty} e(nT)z^{-n} \qquad 10.16$$

where $E(z)$ is defined as the *z-transform* of $e^*(t)$. In general, any continuous function that possesses an s-transform will have an equivalent z-transform and it is common to write

$$E(z) = \mathscr{Z}[e(t)]$$

To derive a pulse transfer function this concept will be applied to Fig. 10.3. The output response for this arrangement, using the definition implied by Eq. 10.16, is

$$C(z) = \sum_{n=0}^{\infty} c(nT)z^{-n} \qquad\qquad 10.17$$

The value of the process output at the sampling instant $t = nT$ is, from Eq. 10.5,

$$c(nT) = g(nT)m(0) + g(nT - T)m(T) + g(nT - 2T)m(2T) + \ldots$$

$$= \sum_{k=0}^{n} g(nT - kT)m(kT) \qquad\qquad 10.18$$

Since $g(nT - kT) = 0$ for values of $k > n$, Eq. 10.18 can be written

$$c(nT) = \sum_{k=0}^{\infty} g(nT - kT)m(kT) \qquad\qquad 10.19$$

Substituting Eq. 10.19 into Eq. 10.17 yields the output response function

$$C(z) = \sum_{n=0}^{\infty} \left[\sum_{k=0}^{\infty} g(nT - kT)m(kT) \right] z^{-n}$$

In view of the fact that $g(nT - kT) = 0$ when $k > n$ this expression is the same as

$$C(z) = \sum_{p=0}^{\infty} g(pT)z^{-p} \sum_{k=0}^{\infty} m(kT)z^{-k}$$

Using the definition of Eq. 10.16, the right hand side of the above equation can be abbreviated to

$$C(z) = G(z)M(z) \qquad\qquad 10.20$$

Equation 10.20 is the z-transform equivalent of the Laplace transform equation given as Eq. 10.7, and $G(z)$ is known as the process *pulse transfer function*.

Although z-transformation is only applicable to discrete signals, it can be applied to a continuous process response if signal values are required at the sampling instants only and no information is needed between sample instants.

To demonstrate the use of Eq. 10.17 for deriving z-transforms two simple examples are given.

Example 10.2. Consider a step disturbance of magnitude K applied at time $t = 0$

$$\text{i.e.} \quad f(t) = K \text{ for } t \geq 0$$

The output of the sampler is then

$$f(nT) = K \text{ for } n = 0, 1, 2, \ldots$$

Hence
$$F(z) = \sum_{n=0}^{\infty} f(nT)z^{-n} = \sum_{n=0}^{\infty} Kz^{-n}$$

$$= K(1 + z^{-1} + z^{-2} + z^{-3} + \ldots)$$

where the term in brackets is the binomial expansion of $(1 - z^{-1})^{-1}$ for $|z^{-1}| < 1$. Hence the z-transform of a step disturbance is

$$F(z) = \frac{Kz}{z - 1}$$

The Laplace transform counterpart is

$$F(s) = \frac{K}{s}$$

Example 10.3. Consider the Laplace transform

$$F(s) = \frac{K}{s^2 + 4s + 8}$$

From Table 2.1 the time response $f(t)$ is

$$f(t) = \tfrac{1}{2}Ke^{-2t} \sin 2t$$

At $t = nT$

$$f(nT) = \tfrac{1}{2}Ke^{-2nT} \sin 2nT$$

$$= \tfrac{1}{2}Ke^{-2nT} \frac{1}{2j} (e^{j2nT} - e^{-j2nT})$$

and hence
$$F(z) = \frac{K}{4j} \left[\sum_{n=0}^{\infty} (e^{-2T}e^{j2T}z^{-1})^n - \sum_{n=0}^{\infty} (e^{-2T}e^{-j2T}z^{-1})^n \right]$$

$$= \frac{K}{4j} \left[\frac{1}{1 - e^{-2T}e^{j2T}z^{-1}} - \frac{1}{1 - e^{-2T}e^{-j2T}z^{-1}} \right]$$

by inspection of Example 10.2.

Hence
$$F(z) = \frac{K}{4j} \left[\frac{e^{-2T}z^{-1}(e^{j2T} - e^{-j2T})}{1 - e^{-2T}z^{-1}(e^{j2T} + e^{-j2T}) + e^{-4T}z^{-2}} \right]$$

$$= \frac{K}{2} \left[\frac{ze^{-2T} \sin 2T}{z^2 - 2ze^{-2T} \cos 2T + e^{-4T}} \right]$$

Some widely used z-transform pairs are listed in Table 10.1.

Table 10.1 Laplace and z-transforms for basic time functions

Time function $f(t)$	Laplace transform $F(s)$	z-transform $F(z)$
$\delta(t)$	1	1
$\delta(t-nT)$	e^{-nTs}	$\dfrac{1}{z^n}$
unit step	$\dfrac{1}{s}$	$\dfrac{z}{z-1}$
t	$\dfrac{1}{s^2}$	$\dfrac{Tz}{(z-1)^2}$
e^{-at}	$\dfrac{1}{s+a}$	$\dfrac{z}{z-e^{-aT}}$
te^{-at}	$\dfrac{1}{(s+a)^2}$	$\dfrac{Tze^{-aT}}{(z-e^{-aT})^2}$
$\sin \omega t$	$\dfrac{\omega}{s^2+\omega^2}$	$\dfrac{z \sin \omega T}{z^2-2z \cos \omega T + 1}$
$\cos \omega t$	$\dfrac{s}{s^2+\omega^2}$	$\dfrac{z^2-z \cos \omega T}{z^2-2z \cos \omega T + 1}$
$e^{-at} \sin \omega t$	$\dfrac{\omega}{(s+a)^2+\omega^2}$	$\dfrac{ze^{-aT} \sin \omega T}{z^2-2ze^{-aT} \cos \omega t + e^{-2aT}}$
$e^{-at} \cos \omega t$	$\dfrac{s+a}{(s+a)^2+\omega^2}$	$\dfrac{z^2-ze^{-aT} \cos \omega T}{z^2-2ze^{-aT} \cos \omega T + e^{-2aT}}$

10.6 Block diagrams

To illustrate the use of Eq. 10.7 and Eq. 10.20 in the derivation and manipulation of block diagrams, the three principal loop arrangements of Fig. 10.7a, b, and c will be studied; other configurations are reducible to combinations of these loop arrangements.

(a) *Processes in cascade—Fig. 10.7a*

The output responses from the two sections are

$$U_2{}^*(s) = G_1{}^*(s)U_1{}^*(s)$$

and

$$C^*(s) = G_2{}^*(s)U_2{}^*(s)$$

Eliminating $U_2{}^*(s)$ gives the starred transfer function

$$\frac{C^*(s)}{U_1{}^*(s)} = G_1{}^*(s)G_2{}^*(s)$$

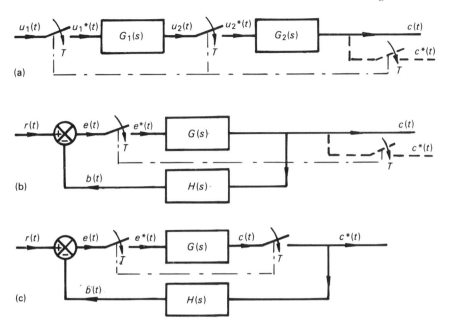

Fig. 10.7 Block diagrams for systems with sampling (a) processes in cascade (b) closed loop with one sampler (c) closed loop with two samplers

and the corresponding pulsed transfer function is

$$\frac{C(z)}{U_1(z)} = G_1(z)G_2(z)$$

i.e. the product of the individual pulsed transfer functions.

(b) *Closed loop with one sampler—Fig. 10.7b*
   The starred error signal is

$$E^*(s) = R^*(s) - B^*(s)$$

where

$$B^*(s) = GH^*(s)E^*(s)$$

Eliminating $B^*(s)$ gives on rearrangement

$$E^*(s) = \frac{R^*(s)}{1 + GH^*(s)}$$

which is the Laplace transform of the sampler output response. The output response from the system at the sample instants is:

$$C^*(s) = G^*(s)E^*(s)$$

Substituting for $E^*(s)$ yields

$$C^*(s) = \frac{G^*(s)R^*(s)}{1 + GH^*(s)}$$

and in terms of the z-transform

$$C(z) = \frac{G(z)R(z)}{1 + GH(z)}$$

The equation only describes the values of the output response at the sampling instants and the term $GH(z)$ is obtained by first multiplying together the $G(s)$ and $H(s)$ functions, then the z-transform of the product is obtained.

(c) *Closed loop with two samplers—Fig. 10.7c*
    The starred error signal is

$$E^*(s) = R^*(s) - B^*(s)$$

Also

$$C^*(s) = G^*(s)\ E^*(s)$$

and

$$B^*(s) = H^*(s)\ C^*(s)$$

Eliminating $E^*(s)$ and $B^*(s)$ gives the starred Laplace transform of the system response as:

$$C^*(s) = \frac{G^*(s)\ R^*(s)}{1 + G^*(s)\ H^*(s)}$$

The corresponding z-transform is

$$C(z) = \frac{G(z)\ R(z)}{1 + G(z)\ H(z)}$$

Note that $G(z)H(z)$ is not the same as $GH(z)$, but is the product of the individual z-transforms of the functions $G(s)$ and $H(s)$.

10.7 Inverse operation

To obtain the time response $f^*(t)$ of a process where $F(z)$ has been evaluated by an equation in the form of Eq. 10.20, a mathematical procedure known as inverse z-transformation must be carried out. The most direct route available to this end is to adopt either a partial fraction or a power series expansion approach.

   The former method requires the expansion of $z^{-1}F(z)$ into partial fractions such that the inverse z-transformation of each term multiplied by z is recognizable from z-transform tables in an analogous manner to Section 2.2 and Chapter 4. In the latter, the easier of the two methods to implement, $F(z)$ is expanded into a power series of z^{-1} by long division; the coefficient of the z^{-n} term corresponds to the value of the time function $f^*(t)$ at the nth sampling instant.

   In order to obtain the value of $f^*(t)$ as time becomes infinite, assuming $F(s)$

has no poles on the imaginary axis or to the right of it in the s-plane, use is made of the final-value theorem:

$$\lim_{t \to \infty} \{f^*(t)\} = \lim_{z \to 1} \left\{ \frac{z-1}{z} F(z) \right\}$$ 10.21

i.e. it is given by the value of $\dfrac{z-1}{z} F(z)$ as z approaches unity.

10.8 Data reconstruction

Reconstruction of continuous data from a sampled record is performed by starting with known data about the signal up to a given sample instant and then estimating by extrapolation data values up to the next sample instant. A mathematical approximation for the signal in the interval $nT \leq t < (n+1)T$ can be derived from the Taylor's power series expansion

$$f_n(t) = f(nT) + \dot{f}(nT)(t-nT) + \frac{\ddot{f}(nT)}{2!}(t-nT)^2 + \ldots$$

where $f_n(t)$ is the estimate for $f(t)$ between the two measured consecutive samples. The most widely used data reconstruction device is the *zero-order hold* in which $f(t)$ across the interval is approximated by the constant value

$$f_n(t) = f(nT) \text{ for } nT \leq t < (n+1)T$$

For the zero-order hold device the output is thus a set of flat-top pulses of width T, as illustrated in Fig. 10.8a. In contrast a *first order hold* device

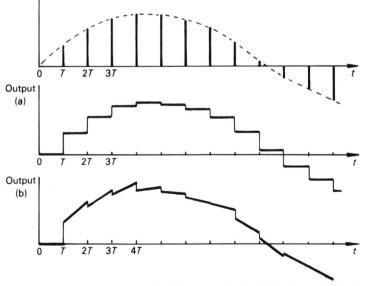

Fig. 10.8 Data reconstruction (a) zero order hold (b) 1st order hold

incorporates the first two terms in the Taylor's power series expansion, Fig. 10.8b.

Mathematically, the zero-order hold device can be described by use of Eq. 2.4 applied to the signal of Fig. 10.8a, which results in the Laplace transform of the output function

$$F(s) = \int_0^T f(0)e^{-st}\,dt + \int_T^{2T} f(T)e^{-st}\,dt + \ldots + \int_{nT}^{(n+1)T} f(nT)e^{-st}\,dt + \ldots$$

$$= \frac{1 - e^{-sT}}{s} \sum_{i=0}^{\infty} f(iT)e^{-isT}$$

$$= \frac{1 - e^{-sT}}{s} F^*(s)$$

The transfer function of a zero-order hold circuit is thus

$$G_{ho}(s) = \frac{1 - e^{-sT}}{s} \qquad\qquad 10.22$$

The frequency response function $G_{ho}(j\omega)$ is obtained by effecting the substitution $s = j\omega$ in Eq. 10.22.

Example 10.4. The open-loop transfer function used in Example 10.1 will be studied further to illustrate the power series expansion method as a means of obtaining the inverse z-transformation, and the use of Eq. 10.21 to determine the steady state value.

The combined transfer function is

$$G_{ho}(s)\,G(s) = \frac{(1 - e^{-sT})}{s}\left(\frac{1}{s^2 + s + 1}\right)$$

and hence

$$G_{ho}G(z) = (1 - z^{-1})\mathscr{L}\left[\frac{1}{s(s^2 + s + 1)}\right]$$

$$= (1 - z^{-1})\,\mathscr{L}\left[\frac{1}{s} - \frac{s+1}{s^2 + s + 1}\right]$$

$$= (1 - z^{-1})\mathscr{L}\left[\frac{1}{s} - \frac{s + 0.5}{(s + 0.5)^2 + 0.866^2} - \frac{0.5}{(s + 0.5)^2 + 0.866^2}\right]$$

From Table 10.1

$$G_{ho}G(z) = (1 - z^{-1})\left[\frac{z}{z - 1} - \frac{z^2 + e^{-0.5T}(0.5774\sin 0.866T - \cos 0.866T)z}{z^2 - 2ze^{-0.5T}\cos 0.866T + e^{-T}}\right]$$

If the sampling interval is chosen to be 1 second, for the reasons given in Example 10.1

$$G_{ho}G(z) = \frac{0.3404z + 0.2415}{z^2 - 0.7859z + 0.3679} = \frac{C(z)}{U(z)}$$

The output response for a unit step input is

$$C(z) = \left(\frac{z}{z-1}\right)\left[\frac{0.3404z + 0.2415}{z^2 - 0.7859z + 0.3679}\right]$$

$$= \frac{0.3404z^2 + 0.2415z}{z^3 - 1.7859z^2 + 1.1538z - 0.3679}$$

This equation can now be expressed in the form

$$C(z) = a_0 + a_1z^{-1} + a_2z^{-2} + \dots$$

by use of manual long division (or a simple computer program) as follows:

$$z^3 - 1.7859z^2 \qquad 0.3404z^{-1} + 0.8494z^{-2} + 1.1241z^{-3} + \dots$$

$+ 1.1538z - 0.3679$	$0.3404z^2$	$+ 0.2415z$	
	$0.3404z^2$	$- 0.6079z$	$+ 0.3928$	$- 0.1252z^{-1}$
		$+ 0.8494z$	$- 0.3928$	$+ 0.1252z^{-1}$
		$0.8494z$	$- 1.5169$	$+ 0.9800z^{-1} + \dots$
			$+ 1.1241$	$- 0.8548z^{-1}$
			1.1241	$- \dots\dots\dots$

$\dots\dots\dots$

Continuing in this way will yield successive coefficients for z^{-n}. The time function at the instants of sampling is therefore given by

$$c^*(t) = 0.34\ \delta(t - T) + 0.85\ \delta(t - 2T) + 1.12\ \delta(t - 3T) + \dots.$$

Using Eq. 10.21 will give the value of $c^*(t)$ as t becomes infinite for a step disturbance in $u(t)$

$$\lim_{t \to \infty} \{c^*(t)\} = \lim_{z \to 1} \left\{\frac{0.3404z + 0.2415}{z^2 - 0.7859z + 0.3679}\right\}$$

$$= 1$$

For comparison the time response to a unit step input disturbance for the continuous data process has been computed, and the continuous and the sampled system responses are both shown in Fig. 10.9b. Because the input disturbance is a step function, no approximation error exists at the output from the hold circuit, hence the sampled-data points are coincident with those from the continuous data process. This will be the case whatever value of sampling interval is chosen. Also included in this figure are typical response

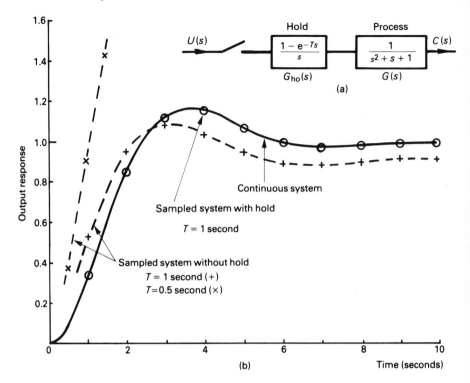

Fig. 10.9 Effect of sampling, Example 10.4 (a) block diagram (b) unit step response curves

curves for the same system but with the hold circuit omitted. These show that the system output signal increases in magnitude for reducing sampling interval, as would be expected as a consequence of the sampler output for a unit step input being a train of unit strength impulses (Eq. 10.1).

Example 10.5. For the closed loop arrangement shown in Fig. 10.10a with sampling interval 1 second estimate the process sampled-data time response to a unit step disturbance for 10 sample intervals, with and without the hold circuit present. Calculate the final steady state value of this output response for both cases.

For Fig. 10.7b it has been established that

$$C(z) = \frac{G(z)R(z)}{1 + GH(z)}$$

hence for Fig. 10.10a the closed loop pulsed transfer function is

$$\frac{C(z)}{R(z)} = \frac{G_{\text{ho}}G(z)}{1 + G_{\text{ho}}G(z)}$$

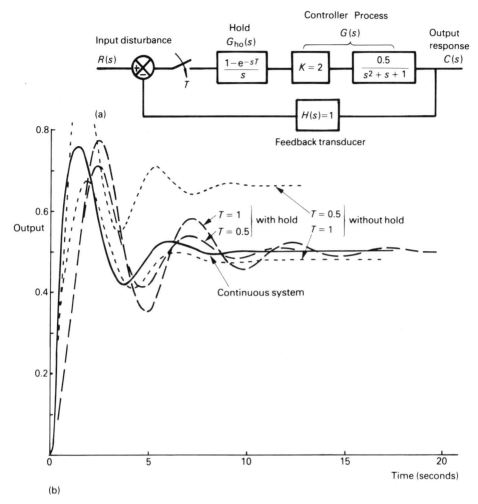

Fig. 10.10 Effect of sampling and hold circuit, Example 10.5 (a) block diagram (b) unit step response curves

and in Example 10.4 where this open loop system is analysed it is shown that

$$G_{ho}G(z) = \frac{0.3404z + 0.2415}{z^2 - 0.7859z + 0.3679}$$

The closed loop pulsed transfer function is therefore

$$\frac{C(z)}{R(z)} = \frac{0.3404z + 0.2415}{z^2 - 0.4455z + 0.6094}$$

and hence for

$$R(z) = \frac{z}{z - 1}$$

$$C(z) = \frac{0.3404z^2 + 0.2415z}{z^3 - 1.4455z^2 + 1.0549z - 0.6094}$$

Using Eq. 10.21 yields the steady state value

$$\lim_{t \to \infty} \{c^*(t)\} = \frac{0.5819}{1.1639} = 0.5$$

With the hold device omitted from the loop the output is

$$C(z) = \frac{0.5335z^2}{z^3 - 1.2524z^2 + 0.6203z - 0.3679}$$

and the steady state value is

$$\lim_{t \to \infty} \{c^*(t)\} = 0.48$$

For each of these $C(z)$ expressions, the power series expansion method gives the coefficients of the terms $\delta(t - nT)$ and these are listed together with the steady values in Table 10.2. For clarity the system output responses are

Table 10.2 Results of Example 10.5, $T = 1$ second

Coefficient n	1	2	3	4	5	6
$c^*(t)$ with hold	0.34	0.734	0.701	0.447	0.354	0.467
$c^*(t)$ without hold	0.534	0.668	0.506	0.415	0.452	0.494
Continuous data system	0.739	0.665	0.461	0.428	0.493	0.524

Coefficient n	7	8	9	10	Steady state value
$c^*(t)$ with hold	0.574	0.553	0.478	0.458	0.5
$c^*(t)$ without hold	0.492	0.475	0.472	0.477	0.48
Continuous data system	0.510	0.494	0.495	0.5	0.5

plotted in Fig. 10.10b. In this figure the continuous output response trace for the sampled system is created by connecting the discrete output sequence by a smooth curve. Such an approximation can be used with confidence if the sampling frequency is substantially higher than the natural frequency of the system. The response curves which correspond to the smaller sampling interval of 0.5 second are also shown. These traces, together with those of Fig. 10.9b, focus attention on the need for adequate data reconstruction in control system design and it is now established practice to introduce a hold circuit after each sampler in a loop to guarantee this end.

10.9 The z-plane

The Laplace transform method is the basic tool for controller design in linear continuous data systems. In a similar manner the z-transform method offers scope for analysis and synthesis of sampled-data systems. A study of the pole-zero configuration of the characteristic equation is one common design approach and requires the facility of being able to transfer root locations in the s-plane to their corresponding positions in the z-plane. This mapping process is achieved by employing the transformation $z = e^{Ts}$, where $T = 2\pi/\omega_s$ is the sampling interval and s the Laplace operator.

If the s-plane is divided into horizontal strips, ω_s wide and symmetrical about the real axis, the perimeter of the first of these strips, shown in Fig. 10.11 and referred to as the primary strip, can be mapped into the z-plane as follows. The path from the origin along the positive imaginary axis in the s-plane becomes

$$z = e^{j(2\pi\omega/\omega_s)}$$

$$= \cos 2\pi \, \omega/\omega_s + j \sin 2\pi \, \omega/\omega_s$$

and substituting all values for ω in the range $0 \le \omega \le \frac{1}{2}\omega_s$ gives the locus ① to ② in Fig. 10.11b.

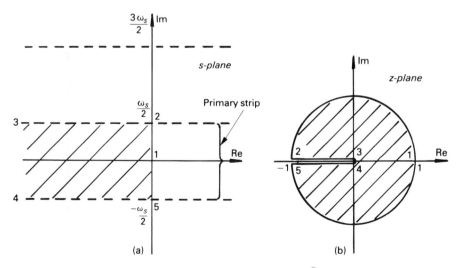

Fig. 10.11 Transformation using mapping function $z = e^{Ts}$ (a) s-plane (b) z-plane

For the boundary $$s = \sigma + \tfrac{1}{2}j\omega_s$$

$$z = e^{2\pi/\omega_s(\sigma + (1/2)j\omega_s)}$$

$$= -e^{(2\pi/\omega_s)\sigma}$$

and for values of $0 \le \sigma \le -\infty$ gives values for z in the range -1 to 0, which determines the route from ② to ③. Continuing in this way around the perimeter enables the route ③—④—⑤—① to be mapped, illustrating that this portion of the left half of the s-plane is mapped into a circle of unit radius centred at the origin in the z-plane. Any root lying in the primary strip must lie within the unit circle.

Transferring the boundary of each of the other strips, referred to as complementary strips, from the s-plane to the z-plane generates the same unit circle. Hence, the boundary for stability is the perimeter of this circle and the circle of unit radius in the z-plane is thus equivalent to the imaginary axis in the s-plane. Roots within the circle give rise to decaying motions while the opposite is true for those that lie outside the unit circle.

10.10 Routh–Hurwitz stability test

The conventional procedure described in Section 8.3 was devised to determine whether the roots of a polynomial equation lie in the left or right half of the s-plane. The method must be adapted to permit testing whether roots lie within or outside the unit circle in the z-plane. To achieve this, a modification can be introduced that maps the interior of the unit circle onto the left half of a third complex plane. This transformation is achieved by use of the mapping function

$$r = \frac{z - 1}{z + 1} \qquad\qquad 10.23$$

where the complex variable

$$r = \sigma_r + j\omega_r \qquad\qquad 10.24$$

If this transformation in r is used, the conventional Routh–Hurwitz test can be applied to the polynomial equation in the variable r.

As was illustrated in Section 10.8 the stability of a sampled data closed loop system is a function of both loop gain K and sampling interval T. The Routh–Hurwitz test is a convenient procedure for locating the stability boundary linking T and K, and the following example illustrates this use.

Example 10.6. Consider the arrangement of Fig. 9.8 modified to include a single sampler and a hold circuit as shown in Fig. 10.12. The open loop

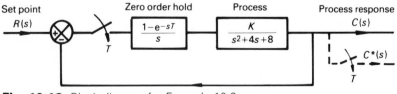

Fig. 10.12 Block diagram for Example 10.6

continuous data transfer function is

$$G(s) = \frac{K}{s^2 + 4s + 8}$$

and the z-transform of the process together with the hold circuit is

$$G_{ho}G(z) = (1 - z^{-1})\mathscr{L}\left\{\frac{K}{s(s^2 + 4s + 8)}\right\}$$

$$= (1 - z^{-1})\mathscr{L}\left\{\frac{K}{8}\left(\frac{1}{s} - \frac{(s + 2)}{(s + 2)^2 + 2^2} - \frac{2}{(s + 2)^2 + 2^2}\right)\right\}$$

Putting $k = \dfrac{K}{8}$, replacing the groups in 's' by the equivalent groups in 'z' using

Table 10.1, and rearranging gives:

$$G_{ho}G(z) = k\left\{\frac{ze^{-2T}(e^{2T} - \sin 2T - \cos 2T) + e^{-2T}(e^{-2T} + \sin 2T - \cos 2T)}{z^2 - 2ze^{-2T}\cos 2T + e^{-4T}}\right\}$$

By definition the characteristic equation is

$$1 + G_{ho}G(z) = 0$$

i.e. $\quad z^2 + ae^{-2T}z + be^{-2T} = 0$

where

$$a = k(e^{2T} - \sin 2T - \cos 2T) - 2\cos 2T$$

and $\qquad b = k(e^{-2T} + \sin 2T - \cos 2T) + e^{-2T}$

Using the mapping function $z = \dfrac{1 + r}{1 - r}$ yields

$$(1 + be^{-2T} - ae^{-2T})r^2 + 2(1 - be^{-2T})r + (1 + ae^{-2T} + be^{-2T}) = 0$$

from which it can be seen that if loop stability is to be achieved

$$1 + be^{-2T} - ae^{-2T} > 0$$

i.e. $\quad k < k_1$

where

$$k_1 = \frac{e^{2T} + e^{-2T} + 2\cos 2T}{e^{2T} - e^{-2T} - 2\sin 2T}$$

and

$$1 - be^{-2T} > 0$$

i.e. $\quad k < k_2$

where

$$k_2 = \frac{e^{2T} - e^{-2T}}{e^{-2T} + \sin 2T - \cos 2T}$$

and

$$1 + ae^{-2T} + be^{-2T} > 0$$

or $\qquad k(e^{2T} + e^{-2T} - 2\cos 2T) > -(e^{2T} + e^{-2T} - 2\cos 2T)$

i.e. $\quad k > k_3$

where $\qquad\qquad\qquad\qquad k_3 = -1$

The profile of the stability region defined for variations in K and T is presented in Fig. 10.13 and this shows very clearly the loss of inherent stability present with the continuous-data system as a direct result of introducing the sample and hold device into the loop.

Time response curves computed using the power series expansion procedure together with Eq. 10.21 to evaluate the steady state value are shown in Fig. 10.14 for a unit step input disturbance. These do confirm the expected change in dynamic behaviour with increasing values of T, as can also be predicted from Fig. 10.13 for the fixed gain value $K = 10$. The corresponding root locus diagram is given in Fig. 10.15. This figure can be made more informative if the contour lines for constant damping factor ζ are mapped across from the s-plane.

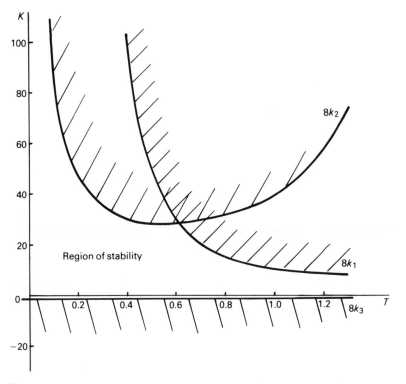

Fig. 10.13 Stability region for Example 10.6

Using Fig. 4.6, it can be seen that a root on a constant damping factor (ζ) line is given by

$$s = -\omega \tan \beta + j\omega$$

where $\beta = 90 - \varphi$.

The mapping function from the s-plane to the z-plane is

$$z = e^{(-\omega \tan \beta + j\omega)T}$$
$$= e^{-\omega T \tan \beta}(\cos \omega T + j \sin \omega T)$$

Expressing this in polar coordinates, gives

$$z = e^{-(2\pi \tan \beta)(\omega/\omega_s)}\underline{/2\pi(\omega/\omega_s)} \qquad 10.25$$

after substitution of $T = 2\pi/\omega_s$. Equation 4.22 gives $\zeta = \cos \varphi$, hence $\zeta = \sin \beta$ and by using Eq. 10.25 the contour lines for constant damping factor can be mapped onto the z-plane. For most practical systems a sampling frequency is chosen such that the forward path transfer function introduces significant attenuation at frequencies higher than $\omega_s/2$, hence only the poles in the strip between $+j\omega_s/2$ and $-j\omega_s/2$ in the s-plane need be mapped across.

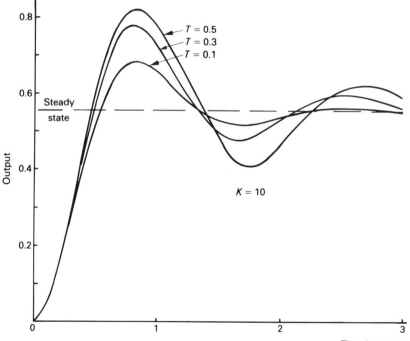

Fig. 10.14 Unit step responses with variation in *T*, for fixed gain value $K = 10$

With the contour lines drawn for constant damping factor ζ, Fig. 10.15 indicates the change in transient response to be expected for increasing values of T and does highlight the usefulness of this figure in control system design.

10.11 Frequency response of sampled-data system

All the properties and rules for the continuous-data system are still valid when applied to the open loop pulsed transfer function $GH(z)$, if the bilinear transformation in r is employed. The plot of $GH(z)$ is made in terms of the magnitude and phase as a function of ω_r, as defined by Eq. 10.24.

For example, consider the transfer function of Example 6.2, i.e.

$$G(s) = \frac{10}{s(1 + 0.5s)(1 + 0.1s)} \qquad 10.26$$

For the sampled process incorporating zero-order hold

$$G_{ho}G(z) = (1 - z^{-1})\mathscr{Z}\left(\frac{10}{s^2(1 + 0.5s)(1 + 0.1s)}\right)$$

$$= (1 - z^{-1})\mathscr{Z}\left(\frac{10.0}{s^2} - \frac{6.0}{s} + \frac{2.85}{(1 + 0.5s)} + \frac{0.15}{(1 + 0.1s)}\right)$$

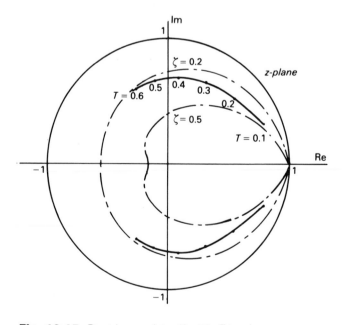

Fig. 10.15 Root locus plot—$K = 10$, T varying

From Table 10.1

$$G_{ho}G(z) = (1 - z^{-1})\left(\frac{10Tz}{(z-1)^2} - \frac{6z}{(z-1)} + \frac{5.7z}{(z-e^{-2T})} + \frac{1.5z}{(z-e^{-10T})}\right)$$

To ensure that the sampling frequency is at least 4 times the bandwidth of the continuous system, choose a value T of 0.3 seconds. Hence, rearrangement of the above equation gives

$$G_{ho}G(z) = \frac{1.2z^3 - 2.91z^2 + 3.86z - 0.86}{(z-1)(z-0.55)(z-0.05)}$$

Employing the bilinear transformation yields

$$G_{ho}G\left(z = \frac{1+j\omega_r}{1-j\omega_r}\right) = \frac{(1.29 - 0.07\omega_r^2) - j\omega_r(8.83\omega_r^2 + 0.59)}{0.86j\omega_r(1 + 3.44j\omega_r)(1 + 1.11j\omega_r)} \qquad 10.27$$

If the gain of Eq. 10.26 is reduced by a factor of 5 the polar plot drawn in Fig. 10.16 for this reduced gain value yields a phase margin of 44° and a gain margin of 16 db. These values suggest a marginally acceptable dynamic behaviour from the closed loop system incorporating this process, and this is

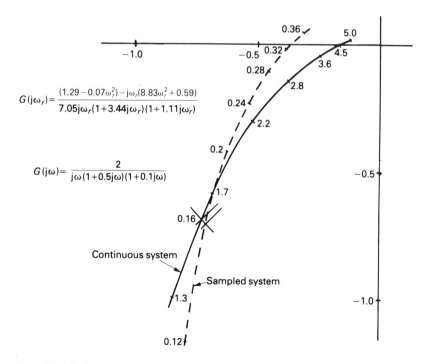

Fig. 10.16 Polar plots for continuous system and equivalent sampled system

confirmed from the step response shown in Fig. 10.17. By reducing the gain of Eq. 10.27 by a factor of 8.2 a phase margin of 45° and a gain margin of 9 db can be achieved. With these values, a step response for the closed loop sampled system should be very similar to that of the continuous system, and this is confirmed in Fig. 10.17.

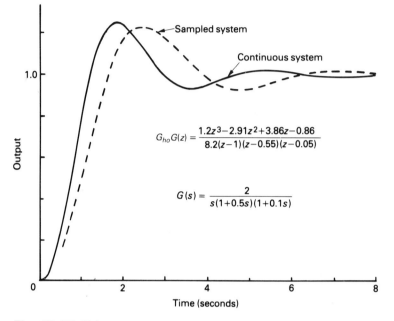

Fig. 10.17 Unit step responses

This result for an arbitrarily selected process demonstrates that the design rules used with the continuous-data system can be extended to the sampled-data system if the bilinear transformation is employed. Hence expertise gained with continuous-data systems can be used in design studies of sampled-data systems.

Similarly, the Bode diagram can be produced and used in the way outlined in Section 6.3 for the continuous-data system.

The pseudo-frequency ω_r can be transformed into the real frequency ω by using the mapping function of Eq. 10.23 and the transform definition $z = e^{sT}$

$$\text{i.e.} \quad j\omega_r = \frac{e^{j\omega T} - 1}{e^{j\omega T} + 1}$$

Using the exponential values of $\sin \theta$ and $\cos \theta$ yields

$$j \tan \theta = \frac{e^{j\theta} - e^{-j\theta}}{e^{j\theta} + e^{-j\theta}} = \frac{e^{j2\theta} - 1}{e^{j2\theta} + 1}$$

then by inspection

$$j\omega_r = j \tan \frac{\omega T}{2}$$

and hence

$$\omega = \frac{2}{T} \tan^{-1} \omega_r \qquad\qquad 10.28$$

11
Design of Closed Loop Systems

The engineer concerned with the design of a control loop will know from the project specifications the prime objectives which are to be attained, and the requirements for acceptable behaviour depend largely on the applications for which the system is to be designed. The aim of the earlier chapters of this book has been to impart an understanding of the nature of dynamic behaviour, to show the general advantages which can be gained by the use of feedback, and to describe some of the analytical techniques available to the design engineer. This final chapter is concerned with synthesis, where the requirement is one of determining what form of closed loop arrangement is necessary to yield a specific form of output response for a given input excitation.

The first section discusses in general terms the principal ways by which systems can be designed in order to achieve specific performance requirements. There are two aspects, that of choosing a form of controller within the loop, and that of determining suitable parameter values for the controller. Sections 11.2 to 11.4 describe the use of proportional, integral and derivative action; the effect of each is explained and guidance is given on the selection of controller settings. The following three sections describe how performance specifications can be achieved by the use of passive compensation networks. Section 11.8 outlines some other forms of control scheme for continuous systems. This is followed by a section to discuss the design of sampled-data systems and digital controllers, and a section to introduce the ideas of state vector feedback control. Section 11.11 describes relay control, a form of control action which is widely used because of its simplicity and hence low cost, and which introduces non-linearity into the feedback loop and thus requires techniques that extend the design methods described earlier. The chapter concludes with a case study illustrating the application to a specific system of the many techniques presented in this book. It describes, in outline, the derivation of a suitable mathematical model for the physical system, the analysis of the dynamic behaviour, and the design of appropriate compensation for the feedback loop.

11.1 The general approach to design

The requirements for a system will be described by some appropriate performance specification, expressed either as time domain requirements (defining the transient and steady state response for a step change or other forcing function) or as frequency domain requirements (phase margin, gain margin, bandwidth, peak magnification, etc.). Although there is no direct analytical relationship between the two sets of performance characteristics for systems of order higher than two there is a broad correspondence between them. A system designed with a value of $M_p = 1.3$ should have a relatively small rise time without large overshoot when subjected to a step input.

There are two basic approaches to design. The older, but still very widely used one is an orderly trial and observation intuitive approach aimed at finding an acceptable, but not necessarily the best possible, design solution. Based on past experience a control loop configuration and form of controller is chosen at the outset and one or more of the analytical techniques described earlier is used to try to determine controller parameters which allow the system to meet the specifications. If the chosen arrangement is not satisfactory then other forms of controller must be investigated. The more complex the controller the greater the number of parameters which can be varied. Previous experience helps in obtaining a satisfactory solution within a reasonable time and within the economic constraints that normally exist in a design project. The alternative approach is one of true synthesis, where an attempt is made to determine a unique solution in accord with a rigidly defined specification in some optimal way. To aim to achieve this is attractive in principle, but it requires a sound knowledge of the analytical methods of modern control theory. Also, the cost of the equipment necessary to implement the resulting control law may prove to be difficult to justify economically, on the grounds of dynamic performance alone.

The simplest and most widely used arrangement is *series compensation* where the controller or compensation device is positioned in the forward loop as shown in Fig. 11.1a. *Parallel* or *feedback compensation* by means of a

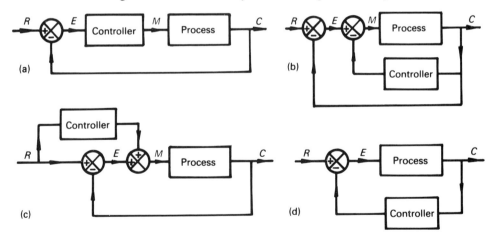

Fig. 11.1 Control loop configurations (a) series or cascade compensation (b) feedback compensation (c) feedforward compensation (d) state feedback control

subsidiary feedback loop (Fig. 11.1b) offers certain advantages; it may also be used in conjunction with series compensation. The next section collects together ideas presented earlier for studying the response of a closed loop system where the loop gain can be adjusted but where otherwise the dynamic characteristics are fixed. Such an arrangement with a series controller which is simply a gain element gives what is termed *proportional control action*. Where no suitable value of gain can be found to achieve the specification, additional loop elements are needed. Section 11.3 looks at the use of *integral action* and *derivative action,* and describes how these modify the response and how the coefficients in the resulting 2-term or 3-term controller may be chosen. Section 11.4 considers the practical side of control by introducing empirical methods used by engineers for selecting the correct amount of control action necessary to achieve a required performance on existing plant. The topic of *system compensation* is then discussed; this is a procedure whereby additional electrical networks or mechanical elements are incorporated within the loop to modify the system behaviour in such a way that it more nearly satisfies the required specification. As an example to illustrate the general features of system compensation, Section 11.6 considers in some detail one of these additional control actions, phase lead series compensation, and the next section discusses some of the differing characteristics of other compensation methods.

The steady state accuracy requirement dictates the form of open loop transfer function and the value of loop gain needed, as described in Section 8.2. Design in the time domain to achieve specific transient response characteristics is facilitated by studies of root locus plots for the system. The aim is to select physically achievable numerical values for the system parameters in such a way that the system poles are placed in suitable regions of the *s*-plane. The dominant poles are the most critical, and considerations of settling time and maximum overshoot in response to a step change dictate the area which should give acceptable behaviour as indicated in Fig. 11.2. The response is, however, influenced both by secondary poles and by any system zeros which are present, and hence root locus studies must be supplemented by simulation studies to confirm that the specifications are satisfied.

Where performance specifications are given as frequency domain characteristics design will employ the analytical methods of Chapter 6. Although they are largely trial and error methods and the earliest ones devised these remain important since they have a number of advantages. They are easy to understand and to apply, they are independent of the order of the system transfer function, and indeed do not require the mathematical model to be known in transfer function form since experimentally obtained harmonic response data is equally acceptable. The Bode diagram is the most useful, with the Nichols chart being used to relate open loop and closed loop data when the system is a simple unity feedback system.

11.2 Proportional control

Consider the control of the output of a process with transfer function $G(s)$ which utilizes feedback principles, and assume that the process characteristics cannot be altered by the designer (for example the speed regulating system shown in Fig. 9.2a). The simplest form of control is one in which the error signal $e(t)$ is multiplied by a constant k_1 to yield a signal called the *manipulated variable* $m(t)$ which is the input to the process; the numerical value of this constant k_1 determines the amount of corrective effort which is applied for a

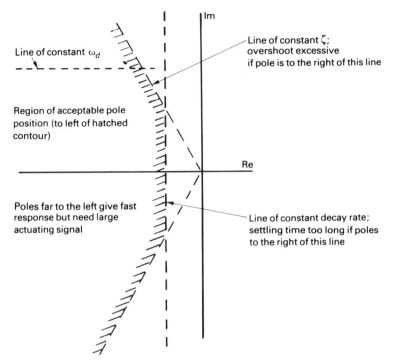

Fig. 11.2 Acceptable region for dominant roots

given magnitude of error. This arrangement is called *proportional control*, and by varying the value of k_1, the dynamic behaviour of the overall system can be altered. For very low values of k_1 the corrective effort is small, and hence the response is likely to be sluggish (Fig. 9.2c); as k_1 increases the response of the system for the same magnitude of error becomes more rapid and, if k_1 is very large, instability is likely to result, or the oscillatory response would be so lightly damped that it would be unsatisfactory for all practical purposes. The significant variable is actually the loop gain K_p, which is the product of k_1 and the steady state gain of the process.

If $G(s)$ has no poles at the origin of the complex s-plane, then the overall system will always have a steady state positional error. This error, as shown in Section 8.2, is proportional to $\dfrac{1}{1 + K_p}$, hence it can be reduced by increasing the loop gain K_p, and can be evaluated by application of the final value theorem for a constant input excitation. Increase in loop gain, however, causes the dominant complex roots (Fig. 9.2b) to move closer to the imaginary axis and to the instability associated with root positions in the right half of the complex s-plane. Provided a value of loop gain K_p can be chosen which gives both an acceptable transient response and a small enough steady state error then the design problem is solved. If these requirements cannot be satisfied simultaneously then the loop must be modified by the inclusion of some other form of control action, of a compensation network, or of a subsidiary feedback loop. If, however, $G(s)$ does have a pole at the origin (a factor s in the denominator) or if additional control action is included to introduce a pole at the origin of the root locus diagram, this reduces the positional error to zero and reduces the velocity error to a value which is inversely proportional to the loop gain. Similarly, a double pole at the origin would yield a positional error and a velocity error which are both zero, and an acceleration error which is inversely proportional to loop gain (Section 8.2).

Example 11.1. For the feedback system shown in Fig. 9.2a, can a suitable value of loop gain be found?

At the limit of stability, the positional error is at the lowest value that it can attain, namely $\dfrac{1}{1 + 315/25} = 0.073$, 7%; this is at the limit of what would be acceptable for a simple speed regulating system. A value of $K_p = 35$ gives a suitable transient response with damping factor $\zeta = 0.64$ for the dominant roots; however, the steady state error is excessive at a value of 42%. For this simple speed control system the design engineer would have to think seriously about the introduction of additional control action.

11.3 Integral and derivative action

(a) *Integral action.* A prime requirement of many control systems is that there should be no error or at worst a very small error in the steady state. It was shown in Section 8.2 that for a type 0 system, one with no factors of s in the denominator of the transfer function, a steady state error always exists for a steady input. This error can be decreased at the expense of a more oscillatory response by an increase in gain, but it may not be possible to attain simultaneously satisfactory steady state and dynamic behaviour (as discussed in Section 11.2). Zero steady state positional error would require the system to be of Type 1, and this can be achieved by introducing integral action within the controller. To the proportional term is added a signal proportional to the time integral of the error; i.e. the controller output $m(t)$ is $[k_1 e(t) + k_2 \int e(t) \, dt]$ and it is this signal which actuates the system. The block diagram is then of the form shown in Fig. 11.3. Since the error signal is integrated within the control-

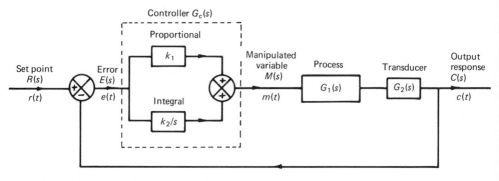

Fig. 11.3 Feedback system with P + I control action

ler, even the smallest error eventually produces a corrective signal of sufficient magnitude to actuate the system to eliminate the error. The system will, theoretically, only come to rest when the error has been reduced to zero.

Consider analytically the effect of integral action on the system of Fig. 11.3 when the process and measuring transducer have transfer function

$$G_1(s)G_2(s) = \frac{1}{(s^2 + 4s + 8)(1 + s)}.$$

With proportional control ($k_2 = 0$) the closed loop transfer function is

$$\frac{C(s)}{R(s)} = \frac{k_1}{s^3 + 5s^2 + 12s + 8 + k_1} \qquad 11.1$$

Hence the steady state error for a unit input is

$$1 - \lim_{s \to 0} s\left[\frac{1}{s} \cdot \frac{k_1}{s^3 + 5s^2 + 12s + 8 + k_1}\right] = \frac{8}{8 + k_1}$$

With proportional plus integral (P + I) control

$$\frac{C(s)}{R(s)} = \frac{k_1 s + k_2}{s^4 + 5s^3 + 12s^2 + (8 + k_1)s + k_2} \qquad 11.2$$

and the steady state error for a unit input is

$$1 - \lim_{s \to 0} s\left[\frac{1}{s} \frac{k_1 s + k_2}{s^4 + 5s^3 + 12s^2 + (8 + k_1)s + k_2}\right] = 0$$

One method by which numerical values for the parameters k_1 and k_2 can be selected is by use of a root locus or root contour plot. If a performance index based on the transient response characteristics, such as rise time, initial overshoot, etc. as described in Section 4.4 is used, then the roots on the dominant loci must lie in some region such as that bounded by the lines drawn for a damping factor of $\zeta = 0.4$ and $\zeta = 0.5$ (corresponding to transient responses shown in Fig. 4.7). This is the hatched region shown in Fig. 11.4, the root contour plot for the system with P + I control. Inspection of this figure shows that values of $k_1 = 8$ and $k_2 = 11$ position the dominant roots in the centre of the hatched area; hence these values of k_1 and k_2 are likely to give the desired transient response. A simulation study would now be made to select better values for k_1 and k_2 that would more nearly give the response shown in Fig. 4.7 for $\zeta = 0.5$, since further adjustment of both these parameters may be necessary to make allowance for the effect of the secondary locus shown in Fig. 11.4 and for the zero in Eq. 11.2. Because of this zero, the root locus pattern cannot be used in isolation during a design study, but must be supplemented by simulation data. The transient response for the parameters given above is shown in Fig. 11.7b. With P + I, the response shown for this typical speed control system would in engineering practice normally be considered 'satisfactory', having a maximum overshoot of 23%, a rise time of 1.5 seconds, and a settling time of 6 seconds. For the process alone, the overshoot would be zero, and the rise time and settling time would each be around 3 to 4 seconds.

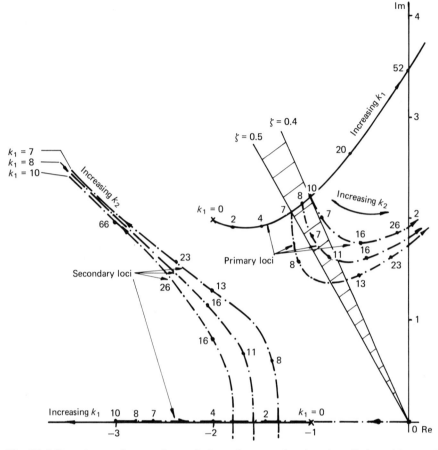

Fig. 11.4 Root locus diagram for variation of proportional action (k_1) and integral action (k_2). $G_1(s)G_2(s) = \dfrac{1}{(s^2 + 4s + 8)(s + 1)}$

(b) *Derivative action.* A form of control action which can increase the effective damping is *derivative action*; this is not used by itself but in conjunction with proportional or proportional plus integral action. To the normal error signal is added a signal proportional to its derivative, giving a 2-term or 3-term controller (Fig. 11.5). The 3-term controller has a transfer function $G_c(s) = (k_1 + k_2/s + k_3 s)$. Alternatively, this is often expressed as

$$G_c(s) = k_c\left(1 + \frac{1}{T_i s} + T_d s\right)$$

in which $k_1 = k_c$, $k_2 = k_c/T_i$ and $k_3 = k_c T_d$. The derivative term contributes an anticipatory type of control action, where the output of the controller is modified when the error is changing rapidly, thus anticipating a large overshoot and making some correction before it occurs. When a system is moving

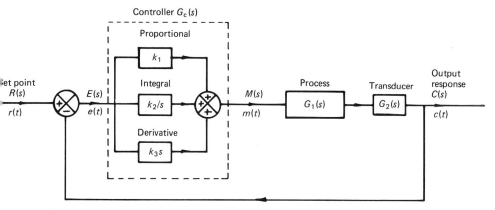

Fig. 11.5 Feedback system with P + I + D control action

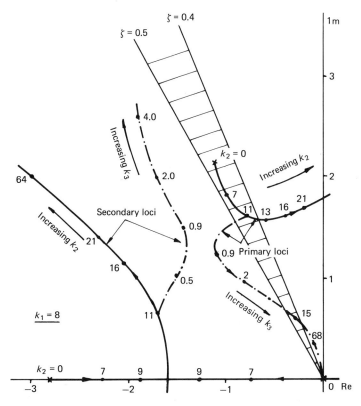

Fig. 11.6 Root locus diagram for variation of integral action (k_2) and derivative action (k_3). $G_1(s)G_2(s) = \dfrac{1}{(s^2 + 4s + 8)(s + 1)}$

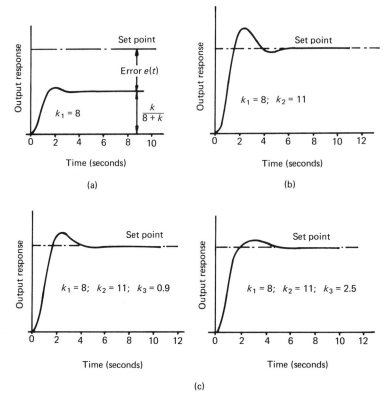

Fig. 11.7 Step responses for system shown in Fig. 11.3 and Fig. 11.5:

$$G_1(s)G_2(s) = \frac{1}{(s^2 + 4s + 8)(s + 1)}$$ (a) P controller (b) P + I controller (c) P + I + D controller

towards a state of zero error $e(t)$, Fig. 11.7b, then $e(t)$ and $\dot{e}(t)$ have opposite signs; hence the derivative term reduces the magnitude of $m(t)$ and thus reduces the signal that is accelerating the output response $c(t)$ towards the zero error state. When the output response has overshot or undershot and is moving away from the zero error condition, then $e(t)$ and $\dot{e}(t)$ have the same sign and the derivative term augments the decelerating signal. When the system comes to rest then $\dot{e}(t)$ is zero and the derivative term has no further influence.

The effect of derivative action on the position of the roots of the characteristic equation can be seen in Fig. 11.6, which shows that the addition of derivative action has as expected improved the relative stability of the system. This is always a highly desirable feature in the design of a control system, since any change in the values of plant parameters over a period of time is less likely to cause the system to drift into instability. The effect on the dynamic behaviour resulting from the additional closed loop zeros must, however, be investigated before any decision on the suitability of, or the need for, derivative action can be taken with confidence. Inspection of Fig. 11.6 suggests that a useful value for k_3 to reduce the overshoot, with minimum effect on the other dynamic characteristics, might be 0.9. However, a simulation study, Fig. 11.7c, indicates that $k_3 = 2.5$ would be a better choice. This required change in the value of k_3 is the direct result of the presence of the closed loop zeros. The poles alone dictate the stability boundary, but both the poles and zeros contribute to the dynamic behaviour of the closed loop system.

(c) *Rate feedback or negative velocity feedback.* To avoid mechanical failure or system malfunctioning, it is essential in all engineering situations to safeguard against the occurrence of large initial transient overshoots. The suppression of these overshoots must not, in general, be at the expense of the system accuracy; therefore it becomes necessary in most designs to introduce additional control action to prevent this. An action similar to that of proportional plus derivative control can be achieved by incorporating within the control loop a minor feedback path which introduces control action known as *velocity feedback*. The block diagram, with velocity feedback included, is then as shown in Fig. 11.8, from which it can be seen that a signal proportional to the derivative of the output rather than the derivative of the error signal is used. The numerical value of these two derivatives will be the same for all unity feedback systems except when adjustment is being made to the set point $r(t)$. The change in the closed loop transfer function can be seen from the following two equations:

$$\frac{C(s)}{R(s)} = \frac{k_1 + k_3 s}{s^3 + 5s^2 + (12 + k_3)s + (8 + k_1)} \qquad 11.3$$

for the system considered earlier with proportional plus derivative control, and

$$\frac{C(s)}{R(s)} = \frac{k_1}{s^3 + 5s^2 + (12 + k_4)s + (8 + k_1)} \qquad 11.4$$

for the system incorporating negative velocity feedback. In practice, Eq. 11.3 would be modified as a result of a small additional time constant associated with the differentiation, necessary to avoid problems of noise amplification and of saturation with step changes of error. Fig. 11.9 shows that the use of

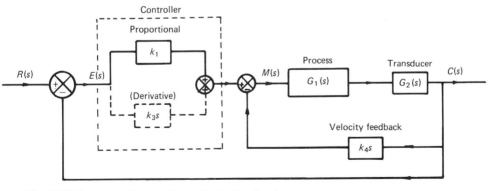

Fig. 11.8 System with negative velocity feedback

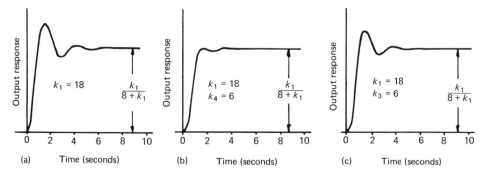

Fig. 11.9 Step responses for change in control action:

$$G_1(s)G_2(s) = \frac{1}{(s^2 + 4s + 8)(s + 1)}$$ (a) P controller (b) P controller and negative velocity
feedback (c) P + D controller

negative velocity feedback instead of derivative action can give a smaller initial overshoot but would do so at the expense of an increase in rise time.

Velocity feedback is chiefly of advantage for servomechanisms in which the output velocity can be measured directly by a tachogenerator or velocity transducer, thus avoiding the problem of noise amplification that can arise when trying to differentiate an error signal. It is always good engineering practice to avoid the use of differentiation, if at all possible, when choosing the type of control action to be incorporated in a design.

11.4 Selecting controller settings on existing process plant

As a result of empirical tests on a wide variety of process plant, Ziegler and Nichols (see Ref. 1, p. 278) propose a simple rule of thumb procedure for estimating the values of controller settings k_1, k_2, and k_3 for existing operating plant in order to achieve an optimum transient response. There are two methods, one based on the step response of the open loop system and the other based on information obtained at the stability limit of the process under proportional control.

In the first method, with the loop opened, the plant is subjected to a step change of manipulated variable and the resulting output response curve is characterized by two measured parameters N and L, shown in Fig. 11.10. N is the maximum slope of the curve for a change M of manipulated variable, and L is the time at which the line of maximum slope intersects the time axis. The recommendations which Ziegler and Nichols put forward for the controller settings are:

$$k_c = \frac{M}{NL} \text{ for P control}$$

$$k_c = 0.9 \frac{M}{NL}, \ T_i = 3.3L \text{ for P + I control}$$

$$k_c = 1.2 \frac{M}{NL}, \ T_i = 2L, \ T_d = 0.5L \text{ for P + I + D control}$$

11.5

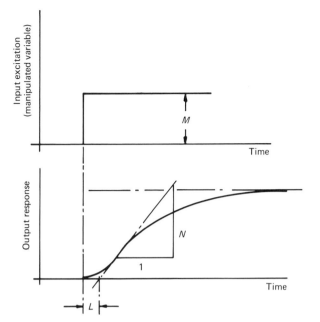

Fig. 11.10 Open loop response parameters for Ziegler–Nichols first method

where k_c, T_i, and T_d are the parameter values of controller gain, integral action time and derivative action time respectively, as they appear in the control law

$$G_c(s) = k_c\left(1 + \frac{1}{T_i s} + T_d s\right)$$ 11.6

The procedure of the second method is to determine experimentally the limiting condition of stability of the closed loop system under proportional control only, and to use the resulting information to calculate controller settings. If the limiting value of gain for stability is k_{crit} and the time period of oscillation is P_{crit}, Fig. 11.11, then the Ziegler–Nichols recommended controller settings are:

$k_c = 0.5\, k_{crit}$ for P control
$k_c = 0.45\, k_{crit}$, $T_i = 0.83\, P_{crit}$ for P + I control
$k_c = 0.6\, k_{crit}$, $T_i = 0.5\, P_{crit}$, $T_d = 0.125\, P_{crit}$ for P + I + D control 11.7

Other workers (see Ref. 2, p. 278) have extended these ideas to show how the commonly used analogue controllers can be replaced by their digital equivalents, and how the analogue settings of Ziegler–Nichols and others can be translated into settings for digital controllers, to achieve satisfactory loop tuning. Most controller manufacturers also provide more specific instruction for the adjustment of their instruments based on these ideas. The settings obtained using these instructions, however, only give a good first estimate and

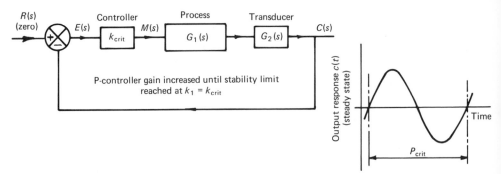

Fig. 11.11 Oscillatory response parameters for Ziegler–Nichols second method

further adjustment is still necessary to meet the control requirements of specific plant.

11.5 System compensation

Most feedback systems are required simultaneously to match performance specifications both for steady state accuracy and for relative stability. The former requires that the steady state error with a given type of input excitation should not exceed some specified value, and this defines a certain minimum value of loop gain, say K_1. To ensure that the system has adequate relative stability, it must have a specified minimum value of phase margin or gain margin, or a specified maximum value of M_p, and this defines a certain maximum value of loop gain, say K_2. If $K_1 > K_2$, then the two requirements are not compatible, and the specifications cannot both be satisfied unless some form of *phase compensation* is introduced.

The way in which the addition of compensating networks can result in compatibility can be illustrated by considering the Nyquist diagram, Fig. 11.12. The general objective is one of reshaping the open loop harmonic response plot so that the low frequency gain is high enough and, in addition, the plot avoids the critical $(-1, \mathrm{j}0)$ point with an adequate safety margin. The locus can be reshaped in the manner shown by

   (i) starting with gain K_1 for the system and introducing phase lead at high frequencies in order to attain the specified phase margin, gain margin, or M_p (*phase lead compensation*), or

  (ii) starting with gain K_2 for the system and introducing phase lag at low frequencies to meet steady state accuracy requirements (*phase lag compensation*) or

 (iii) starting with a gain between K_1 and K_2 and introducing some phase lead at high frequencies and some phase lag at low frequencies (*lag-lead compensation*).

The design task of determining the transfer function required for a suitable compensating network can be carried out in the time domain or in the frequency domain using one or more of the techniques of analysis described in

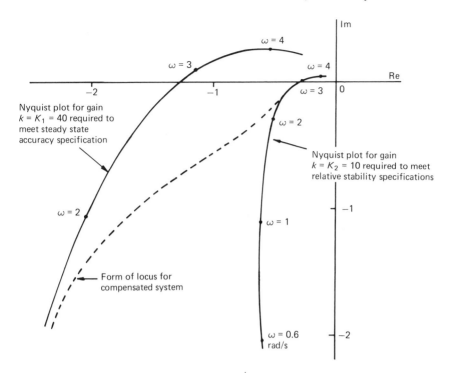

Fig. 11.12 Nyquist diagram for $G(s) = \dfrac{k}{s(s^2 + 4s + 8)}$ illustrating principle of compensation

earlier chapters. Design by means of the Bode plot is particularly useful because of the ease with which the effect of compensation can be evaluated by noting the improvement to stability margins resulting from the addition of magnitude and phase curves for the compensating network being investigated. The design procedures are orderly graphical trial and error procedures, and although this approach is among the earliest of design techniques it is probably still the best for systems with one or two feedback loops. The time domain characteristics are not directly apparent from the Bode plot but are related in a general way to the shape of the plot in the vicinity of the critical 0 dB, -180 degree point. Although a phase margin of 45°, with a gain margin of around 6 to 8 dB, provides no guarantee that the transient behaviour will be acceptable, conditions are not often encountered where it is not. The procedure is usually to establish a tentative design with the aid of a Bode plot, then to simulate the resulting system and, by trial and observation, make adjustments if necessary to achieve an appropriate transient response based on rise time, initial overshoot, etc. The design technique gives no clear guidance at the outset as to which type of compensation would be the best for any given system; hence the designer must use past experience to decide on a method, try it, and if no satisfactory design emerges try another.

11.6 Phase lead series compensation

This section outlines the general features of phase lead series compensation in order to illustrate the procedure of designing a compensation network. The approach with phase lag, lag-lead, or parallel compensation is broadly similar, although the details vary. The phase lead is provided by a compensating device which has a transfer function

$$G_c(s) = \frac{1}{\alpha} \frac{1 + \alpha Ts}{1 + Ts}, \quad \text{where } \alpha > 1.$$

It should be noted that with a passive device the phase lead provided by the zero at $-1/\alpha T$ cannot be obtained without including in addition a pole at $-1/T$. Inherent also is the attenuation $1/\alpha$; hence, when used for compensation, additional amplification is needed to restore the loop gain to the required value.

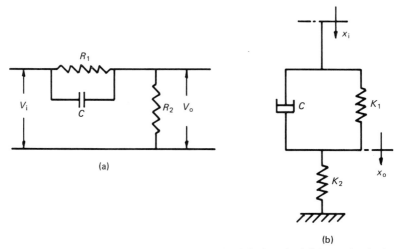

(a)

(b)

Fig. 11.13 Phase lead compensation networks. (a) electrical (b) mechanical

Such a transfer function is valid for the electrical circuit of Fig. 11.13a. That this is so with $\alpha = \dfrac{R_1 + R_2}{2}$, $T = \dfrac{R_1 R_2 C}{R_1 + R_2}$, can be shown by the analytical methods of Chapter 2, provided assumptions are made that any input impedance presented to the circuit will be small, and that the circuit will always be connected to a high impedance output, thus maintaining the input–output properties of an open circuit. The mechanical arrangement sketched in Fig. 11.13b can be shown to be analogous, with $\alpha = (K_1 + K_2)/K_2$, and $T = C/(K_1 + K_2)$. The amount of phase lead, and the frequency band where it is effective, can be selected by appropriate choice of circuit components to obtain the required values of α and T.

What are the characteristics of such a phase lead arrangement? In the s-plane a pole and a zero are introduced on the negative real axis with the zero lying closer to the imaginary axis than the pole (Fig. 11.14a); the position and spacing of the roots is determined by the numerical values of α and T. The effect on a root locus diagram of introducing such a pair of roots, with the zero dominant, is to pull the dominant loci towards the left of the diagram and, as a consequence, improve the relative stability of the system. The extent to which the dominant loci are moved to the left of the diagram will be dictated by the values of α and T chosen at the design stage. On the polar plot, the locus of the unity gain function $\dfrac{1 + j\omega\alpha T}{1 + j\omega T}$ can readily be shown to be a semicircle in the 4th quadrant with a magnitude of 1 at low frequencies, rising to a maximum value of α at high frequencies (Fig. 11.14b). The phase is a lead which increases with increase of frequency from zero to a maximum value determined by the chosen value of α, and then reduces to zero again as the frequency approaches infinity. The tangent drawn to this semicircle from the origin determines the maximum phase lead φ_m that is obtainable, and the frequency ω_m at which it occurs. The angle φ_m increases with increase of α, and tends towards a maximum lead of $90°$ as α approaches infinity. On the Bode plot (Fig. 11.14c), the lead term has a break point at $\omega = 1/\alpha T$ and thus starts to influence the response at about one tenth of this frequency; as frequency increases the effect of the lead term grows but is gradually opposed by the lag term which has its break point at $\omega = 1/T$. As a consequence of symmetry of the phase plot, the frequency ω_m at which the maximum phase lead occurs lies midway between the corner frequencies on the logarithmically scaled frequency axis, hence

$$\log_{10} \omega_m = \tfrac{1}{2}\left(\log_{10} \frac{1}{\alpha T} + \log_{10} \frac{1}{T}\right)$$

or

$$\omega_m = \frac{1}{T\sqrt{\alpha}}$$

The maximum value of phase lead is given by

$$\varphi_m = \tan^{-1} \omega_m \alpha T - \tan^{-1} \omega_m T$$

$$\therefore \quad \tan \varphi_m = \frac{\omega_m \alpha T - \omega_m T}{1 + (\omega_m \alpha T)(\omega_m T)}$$

Substituting

$$\omega_m = \frac{1}{T\sqrt{\alpha}},$$

yields

$$\tan \varphi_m = \frac{\alpha - 1}{2\sqrt{\alpha}}$$

or more conveniently

$$\sin \varphi_m = \frac{\alpha - 1}{\alpha + 1} \qquad 11.8$$

This equation is used to calculate the value of α needed to provide any specific value of phase lead φ_m.

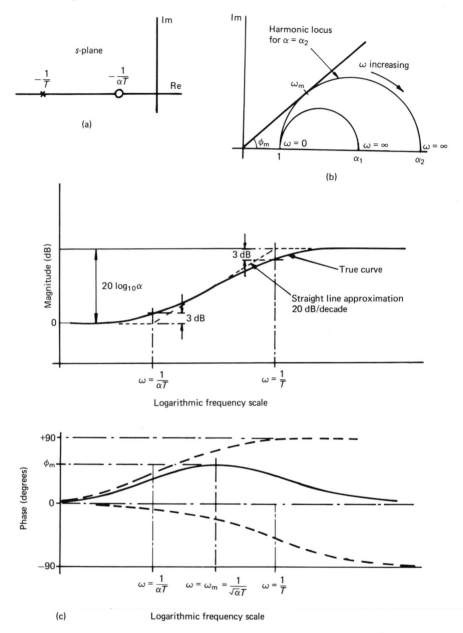

Logarithmic frequency scale

Fig. 11.14 Characteristics of phase lead network $\dfrac{1 + aTs}{1 + Ts}$, $a > 1$ (a) root locus (b) polar plot (c) Bode plot

The design procedure using the Bode diagram is as follows:

1. Plot the Bode diagram for the uncompensated system with the gain chosen to achieve the steady state error requirements.

2. Read from the plot the phase margin, and estimate the phase lead required to give acceptable system response. To make allowance for the increase in gain crossover frequency, caused by the magnitude contribution of the compensation network, approximately 5 degrees should be added to determine a trial design value for φ_m. Calculate the required value of α using Eq. 11.8.

3. To ensure that φ_m is located at the new gain crossover frequency, calculate the high frequency magnification of the function $\dfrac{1 + j\omega\alpha T}{1 + j\omega T}$, find the frequency at which the uncompensated system has an attenuation of half this value, and make ω_m equal to that frequency. Hence $T = \dfrac{1}{\omega_m \sqrt{\alpha}}$, and the break points for the compensation network are at frequencies $\omega_m/\sqrt{\alpha}$ and $\omega_m \sqrt{\alpha}$.

4. Increase the gain by a factor α, to correct for the attenuation inherent in a practical compensation network, and draw the Bode diagram for the compensated system.

5. Check that the required performance specifications are satisfied and, if not, select a larger value of φ_m and repeat the procedure.

Example 11.2. A unity feedback system with open loop transfer function $\dfrac{K}{(1 + 10s)(1 + s)}$ is required to have a phase margin of at least 45 degrees and a steady state positional error which does not exceed 1%. Determine the required value of K and, if the performance specifications cannot be satisfied by appropriate choice of K, design suitable phase lead series compensation for the loop.

The value of K must be chosen to satisfy the steady state error requirements. For a unit step input the steady state error is given by

$$e_{ss} = 0.01 = \lim_{s \to 0} sE(s) = \lim_{s \to 0} \left[\frac{1}{1 + \dfrac{K}{(1 + 10s)(1 + s)}} \right]$$

$$\therefore \quad K = 100, \text{ say.}$$

The Bode diagram for the uncompensated system is drawn by summing the contributions to magnitude and phase of the gain term, and of the two simple lag terms which have break points at frequencies of 0.1 and 1 rad/second:

Magnitude (dB) $= 20 \log_{10} 100 - 20 \log_{10} \sqrt{(1 + (10\omega)^2)} - 20 \log_{10} \sqrt{(1 + \omega^2)}$

Phase $= -\tan^{-1} 10\omega - \tan^{-1} \omega$.

From the Bode diagram (Fig. 11.15) the phase margin is measured to be 19°; hence at least 26° of phase lead is required. To make some allowance for phase

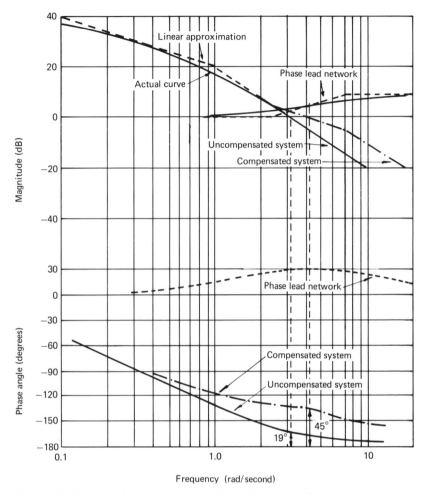

Fig. 11.15 Phase lead compensation—Bode diagram for Example 11.2

reduction resulting from increase of the gain crossover frequency, choose a trial value of $\varphi_m = 30°$. Applying Eq. 11.8:

$$\sin 30° = \frac{\alpha - 1}{\alpha + 1} = 0.5$$

$$\therefore \quad \alpha = 3$$

The transfer function of the phase lead network is therefore

$$G_c(s) = \frac{1}{3} \frac{1 + 3Ts}{1 + Ts}$$

and the value of T must now be determined to ensure that the phase lead of $30°$ is effective at the new gain crossover frequency. At high frequencies, the magnitude of the transfer function $\dfrac{1 + 3Ts}{1 + Ts}$ is

$$20 \log_{10} 3 = 9.6 \text{ dB.}$$

To ensure that φ_m is effective at the new gain crossover frequency, place ω_m at the frequency where the uncompensated system magnitude is $-0.5 \ (9.6) = -4.8$ dB. From Fig. 11.15 this is seen to give $\omega_m = 4.2$ rad/second. Hence the corner frequencies for the compensation network are

$$\frac{1}{\alpha T} = \frac{\omega_m}{\sqrt{3}} = 2.4 \text{ rad/second, and } \frac{1}{T} = \omega_m \sqrt{3} = 7.3 \text{ rad/second}$$

Hence the transfer functions for the compensation network and the system are respectively

$$G_c(s) = \frac{1}{3} \frac{1 + 0.42s}{1 + 0.14s} \text{ and } G(s) = \frac{300}{(1 + 10s)(1 + s)}$$

Addition of the magnitude and phase curves for the compensation network and the uncompensated system in Fig. 11.15 confirms that this compensation network increases the phase margin to $45°$, which is the value required. The gain margin is infinite since the system is of second order.

The improvement to the transient behaviour resulting from compensation can be seen in the step response traces of Fig. 11.16.

This example illustrates that phase lead compensation generally improves the rise time and reduces the amplitude of transient oscillations, but increases the bandwidth, and so may introduce undesirable effects resulting from noise transmission through the system. The compensation network acts as a high pass filter. Much noise is, however, usually suppressed due to the low pass characteristics of most physical systems. It should be noted that by no means all systems can be satisfactorily compensated by means of a phase lead network. A common situation in which the design method fails is where the transfer function of the uncompensated system is of a form which causes the phase lag to increase rapidly near the gain crossover frequency; any phase lead added is then nullified to a large extent by the marked decrease in phase of the uncompensated system at the new gain crossover frequency. The designer may also be constrained by the physical nature of components to be used, or limited by factors such as cost, weight, and space. It may not be possible, because of engineering difficulties, to achieve the large gain required to meet the steady state accuracy specification. Phase lead compensation is not advisable where the system gain must be so high that the uncompensated system is badly unstable.

11.7 Phase lag, and lag-lead series compensation

A phase lag compensation element has the transfer function

$$G_c(s) = \frac{1 + \alpha Ts}{1 + Ts}, \quad \text{where } \alpha < 1$$

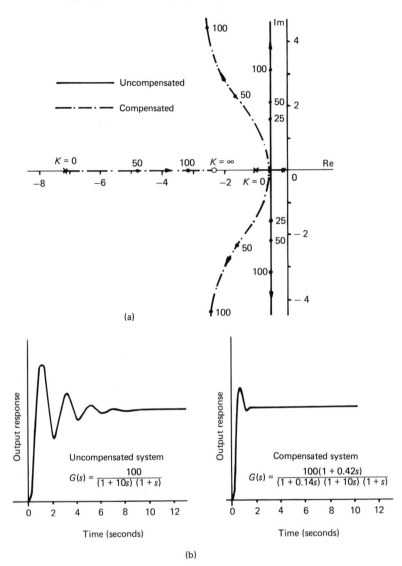

Fig. 11.16 Effect of phase lead compensation (a) root locus diagram (b) step responses

This can be realized by the passive electrical network of Fig. 11.17a provided that the input impedance is small and the output impedance is large; $\alpha = R_2/(R_1 + R_2)$, which is less than unity, and $T = C(R_1 + R_2)$. A spring and damper arrangement as in Fig. 11.17b is equivalent, with $\alpha = K_1/(K_1 + K_2)$ and $T = C_2(K_1 + K_2)/K_1 K_2$. At low frequencies the phase lag element has unity gain and at high frequencies there is an attenuation α. Introduction of such an element adds a real pole and a real zero in the s-plane, the pole being dominant and their position and spacing being determined by the numerical

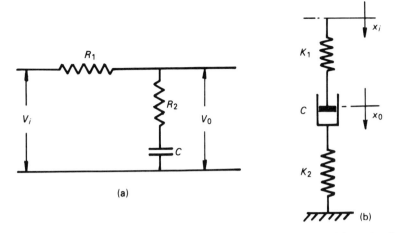

Fig. 11.17 Phase lag compensation networks (a) electrical (b) mechanical

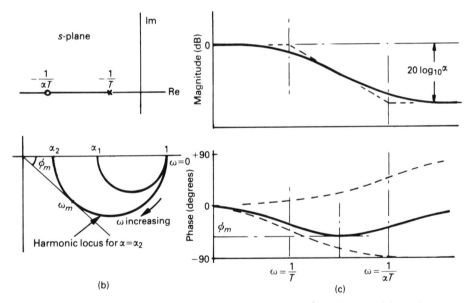

Fig. 11.18 Characteristics of phase lag network $1 + \alpha Ts/1 + Ts$, $\alpha < 1$ (a) root locus plot (b) polar plot (c) Bode plot

values of α and T. The dominant loci of the root locus plot are pushed towards the right, but the values of K for the compensated system are lower giving improved relative stability. The characteristics of a phase lag element, shown in Fig. 11.18, are the inverse of those for a phase lead element. Design of phase lag compensation does not rely on the phase shift of the network, rather it utilizes the characteristic of attenuation at high frequencies.

As with phase lead compensation the starting point in the design process is the uncompensated system with the value of the steady state gain chosen to meet the steady state error requirements. The phase curve of the Bode plot in the region of the gain crossover frequency is kept relatively unchanged and the magnitude is decreased in this region (and at higher frequencies) by means of the lag network so that the gain crossover frequency decreases to give an improved phase margin. (This contrasts with phase lead compensation where the magnitude curve is kept relatively unchanged in the region of the gain crossover frequency and phase lead is introduced to increase the phase margin, making due allowance for the effect on phase margin of the accompanying increase in gain crossover frequency). The design procedure using the Bode diagram is as follows:

1. Plot the Bode diagram for the uncompensated system with the gain chosen to achieve the steady state error requirements.
2. Find the frequency ω_c corresponding to the desired phase margin plus about 5°. The magnitude plot must be altered so that it passes through 0 dB near this frequency. Measure the amplitude G_c of the uncompensated system at this frequency ω_c. The phase lag network must provide an attenuation of G_c.
3. Calculate the value of α to provide this attenuation from the relationship $G_c = -20 \log_{10} \alpha$ dB. Select T so that the phase lag effect is well below ω_c, say $1/\alpha T = 0.1\ \omega_c$, in which case the phase lag introduced by the network at the gain crossover frequency is about 5°, which has already been allowed for in step 2.
4. From the plots for the uncompensated system and the compensation network with α and T chosen in step 3 draw the Bode plot for the compensated system.
5. Check that the required performance specifications are satisfied and if not adjust the selected values to try to attain them.

Example 11.3. A unity feedback system with open loop transfer function $\dfrac{K}{(1 + 10s)(1 + s)(1 + 0.5s)}$ is required to have a phase margin of at least 45° and a steady state positional error which does not exceed 1%. Determine the required value of K and design suitable phase compensation for the loop. (Note that this is the system of Example 11.2 with one additional time constant of 0.5 seconds).

The value of K must be chosen to satisfy the steady state requirements, and remains identical to that for Example 11.2, i.e. $K = 100$. The Bode diagram for the uncompensated system is drawn, as in the previous example, by summing the contributions to the magnitude and phase of the constituent factors of the transfer function:

$$\text{Magnitude (dB)} = 20 \log_{10} 100 - 20 \log_{10} \sqrt{(1 + (10\omega)^2)}$$
$$- 20 \log_{10} \sqrt{(1 + \omega^2)} - 20 \log_{10} \sqrt{(1 + (0.5\omega)^2)}$$
$$\text{Phase} = -\tan^{-1}(10\omega) - \tan^{-1}\omega - \tan^{-1}(0.5\omega)$$

The magnitude and phase can be easily calculated with the aid of a hand calculator. The gain margin and phase margin are both negative (-9 dB and $-23°$, Fig. 11.19) indicating that the uncompensated system with the gain set to achieve the required steady state error is unstable. It can readily be shown by applying the Routh–Hurwitz criterion that the limiting value of K before instability occurs is 34.65.

Phase lead compensation is unlikely to succeed in meeting the stability requirements since the phase in the region of the gain crossover frequency is decreasing rapidly with increase in frequency.

Investigate therefore the benefits of phase lag compensation. The phase is $(180° - 50°) = 130°$ for the frequency $\omega_c = 0.62$ rad/second. The magnitude at this frequency is found from the plot to be 22 dB.

$$\therefore \quad 20 \log_{10} \alpha = -22 \quad \therefore \quad \alpha = 0.08$$

$$\text{also} \quad \frac{1}{\alpha T} = 0.1 \, (0.62) \quad \therefore \quad T = 202 \text{ seconds}$$

A suitable phase lag compensation network should therefore be

$$G_c(s) = \frac{1 + 16s}{1 + 202s}$$

which has magnitude and phase characteristics as shown in Fig. 11.19. Addition of these and the plots for the uncompensated system gives a plot for the

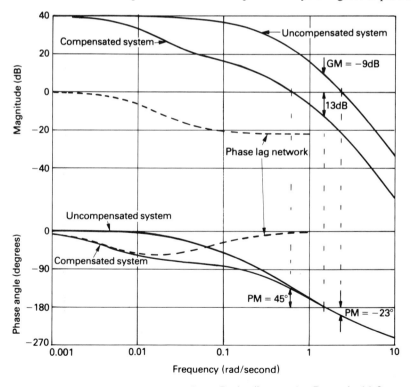

Fig. 11.19 Phase lag compensation—Bode diagram for Example 11.3

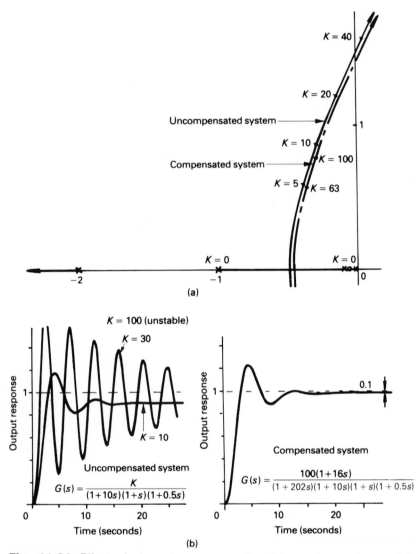

Fig. 11.20 Effect of phase lag compensation (a) root locus diagram (b) step response curves

compensated system, and from this the phase margin is found to be 45° as required and the gain margin is now 13 dB.

The resulting step response can be seen in Fig. 11.20b. The change to the root locus diagram, and to the position of the roots can be seen in Fig. 11.20a—the dominant complex roots are brought from the right half of the s-plane to a position corresponding to $\zeta = 0.36$ and $\omega_n = 0.82$ rad/second at the expense of introducing a real root close to the origin, which makes the response sluggish.

By replotting the harmonic response characteristics on a Nichols chart one can find the closed loop characteristics to be $M_p = 1.4$, $\omega_p = 0.7$ rad/second and bandwidth $= 1.1$ rad/second.

Study of the root locus plot suggests how this may be used for the design of phase lag compensation. Establish on the root locus for the uncompensated system a desirable root position, compare the value of K there with that required to satisfy steady state requirements, and call the ratio α. Choose $1/\alpha T$ to be one order of magnitude at least smaller than the smallest pole of the uncompensated system; the exact location of the additional pole and zero is not critical, only the distance between them.

This study illustrates that phase lag compensation improves the relative stability and reduces overshoot but usually at the expense of a longer rise time since the values of ω_p and bandwidth are decreased. This contrasts with phase lead compensation where the bandwidth is increased thus improving rise time, and perhaps giving problems of noise transmission. Each method has advantages and disadvantages, and where a system cannot be designed to satisfy several requirements simultaneously by using one or the other the desired performance may be attainable by using the two together to gain advantages from each one. This is referred to as *lag-lead compensation*, and can be achieved either by use of separate lag and lead circuits in series, with a buffer amplifier between, or by the use of the single circuit of Fig. 11.21.

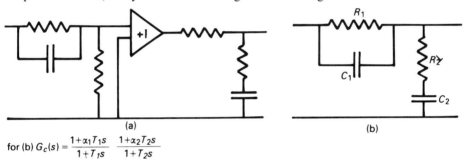

$$\text{for (b) } G_c(s) = \frac{1+\alpha_1 T_1 s}{1+T_1 s}\ \frac{1+\alpha_2 T_2 s}{1+T_2 s}$$

where $\alpha_1 T_1 = R_1 C_1$, $\alpha_2 T_2 = R_2 C_2$ and $\alpha_1 \alpha_2 = 1$

Fig. 11.21 Lag-lead compensation networks

11.8 Pole cancellation and feedforward compensation

Where the dominant roots of a system comprise a pair of complex conjugate poles which are close to the imaginary axis the behaviour will be excessively oscillatory and the amount of improvement available by phase compensation methods is limited. A technique which can sometimes be used is that of *pole cancellation*. In principle the aim is to introduce a compensation network with zeros which cancel the system poles, together with poles which are positioned more suitably in the s-plane. Figure 11.22 shows two compensation networks

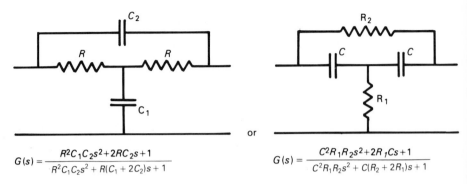

$$G(s) = \frac{R^2 C_1 C_2 s^2 + 2RC_2 s + 1}{R^2 C_1 C_2 s^2 + R(C_1 + 2C_2)s + 1}$$

or

$$G(s) = \frac{C^2 R_1 R_2 s^2 + 2R_1 C s + 1}{C^2 R_1 R_2 s^2 + C(R_2 + 2R_1)s + 1}$$

Fig. 11.22 Compensation networks for pole cancellation

referred to as 'bridged T networks' which can be used for this purpose. Cancellation can seldom be exact since the system poles will not usually be known exactly due to practical limitations in modelling and due to slow changes of system parameters with time. The effect of inexact cancellation is that a pair of roots remains near to the system poles, but the effect is small since the coefficient associated with the roots has a small numerical value.

A different design approach which may be useful if the expected unwanted disturbances are known to act at a specific point in the system is by using *feedforward compensation* in conjunction with the feedback loop (Fig. 11.1c). The disturbance signal is monitored and a control signal derived to cancel out much of the disturbance before it affects the system. The computation of the control action needed requires that a model of the system is available. The more

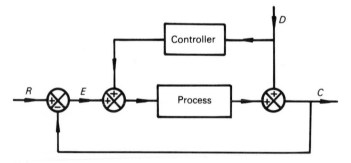

Fig. 11.23 Additional example of feedforward control

closely the disturbance can be monitored and the more accurate the system model, the better will be the control. The arrangement of Fig. 11.23, although apparently containing a minor feedback loop, is in fact another example of feedforward control, the disturbance D here entering at a different point in the system.

11.9 Compensation of sampled-data system

Compensation network design for a sampled-data system is similar to that described in Sections 11.5 to 11.7 for a continuous-data system, and can conveniently be carried out using a Bode diagram.

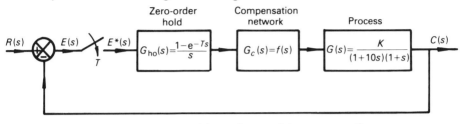

Fig. 11.24 Sampled-data system with continuous-data compensation

Example 11.4. Consider a system with block diagram as in Fig. 11.24 where, for comparison, the open loop transfer function is as used in the continuous data system of Example 11.2.

The z-transform of the uncompensated open loop can be written as

$$G_{ho}G(z) = (1 - z^{-1})\mathscr{Z}\left[\frac{K}{s(1 + 10s)(1 + s)}\right]$$

$$= \frac{K}{9}\left(\frac{z - 1}{z}\right)\mathscr{Z}\left[\frac{9}{s} - \frac{10}{(0.1 + s)} + \frac{1}{(1 + s)}\right]$$

From Table 10.1

$$G_{ho}G(z) = \frac{K}{9}\left(\frac{z - 1}{z}\right)\left(\frac{9z}{z - 1} - \frac{10z}{z - e^{-0.1T}} + \frac{z}{z - e^{-T}}\right)$$

Inspection of Fig. 11.16b would suggest a sampling time of $T = 0.2$ seconds to give a good sampled-data representation of the continuous signal.

$$\therefore \quad G_{ho}G(z) = \frac{K}{9}(z - 1)\left(\frac{9}{z - 1} - \frac{10}{z - 0.9802} + \frac{1}{z - 0.8187}\right)$$

$$= \frac{K}{9}\left(\frac{0.017z + 0.016}{(z - 0.98)(z - 0.819)}\right)$$

Rearranging Eq. 10.23 to make z the subject gives

$$z = \frac{1 + r}{1 - r}$$

Using this mapping function for z, the corresponding open loop r-transform of $G_{ho}G(z)$ is

$$G_{ho}G(r) = \frac{K}{9}\left[\frac{0.017\left(\dfrac{1 + r}{1 - r}\right) + 0.016}{\left(\left(\dfrac{1 + r}{1 - r}\right) - 0.98\right)\left(\left(\dfrac{1 + r}{1 - r}\right) - 0.819\right)}\right]$$

$$\simeq \frac{K(1 - 0.97r)}{(1 + 99r)(1 + 10r)}$$

and $\qquad G_{ho}G(j\omega_r) = \dfrac{K(1 - 0.97j\omega_r)}{(1 + 99j\omega_r)(1 + 10j\omega_r)}$

The break points needed to plot the Bode diagram for $G_{ho}G(j\omega_r)$ occur at $\omega_r = 0.1$ and very close to 0.01 and 1.0 radians per second. If a value of $K = 40$ is selected the phase margin is $19°$ and a direct comparison with Example 11.2 can be made. The Bode diagram for $G_{ho}G(j\omega_r)$ is drawn in Fig. 11.25. For a phase lead network

$$G_c(r) = \frac{1}{\alpha} \frac{1 + \alpha\tau r}{1 + \tau r} \quad \text{where } \alpha > 1$$

As explained in Example 11.2, a suitable trial value for φ_m is $30°$, resulting in the value $\alpha = 3$. The new crossover frequency is positioned at a magnitude value of -4.8 dB and this yields a value for $\omega_m = 0.26$ rad/second. Hence the corner frequencies for the network are located at

$$1/\alpha\tau = 0.26/\sqrt{3} = 0.15 \text{ rad/second}$$
and $\qquad 1/\tau = 0.26\sqrt{3} = 0.45 \text{ rad/second}$

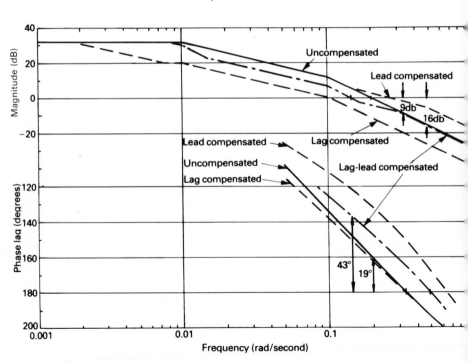

Fig. 11.25 Bode diagram for Example 11.4

For the compensated system

$$\frac{C(r)}{E(r)} = \frac{40(1 - 0.97r)(1 + 6.7r)}{(1 + 99r)(1 + 10r)(1 + 2.2r)}$$

and by making the appropriate substitution for r

$$\frac{C(z)}{E(z)} = \frac{40(0.03z + 1.97)(7.7z - 5.7)(z + 1)}{(100z - 98)(11z - 9)(3.2z - 1.2)}$$

Multiplying the top and bottom of this equation by $(z - 1)$ and separating into partial fractions gives

$$\frac{C(z)}{E(z)} = \left(\frac{z-1}{z}\right)\left(-\frac{42.5z}{(z-0.98)} + \frac{1.9z}{(z-0.818)} + \frac{0.52z}{(z-0.375)} + \frac{40z}{(z-1)}\right)$$

Using Table 10.1, and rearranging gives

$$\frac{C(s)}{E(s)} = \left(\frac{1 - e^{-sT}}{s}\right)\left(\frac{40(1 + 0.65s)}{(1 + 10s)(1 + s)(1 + 0.2s)}\right)$$

from which

$$G_c(s) = \frac{(1 + 0.65s)}{(1 + 0.2s)}$$

The realization of this transfer function can be achieved by use of the compensation networks shown in Fig. 11.13.

The closed loop pulse transfer function is

$$\frac{C(z)}{R(z)} = \frac{9.24z^3 + 609z^2 + 151z - 449}{3529z^3 - 7041z^2 + 5347z - 1507}$$

For a unit step disturbance in $R(z)$, i.e. $R(z) = \dfrac{z}{z-1}$, the output response is

$$C(z) = \frac{9.24z^4 + 609z^3 + 151z^2 - 449z}{3529z^4 - 10\,570z^3 + 12\,388z^2 - 6854z + 1507}$$

From this equation the steady state value of $c(t)$ can be computed as 0.976 by use of Eq. 10.21, and by means of long division the time response can be estimated. This output response is shown in Fig. 11.26 and illustrates the improvement achieved by the addition of the phase lead compensation element.

The compensated Bode diagram, Fig. 11.25, shows that a phase margin of 39° and a gain margin of 10 dB have been achieved. However, the steep slope

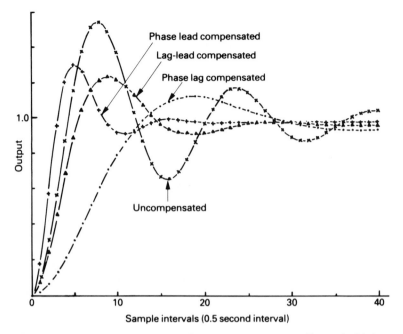

Output

Fig. 11.26 Effect of compensation on step response, Example 11.4

of the phase angle curve suggests that the sampled process is less amenable to phase lead compensation than the original continuous-data system.

If alternatively a phase lag network is incorporated and the procedure described in Section 11.7 is followed, it can be seen that a phase margin of 45° can be realized if the gain crossover frequency is moved to 0.1 rad/second. Since the network does influence marginally the final phase lag, a lower frequency of 0.08 will be used as the crossover value. Thus the network must produce 13 dB of attenuation at this frequency.

Hence

$$20 \log \alpha = -13 \text{ dB}$$

$$\alpha = 10^{-13/20} = 0.22$$

and this fixes the distance between the two corner frequencies of the lag network. The upper corner frequency is located at 1/10 of the new crossover frequency

$$\text{i.e.} \quad \frac{1}{\alpha\tau} = \frac{0.08}{10} = 8.0 \times 10^{-3} \text{ rad/second}$$

$$\text{and} \quad \frac{1}{\tau} = 0.22 \times 8.0 \times 10^{-3} = 1.76 \times 10^{-3} \text{ rad/second}$$

Thus

$$\frac{C(r)}{E(r)} = \frac{40(1 - 0.97r)(1 + 125r)}{(1 + 99r)(1 + 10r)(1 + 568r)}$$

and

$$\frac{C(z)}{R(z)} = \frac{3.78z^3 + 248.28z^2 + 0.22z - 244.28}{15\,651.28z^3 - 43\,481.27z^2 + 40\,584.82z - 12\,746.63}$$

As would be expected the stability margin, Table 11.1, has been improved by use of the lag network but the reduced bandwidth results in a longer rise time as shown by the step response given in Fig. 11.26.

Table 11.1 Harmonic response characteristics, Example 11.4

	PM	GM	Bandwidth
uncompensated	19	9	0.20
lead compensated	38	10	0.37
lag compensated	48	20	0.11
lead-lag compensated	43	16	0.20

A more practical and possibly more versatile approach to sampled-data system compensation may be found in the use of the lag-lead network (or its equivalent) shown in Fig. 11.21 since it contains advantages of both the phase lead and phase lag networks.

The transfer function of a lag-lead network can be written as

$$G_c(r) = \left(\frac{1 + \alpha_1 \tau_1 s}{1 + \tau_1 s} \right) \times \left(\frac{1 + \alpha_2 \tau_2 s}{1 + \tau_2 s} \right)$$

where $\alpha_1 \alpha_2 = 1$, $\alpha_1 > 1$ and $\alpha_2 < 1$

The lag portion will first be established by selecting values for α_2 and τ_2, a purely arbitrary choice in this case.

If the crossover be moved to 0.15 rad/second a phase margin of 30° will result.

i.e. $\quad 5 = -20 \log \alpha_2$

$$\alpha_2 = 10^{-5/20} = 0.5623$$

and $\qquad \dfrac{1}{\alpha_2 \tau_2} = \dfrac{0.15}{10} = 0.015 \text{ rad/second}$

$$\frac{1}{\tau_2} = 8.4 \times 10^{-3} \text{ rad/second}$$

Using the constraint

$$\alpha_1 \alpha_2 = 1$$

gives

$$\alpha_1 = \frac{1}{0.5623} = 1.8$$

The phase lead portion is positioned on the Bode diagram in the same way as described earlier. The attenuation of the lead network is

$$20 \log_{10} 1.8 = 5 \, \text{dB}$$

hence

$$\omega_m = 0.23$$

$$\frac{1}{\tau_1} = 0.23 \sqrt{1.8} = 0.3086$$

$$\frac{1}{\alpha_1 \tau_1} = \frac{0.3086}{1.8} = 0.1714$$

For the compensated system

$$\frac{C(r)}{E(r)} = \frac{40(1 - 0.97r)(1 + 5.8r)(1 + 67r)}{(1 + 99r)(1 + 10r)(1 + 3.2r)(1 + 119r)}$$

and the closed loop pulse transfer function is

$$\frac{C(z)}{R(z)} = \frac{13.87z^4 + 90\,154z^3 - 629.97z^2 - 893.54z + 624.1}{13\,873.87z^4 - 44\,910.26z^3 + 55\,184.45z^2 - 30\,479.94z + 6348.28}$$

The time response for this system is shown in Fig. 11.26 and although an improvement is shown further trials would be necessary to determine if the gain margin could be increased while still maintaining a similar phase margin and bandwidth (Table 11.1).

This example illustrates that the ideas normally associated with continuous-data system design can be extended in all aspects to the sampled-data system by use of z-transformation and the r-transform method.

11.10 State vector feedback control

An exposition of the design of linear systems using the classical methods of Bode diagrams and root locus plots has been given in the earlier sections of this chapter. It will have been observed that in the classical method of design feedback is most generally obtained from one variable, the output. Only when inner feedback loops are used for system compensation is more than one variable employed for feedback control. The conventional controller incorporating P + D, P + I, phase lead or phase lag algorithms is generally unable to control independently all system poles, Fig. 11.6, since the number of free parameters available for adjustment is restricted to two or three in most cases. Therefore, if the process can be described in state vector form, it is logical to extend the power of the classical design approach by providing full state

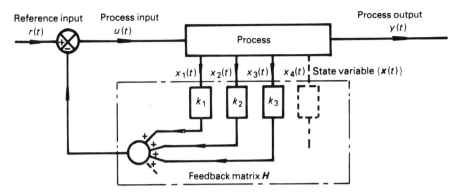

Fig. 11.27 Block diagram for state vector feedback control

feedback. This leads to the concept of *state variable feedback* and is the basis of most design techniques in modern control theory.

Many of the analytical design procedures reduce to problems of (a) finding a suitable variable to manipulate to enable the system output to be changed from some initial state to any other desired state in a finite time, and (b) being able to estimate, with confidence, the process state from observations made over a finite time of the output response. These two properties are classified in the literature as *controllability* and *observability* respectively.

The arrangement shown in Fig. 11.27 is a block diagram representation of a system in which each state variable is fed back through a fixed gain. The state vector $\{x(t)\}$ for the n-dimensional process is fed back through a constant $1 \times n$ matrix H, and the system describing equations can be written

$$u(t) = r(t) - H\{x(t)\}$$

Substituting this in Eq. 5.16, yields

$$\{\dot{x}(t)\} = (A - BH)\{x(t)\} + Br(t)$$

From the analytical results of Section 5.3, the characteristic equation for this closed loop system is

$$|sI - A + BH| = 0 \qquad\qquad 11.9$$

If the system can be shown to be controllable, i.e. if it is possible to change the system state from some initial state $\{x(0)\}$ to a desired equilibrium state in a finite time interval by means of the process input $u(t)$, then the roots of Eq. 11.9 can be chosen arbitrarily. This gives rise to a design procedure known as *pole-placement*.

Although most physical systems are controllable, there are some exceptions and care must be taken in making all-inclusive general statements. In particular, lack of controllability may not be apparent when a transfer function description is used to model a process. The necessary and sufficient condition for controllability is that the composite matrix

$$S = [B \; AB \; A^2B \; \ldots\ldots \; A^{n-1}B]$$

has a rank of n. The rank of matrix S is the order of the largest non-singular matrix (defined in Appendix C) contained in S. For example, if the matrix is

$$S = \begin{bmatrix} 1 & 2 & 3 \\ 2 & 3 & 4 \\ 3 & 5 & 7 \end{bmatrix}$$

then S is of rank 2 because

$$\begin{vmatrix} 1 & 2 \\ 2 & 3 \end{vmatrix} = -1 \quad \text{and} \quad \det S = 0$$

Consider a process described by the state variable Eq. 5.7, i.e.

$$\{\dot{x}(t)\} = \begin{bmatrix} 0 & 1 & 0 \\ 0 & 0 & 1 \\ 0 & -8 & -6 \end{bmatrix} \{x(t)\} + \begin{bmatrix} 0 \\ 0 \\ 1 \end{bmatrix} u(t) \qquad 5.7$$

then

$$S = [B\ AB\ A^2 B] = \begin{bmatrix} 0 & 0 & 1 \\ 0 & 1 & -6 \\ 1 & -6 & 28 \end{bmatrix} = -1$$

which satisfies the controllability requirement of this process, i.e. that S is of order 3 since $n = 3$. It should be noted that Eq. 5.7 is of a special type, known as 'phase-variable canonical form' and as such will always be state controllable (Appendix C, Section (j)).

Example 11.5. For the engine speed regulating system of Fig. 9.2, re-drawn in modified form in Fig. 11.28, derive a state-vector control law that will give

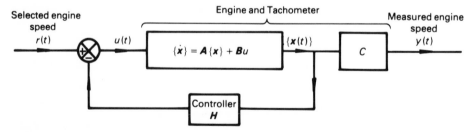

Fig. 11.28 Speed regulating system, Example 11.5

zero steady state error for a step change in selected engine speed and that will also give minimal initial overshoot to this step-input disturbance.

To quicken the process response and reduce the steady state error a gain value of 100 is taken, hence for this example the forward loop transfer function is

$$\frac{Y(s)}{U(s)} = \frac{100}{(s^2 + 9s + 25)(1 + s)}$$

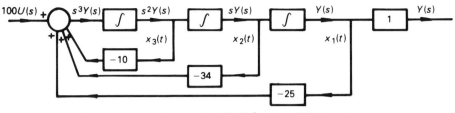

Fig. 11.29 State variable diagram for $100/(s^2 + 9s + 25)(1 + s)$

and the state variable diagram can be drawn as shown in Fig. 11.29. From inspection of Fig. 11.29 the state variable equations are:

$$\dot{x}_1(t) = x_2(t)$$
$$\dot{x}_2(t) = x_3(t)$$
$$\dot{x}_3(t) = -25x_1(t) - 34x_2(t) - 10x_3(t) + 100u(t)$$
$$y(t) = x_1(t)$$

that is

$$A = \begin{bmatrix} 0 & 1 & 0 \\ 0 & 0 & 1 \\ -25 & -34 & -10 \end{bmatrix}, \quad B = \begin{bmatrix} 0 \\ 0 \\ 100 \end{bmatrix}, \quad C = [1 \ 0 \ 0]$$

The constant feedback matrix H can be written

$$H = [h_1 \ h_2 \ h_3]$$

Using Eq. 11.9, the characteristic equation is

$$|sI - A + BH| = s^3 + (10 + 100h_3)s^2 + (34 + 100h_2)s + (25 + 100h_1) = 0$$

Since zero steady state error is a design requirement

$$25 + 100h_1 = 100$$
$$h_1 = 0.75$$

The second requirement of minimal overshoot suggests, by inspection of Fig. 9.2b, that two roots positioned at $-2 \pm 2j$ will help achieve this end. Hence

$$s^3 + (10 + 100h_3)s^2 + (34 + 100h_2)s + 100 = (s + 2 - 2j)(s + 2 + 2j)(s + p)$$
$$= s^3 + (4 + p)s^2 + 4(p + 2)s + 8p$$

Inspection of this equation and equating coefficients yields

$$p = \frac{100}{8} = 12.5$$

$$34 + 100h_2 = 4(12.5 + 2)$$
$$\therefore \quad h_2 = 0.24$$
$$10 + 100h_3 = 4 + 12.5$$
$$\therefore \quad h_3 = 0.065$$

The closed loop transfer function is then

$$\frac{Y(s)}{R(s)} = \frac{100}{s^3 + 16.5s^2 + 58s + 100}$$

The complex roots of the characteristic equation have a damping factor of 0.707 and are dominant since the third root is far to the left. Hence the required specifications have been satisfied and the response (shown in Fig. 11.30) is very similar to that of a second order system.

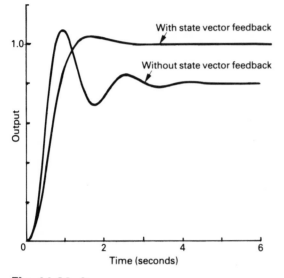

Fig. 11.30 Step response

A weakness of state-vector feedback control in practice is that not all of the state variables will be readily accessible directly from the system, or the cost of monitoring these might be prohibitive. For a high order system there are many state variables and hence many transducers are needed. These problems can be surmounted by estimating individual unavailable state values by use of the *state observer algorithm*. (Luenberger (Ref. 3, p. 278) showed that an nth order process with q independent outputs can be observed by using an $(n - q)$ order linear dynamic system. This condition of observability is defined in a manner analogous to controllability and indicates that an unobservable system will have dynamic modes of operation which do not influence the measured output response in any way.

If the matrix

$$Q = [C^T \, A^T C^T \, (A^T)^2 C^T \, \ldots\ldots \, (A^T)^{n-1} C^T]$$

is of rank n, the system is observable and the state vector can be constructed from linear combinations of the output $\{y(t)\}$, input $u(t)$ and derivatives of these variables. Intuitively, the observer should have the same form of state equation as the original process. The estimated state vector is designated as

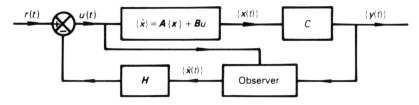

Fig. 11.31 Control loop incorporating observer

$\{\hat{x}(t)\}$ and is used to generate the control variable $u(t)$ through the feedback matrix H, Fig. 11.31, since the observer will be shown to have the capacity to minimize the error between the actual states and the observed states. These requirements can be embodied into a mathematical algorithm that enables the observer block, Fig. 11.31, to be specified in detail. Based on this premise, the appropriate mathematical equations are now presented together with an example to illustrate how these might be used in the design of a state observer.

Defining the observer algorithm as

$$\{\dot{z}(t)\} = E\{z(t)\} + F\{y(t)\} + G\{u(t)\} \qquad 11.10$$

an estimate of the process states can be achieved by use of the linear relation

$$\{z(t)\} = L\{\hat{x}(t)\} \qquad 11.11$$

The orders of the vectors and coefficient matrices, yet to be chosen, are:

$\{z(t)\} = (n - q) \times 1$ vector; $\quad \{y(t)\} = q \times 1$ vector; $\quad \{u(t)\} = p \times 1$ vector

and

$$E = (n - q) \times (n - q) \text{ matrix}; \quad F = (n - q) \times q \text{ matrix};$$

$$G = (n - q) \times p \text{ matrix}; \quad L = (n - q) \times n \text{ matrix}.$$

To be able to use an observer with confidence it is essential that $\{\hat{x}(t)\}$ be driven as close to $\{x(t)\}$ as possible, hence an error vector $\{\varepsilon_x(t)\}$ is defined as,

$$\{\varepsilon_x(t)\} = \{\hat{x}(t)\} - \{x(t)\} \qquad 11.12$$

Substituting from Eq. 11.12 into Eq. 11.11 gives

$$\{z(t)\} = L\{x(t)\} + L\{\varepsilon_x(t)\} \qquad 11.13$$

Differentiating each term with respect to time in Eq. 11.13 gives

$$\{\dot{z}(t)\} = L\{\dot{x}(t)\} + L\{\dot{\varepsilon}_x(t)\} \qquad 11.14$$

Replacing $\{\dot{x}(t)\}$ from Eq. 5.16 yields

$$\{\dot{z}(t)\} = LA\{x(t)\} + LB\{u(t)\} + L\{\dot{\varepsilon}_x(t)\} \qquad 11.15$$

Substituting Eq. 11.13 and Eq. 11.15 into Eq. 11.10, and replacing $\{y(t)\}$ with Eq. 5.17 (matrix $D = 0$), gives on rearrangement

$$L\{\dot{\varepsilon}_x(t)\} = EL\{\varepsilon_x(t)\} + (EL + FC - LA)\{x(t)\} + (G - LB)\{u(t)\} \qquad 11.16$$

The solution of this equation is dictated by the constraints imposed, therefore to ensure that $\{\varepsilon_x(t)\}$ decays with time, Eq. 11.16 will be constrained to be

$$L\{\dot{\varepsilon}_x(t)\} = EL\{\varepsilon_x(t)\} \qquad\qquad 11.17$$

and hence the estimated vector $\{\hat{x}(t)\}$ will converge onto the actual vector $\{x(t)\}$. From Eq. 5.34 the solution of Eq. 11.17 is

$$L\{\varepsilon_x(t)\} = e^{Et}L\{\varepsilon_x(0)\} \qquad\qquad 11.18$$

Now the value of the observer output at time $t = 0$ cannot readily be evaluated because the observer output at the time instant immediately before is not known. It is most simple, therefore, to assume that $\{\hat{x}(0)\}$ is zero, hence

$$\{\varepsilon_x(0)\} = -\{x(0)\}$$

Thus, the error vector at any time instant can be obtained from a knowledge of the initial states of the plant.

For Eq. 11.17 to be true

$$LA - EL = FC \qquad\qquad 11.19$$

and
$$G = LB \qquad\qquad 11.20$$

In order to implement the observer, values must be assigned to the matrices E, F, G and L which are related according to Eq. 11.19 and Eq. 11.20. The approach adopted here is to specify E and F and solve Eq. 11.19 for L and Eq. 11.20 for G.

The observer described is of a reduced order because the information contained in the plant output is utilized to formulate the estimated state vector. Hence by forming an adjoined equation from Eq. 11.13 and Eq. 5.17, with matrix $D = 0$, yields

$$\left[\begin{array}{c} \{z(t)\} \\ \hline \{y(t)\} \end{array}\right] = \left[\begin{array}{c} L \\ \hline C \end{array}\right]\{x(t)\} + \left[\begin{array}{c} L \\ \hline 0 \end{array}\right]\{\varepsilon_x(t)\}$$

and since $\{\varepsilon_x(t)\}$ decays with time, an estimate of the state vector is obtained from

$$\{\hat{x}(t)\} = \left[\begin{array}{c} L \\ \hline C \end{array}\right]^{-1}\left[\begin{array}{c} \{z(t)\} \\ \hline \{y(t)\} \end{array}\right] \qquad\qquad 11.21$$

Example 11.6. Design a state observer suitable for use with the speed regulating system shown in Fig. 11.28.

To confirm that the system is observable the matrix $Q = [C^T \ A^T C^T \ (A^T)^2 C^T]$ must have rank 3.

Now

$$C^T = [1 \quad 0 \quad 0]^T$$

$$(A^T)^2 = \begin{bmatrix} 0 & 0 & -25 \\ 1 & 0 & -34 \\ 0 & 1 & -10 \end{bmatrix}^2 = \begin{bmatrix} 0 & -25 & 250 \\ 0 & -34 & 315 \\ 1 & -10 & 66 \end{bmatrix}$$

and

$$\det \mathbf{Q} = \begin{vmatrix} 1 & 0 & 0 \\ 0 & 1 & 0 \\ 0 & 0 & 1 \end{vmatrix} = 1,$$

hence the necessary condition is satisfied.

If the dependence of the estimated errors upon the observer dynamics is to be accounted for, a number of restrictions must always be imposed on matrices $\mathbf{E}$ and $\mathbf{F}$ in order to reduce the number of independent variables. In this example, these restrictions will be:

(a) $\mathbf{E}$ is a diagonal matrix
(b) the elements of $\mathbf{F}$ are made equal to unity, that is the plant output is fed directly into the observer.

Since the roots of the characteristic equation are at $-2 \pm 2j$ and -12.5, the elements of $\mathbf{E}$ will be arbitrarily chosen to be -3 and -2.

From Eq. 5.37

$$\mathscr{L}(\mathrm{e}^{\mathbf{E}t}) = \frac{\mathrm{adj}\,(s\mathbf{I} - \mathbf{E})}{|s\mathbf{I} - \mathbf{E}|}$$

$$= \begin{bmatrix} \dfrac{1}{(s+3)} & 0 \\ 0 & \dfrac{1}{(s+2)} \end{bmatrix}$$

hence

$$\mathrm{e}^{\mathbf{E}t} = \mathscr{L}^{-1} \begin{bmatrix} \dfrac{1}{(s+3)} & 0 \\ 0 & \dfrac{1}{(s+2)} \end{bmatrix}$$

$$= \begin{bmatrix} \mathrm{e}^{-3t} & 0 \\ 0 & \mathrm{e}^{-2t} \end{bmatrix}$$

hence Eq. 11.8 gives the error vector

$$L\{\varepsilon_x(t)\} = \begin{bmatrix} \mathrm{e}^{-3t} & 0 \\ 0 & \mathrm{e}^{-2t} \end{bmatrix} L\{\varepsilon_x(0)\}$$

The largest state error is less than 2% of the initial value after 2 seconds, therefore these values for the elements of $\mathbf{E}$ will be used in the observer design for this speed regulating system.

Expressing

$$\mathbf{L} = \begin{bmatrix} l_1 & l_2 & l_3 \\ l_4 & l_5 & l_6 \end{bmatrix},$$

then

$$LA = \begin{bmatrix} l_1 & l_2 & l_3 \\ l_4 & l_5 & l_6 \end{bmatrix} \begin{bmatrix} 0 & 1 & 0 \\ 0 & 0 & 1 \\ -25 & -34 & -10 \end{bmatrix}$$

$$= \begin{bmatrix} -25\, l_3 & l_1 - 34\, l_3 & l_2 - 10\, l_3 \\ -25\, l_6 & l_4 - 34\, l_6 & l_5 - 10\, l_6 \end{bmatrix}$$

Similarly

$$EL = \begin{bmatrix} -3\, l_1 & -3\, l_2 & -3\, l_3 \\ -2\, l_4 & -2\, l_5 & -2\, l_6 \end{bmatrix}$$

and

$$LA - EL = \begin{bmatrix} -25\, l_3 + 3\, l_1 & l_1 - 34\, l_3 + 3\, l_2 & l_2 - 10\, l_3 + 3\, l_3 \\ -25\, l_6 + 2\, l_4 & l_4 - 34\, l_6 + 2\, l_5 & l_5 - 10\, l_6 + 2\, l_6 \end{bmatrix}$$

$$FC = \begin{bmatrix} 1 \\ 1 \end{bmatrix} \begin{bmatrix} 1 & 0 & 0 \end{bmatrix} = \begin{bmatrix} 1 & 0 & 0 \\ 1 & 0 & 0 \end{bmatrix}$$

By equating the individual elements of Eq. 11.19

$$L = \begin{bmatrix} 0.93 & 0.5 & 0.07 \\ 1.64 & 0.73 & 0.09 \end{bmatrix}$$

From Eq. 11.20

$$G = \begin{bmatrix} 7 \\ 9 \end{bmatrix}$$

Now

$$\begin{bmatrix} L \\ \hline C \end{bmatrix} = \begin{bmatrix} 0.93 & 0.5 & 0.07 \\ 1.64 & 0.73 & 0.09 \\ 1 & 0 & 0 \end{bmatrix}$$

From Appendix C

$$\text{Adj} \begin{bmatrix} L \\ \hline C \end{bmatrix} = \begin{bmatrix} 0 & 0 & -0.0061 \\ 0.09 & -0.07 & 0.0311 \\ -0.73 & 0.50 & -0.1461 \end{bmatrix}$$

$$\det \begin{bmatrix} L \\ \hline C \end{bmatrix} = -0.0061$$

and

$$\begin{bmatrix} L \\ \hline C \end{bmatrix}^{-1} = \begin{bmatrix} 0 & 0 & 1 \\ -14.75 & 11.48 & -5.1 \\ 119.67 & -81.97 & 24 \end{bmatrix}$$

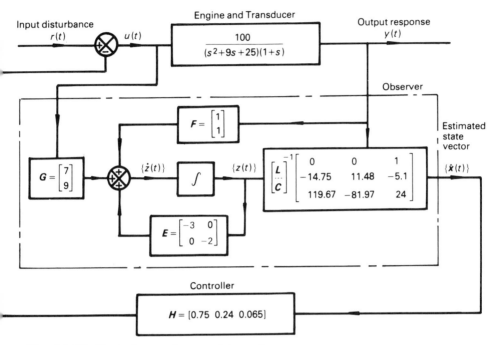

Fig. 11.32 Block diagram for complete system

From Eq. 11.21, the estimated state vector is

$$
\begin{bmatrix} \hat{x}_1(t) \\ \hat{x}_2(t) \\ \hat{x}_3(t) \end{bmatrix} = \begin{bmatrix} 0 & 0 & 1 \\ -14.75 & 11.48 & -5.1 \\ 119.67 & -81.97 & 24 \end{bmatrix} \begin{bmatrix} z_1(t) \\ z_2(t) \\ y(t) \end{bmatrix}
$$

With this information the complete system diagram can be drawn as shown in Fig. 11.32. The time response for this arrangement is almost identical to that shown in Fig. 11.30 for the system with state vector feedback indicating the power of this approach in control algorithm design.

11.11 Relay control

A simple low cost form of feedback control action that makes use of a switched relay has found wide industrial application. The magnitude of the corrective action is independent of the size of the error, but the sign of this constant corrective action is directly dependent on the sign of the error signal. The most familiar relay control system is a room temperature control (Fig. 11.33); this employs a thermostat to switch the heat on when the temperature is too low and off again when the temperature exceeds the desired value (cooling would be needed where the desired temperature is below that of the prevailing ambient temperature).

Inherent within all relay elements is a certain amount of dead-band, and this is used to ensure that as long as the error magnitude is less than some defined

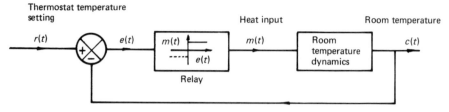

Fig. 11.33 Relay control of room temperature

value there is no corrective action. In an electrical relay this dead-band arises because the coils require a finite amount of current to actuate the relay contacts; in a hydraulic system valve overlap may be present to reduce fluid leakage at porting, and this creates a dead-band. The presence of dead-band may cause the system to exhibit self-sustained oscillations of constant amplitude and frequency, referred to as *limit cycles*. Control over the size of the dead-band to prevent limit cycles can only be exercised if the magnitudes of the signals within a system are known. A change to a set-point could, for example, be responsible for the onset of a limit cycle oscillation. However, analytical methods do exist which enable the engineer to predict the dead-band widths for given signal magnitudes which would cause limit cycle conditions. The limit cycle phenomenon can be used to advantage in certain industrial situations to overcome problems of valve stiction which may otherwise lead to malfunction and component failure.

The dynamic behaviour of systems such as those above, which include straight-forward non-linearities, can be analysed by three techniques; these are extensions of the linear techniques described earlier in this book, and are no more difficult to understand. The system can be simulated on an analogue computer using appropriate non-linear units, and the output response noted for different forcing functions. In the time domain, the step response can be studied by means of the *phase plane technique*, where a phase trajectory (similar to Fig. 2.10, but with discontinuities of slope arising from the switching) is drawn by graphical or analytical means. This method is limited to second order systems since higher order trajectories cannot be drawn on paper. Phase trajectories can be obtained directly from an analogue simulation and are particularly useful for giving a physical insight into the form of the transient behaviour and the effect of the non-linearity. The third technique is a frequency domain method, suitable for any order of system but restricted to a single group of non-linearities, in which the non-linearity is approximated by a *describing function*. This is a function analogous to $G(j\omega)$ but whose magnitude and phase are, in general, functions of input amplitude in addition to frequency (they are the amplitude and phase of the first harmonic component of the output, it being assumed that higher harmonics are attenuated in their passage round the loop).

In contrast to linear systems, the response of a non-linear system to an input excitation of known magnitude and form is no guide to its behaviour for other input signals, since the principle of superposition no longer holds. The stability of linear systems is determined solely by the location of the roots of the characteristic equation; for non-linear systems the situation is not so clear and is very much dependent on the input signal and the initial system state.

It can be concluded that in the design of a nonlinear system, information is required about the type and amplitude of all anticipated inputs, and the initial operating condition of the system about which the design study takes place, in addition to the usual detailed knowledge of the physical process from which the mathematical model is derived. With this information a full analytical and simulation study can be conducted and results obtained which can be used with confidence.

11.12 Case study of electrohydraulic servomechanism

As a conclusion to the book, this final section attempts to improve the reader's physical understanding of the rather abstract concepts of system modelling, analysis, and control, and to further illustrate the interrelationship between the many different topics by describing a case study of a specific practical system. The study outlines the analysis and design of an electrohydraulic servomechanism used for positioning the slideway of a numerically controlled machine tool. The first stage is concerned with obtaining a mathematical model suitable for analysis. This is followed by the determination of system accuracy and dynamic response, and the design of appropriate compensation to achieve a performance which is deemed to be 'satisfactory'.

(a) *Modelling of system.* With a numerically controlled machine tool, the required machining operations are specified by a set of coded instructions read from paper tape or other storage medium. The machining is then carried out by moving the workpiece relative to the cutting tool in the appropriate direction at the required feed rate by means of positional servomechanisms; the servomechanisms convert electrical signals specifying the desired position into an actual position. The subject of this study is a milling machine (shown schematically in Fig. 11.34) in which the cutter rotates about a fixed axis and the workpiece is moved relative to it. The workpiece is mounted on a slideway which has three axes of movement, and the movement is effected for each axis by a ram (or rams) controlled by an electrohydraulic servovalve. To achieve accurate positioning and hence accurate machining, feedback is essential; thus the actual position of the slideway is compared with the desired position to generate an error signal; this is amplified and acts as input signal to the servovalve. A simple block diagram representation is shown in Fig. 11.35, omitting at this stage any minor loop or other compensation feature. The control loops for all three axes are similar, except that the masses to be moved and the actuating ram areas have different numerical values; hence for illustrative purposes only one of the loops need be studied.

The system chosen is one in which, for a preliminary study, the nonlinearities inherently present can be ignored, and small perturbation analysis can be employed to derive a linear model. Once a general understanding of the form of the behaviour of the linearized system has been obtained, then the model can if required be refined to include certain of the non-linearities and the less dominant effects. To enable an analysis to be carried out, a transfer

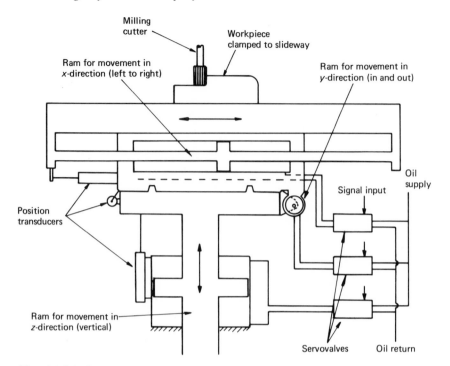

Fig. 11.34 Schematic arrangement of servomechanisms for positioning of machine tool slideway on three axes

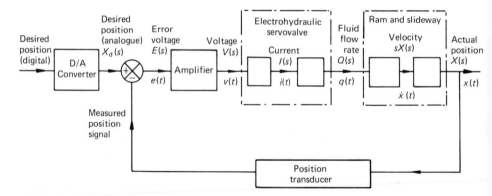

Fig. 11.35 Block diagram of electrohydraulic servomechanism (without compensation)

function description must be determined for each of the blocks in the loop, the transfer functions being obtained on the basis of theoretical considerations, experimental testing, or a combination of the two. It is likely that the dynamic characteristics of the mechanical components will be dominant, and that the transducer and amplifier can effectively be thought of as having constant gains and negligible phase shifts within the bandwidth of the remainder of the system.

The form of the transfer function for the hydraulic ram and slideway can be determined theoretically by application of the appropriate physical equations—in this case Newton's second law of motion, and a flow continuity equation. Allowing for the presence of leakage, and for a fluid which is not completely incompressible, the transfer function can be derived (Section 2.5, Eq. 2.36) in the form

$$\frac{X(s)}{Q(s)} = \frac{1}{s\left\{\dfrac{Mv}{K_B A}s^2 + \left(\dfrac{K_L M}{A} + \dfrac{\mu v}{K_B A}\right)s + \left(\dfrac{K_L \mu}{A} + A\right)\right\}} \qquad 11.22$$

where $X(s)$ and $Q(s)$ are the Laplace transforms of the actual position and the fluid volumetric flow rate respectively, M is the total mass being moved, A the effective ram area, K_B the bulk modulus of the fluid, v the volume of fluid between the servovalve and the ram, K_L a leakage coefficient (flow/unit pressure difference), and μ a friction coefficient (force/unit velocity). A is constant and M nearly so (varying only by virtue of the different masses of workpieces); K_B is dependent on the type of fluid used and the amount of entrained air which is assumed to be present; v varies with ram position; K_L and μ are likely to be unknown, but order of magnitude estimates can probably be made. If leakage is assumed to be negligible for a first study, then the transfer function simplifies to

$$\frac{X(s)}{Q(s)} = \frac{1}{s\left\{\dfrac{Mv}{K_B A}s^2 + \dfrac{\mu v}{K_B A}s + A\right\}} = \frac{\dfrac{1}{A}\left(\dfrac{K_B A^2}{Mv}\right)}{s\left\{s^2 + \dfrac{\mu}{M}s + \dfrac{K_B A^2}{Mv}\right\}} \qquad 11.23$$

The relationship between slideway velocity and ram input flowrate is thus of second order with undamped natural frequency $\omega_n = \sqrt{\dfrac{K_B A^2}{Mv}}$, damping factor $\zeta = \dfrac{\mu}{2A}\sqrt{\dfrac{v}{MK_B}}$, and gain $= \dfrac{1}{A}$. The 'spring' effect arises from the compressibility of the fluid giving an effective stiffness $= \dfrac{K_B A^2}{v}$. It can also be seen that ω_n is a function of ram position and will be a minimum when v is a maximum, i.e. when the ram is in the midposition with equal volumes of fluid at each side. The damping which is assumed to arise primarily from viscous drag in the lubricating film will be small, and an accurate assessment of ζ can only follow from experimental testing. Comparing the two transfer functions, the effect of any leakage can be seen to be to increase ω_n, increase the effective ζ, and reduce the gain.

The flow to the ram is controlled by an electrohydraulic servovalve. A typical valve is shown schematically in Fig. 11.36, and its mode of operation is described briefly in this paragraph, with terminology as used in the diagram. The valve is designed to give an output flow rate proportional to input current

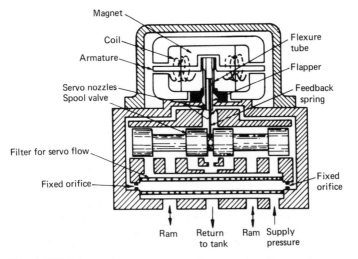

Fig. 11.36 Schematic arrangement of servovalve (Dowty Series 4551)

and to have a 'good' dynamic response (one that is fast relative to the system); it utilizes the principle of feedback to achieve this. The input signal, the current flowing through the coil, induces an electromagnetic force on the armature which tilts the armature-flapper assembly slightly about an effective pivot provided by the flexure tube, thus causing an increase of flow area at one nozzle and a decrease at the other. This creates a differential pressure across the ends of the spool valve, and results in spool displacement which, in turn, causes a restoring torque to be applied to the armature assembly via the feedback spring. Spool movement continues until the feedback torque balances the input signal torque, and the armature-flapper assembly, with forces in equilibrium, returns to its null position with the flapper mid-way between the nozzles, the pressure difference across the spool dropping to zero. The resulting spool position is then proportional to the input current. If the pressure difference between the supply pressure and the ram pressure is substantially constant, then the output flow rate is proportional to the input current.

Any attempt at deriving a transfer function for such a valve, using the fundamental physical equations, would require many assumptions to be made about magnitudes of effective inertias, damping forces, etc. It would therefore be essential to validate the theoretical model by experimental testing. A model derived by this means would probably be more complex than necessary, and would include dynamic effects that are only of significance at frequencies beyond the system bandwidth. For such a component, therefore, direct practical testing and fitting of an appropriate low order transfer function to the test results would probably be more relevant. Typical harmonic response information (Fig. 11.37), together with parameters for an equivalent second order transfer function, are provided on the manufacturer's data sheet. A first order transfer function can give a reasonable approximation for frequencies up to about 40 Hz (Fig. 11.37a) which could be useful if the system bandwidth is less than this and if a very simple model is needed. The second order transfer

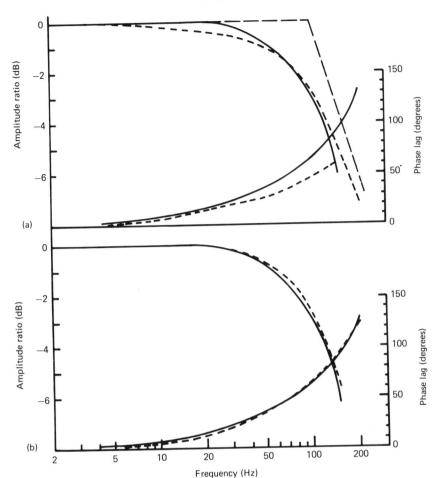

Fig. 11.37 Typical servovalve frequency response with first and second order transfer function fits. (a) first order fit (b) second order fit

function suggested by the manufacturer (ω_n = 140 Hz, ζ = 0.9) can be seen to provide a very good fit to both the magnitude and the phase curves over the full frequency range for which harmonic information is given (Fig. 11.37b). The transfer function of the servovalve can thus be written as

$$\frac{Q(s)}{I(s)} = k_v\left(\frac{1}{1 + 0.0016s}\right) \qquad 11.24$$

or

$$\frac{Q(s)}{I(s)} = \frac{k_v(775\,000)}{s^2 + 1580s + 775\,000} \qquad 11.25$$

where k_v is the valve static gain at zero load pressure, also available from the data sheet as 2.5 in^3/second/mA. The valve harmonic information and the transfer function derived from it relates to a current input. If the error amplifier is a voltage amplifier, then an additional block relating current $I(s)$ to voltage $V(s)$ must be included in the block diagram. The dynamics of this arise from the inductance of the coil of the servovalve torque motor, and it can easily be shown that the transfer function is

$$\frac{I(s)}{V(s)} = \frac{\dfrac{1}{R}}{1 + \dfrac{L}{R}s} \qquad\qquad 11.26$$

where R and L are the resistance and inductance respectively. For the valve used, $R = 200 \ \Omega$ and $L = 1$ H, hence the gain term is 5 mA/volt and the time constant is 0.005 seconds. This is larger than the primary time constant of the valve, Eq. 11.24, and would thus dominate. In practice, the error amplifier would normally be a power amplifier in which case the time constant relating current output and voltage input is likely to be very small in comparison to the effective time constant of the ram and slideway; thus the amplifier will have a flat response to a frequency well above the system bandwidth, will have negligible phase shift, and can be considered to have a transfer function which is a constant k_a. Similarly the position transducer can be assumed to be a pure gain term k_t.

To confirm the form of the ram and slideway transfer function, to check the estimated value of ω_n, and to determine the value of ζ it is necessary to carry out some practical testing. Testing can be carried out with the loop opened, by applying a forcing voltage to the amplifier input or directly to the servovalve using a separate drive amplifier, and recording slideway position or velocity with the existing transducer or with a test transducer. To eliminate errors arising from non-linearities caused by Coulomb friction, and to avoid the danger of damage to the bearing surface which might result from long testing with small amplitudes close to any given position, the testing is best carried out by superimposing steps and sine waves on slow ramp inputs, and taking measurements at a fixed point as the slideway passes it, while moving between two limiting positions on either side. Typical results for step response tests (Fig. 11.38) and frequency response tests (Fig. 11.39) confirm the existence of

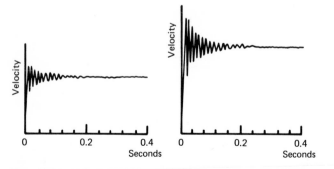

Fig. 11.38 Typical step responses of velocity

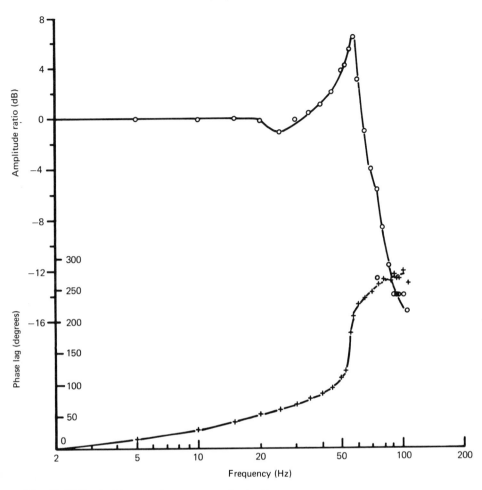

Fig. 11.39 Typical harmonic response of velocity

the very lightly damped second order component of response expected from the considerations above. A good estimate of the value of ω_n for the ram and slideway can be obtained directly from the step response trace and, as the damping is very small, the damping factor ζ can be determined by application of the logarithmic decrement method. As a consequence of the averaging inherent in frequency response testing, these values can be estimated more accurately from the harmonic response curves, and the value of the servovalve time constant confirmed, by seeking asymptotes on the magnitude plot and by trial and error curve fitting. At this stage, a digital computer program for evaluating the harmonic response for a known transfer function can be of great help, and would be used in conjunction with some appropriate criterion of 'goodness of fit', to determine a transfer function whose harmonic response is a good fit to the experimental curves (e.g. Levy's method (see ref. 4, p. 278).

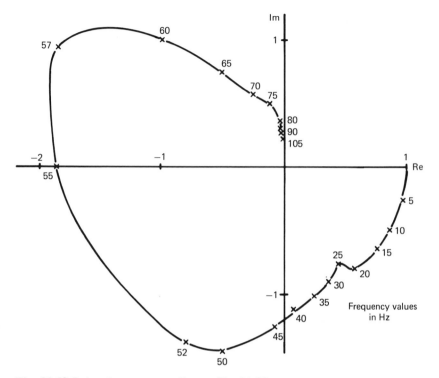

Fig. 11.40 Polar plot corresponding to Fig. 11.39

Study of the phase plot in relation to the gain plot will show whether any significant nonminimum phase effects are present. The corresponding polar diagram (Fig. 11.40) is of interest and highlights the rapid phase change which occurs in the region of the resonant frequency, and the nominally flat response up to about 20 Hz.

(b) *Analysis of response and design of compensation.* From a combination of theoretical analysis, experimental testing and manufacturers' published data, a linearized mathematical model can thus be developed. If it is assumed that the amplifier is a power amplifier with negligible time constant, that the servovalve can initially be represented by the first order approximation derived above, and that the transducer gain k_t is lumped with the amplifier gain (i.e. the desired position signal becomes the actual desired position) then the block diagram Fig. 11.35 takes the form shown in Fig. 11.41. The dynamic behaviour of the system can now be investigated theoretically with a view to determining how parameter variations or higher order transfer function representations affect the system behaviour, and how different forms of compensation might change this behaviour.

Thought must be given at this stage to what type of response is required, bearing in mind that the end result is a machining operation. Qualitatively, the desired form of behaviour can be described as one which responds rapidly to

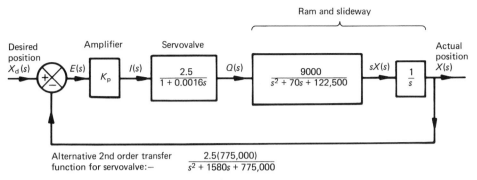

Fig. 11.41 Simplified block diagram of system

any change of desired position, with negligible overshoot and with a very small steady state error. The positional error should be zero and the velocity error as small as conveniently possible to allow accurate contouring at fast feed rates. It is thus desirable to undertake an investigation into transient response and steady state accuracy for the basic system, and for the system with various forms of compensation. The transient behaviour can conveniently be determined by means of an analogue computer simulation or a digital computer simulation (Chapter 3), using root locus plots to aid the interpretation of the results (Chapter 9). The corresponding steady state accuracy can be determined by application of the final value theorem of Laplace transform theory (Chapter 8).

Consider first the basic system (Fig. 11.41) in which there is scope for alteration of the value of the loop gain. The positional error is zero as a consequence of the presence of the integration term inherent in the operation of the ram, and the velocity error is inversely proportional to K_p. The root locus diagram (Fig. 11.42a) can be sketched relatively quickly by hand using the aids to construction described in Section 9.3 or can be computed accurately if a digital computer package is available. Its form suggests that for very low values of K_p (and hence large velocity errors) the response will be very sluggish because of the dominance of the real root very close to the origin. As K_p increases, the very lightly damped superimposed oscillation soon becomes dominant, and for a relatively small loop gain the response will become unstable (Fig. 11.43). The limiting value of K_p can be found by using the Routh–Hurwitz criterion; it determines the smallest achievable velocity error. No value of gain appears to be suitable. It is clear that the very lightly damped ram and slideway poles present a problem, and that any compensation used should have the effect of moving these portions of locus further from the imaginary axis towards the left of the s plane. Representation of the servovalve by the second order transfer function, which is valid over a wider frequency range (Fig. 11.42b), makes negligible difference to the result, since the appropriate poles are so far to the left that they cause no marked alteration to the dominant portions of the root locus.

There is little scope, even at the design stage, for altering the physical parameters of the ram and slideway in order to move the complex poles

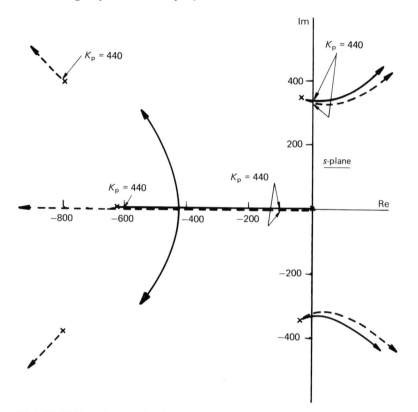

Fig. 11.42 Root locus plot for uncompensated system (a) with first order servovalve representation (———) (b) with second order servovalve representation (– – –)

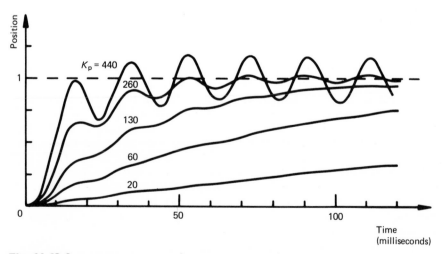

Fig. 11.43 Step response curves for uncompensated system with varying K_p

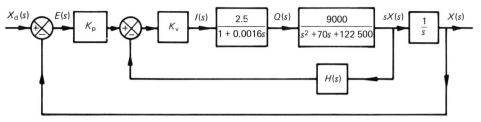

Fig. 11.44 System with minor loop compensation

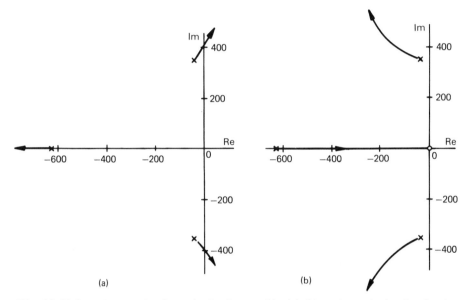

Fig. 11.45 Root locus plot for velocity loop with (a) Negative velocity feedback (b) Negative acceleration feedback

farther to the left, and hence increase the damping of the oscillation which dominates the transient response, and allow the loop gain and hence accuracy to be increased. The poles can, however, effectively be moved by introducing a minor feedback loop around the block whose transfer function contains them; this can conveniently be done by feeding back some function of velocity as shown in Fig. 11.44. The aim is to choose the form of inner loop compensation $H(s)$, the parameter values of $H(s)$, and the inner loop gain variable K_v to be such that the roots of the inner loop (velocity loop) which lie near to the ram and slideway poles, and which are poles of the main loop (position loop), are positioned as far to the left as possible. For any given form of transfer function $H(s)$, a root locus diagram for the velocity loop will show whether any improvement is possible, and step response traces for the simulated velocity loop can be used to confirm the expected changes in transient behaviour.

Three forms of transfer function $H(s)$ are probably worth investigating—negative velocity feedback, $H(s) = \text{constant} = k_1$, negative acceleration feed-

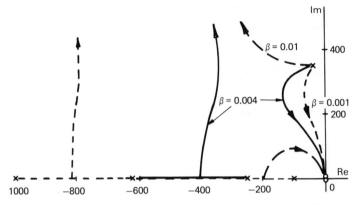

Fig. 11.46 Root locus plot for velocity loop with negative transient acceleration feedback

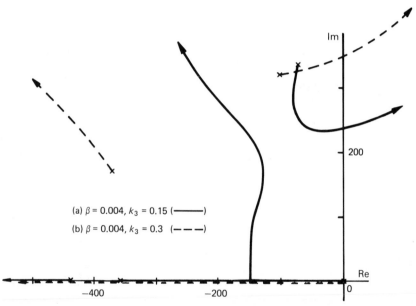

Fig. 11.47 Root locus plot for position loop with NTA compensation

back, $H(s) = k_2 s$, and negative transient acceleration feedback, $H(s) = \dfrac{k_3 s^2}{1 + \beta s}$.

A root locus diagram for the velocity loop immediately shows that, with negative velocity feedback, the dominant roots move towards the right in the s-plane (Fig. 11.45a), causing the behaviour to be even more oscillatory. For negative acceleration feedback, however, the corresponding portions of root locus move towards the left, suggesting that some degree of improvement is possible (Fig. 11.45b). The root locus plot for negative transient acceleration feedback is more complicated, since a different set of loci arises for each value of the time constant β (Fig. 11.46). There appears to be an optimum value of β where the damping factor of the dominant roots increases most rapidly with increase in gain. For any of the forms of compensation with given parameter values, the root locus plot for the position loop can now be drawn, the poles of this plot being the roots of the velocity loop instead of those used in Fig. 11.42 (e.g. Fig. 11.47). If $H(s)$ has been chosen well, then the result is a much improved transient response (Fig. 11.48). Other forms of compensation can also be investigated, such as the possible use of phase compensation within the minor loop or in the forward loop, and the potential available in a cancellation compensation approach.

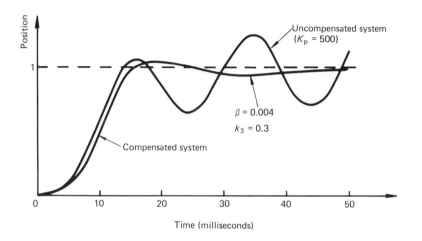

Fig. 11.48 Step response curve for system with NTA compensation with parameters chosen to give fast well damped response

For any of the compensation methods studied, some study of the effect on gain and phase margin will improve understanding of system harmonic response, and the relationship between transient and harmonic response. Analysis of system accuracy in terms of loop gains and forms of compensation will fill in a further part of the picture, and will highlight the conflict between achieving good dynamic behaviour and good steady state accuracy. In a design situation it would then be necessary to attempt to choose a good and realizable compensation method, and to optimize the system parameters with respect to the chosen performance criteria. The large numerical values, which tend to occur here, highlight the scaling which commonly is necessary or desirable when analysing a real system, as opposed to a hypothetical system, where convenient numerical values are chosen.

A full and detailed description of the analysis of this system, comparison of different compensation methods, and design of suitable compensation, requires more space than is available here. The reader is therefore left to carry out such an investigation, for the model given in Fig. 11.41, as an exercise to consolidate the material learnt in this book.

Specific references in Chapter 11.
1 Ziegler, J. G., and Nichols, N. B. *Trans A.S.M.E.* Vol. 64, pages 759–68, 1942.
2 *Quarterly Journal of Automatic Control*, Journal 4, Vol. XVI, No. 2, pages 53–67, 1975.
3 Luenberger, D. G. 'Observing the State of a Linear System', *IEEE Transactions of Military Electronics*, Vol. MIL-8, pages 74–80, 1964.
4 Levy, E. C. 'Complex Curve Fitting', *IRE Trans* Vol. AC–4, pages 37–43, 1959.

Appendix A
Problems

1 In a hydraulic spool valve leakage occurs in an axial direction through the narrow gap between the valve and the housing. Such flow is normally laminar and the flow rate q can be evaluated by applying the Poiseuille equation. This can be written as

$$q = \frac{\pi d h^3}{12\eta} \frac{p_1 - p_2}{l}$$

where $p_1 - p_2$ is the pressure difference between the inlet and outlet of the leakage gap, η is the fluid viscosity, l the length of the leakage path, d the valve diameter and h the leakage gap (the radial clearance). If d and h are constant obtain a linearized equation for the flow rate in terms of the remaining variables and the constants. What is the significance of this equation, and why is it used?

2 Determine the transfer functions relating the applied force f to the position y, and the applied torque T to the angular position θ for the translational and rotational mechanical systems shown in Fig. P1. K_1, K_2, K_3, and K are stiffness coefficients, C is a damping coefficient, M is a mass, and J_1 and J_2 are moments of inertia. State what assumptions are made.

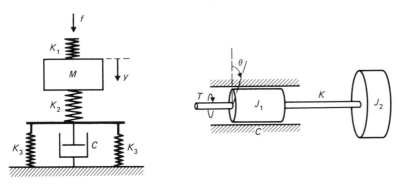

Fig. P1

3 Fig. P2 shows three passive electrical networks which can be used for system compensation. On the assumption that the input impedance is zero and the output impedance is infinite derive the transfer function relating input and output voltages (relative to earth potential) for each circuit.

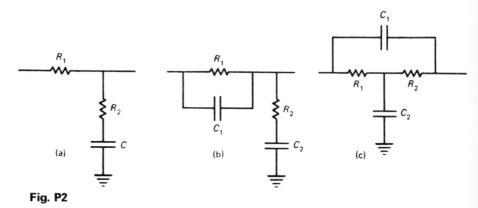

Fig. P2

4 A thermometer of thermal capacity W_1 (joules/°C) is inserted in a mercury filled protective pocket of thermal capacity W_2 (joules/°C). If the overall coefficient of heat transfer from the mercury in the pocket to the fluid in the thermometer is H_1 (joules/second °C) and from the external fluid to the mercury in the pocket is H_2 (joules/second °C), determine the transfer function relating indicated temperature to actual temperature.

5 Fig. P3 shows schematically a component of a hydraulic system in which oil at pressure p is used to obtain angular movement θ of a lever. Explain the significance of the expression 'small perturbation analysis' with particular reference to this arrangement. Hence derive the transfer function, assuming the piston to be frictionless and leak-free, and the fluid to be incompressible. What effect would leakage past the piston and viscous drag on the piston have on the derived transfer function?

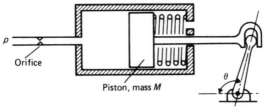

Fig. P3

6 With the aid of a schematic diagram describe briefly the principle of operation of a hydraulic positional servomechanism. Derive the form of the transfer function assuming that account must be taken of the effects of fluid compressibility, fluid leakage, and inertia. Derive also the simplified form of transfer function which results if these effects are neglected.

7 Fig. P4 shows schematically an arrangement for controlling the temperature of a steam-heated oven, utilizing temperature sensitive bellows and a hydraulic servomechanism. The desired temperature is set by adjustment of the position x of a pointer attached to one end of the bellows. An increase in oven temperature θ causes the bellows to expand, the movement being the input signal to the hydraulic servomechanism whose output y actuates a valve to decrease the steam inlet flow. Determine the transfer function relating valve position y to oven temperature θ. Assume servo valve flow for unit displacement is Q_v, area of ram is A, overall coefficient of heat transfer across bellows wall is H, specific heat and mass of bellows fluid are c and m respectively, and bellows extension is L for unit temperature rise of bellows fluid. Neglect fluid compressibility, fluid leakage, and inertia of moving parts. Suggest briefly the way in which the transfer function would differ if secondary effects such as the above were included.

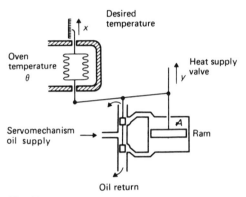

Fig. P4

8 What is an analogue computer, and in what main ways does it differ from a digital computer? Two variables y and x are both functions of time and are related by the differential equation

$$\frac{d^4 y}{dt^4} + 5.8 \frac{d^3 y}{dt^3} + 0.03 \frac{d^2 y}{dt^2} + 12 \frac{dy}{dt} + 120y = 20x$$

Derive an analogue computer circuit diagram for this equation, and explain how it could be used. Assume that the operational amplifiers available have two inputs with a gain of 10 and two inputs with a gain of unity.

9 The output of a system component whose transfer function is known to be

$$G_1(s) = \frac{20}{s^2 + 1.2s + 0.2}$$

is monitored by means of a transducer with transfer function

$$G_2(s) = \frac{0.06}{1 + 0.1s}$$

as shown in Fig. P5.

Input $U(s)$	System component $G_1(s) = \dfrac{20}{s^2 + 1.2s + 0.2}$	Actual output $C(s)$	Transducer $G_2(s) = \dfrac{0.06}{1 + 0.1s}$	Measured output $C_m(s)$

Fig. P5

Write down the differential equations for the system component and for the transducer, and derive an analogue computer circuit diagram which could be used to study the response of the system component and the effect of the transducer dynamic behaviour on the measured response. Explain how the circuit might be used. How would the circuit differ to permit investigation of the effect of a change of transducer time constant to 0.04 seconds?

10 The feedback system shown in block diagram form in Fig. P6 controls the output variable $c(t)$ of a plant. The plant dynamic behaviour is thought to be adequately described by the linear differential equation

$$\dddot{c}(t) + 5.2\ddot{c}(t) + 17.5\dot{c}(t) + 0.77c(t) = u(t)$$

The amplifier has an adjustable gain K and a negligible time constant, and the transducer is known to approximate to a second order linear system component with unity gain, damping factor 0.3, and undamped natural frequency 5 rad/second. Draw an analogue computer circuit diagram which could be used to investigate the dynamic behaviour of this system. What studies might be carried out, and what checks could be made to ensure the validity of the results? Use operational amplifier notation and assume that amplifier input gains of 1 and 10 are available.

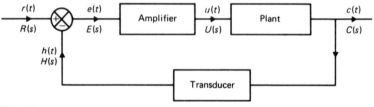

Fig. P6

11 Draw an analogue computer circuit diagram for a dynamic process represented by the overall transfer function

$$\frac{Y(s)}{U(s)} = \frac{4.2(s + 3.4)}{s^5 + 8.6s^4 + 0.15s^3 + 10.3s^2 + 100s + 5}$$

Assume that the amplifiers available have three inputs with gain 1 and two inputs with gain 10. What are the limitations of this diagram, and what additional information is needed to enable a more useful diagram to be prepared?

12 For the block diagram shown in Fig. P7 obtain an analogue computer circuit diagram which could be used to investigate the effect on transient behaviour of the system of changes in settings of the proportional plus integral plus derivative governor. Use operational amplifier notation and assume that amplifiers are available only with inputs of gain 1 or 10.

13 Write a digital computer program which could be used to investigate the dynamic behaviour of the system of Problem 9. (This requires familiarity with Fortran, Pascal or some other high level programming language.)

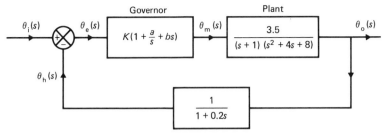

Fig. P7

14 Write a program using the simulation language CSMP to simulate the system of Problem 10. (A program with the correct general form can be written with the information in Section 3.9, but to ensure freedom from errors a CSMP reference manual or textbook is required.)

15 'A component part of a physical system when tested experimentally was found to be closely approximated by a first order transfer function with time constant 10 seconds.'

Explain clearly the significance of this statement, in particular
(i) what is meant by a 'first order transfer function with time constant 10 seconds',
(ii) in what ways the system component could have been tested,
(iii) how it would have been shown to be approximated by a first order transfer function,
(iv) how the numerical value of time constant could have been obtained.

16 A step change of magnitude unity is applied to a dynamic system consisting of two elements in series with transfer functions $\dfrac{1}{1+s}$ and $\dfrac{1}{s^2 + 7s + 10}$ respectively. Obtain an expression for the output response as a function of time. Hence find the steady state value of the output, and check the result using the final value theorem. Find also the maximum overshoot and the approximate time taken to settle within 5% of the steady value.

17 A system component has a transfer function

$$G(s) = \frac{1}{(s+1)(s^2 + s + 1)}$$

Obtain an expression for the output as a function of time resulting from a unit step change of input. Plot the response curve for the transient. Explain the significance of the result with reference to the values of the poles of the transfer function. Sketch also the likely form of the step response for

$$G(s) = \frac{1}{(s+1)(s^2 + 4s + 16)}$$

18 For the simple closed loop system represented by the block diagram of Fig. P8 determine the response c as a function of time t for (a) a unit step change of input (b) a steadily changing input $r = 4t$ for $t \geq 0$. Hence determine the initial rates of change of $c(t)$, the approximate times to settle within 5% of steady

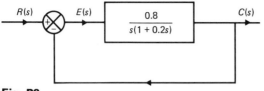

Fig. P8

state, and the steady state errors. How would the response differ if the forward loop gain were increased?

19 What is the 'principle of superposition' and why is it important in control systems analysis?

A thermocouple mechanically strengthened by encapsulation is used to measure the temperature of the fluid flowing in a pipe. It has been established by experimental testing that the response of the encapsulated thermocouple is closely represented by a first order transfer function with time constant of magnitude 2 seconds. The fluid temperature rises suddenly by 20 °C from a constant temperature, and thereafter rises at a constant rate of 2 °C per second for 20 seconds before becoming constant again. Sketch the form of the output response of the thermocouple. Obtain an equation expressing indicated temperature as a function of time, and hence determine the maximum error in the reading and the time at which the error first becomes less than 1 °C and remains less than this value.

20 A system component is known to be represented by the transfer function

$$G(s) = \frac{10}{(1 + s)(1 + 4s)}$$

The input signal to the component increases suddenly from a datum value to a new value 10 units higher, and then 4 seconds later changes suddenly back to the datum value. Sketch approximately to scale the general form of the response of the output which you would expect and explain in some detail why you have drawn it as you have. Derive an analytical expression for the output as a function of time.

21 Fig. P9 shows the output responses recorded when two different system components were subjected in turn to a unit step input function. Estimate the transfer functions of the components, and indicate on a sketch the position of the roots in the s-plane.

22 Describe in state variable form a system characterized by the differential equation

$$\frac{d^3y}{dt^3} + 4.6 \frac{d^2y}{dt^2} + 39.6 \frac{dy}{dt} + 36y = 36u$$

Draw the block diagram representation of the state model.

23 A feedback control system has transfer function

$$G(s) = \frac{s^2 + 3s + 2}{s(s^2 + 7s + 12)}$$

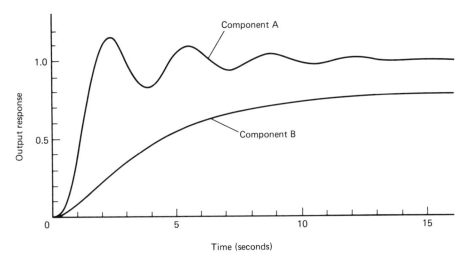

Time (seconds)

Fig. P9

Derive two different state models for this system and give the state variable diagram for each.

24 A multitank system consists of four tanks with cross-sectional areas a_1, a_2, a_3, and a_4 interconnected by pipes with flow resistances R_1, R_2, and R_3. Fluid is normally supplied to tanks 1 and 4 at flow rates $q_1(t)$ and $q_4(t)$, and drawn from tanks 2 and 3 at flow rates $q_2(t)$ and $q_3(t)$ as shown in Fig. P10. These

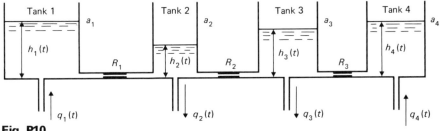

Fig. P10

flow rates are independent of the liquid levels in the tanks, while the flow rate from one tank to another is equal to the difference in liquid levels divided by the flow resistance value. If the controlled or output variables are stated to be $h_2(t)$ and $h_3(t)$ derive the state equations for the three situations when the manipulated or input variables are defined as

(a) $q_1(t)$, $q_2(t)$, $q_3(t)$ and $q_4(t)$
(b) $h_1(t)$, $h_4(t)$, $q_2(t)$ and $q_3(t)$
(c) $h_1(t)$ and $h_4(t)$, with $q_2(t) = q_3(t) = 0$

25 What is the transfer function matrix of a process? Derive the transfer function matrix of the multitank arrangement of Problem 24(c). Assume that $a_1 = a_2 = a_3 = a_4 = a$ and that $R_1 = R_2 = 2R_3 = R$.

26 Describe the system represented by the transfer function

$$G(s) = \frac{10(1 + s)}{s^2 + 7s + 10}$$

using a first order set of state equations in matrix form. Discuss briefly the uniqueness of your realization and derive the analytical expression for the system output response when a unit step is applied to the input.

27 Explain what you understand by a transition matrix and how it is used in the solution of a state vector differential equation. Derive the transition matrix and hence the solution for a unit step input for the following state vector equation

$$\{\dot{x}(t)\} = \begin{bmatrix} 0 & 1 \\ -1 & -1 \end{bmatrix} \{x(t)\} + \begin{bmatrix} 0 \\ 1 \end{bmatrix} u(t)$$

28 A linear time invariant system is represented by the state equation

$$\{\dot{x}(t)\} = \begin{bmatrix} -1 & 0 & 0 \\ 0 & -4 & 0 \\ 0 & 0 & -2 \end{bmatrix} \{x(t)\} + \begin{bmatrix} 1 \\ 1 \\ 1 \end{bmatrix} u(t)$$

Evaluate the solution matrix, and hence obtain the solution of the state equation for an input $u(t) = 1$ and an initial state

$$\{x(0)\} = \begin{bmatrix} 0 \\ 0 \\ 1 \end{bmatrix}$$

Confirm the result by means of the Laplace transform method of solution. If the output is

$$\{y(t)\} = \begin{bmatrix} 1 & 2 & 1 \\ 0 & 1 & 1 \end{bmatrix} \{x(t)\}$$

what is the system matrix transfer function?

29 Given that the coefficient matrix of a process is

$$A = \begin{bmatrix} 0 & 1 \\ -4 & -2 \end{bmatrix}$$

evaluate the solution matrix e^{At} using the first five terms of the series expansion. Calculate numerical values for the elements of the solution matrix for the discrete cases when $t = 1$ second and when $t = 0.5$ second, and say whether the series expansion approximation seems sufficiently accurate.

30 Obtain by calculation the harmonic response characteristics for system components with transfer functions

(a) $G(s) = \dfrac{100}{(s + 1)(s + 2)(s^2 + 3s + 16)}$ (b) $G(s) = \dfrac{1 + 0.1s}{s(1 + 0.02s)(1 + 0.01s)}$

Plot the results on a polar diagram, and explain their significance.

31 Using straight line approximations draw Bode diagrams for the transfer functions of Problem 30. Sketch also more accurate estimates of the harmonic response curves.

32 The information given in Table P1 is harmonic data obtained by frequency response testing a practical system. It is known that the transducer used to measure the output has second order characteristics with $\omega_n = 100$ rad/second, damping factor = 0.1, and gain = 30. Magnitude and phase information for a second order system with damping factor 0.1 is given in Table P2.

Display the test data on a Bode diagram and obtain the harmonic information for the system itself. Hence derive an approximate transfer function for the system. Explain clearly the significance of any curves drawn.

Table P1

Frequency (rad/s)	0.1	0.2	0.4	0.7	1.0	2	4
Amplitude ratio	98.5	47.3	24.5	13.8	8.92	3.55	1.08
Phase lag (deg)	90	95	103	111	119	135	155

Frequency (rad/s)	7	10	20	40	60	80
Amplitude ratio	0.38	0.19	0.05	0.014	0.008	0.0075
Phase lag (deg)	166	170	180	185	192	205

Table P2

$\dfrac{\omega}{\omega_n}$	0.2	0.4	0.6	0.8	1.0
Magnitude	1.04	1.19	1.49	2.54	5
Phase (deg)	0	−5	−14	−24	−90

33 Table P3 lists the experimentally obtained harmonic response information for a component part of a system. Estimate from this the component transfer function, explaining clearly how you obtain your result. Describe the significance of the data tabulated and of the transfer function obtained.

Table P3

Frequency (Hz)	0.01	0.02	0.04	0.07	0.1	0.15	0.2	0.3	0.5
Magnitude (dB)	−8.5	−8.1	−7.4	−6.0	−4.4	−2.0	−0.5	1.0	2.0
Phase (deg)	11	16	24	29	33	34	31	22	12

Frequency (Hz)	0.7	1	2	3	5	7	10	20	30
Magnitude (dB)	2.6	3.0	5.3	6.0	2.3	−5.0	−12.7	−25	−32
Phase (deg)	7	2	−23	−53	−113	−134	−150	−158	−161

34 Define the term 'autocorrelation function' and explain its role in system identification. List the most important properties of such a function and outline the significance of each.

Obtain the autocorrelation function of the variable

$$y = A \sin \omega t + B \cos \left(3\omega t + \frac{\pi}{4} \right) + C$$

where A, B, and C are constants.

35 Derive expressions for the autocorrelation function of
(a) a sine wave $A \sin (\omega t + \varphi)$
(b) white noise with a band limit of ω_c
Hence sketch the form of autocorrelation function which you would expect when signal (a) is contaminated by signal (b), indicating qualitatively the differences which would arise with different ratios of ω_c/ω.

36 Determine the waveform of a pseudo random binary sequence of length 31 bits, and confirm that it satisfies certain laws of randomness. Sketch the form of the autocorrelation function and of the power spectral density for such a sequence with period 6.2 seconds, and explain the significance of each plot.

37 Describe clearly what is meant by the term 'pseudo random binary sequence', and why it is useful for system identification. A practical system has been tested using a PRBS input signal consisting of a 15 bit sequence with a bit interval of 10 seconds. After the initial transient had died out, the input and output traces were recorded; the values of the output measured at the mid-point of each bit interval are given in Table P4. Determine from these the impulse response of the system, and suggest the form of transfer function which the system is likely to have, with values of parameters where these can be estimated.

Table P4

Input	+1	+1	+1	+1	−1	−1	−1	+1	−1	−1	+1	+1	−1	+1	−1
Output	11	10	9	8	8	11	14	14	10	3	0	4	11	11	10

38 Determine the steady state error which would be present with different forms of input excitation for a unity feedback system in which the forward loop transfer function is

(a) $G(s) = \dfrac{15}{s(s + 3)(s^2 + 5s + 10)}$

(b) $G(s) = \dfrac{1}{s^3 + 5s^2 + 6s + 10}$

Describe how this error could be reduced in each case and explain what side effects result.

39 A feedback control system incorporating a 3-term controller has the block diagram representation shown in Fig. P11. Determine by means of the Routh–Hurwitz criterion the ranges of values of the gain K for which the system is stable

(i) when $a = b = 0$ (proportional control)
(ii) when $a = 1, b = 0$ (proportional + integral control)
(iii) when $a = b = 1$ (proportional + integral + derivative control)

Obtain also the frequencies of sustained oscillations where these occur. What would be the magnitude of the lowest achievable steady state error in each of the above cases for a step input and for a ramp input?

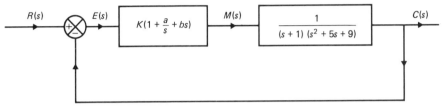

Fig. P11

40 A temperature controller is represented schematically by the block diagram of Fig. P12. All components are assumed to be linear and to have transfer functions as shown. Draw a Bode diagram for the system and hence determine the values of gain margin and phase margin. Straight line approximations may be used but, in assessing the gain and phase margin, an estimate should be made of the inaccuracy arising from the difference between the true curves and the straight line approximations. Discuss the significance of the values obtained.

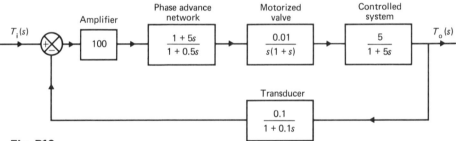

Fig. P12

41 The open loop harmonic response data obtained experimentally for the forward path of a unity feedback control system are given in Table P5. By plotting the magnitude information on a Bode diagram, estimate the likely form of the system transfer function. Plot a Nyquist diagram for the range 2 to 20 rad/s and use it to obtain a plot of closed loop magnification against frequency. Hence determine the values of peak magnification and bandwidth, and explain the significance of the values obtained.

Table P5

Frequency (rad/s)	0.3	0.6	1.0	2	3	4	5	6
Magnitude (dB)	26.5	20.5	16.0	9.5	6.0	1.0	−2.2	−5.0
Phase lag (deg)	95	100	109	124	135	147	156	164

Frequency (rad/s)	8	10	15	20	30	40	60	80
Magnitude (dB)	−9.0	−13.0	−20.0	−27.0	−36.0	−42.5	−51.5	−59.0
Phase lag (deg)	176	185	—	230	—	252	—	—

42 A feedback system with $H(s) = 1$ has forward loop transfer function given by

$$G(s) = \frac{35}{s(3s + 1)(s^2 + 2s + 10)}$$

Determine the open loop frequency response by any appropriate method and hence estimate the values of gain margin and phase margin. Sketch the form of the closed loop magnitude against frequency relationship. Comment on the significance of the results.

43 The open loop transfer function of a unity-feedback control system is given by

$$\dot{G}(s) = \frac{K}{s(1 + 0.1s)(1 + 0.01s)}$$

Evaluate the gain margin and phase margin in terms of K, and hence find the limiting value of K for stability. Check the result by means of the Routh–Hurwitz criterion. What are the magnitudes of the gain and phase margins when K is half of the limiting value?

44 A unity feedback servomechanism has an open loop harmonic response described by

$$G(j\omega) = \frac{-200(1 + 0.1j\omega)}{\omega^2(1 + 0.01j\omega)(1 + 0.02j\omega)}$$

By plotting the harmonic response information on a Nichols chart evaluate the gain and phase margins, and the values of M_p, ω_p, and bandwidth. Plot also the overall magnitude and phase of the servomechanism against an abscissa of frequency. Explain the significance of the results.

45 The regulator system shown in Fig. P13 controls the output response $c(t)$ of a process plant. The harmonic response characteristics of the plant alone,

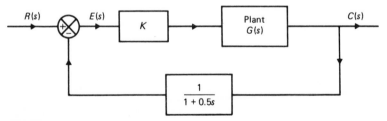

Fig. P13

obtained experimentally, are given by the values listed in Table P6. There is a simple lag with time constant 0.5 second associated with the measurement of the system output $c(t)$, and a gain term K operating on the error signal. Draw

Table P6

ω(rad/second)	0.3	0.5	0.8	1.0	1.2	1.5	2	3	5
$\|G(j\omega)\|$	1.48	1.65	1.88	1.75	1.25	0.73	0.41	0.18	0.06
$\angle G(j\omega)$	$-15°$	$-28°$	$-61°$	$-93°$	$-115°$	$-136°$	$-152°$	$-162°$	$-170°$

the open loop Nyquist diagram for the system and from the plot determine the value of K required for a gain margin of 8 dB. For this value of K determine the variation of closed loop magnification with frequency. Discuss what effect the transducer time constant has on the steady state and dynamic behaviour of the overall system.

46 Sketch the form of the root locus plot corresponding to each of the following open loop transfer functions $G(s)H(s)$, determining as appropriate the numerical values of the salient features which indicate the shape of each plot. Describe in a short paragraph for each how the transient response of the closed loop system might be expected to change with variation of gain constant K.

(i) $$\frac{K}{s(s + 4)(s^2 + 16s + 100)}$$

(ii) $$\frac{K}{s(s + 20)(s^2 + 16s + 100)}$$

(iii) $$\frac{K(s + 3)}{(s + 1)(s + 2)(s + 6)}$$

(iv) $$\frac{K(1 + 10s)}{s^2(1 + 5s)(1 + s)}$$

(v) $$\frac{K(1 + 2s + 3/s)}{(1 + 0.5s)(1 + s)(1 + 3s)}$$

(vi) $$\frac{K}{s(1 + 0.1s)^2}$$

(vii) $$\frac{K(s + 5)}{s^2(s + 20)}$$

(viii) $$\frac{K(s^2 + 2s + 16)}{s(s + 1)(s^2 + 4s + 16)}$$

47 Sketch the general form of the root locus plot for the temperature control system shown in Fig. P12 for variation of the amplifier gain K, indicating clearly the important features. Draw accurately sufficient of the plot to permit determination of the value K required to give a damping factor of 0.7 for the dominant roots, and to determine the value of ω_n for these roots. Mark on the plot the approximate positions of the remaining roots, and comment on the significance of their contribution to the transient response.

48 A feedback system has

$$G(s) = \frac{K}{(1 + s)(1 + 0.08s)(s^2 + 4s + 5)}, \quad H(s) = \frac{1}{1 + 0.1s}$$

By plotting a root locus diagram, determine the approximate value of K required to ensure that the dominant mode of oscillation has a damping factor of 0.7. For this value of K write down an expression for $C(s)$, the Laplace transform of the output response, when the input is subjected to a step change of magnitude unity. By studying the root locus plot to decide which roots have negligible influence, write down a simplified expression for $C(s)$ from which a good approximation to $c(t)$, the output response, could be obtained by Laplace inversion. Estimate the value of the settling time.

49 Fig. P14 shows the block diagram representation of a temperature control loop for an exothermal reaction process. Draw a root locus diagram indicating clearly the important features of the plot. Describe fully what the plot shows about the transient behaviour and stability of the system, and hence determine approximately what is likely to be the most suitable value of controller gain K_c. State clearly your criterion for suitability.

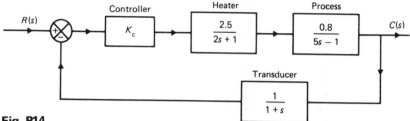

Fig. P14

50 The open loop transfer function of a unity feedback positional servomechanism with the gain adjusted so that the maximum allowable steady state error is not exceeded is

$$G(s) = \frac{20}{s(1 + 0.1s)(1 + 0.2s)}$$

Sketch the root locus plot and determine the undamped natural frequency and damping factor of the dominant roots. Show how the plot is modified by the introduction in the forward loop of a series compensating network with transfer function $\dfrac{1 + 4s}{1 + 30s}$. What are the new values of natural frequency and damping factor for the dominant roots? Explain the significance of the results.

51 A feedback system, Fig. P15, has open loop transfer function

$$G(s)H(s) = \frac{K(1 + Ts)}{s(1 + 0.1s)(1 + 0.02s)}$$

Sketch a root locus diagram to show the variation of the values of the roots of the characteristic equation as the magnitude of the lead term time constant T is altered from zero to a very large value, for a constant value of gain $K = 50$. Draw on the same plot the corresponding loci for values of $K = 20$ and $K = 100$.

52 A closed loop system (Fig. P15) has feedforward and feedback transfer functions given by

$$G(s) = \frac{100(1 + s)}{(1 + 2s)(1 + 4s)} \quad \text{and } H(s) = \frac{1}{1 + \tau s}$$

Sketch the form of the root locus plot for variation of the time constant τ. Comment on the significance of the plot.

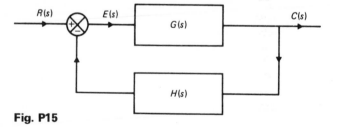

Fig. P15

53 What role does the z-transform serve in the analysis of sampled-data systems? Obtain the z-transform of the transfer function

$$G(s) = \frac{s + 2}{s^2 + 4s + 8}$$

54 For the error sampled unity feedback arrangement shown in Fig. P16 obtain

    (i) the z-transform of the output response, $C(z)$
    (ii) the output response $c^*(t)$ up to the 5th sampling instant, and
    (iii) the final value of the output response

when the input disturbance is a unit step.

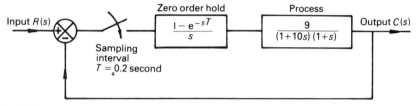

Fig. P16

55 Explain why the transformation $z = \dfrac{r + 1}{r - 1}$ is used in the analysis of sampled-data systems. Show by application of the Routh–Hurwitz criterion that the limiting conditions for stability of the system shown in Fig. P17 are given by

$$K > 0, \quad K < \frac{2(1 + e^{-T})}{1 - e^{-T}}$$

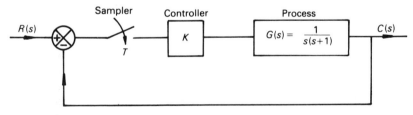

Fig. P17

56 The open loop pulse transfer function of a unity feedback sampled-data control system is given by

$$G(z) = \frac{K(z + 3)}{z(z^2 + 2z + 2)(z + 5)(z + 6)}$$

Sketch the root loci of the system indicating clearly all important features and determine the marginal value of K for stability.

57 The open loop pulsed transfer function for an error sampled control system is

$$GH(z) = \frac{0.792zK}{(z - 1)(z - 0.208)}$$

where $K = 1.57$. Use the bilinear transformation $z = \dfrac{r + 1}{r - 1}$ and plot the polar diagram for this system. From the diagram estimate the phase margin, the gain margin, and the limiting value of K for stability. Comment on the suitability of the system.

58 Explain why proportional, integral and derivative action are of use in a controller in a closed loop system, and how each affects the response of the system. A process consists of four non-interacting stages in series, these being closely represented by simple lags of time constant 3, 5, 1, and 5 minutes and gains of 1, 0.4, 1, and 5 respectively. The process is controlled by a proportional controller of gain 2.5 in a unity feedback system. Is the system stable or not? If integral action time with $T_i = 10$ minutes is added, will the system be stable? If for simulation purposes the time constants and integral action time are considered to be in seconds, what is the effect on stability?

59 Sketch the root locus plot for the process of Problem 58 under the action of a proportional controller of gain K. Show how the plot differs when a 2-term or 3-term controller is used, by sketching qualitatively the form of the plot for various orders of magnitude of integral action time T_i and derivative action time T_d.

60 A regulator system employs rate feedback, as shown in block diagram form in Fig. P18. For the transfer functions shown, and assuming in the first instance that the time constant T is negligible, determine the values of K and k required for the following specification: the steady state error for a step change of input should not exceed 4%, and any dominant complex roots should have a damping factor as large as possible, but not greater than 0.8. How different are the results if $T = 0.05$ seconds?

61 A closed loop system employing minor loop compensation has a block diagram of the form shown in Fig. P18 but with

$$G_1(s) = \frac{K}{s(1 + 0.1s)} \quad \text{and } H_1(s) = \frac{0.02s}{1 + 0.02s}$$

Determine the value of forward loop gain K required to ensure that the peak magnification has a value in the range 1.3 to 1.4. What are the values of resonant frequency, bandwidth, gain margin and phase margin?

62 A feedback system incorporates acceleration feedback, and has a block diagram of the form shown in Fig. P18 with transfer functions

$$G_1(s) = \frac{80}{s(s + 1)(s + 2)(s + 4)}, \quad H_1(s) = ks^2$$

Draw a root locus diagram which shows the variation in the roots of the characteristic equation with variation of the constant k. What information does the plot give about the dynamic performance of the system?

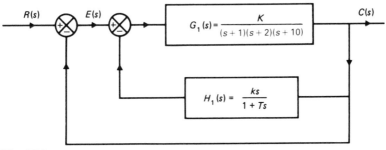

Fig. P18

63 Draw the Bode diagram for the servomechanism of Problem 50 both without and with the compensation element in the loop. What effect does the given phase lag series compensation network have on the values of gain margin and phase margin?

64 Design a phase lead series compensation network in order that the closed loop system shown in Fig. P15, with

$$G(s) = \frac{K}{s(1 + 0.25s)}, \quad H(s) = 1$$

has a velocity error constant of at least 100 second^{-1}, and a phase margin of at least 45°. Draw a block diagram for the compensated system, showing the transfer function of each block.

65 A servomechanism (Fig. P15) has forward path transfer function

$$G(s) = \frac{0.05}{s(1 + 1.25s)}$$

and feedback path transfer function

$$H(s) = \frac{10}{1 + 0.01s}.$$

It is required that the velocity error coefficient K_v be 15 second^{-1} and the phase margin be 45° minimum. Design a phase lead series network to enable this specification to be met. Compare the values of gain margin and phase margin before and after compensation, and comment on the significance.

66 For the system used in Example 11.3, design a state variable feedback loop so that the maximum overshoot does not exceed 20% of a step input disturbance and the steady state error does not exceed 1%. Take a value of $K = 10$.

67 A regulator system using state variable feedback is described by the following state equations

$$\{\dot{x}\} = \begin{bmatrix} 1 & -3 \\ 5 & 0 \end{bmatrix} \{x\} + \begin{bmatrix} 0 \\ 1 \end{bmatrix} u$$

$$u = -[h_1 h_2]\{x\}$$

Find the equation relating h_1 to h_2 when

(i) the system has an undamped natural frequency of $\sqrt{2}$ rad/second
(ii) the system has a damping factor of 0.707.

Evaluate the coefficients of the feedback matrix if the system has a natural frequency of $\sqrt{2}$ rad/second and a damping factor of 0.707.

68 Describe the advantages to be gained by employing feedback in control systems, give the reasons why analysis is necessary in the design stage, and outline the general form which such analysis could take for any given physical system.

Appendix B
Bibliography

A selected list of books for further reading

General texts on feedback control theory which are complementary to this book
1   Auslander, D. M., Takahashi, Y., and Rabins, M. J. *Introducing Systems and Control*, McGraw-Hill, 1974.
    Broadly similar coverage, with emphasis on state representation and digital computer solution; very useful, and presents ideas in a different way.
2   Kuo, B. C. *Automatic Control Systems*, Prentice Hall, (4th Ed.), 1982.
    Both classical and state variable approach; the 4th edition has increased emphasis on digital control and design.
3   Raven, F. H. *Automatic Control Engineering*, McGraw-Hill, (3rd Ed.), 1978.
    Mainly classical approach; additional material on practical components, state space, digital control, and non-linear systems.
4   D'Azzo, J. J., and Houpis, C. H. *Feedback Control System Analysis and Synthesis*, McGraw-Hill, (2nd Ed.), 1966.
    Very detailed treatment of classical linear control theory.
5   D'Azzo, J. J., and Houpis, C. H. *Linear Control System Analysis and Design*, McGraw-Hill, 1975.
    Both the classical and modern approach.
6   Shinners, S. M. *Modern Control System Theory and Application*, Addison Wesley, 1972.
    Aims to bridge the gap between the classical and modern approaches.
7   Towill, D. R. *Transfer Function Techniques for Control Engineers*, Iliffe, 1970.
    Very useful for clarifying the relationship between root locus plots and transient response.
8   Healey, M. *Principles of Automatic Control*, EUP, (3rd Ed.), 1975.
    Introduces the main principles of a wide range of control engineering topics.
9   Truxall, J. G. *Automatic Feedback Control System Synthesis*, McGraw-Hill, 1955.
    A classic early text with much useful information.
10 Eveleigh, V. W. *Introduction to Control Systems Design*, McGraw-Hill, 1972.
    A comprehensive basic text.

11   Emanuel, P., and Leff, E. *Introduction to Feedback Control Systems*, McGraw-Hill, 1979.
An elementary introduction by the classical approach, with inclusion of data acquisition and interfacing between computer and control system.

12   Sante, D. P. *Automatic Control System Technology*, Prentice Hall, 1980.
Elementary text, with particular reference to electrical systems.

13   Miller, R. W. *Servomechanisms, Devices and Fundamentals*, Reston, 1977.
Elementary, and largely hardware oriented.

Texts of particular relevance to specific chapters
14   Mayr, O. *The Origins of Feedback Control*, MIT Press, 1970.
History of the early development of practical feedback control systems.

15   Johnson, C. L. *Analog Computer Techniques*, McGraw-Hill, (2nd Ed.), 1963.

16   Wilkins, B. R. *Analogue and Iterative Methods*, Chapman and Hall, 1970.
This and the previous book give a more detailed treatment of basic analogue computation.

17   Dorn, W. S., and McCracken, D. D. *Numerical Methods with Fortran IV Case Studies*, John Wiley, 1972.

18   Korn, G. A., and Wait, J. V. *Digital Continuous System Simulation*, Prentice Hall, 1978.

19   Speckhart, F. H., and Green, W. L. *A Guide to Using CSMP*, Prentice Hall, 1976.

20   Davies, W. D. T. *System Identification for Self-Adaptive Control*, Wiley Interscience, 1970.
Statistical system identification and its use for automatic identification.

21   Thaler, G. J. *Design of Feedback Systems*, Dowden Hutchinson and Ross, 1973.
An excellent treatment of system design.

22   Hohn, F. E. *Elementary Matrix Algebra*, Macmillan, (3rd Ed.), 1973.

23   Hildebrand, F. B. *Methods of Applied Mathematics*, Prentice Hall, (2nd Ed.), 1965.
These two books contain a more complete treatment of matrix algebra.

24   Jury, E. I. *Sampled-Data Control Systems*, John Wiley, 1958.

25   Kuo, B. C. *Analysis and Synthesis of Sampled-Data Control Systems*, Prentice Hall, 1963.

More advanced texts which extend the basic theory included here
26   MacFarlane, A. G. J. *Dynamical Systems Models*, Harrap, 1970.

27   Nicholson, H. (Ed.) *Modelling of Dynamical Systems*, Institution of Electrical Engineers, 1980.

28   Bishop, A. B. *Introduction to Discrete Linear Controls*, Academic Press, 1975.

29   Newland, D. E. *Random Vibrations and Spectral Analysis*, Longman, 1975.

30   Rosenbrock, H. H. *State-space and Multivariable Theory*, Nelson, 1970.

31   Mishkin, E., and Braun, L. *Adaptive Control Systems*, McGraw-Hill, 1961.

32   Graupe, D. *Identification of Systems*, Van Nostrand Reinhold, 1972.

33   Kirk, D. E. *Optimal Control Theory*, Prentice Hall, 1970.

34 Chu, Y. *Digital Simulation of Continuous Systems*, McGraw-Hill, 1969.

35 Ord-Smith, R. J., and Stephenson, J. *Computer Simulation of Continuous Systems*, Cambridge University Press, 1975.

36 Chestnut, H. *Systems Engineering Tools*, John Wiley, 1965.

37 Lee, T. H., Adams, G. E., and Gaines, W. M. *Computer Process Control: Modelling and Optimisation*, John Wiley, 1968.

38 Kuo, B. C. *Digital Control Systems*, Holt, Rinehart and Winston, 1980.

39 Rosenbrock, H. H. *Computer Aided Control System Design*, Academic Press, 1974.

Appendix C
Introduction to Matrix Algebra

This appendix presents definitions of some terms used in matrix algebra and of elementary matrix operations, and provides a foundation for understanding the mathematical material included in Chapter 5 and Section 11.10, for those readers unfamiliar with matrix algebra.

(a) *Matrix.* A matrix is a set of elements consisting of real or complex numbers, functions or operators, arranged in a rectangular formation of rows and columns which is denoted by square brackets and is of the form

$$A = \begin{bmatrix} a_{11} & a_{12} & . & . & a_{1n} \\ a_{21} & & & & a_{2n} \\ . & & & & . \\ . & & & & . \\ a_{m1} & a_{m2} & . & . & a_{mn} \end{bmatrix}$$

This matrix with m rows and n columns is said to be a matrix of order $m \times n$, and the symbol a_{ij} is used to denote the element located in the ith row and the jth column. If $n = 1$, the matrix has only one column and is known as a column vector; if $m = 1$ it is called a row vector. When $m = n$ the matrix is described as square, and of order n.

For the special case when $m = n$, and all the off-diagonal elements are equal to zero ($a_{ij} = 0$ for $i \neq j$), the matrix reduces to a diagonal matrix of the form

$$\begin{bmatrix} a_{11} & 0 & 0 & 0 & . & 0 \\ 0 & a_{22} & 0 & 0 & . & 0 \\ 0 & 0 & a_{33} & 0 & . & 0 \\ 0 & 0 & 0 & a_{44} & . & 0 \\ . & . & . & . & . & . \\ 0 & 0 & 0 & 0 & . & a_{nn} \end{bmatrix}$$

A diagonal matrix, where all the diagonal elements have the value unity ($a_{ii} = 1$), is called a unit matrix or an identity matrix and given the symbol I.

(b) *Determinant.* For any square matrix, a determinant can be evaluated from the elements of the matrix. For example, if

$$A = \begin{bmatrix} 3 & -2 & 4 \\ 1 & 5 & 6 \\ 2 & 1 & 7 \end{bmatrix}$$

then

$$\det A = |A| = 3 \begin{vmatrix} 5 & 6 \\ 1 & 7 \end{vmatrix} - (-2) \begin{vmatrix} 1 & 6 \\ 2 & 7 \end{vmatrix} + 4 \begin{vmatrix} 1 & 5 \\ 2 & 1 \end{vmatrix}$$

$$= 3(29) + 2(-5) + 4(-9) = 41$$

When the determinant of a matrix is zero, the matrix A is called singular.

(c) *Transpose of a matrix.* The transpose of matrix A, denoted by A^T, is the matrix formed by interchanging rows and columns of A. If the original matrix is an $m \times n$ matrix, its transpose is an $n \times m$ matrix.

$$A^T = \begin{bmatrix} a_{11} & a_{12} & \cdot & \cdot & a_{1n} \\ a_{21} & a_{22} & & & a_{2n} \\ \cdot & & & & \cdot \\ \cdot & & & & \cdot \\ a_{m1} & a_{m2} & \cdot & \cdot & a_{mn} \end{bmatrix}^T = \begin{bmatrix} a_{11} & a_{21} & \cdot & \cdot & a_{m1} \\ a_{12} & a_{22} & & & a_{m2} \\ \cdot & & & & \cdot \\ \cdot & & & & \cdot \\ a_{1n} & a_{2n} & \cdot & \cdot & a_{mn} \end{bmatrix}$$

The transpose of a column vector is a row vector and vice versa.

(d) *Multiplication of a matrix by a scalar quantity.* A matrix is said to be multiplied by a scalar K if all elements a_{ij} are multiplied by K.

(e) *Addition and subtraction of matrices.* Addition and subtraction of two matrices can only be performed if the two matrices have the same order. Addition of two matrices A and B results in a new matrix C with its elements c_{ij} equal to the sum of the corresponding elements a_{ij} and b_{ij}. Further

$$(A + B)^T = A^T + B^T$$

Similar arguments apply for subtraction of matrices.

(f) *Multiplication of matrices.* The multiplication of two matrices is possible only if the number of columns of the first matrix is equal to the number of rows of the second. If an $m \times n$ matrix A is post multiplied by an $n \times p$ matrix B, then the result will be a matrix C of order $m \times p$. For example,

$$\begin{bmatrix} a_{11} & a_{12} & a_{13} \\ a_{21} & a_{22} & a_{23} \\ a_{31} & a_{32} & a_{33} \\ a_{41} & a_{42} & a_{43} \end{bmatrix} \begin{bmatrix} b_{11} & b_{12} \\ b_{21} & b_{22} \\ b_{31} & b_{32} \end{bmatrix} =$$

(4 × 3 matrix) (3 × 2 matrix)

$$\begin{bmatrix} a_{11}b_{11} + a_{12}b_{21} + a_{13}b_{31} & a_{11}b_{12} + a_{12}b_{22} + a_{13}b_{32} \\ a_{21}b_{11} + a_{22}b_{21} + a_{23}b_{31} & a_{21}b_{12} + a_{22}b_{22} + a_{23}b_{32} \\ a_{31}b_{11} + a_{32}b_{21} + a_{33}b_{31} & a_{31}b_{12} + a_{32}b_{22} + a_{33}b_{32} \\ a_{41}b_{11} + a_{42}b_{21} + a_{43}b_{31} & a_{41}b_{12} + a_{42}b_{22} + a_{43}b_{32} \end{bmatrix}$$

(4 × 2 matrix)

That is, the elements c_{ij} are found by multiplying the elements of the ith row of A with the elements of the jth column of B and then summing these element products. It is important to note that generally in matrix multiplication

$$AB \neq BA$$

hence it is always necessary to specify the relative position of the matrices to be multiplied. Multiplication of any matrix by a unit matrix results in the original matrix $(AI = A)$. The transpose of the product of two matrices is the product of their transposes in reverse order, i.e.

$$(AB)^T = B^T A^T$$

(g) *Cofactor and adjoint of a matrix.* The cofactor A_{ij} of a matrix A is defined as

$$A_{ij} = (-1)^{i+j} M_{ij}$$

where M_{ij} is the minor determinant of the A matrix. The minor M_{ij} of an $n \times n$ matrix is the determinant of the $(n-1) \times (n-1)$ matrix formed by deleting the ith row and jth column of the $n \times n$ matrix.

The adjoint matrix is found by replacing each element a_{ij} of matrix A by its cofactor A_{ij} and then transposing. For example,

$$\text{Adj} \begin{bmatrix} 3 & -2 & 4 \\ 1 & 5 & 6 \\ 2 & 1 & 7 \end{bmatrix} = \begin{bmatrix} \begin{vmatrix} 5 & 6 \\ 1 & 7 \end{vmatrix} & -\begin{vmatrix} 1 & 6 \\ 2 & 7 \end{vmatrix} & \begin{vmatrix} 1 & 5 \\ 2 & 1 \end{vmatrix} \\ -\begin{vmatrix} -2 & 4 \\ 1 & 7 \end{vmatrix} & \begin{vmatrix} 3 & 4 \\ 2 & 7 \end{vmatrix} & -\begin{vmatrix} 3 & -2 \\ 2 & 1 \end{vmatrix} \\ \begin{vmatrix} -2 & 4 \\ 5 & 6 \end{vmatrix} & -\begin{vmatrix} 3 & 4 \\ 1 & 6 \end{vmatrix} & \begin{vmatrix} 3 & -2 \\ 1 & 5 \end{vmatrix} \end{bmatrix}^T$$

$$= \begin{bmatrix} 29 & 5 & -9 \\ 18 & 13 & -7 \\ -32 & -14 & 17 \end{bmatrix}^T = \begin{bmatrix} 29 & 18 & -32 \\ 5 & 13 & -14 \\ -9 & -7 & 17 \end{bmatrix}$$

(h) *Inverse, or reciprocal, of a matrix.* The inverse of a square matrix A is written as A^{-1} and defined by

$$AA^{-1} = A^{-1}A = I$$

The inverse of matrix A is evaluated numerically by dividing its adjoint matrix by its determinant

$$A^{-1} = \frac{\text{adj } A}{\text{det } A}$$

(i) *Matrix Calculus.* The derivative of an $m \times n$ matrix $A(t)$ is defined to be

$$\frac{d}{dt} A(t) = \begin{bmatrix} \dfrac{d}{dt} a_{11}(t) & \dfrac{d}{dt} a_{12}(t) & \cdot & \cdot & \dfrac{d}{dt} a_{1n}(t) \\ \dfrac{d}{dt} a_{21}(t) & \dfrac{d}{dt} a_{22}(t) & \cdot & \cdot & \dfrac{d}{dt} a_{2n}(t) \\ & \cdot & & & \\ & \cdot & & & \\ \dfrac{d}{dt} a_{m1}(t) & \dfrac{d}{dt} a_{m2}(t) & \cdot & \cdot & \dfrac{d}{dt} a_{mn}(t) \end{bmatrix}$$

Similarly the integral of an $m \times n$ matrix $A(t)$ is defined as

$$\int A(t)\, dt = \begin{bmatrix} \int a_{11}(t)\, dt & \int a_{12}(t)\, dt & . & . & \int a_{1n}(t)\, dt \\ \int a_{21}(t)\, dt & \int a_{22}(t)\, dt & . & . & \int a_{2n}(t)\, dt \\ . & & & & . \\ . & & & & . \\ . & & & & . \\ \int a_{m1}(t)\, dt & \int a_{m2}(t)\, dt & . & . & \int a_{mn}(t)\, dt \end{bmatrix}$$

(j) *Phase-variable canonical form*

Consider the linear time invariant system described by the nth order differential equation:

$$\frac{d^n c(t)}{dt^n} + a_1 \frac{d^{n-1} c(t)}{dt^{n-1}} + \ldots + a_n c(t) = r(t)$$

For this equation it is possible to define the state variables as:

$$x_1(t) = c(t)$$

$$x_2(t) = \frac{dc(t)}{dt}$$

.

.

.

$$x_n(t) = \frac{d^{n-1} c(t)}{dt^{n-1}}$$

and write the nth order differential equation as a set of 1st order equations, viz

$$\dot{x}_1(t) = x_2(t)$$

$$\dot{x}_2(t) = x_3(t)$$

.

.

.

$$\dot{x}_{n-1}(t) = x_n(t)$$

$$\dot{x}_n(t) = -a_n x_1(t) - a_{n-1} x_2(t) \ldots - a_1 x_n(t) + r(t)$$

Writing these in the concise form of Eq. 5.16 yields

$$A = \begin{bmatrix} 0 & 1 & 0 & 0 & \cdots & 0 \\ 0 & 0 & 1 & 0 & \cdots & 0 \\ 0 & 0 & 0 & 1 & \cdots & 0 \\ . & . & . & . & \cdots & . \\ . & . & . & . & \cdots & . \\ 0 & 0 & 0 & 0 & \cdots & 1 \\ -a_n & -a_{n-1} & -a_{n-2} & -a_{n-3} & \cdots & -a_1 \end{bmatrix} \, ; \quad B = \begin{bmatrix} 0 \\ 0 \\ 0 \\ . \\ . \\ 0 \\ 1 \end{bmatrix}$$

With the coefficient matrix of the process and its driving matrix arranged in this way, Eq. 5.16 is said to be written in 'phase-variable canonical form'.

The matrix operations presented in this appendix can readily be carried out on a digital computer using the standard sub-routine programs available on most commercial machines.

Appendix D
Answers to Problems

1
$$q' = C_1(p_1' - p_2') + C_2\eta' + C_3l'$$

where all variables are relative to a datum, and with constants

$$C_1 = \left[\frac{\pi dh^3}{12\eta l}\right]_0, \quad C_2 = \left[\frac{\pi dh^3(p_1 - p_2)}{12\eta^2 l}\right]_0, \quad C_3 = \left[\frac{\pi dh^3(p_1 - p_2)}{12\eta l^2}\right]_0$$

where [ ]$_0$ indicates that the expressions are evaluated using absolute values of d, h, η etc. for the datum condition.

2
$$\frac{Cs + (K_2 + 2K_3)}{CMs^3 + (K_2M + 2K_3M)s^2 + K_2Cs + 2K_2K_3},$$

$$\frac{J_2s^2 + K}{s(J_1J_2s^3 + CJ_2s^2 + K(J_1 + J_2)s + CK)}$$

3
$$\frac{1 + R_2Cs}{1 + (R_1 + R_2)Cs}, \quad \frac{(1 + R_1C_1s)(1 + R_2C_2s)}{1 + (R_1C_1 + R_2C_2 + R_1C_2)s + R_1R_2C_1C_2s^2},$$

$$\frac{1 + C_1(R_1 + R_2)s + R_1R_2C_1C_2s^2}{1 + (R_1C_1 + R_1C_2 + R_2C_1)s + R_1R_2C_1C_2s^2}$$

4
$$\frac{1}{\dfrac{W_1W_2}{H_1H_2}s^2 + \left(\dfrac{W_1}{H_1} + \dfrac{W_1}{H_2} + \dfrac{W_2}{H_2}\right)s + 1}$$

5
$$\frac{\dfrac{AC_1C_2}{K(C_1 + K_L)}}{\dfrac{M}{K}s^2 + \left(\dfrac{\mu}{K} + \dfrac{A^2}{K(C_1 + K_L)}\right)s + 1}$$

where A is piston area,
    K is spring stiffness,
    K_L and μ are leakage and viscous drag coefficients,
and C_1 and C_2 are coefficients in linearized orifice and lever equations.

6

$$\frac{1}{\dfrac{vM}{AK_BC}s^3 + \left(\dfrac{2K_LM}{AC} + \dfrac{v\mu}{AK_BC}\right)s^2 + \left(\dfrac{2A}{C} + \dfrac{2K_L\mu}{AC}\right)s + 1}$$

where the symbols are as defined on pages 22–26.

7

$$\frac{Y(s)}{\theta(s)} = \frac{L}{(1 + \tau_1 s)(1 + \tau_2 s)} \quad \text{where } \tau_1 = \frac{2A}{Q_v}, \ \tau_2 = \frac{cm}{H}$$

8

9

10

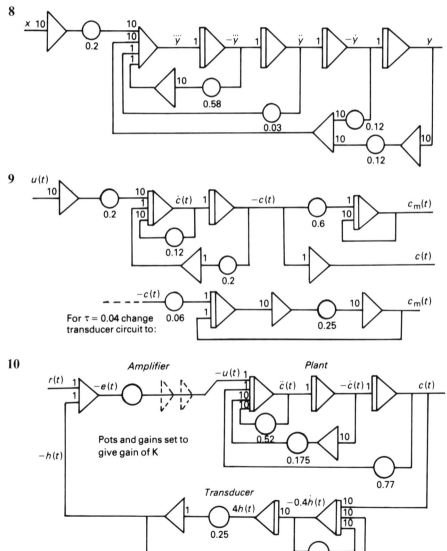

11

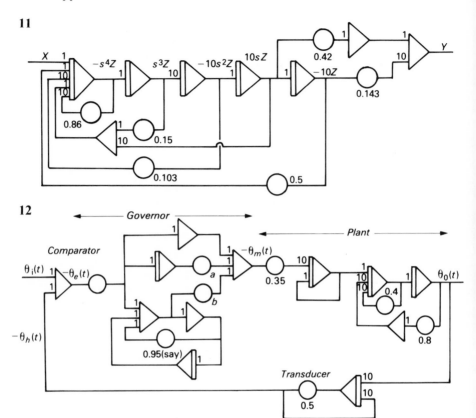

12

16 $$c(t) = \tfrac{1}{10} - \tfrac{1}{4}e^{-t} + \tfrac{1}{6}e^{-2t} - \tfrac{1}{60}e^{-5t}$$
$$c(\infty) = 0.1. \quad \text{No overshoot.} \quad 3.9 \text{ seconds}$$

17 $$c(t) = 1 - e^{-t} - 1.155e^{-0.5t} \sin 0.866t$$

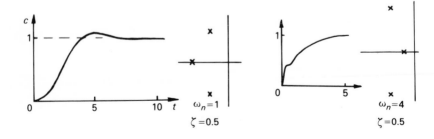

18   (a) $c(t) = 1 - \tfrac{4}{3}e^{-t} + \tfrac{1}{3}e^{-4t}$
        (b) $c(t) = 4t - 5 + \tfrac{16}{3}e^{-t} - \tfrac{1}{3}e^{-4t}$
        zero;   3.3 seconds;   0 and 5.

19
$$6 + 2t - 6e^{-0.5t} \text{ for } t \leq 20$$
$$50 - 4e^{-0.5(t-20)} \text{ for } t > 20$$

Maximum error is $10°$ at $t = 0$. Error $< 1°$ when $t > 22.8$ seconds.

20
$$100(1 - 1.33e^{-0.25t} + 0.33e^{-t}) \text{ for } 0 \leq t \leq 4$$
$$100(2.29e^{-0.25t} + 17.87e^{-t}) \text{ for } t \geq 4$$

21
$$\frac{4}{(s+1)(s^2+0.6s+4)}, \quad \frac{0.8}{(1+3.5s)(1+0.8s)}$$

22

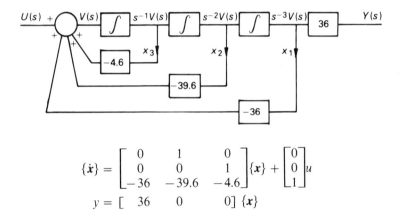

$$\{\dot{x}\} = \begin{bmatrix} 0 & 1 & 0 \\ 0 & 0 & 1 \\ -36 & -39.6 & -4.6 \end{bmatrix} \{x\} + \begin{bmatrix} 0 \\ 0 \\ 1 \end{bmatrix} u$$
$$y = \begin{bmatrix} 36 & 0 & 0 \end{bmatrix} \{x\}$$

23

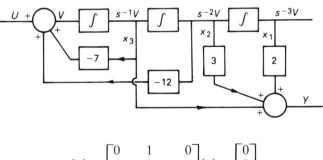

$$\{\dot{x}\} = \begin{bmatrix} 0 & 1 & 0 \\ 0 & 0 & 1 \\ 0 & -12 & -7 \end{bmatrix} \{x\} + \begin{bmatrix} 0 \\ 0 \\ 1 \end{bmatrix} u$$
$$y = \begin{bmatrix} 2 & 3 & 1 \end{bmatrix} \{x\}$$

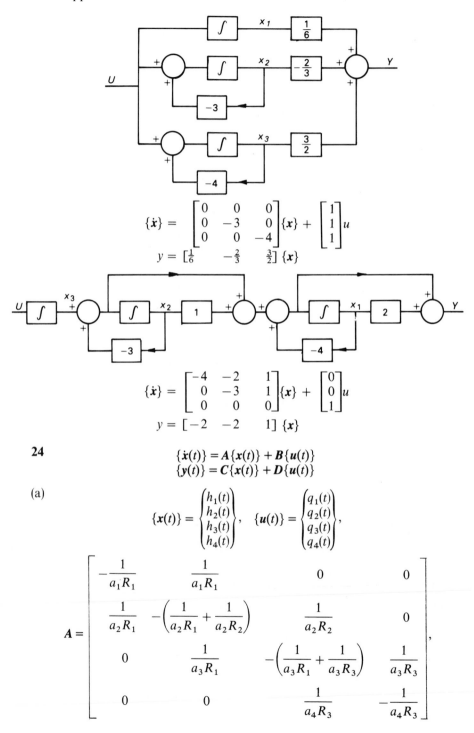

$$\{\dot{x}\} = \begin{bmatrix} 0 & 0 & 0 \\ 0 & -3 & 0 \\ 0 & 0 & -4 \end{bmatrix} \{x\} + \begin{bmatrix} 1 \\ 1 \\ 1 \end{bmatrix} u$$

$$y = \begin{bmatrix} \frac{1}{6} & -\frac{2}{3} & \frac{3}{2} \end{bmatrix} \{x\}$$

$$\{\dot{x}\} = \begin{bmatrix} -4 & -2 & 1 \\ 0 & -3 & 1 \\ 0 & 0 & 0 \end{bmatrix} \{x\} + \begin{bmatrix} 0 \\ 0 \\ 1 \end{bmatrix} u$$

$$y = \begin{bmatrix} -2 & -2 & 1 \end{bmatrix} \{x\}$$

24

$$\{\dot{x}(t)\} = A\{x(t)\} + B\{u(t)\}$$
$$\{y(t)\} = C\{x(t)\} + D\{u(t)\}$$

(a)

$$\{x(t)\} = \begin{Bmatrix} h_1(t) \\ h_2(t) \\ h_3(t) \\ h_4(t) \end{Bmatrix}, \quad \{u(t)\} = \begin{Bmatrix} q_1(t) \\ q_2(t) \\ q_3(t) \\ q_4(t) \end{Bmatrix},$$

$$A = \begin{bmatrix} -\dfrac{1}{a_1 R_1} & \dfrac{1}{a_1 R_1} & 0 & 0 \\[2ex] \dfrac{1}{a_2 R_1} & -\left(\dfrac{1}{a_2 R_1} + \dfrac{1}{a_2 R_2}\right) & \dfrac{1}{a_2 R_2} & 0 \\[2ex] 0 & \dfrac{1}{a_3 R_1} & -\left(\dfrac{1}{a_3 R_1} + \dfrac{1}{a_3 R_3}\right) & \dfrac{1}{a_3 R_3} \\[2ex] 0 & 0 & \dfrac{1}{a_4 R_3} & -\dfrac{1}{a_4 R_3} \end{bmatrix},$$

$$B = \begin{bmatrix} 1 & 0 & 0 & 0 \\ 0 & -1 & 0 & 0 \\ 0 & 0 & -1 & 0 \\ 0 & 0 & 0 & 1 \end{bmatrix}, \quad C = \begin{bmatrix} 0 & 1 & 0 & 0 \\ 0 & 0 & 1 & 0 \end{bmatrix}, \quad D = 0$$

(b)

$$\{x(t)\} = \begin{Bmatrix} h_2(t) \\ h_3(t) \end{Bmatrix}, \quad \{u(t)\} = \begin{Bmatrix} h_1(t) \\ q_2(t) \\ q_3(t) \\ h_4(t) \end{Bmatrix},$$

$$A = \begin{bmatrix} -\left(\dfrac{1}{a_2 R_1} + \dfrac{1}{a_2 R_2}\right) & \dfrac{1}{a_2 R_2} \\ \dfrac{1}{a_3 R_1} & -\left(\dfrac{1}{a_3 R_1} + \dfrac{1}{a_3 R_3}\right) \end{bmatrix}$$

$$B = \begin{bmatrix} \dfrac{1}{a_2 R_1} & -1 & 0 & 0 \\ 0 & 0 & -1 & \dfrac{1}{a_3 R_3} \end{bmatrix}, \quad C = \begin{bmatrix} 1 & 0 \\ 0 & 1 \end{bmatrix}, \quad D = 0$$

(c)

$$\{x(t)\} = \begin{Bmatrix} h_2(t) \\ h_3(t) \end{Bmatrix}, \quad \{u(t)\} = \begin{Bmatrix} h_1(t) \\ h_4(t) \end{Bmatrix}$$

$$A = \begin{bmatrix} -\left(\dfrac{1}{a_2 R_1} + \dfrac{1}{a_2 R_2}\right) & \dfrac{1}{a_2 R_2} \\ \dfrac{1}{a_3 R_1} & -\left(\dfrac{1}{a_3 R_1} + \dfrac{1}{a_3 R_3}\right) \end{bmatrix}$$

$$B = \begin{bmatrix} \dfrac{1}{a_2 R_1} & 0 \\ 0 & \dfrac{1}{a_3 R_3} \end{bmatrix}, \quad C = \begin{bmatrix} 1 & 0 \\ 0 & 1 \end{bmatrix}, \quad D = 0$$

25

$$G(s) = \begin{bmatrix} \dfrac{aRs + 3}{a^2 R^2 s^2 + 5aRs + 5} & \dfrac{2}{a^2 R^2 s^2 + 5aRs + 5} \\ \dfrac{1}{a^2 R^2 s^2 + 5aRs + 5} & \dfrac{2aRs + 4}{a^2 R^2 s^2 + 5aRs + 5} \end{bmatrix}$$

26

$$\{\dot{x}(t)\} = \begin{bmatrix} 0 & 1 \\ -10 & -7 \end{bmatrix}\{x(t)\} + \begin{bmatrix} 0 \\ 1 \end{bmatrix}u(t), \quad y(t) = [10 \quad 10]\{x(t)\}$$

$$\text{or} \quad \{\dot{x}(t)\} = \begin{bmatrix} -5 & 0 \\ 0 & -2 \end{bmatrix}\{x(t)\} + \begin{bmatrix} 1 \\ 1 \end{bmatrix}u(t), \quad y(t) = [\tfrac{40}{3} \quad -\tfrac{10}{3}]\{x(t)\}$$

$$\text{or} \quad \{\dot{x}(t)\} = \begin{bmatrix} -5 & 10 \\ 0 & -2 \end{bmatrix}\{x(t)\} + \begin{bmatrix} 0 \\ 1 \end{bmatrix}u(t), \quad y(t) = [-4 \quad 10]\{x(t)\}$$

$$\text{or} \quad \{\dot{x}(t)\} = \begin{bmatrix} -2 & 10 \\ 0 & -5 \end{bmatrix}\{x(t)\} + \begin{bmatrix} 0 \\ 1 \end{bmatrix}u(t), \quad y(t) = [-1 \quad 10]\{x(t)\}$$

$$c(t) = 1 + \tfrac{5}{3}e^{-2t} - \tfrac{8}{3}e^{-5t}$$

27

$$\varphi(t) = \begin{bmatrix} e^{-0.5t}(\cos\theta + 0.577\sin\theta) & e^{-0.5t}(1.155\sin\theta) \\ e^{-0.5t}(-1.555\sin\theta) & e^{-0.5t}(\cos\theta - 0.577\sin\theta) \end{bmatrix}$$

where $\theta = 0.866t$

$$x_1(t) = 1 - 1.155e^{-0.5t}\sin\left(0.866 + \frac{\pi}{3}\right); \quad x_2(t) = \dot{x}_1(t)$$

28

$$\varphi(t) = \begin{bmatrix} e^{-t} & 0 & 0 \\ 0 & e^{-4t} & 0 \\ 0 & 0 & e^{-2t} \end{bmatrix} \qquad \begin{array}{l} x_1(t) = 1 - e^{-t} \\ x_2(t) = \tfrac{1}{4} - \tfrac{1}{4}e^{-4t} \\ x_3(t) = \tfrac{1}{2} + \tfrac{1}{2}e^{-2t} \end{array}$$

$$G(s) = \begin{bmatrix} \dfrac{4s^2 + 14s + 14}{(s+1)(s+2)(s+4)} \\ \dfrac{2(s+3)}{(s+2)(s+4)} \end{bmatrix}$$

29

$$\varphi(t) = e^A = \begin{bmatrix} 1 - 2t^2 + \tfrac{4}{3}t^3 + \dots & t - t^2 + \tfrac{1}{3}t^4 + \dots \\ -4t + 4t^2 - \tfrac{4}{3}t^4 + \dots & 1 - 2t + \tfrac{4}{3}t^3 - \tfrac{2}{3}t^4 + \dots \end{bmatrix}$$

For $t = 1$ second this gives poor accuracy since further terms could make a significant difference, but for $t = 0.5$ second it is a reasonable approximation, since the terms reduce rapidly in magnitude.

30

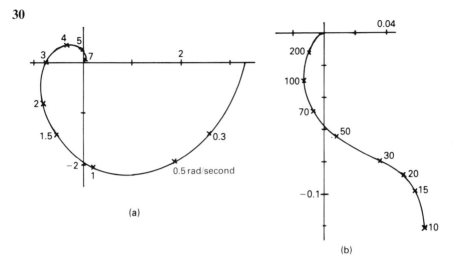

(a)

(b)

31 Same information as Problem 30 plotted on a Bode diagram.

32 $G(s) = \dfrac{0.33}{s(1 + 0.5s)}$ The transducer bandwidth is significantly higher than that of the system.

33 $$G(s) = \frac{220(1 + 2.6s)}{(1 + 0.65s)(s^2 + 20s + 580)}$$

34 $$\varphi_{yy}(\tau) = \frac{A^2}{2} \cos \omega t + \frac{B^2}{2} \cos 3\omega\tau + C^2$$

35 (a) $\dfrac{A^2}{2} \cos \omega\tau$ (b) $\dfrac{B}{\pi\tau} \sin \omega_c \tau$

36

$\phi_{xx}(\tau)$

$\frac{1}{31}$

0.2

6.2s

$\Phi_{xx}(\omega)$

Relatively flat (within 3 dB) to frequency 5/3 Hz

Smallest frequency component $\dfrac{1}{6.2}$ Hz

Spacing of spectral lines $\dfrac{1}{6.2}$ Hz

0   5   10 Hz ω

37 $G(s) = Ke^{-0.5s}\left(\dfrac{40}{s^2 + 2s + 40}\right)$,   with time in minutes.

38 0 and $\frac{10}{11}$ with steady unit input; 2 and ∞ with unit ramp; ∞ for both with acceleration input.

39 (i) $0 < K < 75$, 3.74, 0.107, ∞
(ii) $0 < K < 45$, 3, 0, 0.2
(iii) $0 < K < \infty$, $-$, 0, 0

40 11 dB, $42°$ (from straight line approximation)
13.4 dB, $50.4°$ (by calculation)

41 $G(s) = \dfrac{6.3}{s(1 + 0.25s)(1 + 0.05s)}$, $M_p = 1.9$, bandwidth $= 7$ rad/second.

42 1 dB, $2.5°$. Close to instability.

43 $$20 \log_{10} \frac{110}{K};\quad \tan^{-1}\left(\frac{1 - 0.001\omega_1{}^2}{0.11\omega}\right)$$

where ω_1 is given by

$$0.000\,001\omega_1{}^4 + 0.0101\omega_1{}^2 + 1 = \frac{K^2}{\omega_1{}^2};\quad 110;\quad 6 \text{ dB}, 12°.$$

44 14.5 dB, $30°$; 6 dB, 0.2 rad/second, 0.45 rad/second. Rather poor stability, little improvement possible by change in gain alone.

45 $K = 0.8$. Transducer time constant is significant. With lag GM $= 8$ dB, PM $= 45°$ for $K = 0.8$, e_{ss} is 50%. Without lag GM $= \infty$, PM $= 45°$ for $K = 1.37$, e_{ss} is 37%.

46

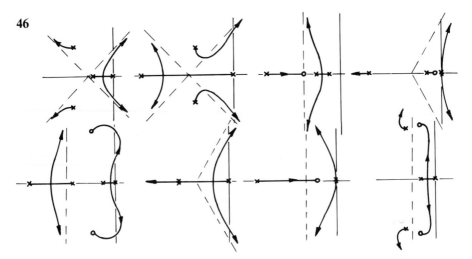

47 60; 0.52 rad/second; -2.3, -10, negligible effect.

48 1.78; $C(s) = \dfrac{225}{s(s^2 + 2.17s + 2.4)(s + 2.9)(s + 10)(s + 12.5)}$

$\simeq \dfrac{1.78}{s(s^2 + 2.17s + 2.4)(s + 2.9)}$

3.7 seconds.

49 Conditionally stable; stable for $0.5 < K_c < 1.8$, approximately second order. For $K_c = 0.57$ dominant roots have $\zeta \simeq 0.7$.

50 Unstable. 3.3 rad/second, 0.47 (with compensation).

51

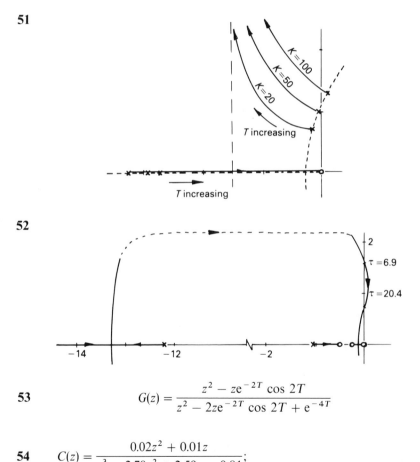

53 $G(z) = \dfrac{z^2 - ze^{-2T} \cos 2T}{z^2 - 2ze^{-2T} \cos 2T + e^{-4T}}$

54 $C(z) = \dfrac{0.02z^2 + 0.01z}{z^3 - 2.78z^2 + 2.59z - 0.81};$

$c^*(t) = 0.02(t - T) + 0.07(t - 2T) + 0.14(t - 3T) + 0.224(t - 4T)$
$+ 0.317(t - 5T) + \ldots\ldots; 1.$

56 Unstable for all K

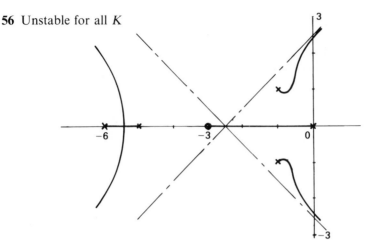

57 PM $= 38°$, GM $= 5.76$ dB;   limiting $K = 3.05$.

58 Stable;   unstable;   no effect.

59

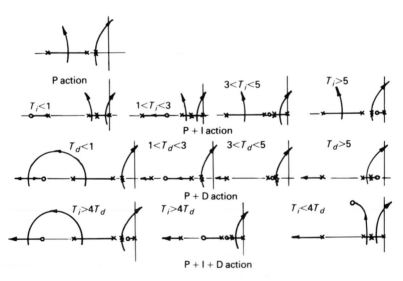

60 For $T = 0$, $K = 480$ for 4% error, $k = 0.26$ gives a maximum ζ of 0.40 for the dominant roots. For $T = 0.05$, $K = 480$ as before, but maximum attainable ζ is 0.16 for $k = 0.18$.

61 $K = 50$ gives $M_p \simeq 1.22$, and 20 rad/second, 33 rad/second, ∞, $47°$. Required M_p is not attainable by change in K alone.

62

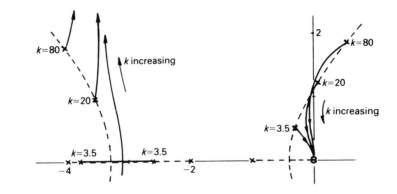

63 -1 dB, $-5°$ (unstable) improved to 16 dB, $45°$.

64
$$G_c(s) = \frac{1}{4.2}\left(\frac{1 + 0.070s}{1 + 0.017s}\right), \quad G(s) = \frac{420}{s(1 + 0.25s)}$$

65
$$G_c(s) = \frac{1}{3.7}\left(\frac{1 + 0.41s}{1 + 0.11s}\right), \quad G(s) = \frac{5.5}{s(1 + 1.25s)}$$

17 dB, $11°$ improved to 24 dB, $45°$

66
$$\{\dot{x}\} = \begin{bmatrix} 0 & 1 & 0 \\ 0 & 0 & 1 \\ -0.2 & -2.3 & -3.1 \end{bmatrix}\{x\} + \begin{bmatrix} 0 \\ 0 \\ 2 \end{bmatrix}u$$

$\boldsymbol{H} = [0.89 \quad 0.94 \quad 0.55]$, Overshoot $= 16\%$

67
$$h_2 = 13 - 3h_1; \quad h_2^2 = 29 - 6h_1; \quad \boldsymbol{H} = [3\tfrac{1}{3} \quad 3]$$

Index